Stand Out 4

Lesson Planner

Second Edition

Staci Johnson

Rob Jenkins

THOMSON

HEINLE ™

...co · Singapore · Spain · United Kingdom · United States

THOMSON

HEINLE ™

Stand Out 4
Lesson Planner
Staci Johnson and Rob Jenkins

Editorial Director: *Joe Dougherty*
Publisher, ESL and Dictionaries: *Sherrise Roehr*
Acquisitions Editor: *Tom Jefferies*
VP, Director of Content Development: *Anita Raducanu*
Development Editor: *John Hicks*
Director of Product Marketing: *Amy T. Mabley*
Executive Marketing Manager, U.S.: *Jim McDonough*
Senior Field Marketing Manager: *Donna Lee Kennedy*
Product Marketing Manager: *Katie Kelley*
Content Project Manager: *Dawn Marie Elwell*
Senior Content Project Manager: *Maryellen Killeen*

Senior Print Buyer: *Mary Beth Hennebury*
Development Editor: *Kasia McNabb*
Development Editor: *Catherine Mazur-Jefferies*
Project Manager: *Tunde Dewey*
Composition: *Pre-Press PMG*
Cover and Interior Design: *Studio Montage*
Cover Art: *©Lisa Henderling/Getty Images*
Illustrators: *James Edwards; S.I. International*
Photo Researcher: *Erika Hokanson*
Printer: *Quebecor Dubuque*

For more information contact Heinle, 25 Thomson Place, Boston, Massachusetts 02210 USA, or you can visit our Internet site at elt.heinle.com

Credits appear on page 176, which constitutes a continuation of the copyright page.

For permission to use material from thi
submit a request online at http://www

Any additional questions about perm
submitted by email to thomsonrigh

ISBN-10: 1-4240-0263-X
ISBN-13: 978-1-4240-1936

ACKNOWLEDGMENTS

Elizabeth Aderman
New York City Board of Education, New York, NY

Lisa Agao
Fresno Adult School, Fresno, CA

Sharon Baker
Roseville Adult School, Roseville, CA

Lillian Barredo
Stockton School for Adults, Stockton, CA

Linda Boice
Elk Grove Adult Education, Elk Grove, CA

Chan Bostwick
Los Angeles Unified School District, Los Angeles, CA

Debra Brooks
Manhattan BEGIN Program, New York, NY

Anne Byrnes
North Hollywood-Polytechnic Community Adult School, Sun Valley, CA

Rose Cantu
John Jay High School, San Antonio, TX

Toni Chapralis
Fremont School for Adults, Sacramento, CA

Melanie Chitwood
Miami-Dade College, Miami, FL

Geri Creamer
Stockton School for Adults, Stockton, CA

Stephanie Daubar
Harry W. Brewster Technical Center, Tampa, FL

Irene Dennis
San Antonio College, San Antonio, TX

Eileen Duffell
P.S. 64, New York, NY

Nancy Dunlap
Northside Independent School District, San Antonio, TX

Gloria Eriksson
Grant Skills Center, Sacramento, CA

Marti Estrin
Santa Rosa Junior College, Santa Rosa, CA

Lawrence Fish
Shorefront YM-YWHA English Language Program, Brooklyn, NY

Victoria Florit
Miami-Dade College, Miami, FL

Sally Gearheart
Santa Rosa Junior College, Santa Rosa, CA

Rhoda Gilbert
New York City Board of Education, New York, NY

Debbie Glass
Merced Adult School, Merced, CA

Laurie Hartwick
Lawrence High School/Adult Learning Center, Lawrence, MA

Kathleen Jimenez
Miami-Dade College, Miami, FL

Nancy Jordan
John Jay High School Adult Education, San Antonio, TX

Renee Klosz
Lindsey Hopkins Technical Education Center, Miami, FL

David Lauter
Stockton School for Adults, Stockton, CA

Patricia Long
Old Marshall Adult Education Center, Sacramento, CA

Daniel Loos
Seattle Community College, Seattle, WA

Maria Miranda
Lindsey Hopkins Technical Education Center, Miami, FL

Karen Moore
Stockton School for Adults, Stockton, CA

George Myskiw
Malcolm X College, Chicago, IL

Dr. Betty Payne
Montgomery College, Rockville, MD

Heidi Perez
Lawrence Public Schools Adult Learning Center, Lawrence, MA

Marta Pitt
Lindsey Hopkins Technical Education Center, Miami, FL

Sylvia Rambach
Stockton School for Adults, Stockton, CA

Eric Rosenbaum
BEGIN Managed Programs, New York, NY

Laura Rowley
Old Marshall Adult Education Center, Sacramento, CA

Stephanie Schmitter
Mercer County Community College, Trenton, NJ

Amy Schneider
Pacoima Skills Center, Pacoima, CA

Sr. M. B. Theresa Spittle
Stockton School for Adults, Stockton, CA

Andre Sutton
Belmont Adult School, Los Angeles, CA

Jennifer Swoyer
Northside Independent School District, San Antonio, TX

Marcia Takacs
Coastline Community College, Fountain Valley, CA

Claire Valier
Palm Beach County School District, West Palm Beach, FL

Sarah Young
Arlington Education and Employment Program (REEP), Arlington, VA

Staci Johnson

Rob Jenkins

Ever since I can remember, I've been fascinated with other cultures and languages. I love to travel and every place I go, the first thing I want to do is meet the people, learn their language, and understand their culture. Becoming an ESL teacher was a perfect way to turn what I love to do into my profession. There's nothing more incredible than the exchange of teaching and learning from one another that goes on in an ESL classroom. And there's nothing more rewarding than helping a student succeed.

I love teaching. I love to see the expressions on my students' faces when the light goes on and their eyes show such sincere joy of learning. I knew the first time I stepped into an ESL classroom that this was where I needed to be and I have never questioned that resolution. I have worked in business, sales, and publishing, and I've found challenge in all, but nothing can compare to the satisfaction of reaching people in such a personal way.

W e are so happy that instructors and agencies have embraced the lesson planning and project-based activities that we introduced in the first edition and are so enthusiastically teaching with **Stand Out**. It is fantastic that so many of our colleagues are as excited to be in this profession as we are.
After writing over 500 lesson plans and implementing them in our own classrooms and after personal discussions with thousands of instructors all over the United States and in different parts of the world, we have found ourselves in a position to improve upon our successful model. One of the most notable things in the new edition is that we have continued to stress integrating skills in each lesson and have made this integration more apparent and obvious. To accomplish any life skill, students need to incorporate a combination of reading, writing, listening, speaking, grammar, pronunciation, and academic skills while developing vocabulary and these skills should be taught together in a lesson! We have accomplished this by extending the presentation of lessons in the book, so each lesson is more fully developed. You will also notice an extended list of ancillaries and a tighter correlation of these ancillaries to each book. The ancillaries allow you to extend practice on particular skill areas beyond the lesson in the text. We are so excited about this curriculum and know that as you implement it, you and your students will *stand out*.

Our goal is to give students
challenging opportunities
to be successful in their
language-learning experience
so they develop confidence
and become independent,
lifelong learners.

Staci Johnson
Rob Jenkins

ABOUT THE SERIES

The **Stand Out** series is designed to facilitate *active* learning while challenging students to build a nurturing and effective learning community.

The student books are divided into eight distinct units, mirroring competency areas most useful to newcomers. These areas are outlined in CASAS assessment programs and different state model standards for adults. Each unit in *Stand Out 4* is then divided into five lessons, a review, and a team project. Lessons are driven by performance objectives and are filled with challenging activities that progress from teacher-presented to student-centered tasks.

SUPPLEMENTAL MATERIALS

- The *Stand Out 4 Lesson Planner* is in full color with 60 complete lesson plans, taking the instructor through each stage of a lesson from warm-up and review through application.
- The *Stand Out 4 Activity Bank CD-ROM* has an abundance of customizable worksheets. Print or download and modify what you need for your particular class.
- The *Stand Out 4 Grammar Challenge* is a workbook that gives additional grammar explanation and practice in context.
- The *Reading and Writing Challenge* workbooks are designed to capture the principle ideas in the student book, and allow students to improve their vocabulary, academic, reading, and writing skills.
- The *Stand Out 4 Assessment CD-ROM with ExamView®* allows you to customize pre- and post-tests for each unit as well as a pre- and post-test for the book.
- Listening scripts are found in the back of the student book and in the Lesson Planner. CDs are available with focused listening activities described in the Lesson Planner.

STAND OUT 3 LESSON PLANNER

The *Stand Out 4 Lesson Planner* is a new and innovative approach. As many seasoned teachers know, good lesson planning can make a substantial difference in the classroom. Students continue coming to class, understanding, applying, and remembering more of what they learn. They are more confident in their learning when good lesson planning techniques are incorporated.

We have developed lesson plans that are designed to be used each day and to reduce preparation time. The planner includes:

- Standard lesson progression (Warm-up and Review, Introduction, Presentation, Practice, Evaluation, and Application)

- A creative and complete way to approach varied class lengths so that each lesson will work within a class period.
- 180 hours of classroom activities
- Time suggestions for each activity
- Pedagogical comments
- Space for teacher notes and future planning
- Identification of LCP standards in addition to SCANS and CASAS standards

USER QUESTIONS ABOUT *STAND OUT*

- **What are SCANS and how do they integrate into the book?**
  SCANS is the Secretary's Commission on Achieving Necessary Skills. SCANS was developed to encourage students to prepare for the workplace. The standards developed through SCANS have been incorporated throughout the **Stand Out** student books and components.

  Stand Out addresses SCANS a little differently than do other books. SCANS standards elicit effective teaching strategies by incorporating essential skills such as critical thinking and group work. We have incorporated SCANS standards in every lesson, not isolating these standards in the work unit. All new texts have followed our lead.

- **What about CASAS?** The federal government has mandated that states show student outcomes as a prerequisite to receiving funding. Some states have incorporated the **C**omprehensive **A**dult **S**tudent **A**ssessment **S**ystem (CASAS) testing to standardize agency reporting. Unfortunately, many of our students are unfamiliar with standardized testing and therefore struggle with it. Adult schools need to develop lesson plans to address specific concerns. **Stand Out** was developed with careful attention to CASAS skill areas in most lessons and performance objectives.

- **Are the tasks too challenging for my students?**
  Students learn by doing and learn more when challenged. **Stand Out** provides tasks that encourage critical thinking in a variety of ways. The tasks in each lesson move from teacher-directed to student-centered so the learner clearly understands what's expected and is willing to "take a risk." The lessons are expected to be challenging. In this way, students learn that when they work together as a learning community, anything becomes possible. The satisfaction of accomplishing something both as an individual and as a member of a team results in greater confidence and effective learning.

- **Do I need to understand lesson planning to teach from the student book?** If you don't understand lesson planning when you start, you will when you finish! Teaching from **Stand Out** is like a course on lesson planning, especially if you use the Lesson Planner on a daily basis.

  Stand Out does *stand out* because, when we developed this series, we first established performance objectives for each lesson. Then we designed lesson plans, followed by student book pages. The introduction to each lesson varies because different objectives demand different approaches. **Stand Out's** variety of tasks makes learning more interesting for the student.

- **What are team projects?** The final lesson of each unit is a **team project**. This is often a team simulation that incorporates the objectives of the unit and provides an additional opportunity for students to actively apply what they have learned. The project allows students to produce something that represents their progress in learning. These end-of-unit projects were created with a variety of learning styles and individual skills in mind. The team projects can be skipped or simplified, but we encourage instructors to implement them, enriching the overall student experience.

- **What do you mean by a customizable Activity Bank?** Every class, student, teacher, and approach is different. Since no one textbook can meet all these differences, the *Stand Out Activity Bank CD-ROM* allows you to customize **Stand Out** for your class. You can copy different activities and worksheets from the CD-ROM to your hard drive and then:

  - change items in supplemental vocabulary, grammar, and life skill activities;

  - personalize activities with student names and popular locations in your area;

  - extend every lesson with additional practice where you feel it is most needed.

  The Activity Bank also includes the following resources:

  - Multilevel worksheets – worksheets based on the standard worksheets described above, but at one level higher and one level lower.

  - Graphic organizer templates – templates that can be used to facilitate learning. They include graphs, charts, VENN diagrams, and so on.

  - Computer worksheets – worksheets designed to supplement each unit and progress from simple

    to complex operations in word processing; and spreadsheets for labs and computer enhanced classrooms.

  - Internet Worksheets – worksheets designed to supplement each unit and provide application opportunities beyond the lessons in the book.

- **Is *Stand Out* grammar-based or competency-based?** **Stand Out** is a competency-based series; however, students are exposed to basic grammar structures. We believe that grammar instruction in context is extremely important. Grammar is a necessary component for achieving most competencies; therefore it is integrated into most lessons. Students are first provided with context that incorporates the grammar, followed by an explanation and practice. At this level, we expect students to learn basic structures, but we do not expect them to acquire them. It has been our experience that students are exposed several times within their learning experience to language structures before they actually acquire them. For teachers who want to enhance grammar instruction, the *Activity Bank CD-ROM* and/or the *Grammar Challenge* workbooks provide ample opportunities.

  The six competencies that drive **Stand Out** are basic communication, consumer economics, community resources, health, occupational knowledge, and lifelong learning (government and law replace lifelong learning in Books 3 and 4).

- **Are there enough activities so I don't have to supplement?** **Stand Out** stands alone in providing 180 hours of instruction and activities, even without the additional suggestions in the Lesson Planner. The Lesson Planner also shows you how to streamline lessons to provide 90 hours of classwork and still have thorough lessons if you meet less often. When supplementing with the *Stand Out Activity Bank CD-ROM*, the *Assessment CD-ROM with ExamView®* and the *Stand Out Grammar Challenge* workbook, you gain unlimited opportunities to extend class hours and provide activities related directly to each lesson objective. Calculate how many hours your class meets in a semester and look to **Stand Out** to address the full class experience.

  Stand Out is a comprehensive approach to adult language learning, meeting needs of students and instructors completely and effectively.

CONTENTS

• Grammar points that are explicitly taught   ◊ Grammar points that are presented in context   △ Grammar points that are being recycled

	Numeracy/ Academic Skills	EFF	SCANS	CASAS
Pre-Unit	• Writing a paragraph • Comparing and contrasting • Setting goals • Using a bar graph	Most EFF skills are incorporated into this unit with an emphasis on: • Taking responsibility for learning • Reflecting and evaluating • Conveying ideas in writing (Technology is optional.)	Many SCAN and EFF skills are incorporated in this unit with an emphasis on: • Understanding systems • Decision making	**1:** 0.1.2; 0.1.4; 0.2.1; 0.2.2 **2:** 0.2.1; 7.2.6 **3:** 0.1.2, 0.1.6, 0.2.1, 7.1.1
Unit 1	• Active reading • Focused listening • Writing a paragraph • Brainstorming • Using context clues • Using an outline • Comparing and contrasting • Reviewing	Most EFF skills are incorporated into this unit with an emphasis on: • Taking responsibility for learning • Reflecting and evaluating • Solving problems and making decisions • Planning (Technology is optional.)	Many SCAN and EFF skills are incorporated in this unit with an emphasis on: • Allocating time • Understanding systems • Applying technology to task • Responsibility • Self management • Writing • Decision making	**1:** 0.1.2, 0.2.4 **2:** 7.1.1, 7.1.2, 7.1.3, 7.2.5, 7.2.6 **3:** 7.1.1, 7.1.2, 7.1.3, 7.2.5, 7.2.6 **4:** 0.1.5, 7.4.1, 7.4.3, 7.4.5 **5:** 7.4.2 **R:** 7.2.1 **TP:** 4.8.1., 4.8.5., 4.8.6.
Unit 2	• Comparing and contrasting • Writing a business letter • Active reading • Focused listening • Calculating budgets • Reviewing	Most EFF skills are incorporated into this unit with an emphasis on: • Learning through research • Using mathematics in problem solving and communication • Planning (Technology is optional.)	Many SCAN skills are incorporated in this unit with an emphasis on: • Responsibility • Participating as a member of a team • Acquiring and evaluating information • Organizing and maintaining information • Decision making • Reasoning	**1:** 0.1.2, 1.3.7 **2:** 1.2.1 **3:** 1.2.1, 1.2.2 **4:** 1.3.1 **5:** 1.2.5 **R:** 7.2.1 **TP:** 4.8.1., 4.8.5., 4.8.6.

Contents   **ix**

CONTENTS

• Grammar points that are explicitly taught   ◊ Grammar points that are presented in context   △ Grammar points that are being recycled

	Numeracy/ Academic Skills	EFF	SCANS	CASAS
Unit 3	• Pronunciation: Rising and Falling intonation • Active reading • Focused listening • Reading a bar graph • Sequencing • Writing about preferences • Summarizing a process • Comparing and contrasting • Using context clues • Reviewing	Most EFF skills are incorporated into this unit with an emphasis on: • Learning through research • Listening actively • Reading with understanding • Solving problems and making decisions • Planning (Technology is optional.)	Many SCAN skills are incorporated in this unit with an emphasis on: • Allocating money • Understanding systems • Monitoring and correcting performance • Interpreting and communicating information • Reading • Writing • Decision making	**1:** 1.4.1, 1.4.2 **2:** 1.4.2, 7.2.7 **3:** 1.4.4, 1.5.3 **4:** 1.5.1, 6.0.3, 6.0I.5, 6.1.1, 6.1.2 **5:** 1.4.7 **R:** 7.2.1 **TP:** 4.8.1, 4.8.5, 4.8.6.
Unit 4	• Pronunciation: Annunciation and Intonation • Focused listening • Making inferences • Reviewing	Most EFF skills are incorporated into this unit with an emphasis on: • Learning through research • Speaking so others can understand • Listening actively • Guiding others • Cooperating with others (Technology is optional.)	Many SCAN skills are incorporated in this unit with an emphasis on: • Understanding systems • Interpreting and communicating information • Writing • Decision making • Seeing things in the mind's eye	**1:** 0.1.2 **2:** 1.8.5, 2.5.6 **3:** 2.2.1, 2.2.5 **4:** 7.2.6 **5:** 7.2.2 **R:** 7.2.1 **TP:** 4.8.1, 4.8.5, 4.8.6
Unit 5	• Focused listening • Active reading • Using a bar graph • Calculating percentages • Skimming • Reviewing	Most EFF skills are incorporated into this unit with an emphasis on: • Learning through research • Reading with understanding • Using mathematics in problem solving and communication • Advocating and influencing (Technology is optional.)	Many SCAN skills are incorporated in this unit with an emphasis on: • Understanding systems • Self management • Acquiring and evaluating information • Interpreting and communicating information	**1:** 3.1.1, 3.1.3, 3.2.1 **2:** 3.1.1 **3:** 3.4.2, 3.5.9 **4:** 3.5.1, 3.5.3, 3.5.5 3.5.9, 6.7.3 **5:** 3.5.9 **R:** 7.2.1 **TP:** 4.8.1, 4.8.5, 4.8.6.

CONTENTS

• Grammar points that are explicitly taught   ◊ Grammar points that are presented in context   △ Grammar points that are being recycled

	Numeracy/ Academic Skills	EFF	SCANS	CASAS
Unit 6	• Active reading • Focused listening • Writing a resume • Writing a cover letter • Reviewing	Most EFF skills are incorporated into this unit, with an emphasis on: • Taking responsibility for learning • Conveying ideas in writing • Speaking so others can understand • Observing critically • Planning • Cooperating with others (Technology is optional.)	Most SCAN skills are incorporated in this unit with an emphasis on: • Self-esteem • Sociability • Acquiring and evaluating information • Speaking • Decision making	**1:** 4.1.8 **2:** 4.1.9 **3:** 4.1.3 **4:** 4.1.2 **5:** 4.1.5, 4.1.7 **R:** 7.2.1 **TP:** 4.8.1, 4.8.5, 4.8.6.
Unit 7	• Focused listening • Active reading • Reading a flowchart • Writing a description of a situation • Reviewing	Most EFF skills are incorporated into this unit with an emphasis on: • Speaking so others can understand • Listening actively • Observing critically • Solving problems and making decisions • Resolving conflict and negotiating • Cooperating with others (Technology is optional.)	Most SCAN skills are incorporated in this unit with an emphasis on: • Understanding systems • Participating as a member of a team • Acquiring and evaluating information	**1:** 4.1.9, 4.4.1 **2:** 4.2.1, 4.4.3 **3:** 4.2.1 **4:** 4.3.3, 4.3.4, 4.5.1 **5:** 4.4.1, 4.6.1 **R:** 7.2.1 **TP:** 4.8.1, 4.8.5, 4.8.6
Unit 8	• Focused listening • Active reading • Writing a paragraph • Writing a speech • Reading a flowchart • Writing a letter to a local official • Reviewing	Most EFF skills are incorporated into this unit with an emphasis on: • Taking responsibility for learning • Learning through research • Solving problems and making decisions (Technology is optional.)	Most SCAN skills are incorporated in this unit with an emphasis on: • Listening • Speaking • Responsibility • Self-esteem	1: 5.1.6 2: 5.1.4, 5.1.6 3: 5.1.4, 5.2.1 4: 5.5.7, 5.5.8 5: 5.1.6 R: 7.2.1 TP: 4.8.1, 4.8.5, 4.8.6.

Welcome to Stand Out, Second Edition

Stand Out works.

And now it works even better!

Built from the standards necessary for adult English learners, the second edition of *Stand Out* gives students the foundation and tools they need to develop confidence and become independent, lifelong learners.

- **Grammar** Charts clearly explain grammar points, and are followed by personalized exercises.
- Clear **grammar** explanations are followed by immediate practice, with a variety of activity types

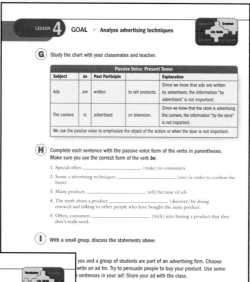

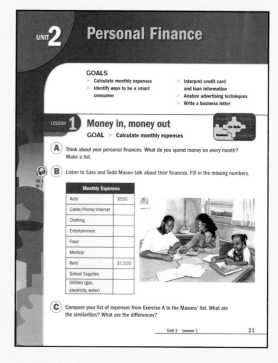

- Clearly defined **goals** provide a roadmap of learning for the student.
- State and federally required **life skills and competencies** are taught, helping students meet necessary benchmarks.

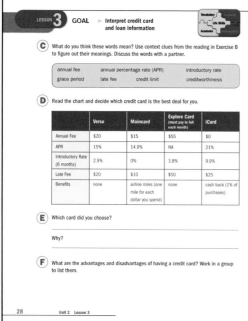

- A variety of **examples from real life**, like bank checks, newspaper ads, money, etc. help students learn to access the information and resources in their community.

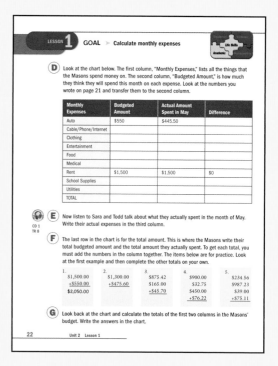

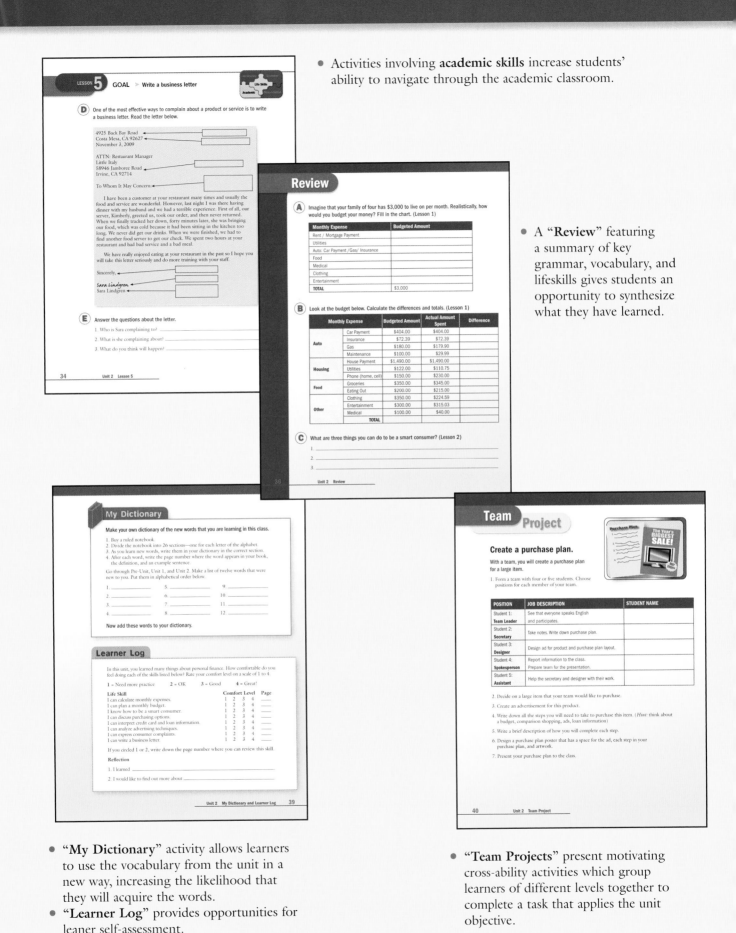

- Activities involving **academic skills** increase students' ability to navigate through the academic classroom.

- A **"Review"** featuring a summary of key grammar, vocabulary, and lifeskills gives students an opportunity to synthesize what they have learned.

- **"My Dictionary"** activity allows learners to use the vocabulary from the unit in a new way, increasing the likelihood that they will acquire the words.
- **"Learner Log"** provides opportunities for leaner self-assessment.

- **"Team Projects"** present motivating cross-ability activities which group learners of different levels together to complete a task that applies the unit objective.

The ground-breaking *Stand Out* Lesson Planners take the guesswork out of meeting the standards while offering high-interest, meaningful language activities, and three levels of pacing for each book. A complete **lesson plan** for each lesson in the student book is provided, following the *Stand Out* methodology – **Warm-up and Review, Introduction, Presentation, Practice, Evaluation,** and **Application** (see page xviii).

- An **at-a-glance prep** section for each lesson ensures that instructors have a clear knowledge of what will be covered in the lesson. References to **unit-specific resources** are also included.

- Clear **pacing guide** icons offer three different pacing strategies.

  ■ = for 1 ½-hour classes

  ■ = for 2 ½-hour classes

  ■ = for 3-hour or more classes

- **Standards Correlations** appear directly on the page, detailing how *Stand Out* meets CASAS, SCANS, and EFF standards.

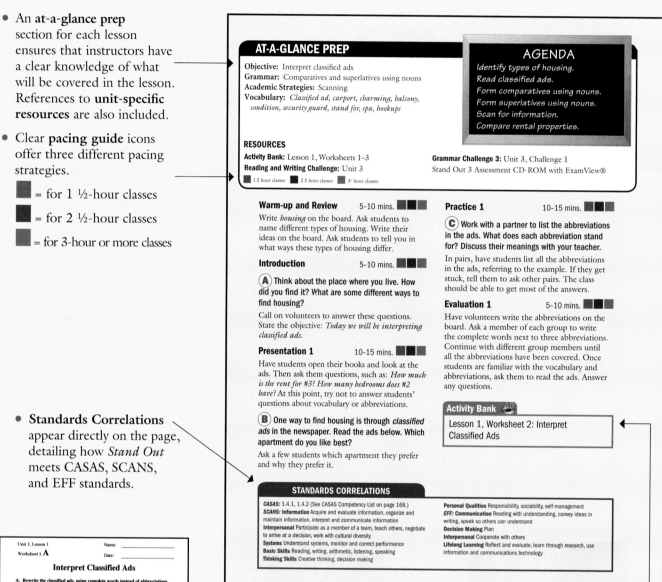

AT-A-GLANCE PREP

Objective: Interpret classified ads
Grammar: Comparatives and superlatives using nouns
Academic Strategies: Scanning
Vocabulary: *Classified ad, carport, charming, balcony, condition, security guard, stand for, spa, hookups*

AGENDA
Identify types of housing.
Read classified ads.
Form comparatives using nouns.
Form superlatives using nouns.
Scan for information.
Compare rental properties.

RESOURCES
Activity Bank: Lesson 1, Worksheets 1–3
Reading and Writing Challenge: Unit 3
Grammar Challenge 3: Unit 3, Challenge 1
Stand Out 3 Assessment CD-ROM with ExamView®

■ 1.5 hour classes   ■ 2.5 hour classes   ■ 3⁺ hour classes

Warm-up and Review   5–10 mins. ■■■
Write *housing* on the board. Ask students to name different types of housing. Write their ideas on the board. Ask students to tell you in what ways these types of housing differ.

Introduction   5–10 mins. ■■■
(A) Think about the place where you live. How did you find it? What are some different ways to find housing?
Call on volunteers to answer these questions. State the objective: *Today we will be interpreting classified ads.*

Presentation 1   10–15 mins. ■■■
Have students open their books and look at the ads. Then ask them questions, such as: *How much is the rent for #3? How many bedrooms does #2 have?* At this point, try not to answer students' questions about vocabulary or abbreviations.

(B) One way to find housing is through *classified ads* in the newspaper. Read the ads below. Which apartment do you like best?
Ask a few students which apartment they prefer and why they prefer it.

Practice 1   10–15 mins. ■■■
(C) Work with a partner to list the abbreviations in the ads. What does each abbreviation stand for? Discuss their meanings with your teacher.
In pairs, have students list all the abbreviations in the ads, referring to the example. If they get stuck, tell them to ask other pairs. The class should be able to get most of the answers.

Evaluation 1   5–10 mins. ■■■
Have volunteers write the abbreviations on the board. Ask a member of each group to write the complete words next to three abbreviations. Continue with different group members until all the abbreviations have been covered. Once students are familiar with the vocabulary and abbreviations, ask them to read the ads. Answer any questions.

Activity Bank
Lesson 1, Worksheet 2: Interpret Classified Ads

STANDARDS CORRELATIONS

CASAS: 1.4.1, 1.4.2 (See CASAS Competency List on page 168.)
SCANS: Information Acquire and evaluate information, organize and maintain information, interpret and communicate information
Interpersonal Participate as a member of a team, teach others, negotiate to arrive at a decision, work with cultural diversity
Systems Understand systems, monitor and correct performance
Basic Skills Reading, writing, arithmetic, listening, speaking
Thinking Skills Creative thinking, decision making

Personal Qualities Responsibility, sociability, self-management
EFF: Communication Reading with understanding, convey ideas in writing, speak so others can understand
Decision Making Plan
Interpersonal Cooperate with others
Lifelong Learning Reflect and evaluate, learn through research, use information and communications technology

41a   Lesson Planner: Unit 3, Lesson 1

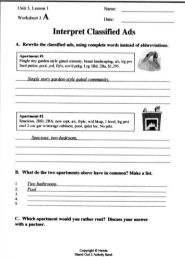

Unit 3, Lesson 1
Worksheet 2 **A**
Name: _____
Date: _____

Interpret Classified Ads

A. Rewrite the classified ads, using complete words instead of abbreviations.

Apartment #1
Single stry garden-style comnty, beaut landscaping, a/c, lrg pvt fncd patio, pool, yrd, f/p's, cov'd prkg. Lrg 3Bd, 2Ba, $1,295.

Single story garden-style gated community.

_____
_____

Apartment #2
Spacious, 2BD, 2BA, new crpt, a/c, frplc, w/d hkup, 1 level, lrg pvt encl 2-car gar w/storage cabinets, pool, quiet loc. No pets.

Spacious, two-bedroom.

_____
_____

B. What do the two apartments above have in common? Make a list.

1. *Two bathrooms*
2. *Pool*
3. _____
4. _____
5. _____

C. Which apartment would you rather rent? Discuss your answer with a partner.

The *Activity Bank CD-ROM* includes Activity Bank worksheets that can be downloaded and modified to meet the needs of your class. Included are:

- supplemental reading and writing activities.
- additional listening practice activities with accompanying audio CD.
- literacy practice sheets designed to help students who need introductory-level written language tasks.
- **multilevel activity masters** for each lesson that can be printed or downloaded and modified for classroom needs.

Presentation 2   10–15 mins. ■■■

Ask students to imagine they are moving to a new home. Tell them they need to cancel the electricity in their current home and get it turned on at their new home. Ask them how they would do this. (Call the electric company.) Ask what sort of information they would need to give to the company's representative to make this happen.

Practice 2   5–10 mins. ■■■

Tell students they will be listening to Vu call the electric company to prepare for his family's move. Direct their attention to Exercise C and tell them they will be listening for four pieces of information.

Teaching Tip

Focused listening

The purpose of teaching focused listening is to help students learn how to understand the main ideas in a conversation even when they don't understand every word.

It's important to remind students that they will not understand every word each time they do a focused listening activity. Otherwise, they may become frustrated and stop listening all together. Preparing students for the listening activity will make them much more effective listeners.

1. Explain the context of the conversation.
2. Ask students what they think they might hear.
3. Show students specifically what they are listening for.

(C) Vu and his family are getting ready to move. Vu calls the electric company to speak to a customer service representative. Listen to the recording and write short answers for the following information.

 Listening Script   CD 1, Track 8

Recording: Thank you for calling Texas Electric. Your call is very important to us. Please choose from the following options. For new service or to cancel your existing service, press 1. To report a problem with your service, press 2. If you have questions about your bill, press 3. For all other questions, press 4. (Vu presses 1.) Thank you. Just one moment.

Representative: *Hello, my name is Kristen. How may I help you?*
Vu: *Um, yes. My family is moving next week. We need to cancel our current service and get service in our new home.*
Representative: *What is your current address?*
Vu: *3324 Maple Road.*
Representative: *Are you Vu Nguyen?*
Vu: *Yes.*
Representative: *When would you like the service turned off?*
Vu: *Next Wednesday, please.*
Representative: *And what is your new address?*
Vu: *5829 Bay Road.*
Representative: *And when would you like the service turned on?*
Vu: *This Monday, please.*
Representative: *OK. Your current service will be turned off sometime between 8 and 12 on Wednesday the 11th. Your new service will be on before 9 on Monday morning the 9th. Is there anything else I can do for you?*
Vu: *No, that's it.*
Representative: *Thank you for calling Texas Electric. Have a nice day.*
Vu: *You, too.*

(D) Listen to the recording again and answer the questions.

Prepare students for the information they are to listen for. (CD 1, Track 8)

Evaluation 2   5 mins. ■■

Go over the answers with the class.

Pronunciation

Rising and Falling Intonation

Ask students a few information questions. Ask if your voice goes up or down at the end of each question. Students should be able to recognize the rising and falling intonation. Explain that this rising and falling intonation helps the listener know that you are asking a question that requires an answer.

Go over the examples in the box in the student book, emphasizing the intonation. Have students practice by repeating after you, first as a class and then individually.

Lesson Planner: Unit 3, Lesson 3   **48a**

- **Teaching Tips** and **Culture Tips** provide ideas and strategies for teaching diverse learners in the classroom.

- **Listening Scripts** from the *Audio CD* are included next to the student book page for ease-of-use.

- *Grammar Challenge* workbooks include supplemental activities for students who desire even more **contextual grammar** and **vocabulary practice.**

- *Reading & Writing Challenge* workbooks provide challenging materials and exercises for students who want even **more practice in reading, vocabulary development,** and **writing.**

- **ExamView® Test Bank** allows you to create **customizable pre- and post- tests for every unit.** The questions are correlated to CASAS and state standards and include multiple choice, true/false, numeric response, and matching types. Listening questions are included along with an audio CD.

The *Stand Out* Lesson Planner methodology ensures success!

Stand Out ensures student success through good lesson planning and instruction. Each of the five Lessons in every Unit has a lesson plan. Unlike most textbooks, the Lesson Planner was written before the student book materials. A lot of learning occurs with the student books closed so by writing the lesson plans first, we could ensure that each objective was clearly achieved. Each lesson plan follows a systematic and proven format:

W Warm-up and/or review

I Introduction

P Presentation

P Practice

E Evaluation

A Application

WARM-UP AND/OR REVIEW
The warm-up activities establish a context and purpose to the lesson. Exercises use previously learned content and materials that are familiar to students from previous lessons.

INTRODUCTION
In the introduction step, exercises focus the students' attention on the goals of the lesson by asking questions, showing visuals, telling a story, etc. Instructors should state the objective of the lesson and tell students what they will be doing. The objective should address what students are expected to be able to do by the end of the lesson.

PRESENTATION
The presentation activities provide students with the building blocks and skills they need to achieve the objectives set in the introduction. The exercises introduce new information to the students through visuals, realia, description, listenings, explanation, or written text. This is the time to check students' comprehension.

PRACTICE
Practice activities provide meaningful tasks for students to practice what they have just learned through different activities. These activities can be done as a class, in small groups, pairs, or individually. All of these activities are student centered and involve cooperative learning. Instructors should model each activity, monitor progress, and provide feedback.

EVALUATION
Evaluation ensures that students are successful. Instructors should evaluate students on attainment of the objective set at the start of the lesson. This can be done by oral, written, or demonstrated performance. At this point, if students need more practice, instructors can go back and do additional practice activities before moving onto the application.

APPLICATION
Application activities help students apply new knowledge to their own lives or new situations. This is one of the most important steps of the lesson plan. If students can accomplish the application task, it will build their confidence to be able to sue what they've learned out in the community. The Team Projects are an application of unit objectives that involves task-based activities with a product.

In addition to each lesson plan following the WIPPEA model, each Unit in *Stand Out* follows this same approach. The first lesson is always in Introduction to the Unit, introducing new vocabulary and the basic concepts that will be expanded upon in the unit. The following four lessons are the Presentations and Practices for the unit topic. Following the five lessons is a Review lesson, which allows students to do more practice with everything they already learned. The final lesson is an Application for everything they learned in the unit, a team project.

AT-A-GLANCE PREP

Objective: Fill out an admission application
Grammar: Information questions
Vocabulary: *meet, admission application, foreign country, maiden name, present stay, tidbit, achieved, goal*

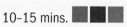

AGENDA

Learn class information.
Fill out an admission application.
Meet your classmates.
Write questions.
Meet more classmates.

RESOURCES

Activity Bank: Pre-Unit, Lesson 1, Worksheets 1–2
Grammar Challenge 4: Pre-Unit, Challenge 1

Audio: CD 1, Track 1

 1.5 hour classes ■ 2.5 hour classes ■ 3⁺ hour classes

 Preassessment *(optional)*

Use the Stand Out 4 Assessment CD-ROM with Exam*View*® to create a pretest for Pre-Unit.

Warm-up and Review   5-10 mins.

As students enter your class for the first time, introduce yourself by saying, *Nice to meet you,* and shaking hands.

Introduction   5-10 mins.

Introduce yourself to the whole class and give students any practical class or schedule information they need for the length of the course. State the objective: *Today we will learn how to fill out a college admission application and start meeting your classmates.*

Presentation 1   10-15 mins.

Ask students how they registered for school. Lead them to the idea of filling out an application. Ask them what information they put on their applications. Make a list of their ideas on the board.

Have students look at the application in Exercise A and go over each part with them, making sure they understand what to write on each blank.

Practice 1   10-15 mins.

(A) Imagine that you have decided to take classes at a college. Fill out the admission application below.

Evaluation 1   10-15 mins.

Walk around the classroom and make sure students are filling out the application correctly.

Getting to Know You

GOALS

➤ Fill out an admission application
➤ Identify learning strategies
➤ Write about your goals

LESSON **1**

Tell me something about yourself.

GOAL ➤ Fill out an admission application

 Imagine that you have decided to take classes at a college. Fill out the admission application below. (Answers will vary.)

❧ CANYON COUNTY COLLEGE ❧
Admission Application

1. _____ _____ _____
   Last Name   *First Name*   *Middle Name*

2. Date of Birth ____/____/____ ____ *Mo Day Year Age*	3. _____-____-_____ *ID Number*	4. Place of Birth _____ *City, State or Foreign Country*

5. Current address

Number and Street / Apt # _____ *City* _____ *State* ____ *Zip Code* ____

6. (____) ____-_____ *(Area Code) Telephone Number*	7. _____ *Mother's Maiden Name*

8. Citizen of what country?

9. What is the highest level of education you have achieved?

10. What is your educational goal?

LESSON **1**   **GOAL** ➤ **Fill out an admission application**

CD 1
TR 1

B **Read the conversation. Then, listen to the conversation.**

Bita: Hi. My name is Bita. What's your name?
Minh: I'm Minh. Nice to meet you.
Bita: Where are you from, Minh?
Minh: I'm from Vietnam. And you?
Bita: I'm from Iran.
Minh: Interesting. I've never been to Iran. Tell me something about yourself.
Bita: Well, I'm studying English because I want to be an architect in the United States.
Minh: Wow! That's ambitious. Good for you!
Bita: And tell me something about yourself, Minh.
Minh: In my free time, I make jewelry and sell it to help raise money for my grandchildren to go to college.
Bita: That's wonderful! I'd love to see your jewelry sometime.
Minh: I'd be more than happy to show it to you.

C Talk to three classmates. Find out their first names, where they are from, and one other piece of interesting information (a tidbit) about them. Then, introduce your new friends to another group of students. (Answers will vary.)

First Name	Country	Interesting Tidbit

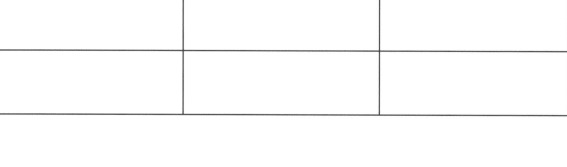

Presentation 2   10–15 mins. ■■■□

 B Read the conversation. Then, listen to the conversation.

Play the recording and have students follow along. Talk about the conversation and answer any questions students have about vocabulary. Practice the conversation as a class.

> 🎧 **Listening Script**   *CD 1, Track 1*
>
> The listening script matches the conversation in Exercise B.

Teaching Tip

Choral drills

A choral drill is when you say something and the whole class repeats after you. You might use this for individual vocabulary words as well as sentences and phrases in a conversation. This method gives students a chance to practice their pronunciation in a group, which is less intimidating than if they repeat individually. It also allows them to hear the intonation and inflection in your voice, which they can try to replicate.

Have students practice the conversation with a partner.

Practice 2   10–15 mins. ■■□

 C Talk to three classmates. Find out their first names, where they are from, and one other piece of interesting information (a tidbit) about them. Then, introduce your new friends to another group of students.

Remind students they can use the conversation in Exercise B as a model but that they shouldn't repeat it word-for-word. For example, many of your students may be from the same country, in which case they wouldn't say Minh's line *I've never been to _____*.

Evaluation 2   10–15 mins. ■■□

Walk around the classroom and listen to the conversations. When students have finished, ask volunteers to introduce a classmate to the whole class. To help students with introduction forms, write the following statements on the board:

This is _____. He/She is from _____. An interesting tidbit about him/her is _____.

Instructor's Notes

_____

_____

_____

_____

_____

_____

_____

_____

_____

_____

_____

_____

_____

_____

_____

_____

_____

_____

_____

_____

_____

_____

_____

_____

_____

_____

Presentation 3   5–10 mins.

Write the following questions on the board and call on a few volunteers to answer them:

What is your educational goal?
What is the highest level of education you have completed?
Where were you born?
What is your mother's maiden name?

Read the directions to Exercise D out loud. In preparation for this activity, brainstorm some other questions students might ask from the admission application as a class.

Practice 3   10–15 mins. ▪

D Find the first three students you talked to in Exercise C. Ask them questions about what they wrote on their applications on page P1. Use the questions below to help you get started.

What are some other questions you might ask about their applications? Write two more questions below.

First, have students find the first three students they met and ask them the questions that are in their books. Then, have students write two additional questions. When they have finished, have them ask these new questions to the same three students.

 Refer students to *Stand Out 4 Grammar Challenge,* Pre-Unit, Challenge 1 for practice with information questions.

Evaluation 3   5–10 mins. ▪

Walk around the classroom and observe the conversations. When students have finished, ask volunteers to tell the class something they learned about another classmate.

Application   10–20 mins. ▪▪▪

E Work with a group of four students. Write three questions you want to ask your classmates to help you get to know them.

Encourage the groups to come up with questions they haven't already asked so they can learn something new about their classmates.

F Interview four *other* classmates and write their answers to your group's questions in the chart below. Go back to your group and share the information. At the end of this exercise, your group should have information about sixteen students!

Explain to students how this exercise will work, making sure they understand that each person in the group will interview four other students. When students have finished, have them regroup and share what they learned about their classmates.

Activity Bank

Lesson 1, Worksheet 1: Meet Your Classmates
Lesson 1, Worksheet 2: Admission Application

Instructor's Notes

_____
_____
_____
_____
_____
_____
_____
_____
_____
_____
_____
_____
_____
_____
_____
_____
_____

D Find the first three students you talked to in Exercise C. Ask them questions about what they wrote on their applications on page P1. Use the questions below to help you get started.

What is your educational goal?
What is the highest level of education you have achieved?
Where were you born?
What is your mother's maiden name?

What are some other questions you might ask about their applications? Write two more questions below. (Answers will vary.)

1. _____

2. _____

E Work with a group of four students. Write three questions you want to ask your classmates to help you get to know them. (Answers will vary.)

1. _____

2. _____

3. _____

F Interview four *other* classmates and write their answers to your group's questions in the chart below. Go back to your group and share the information. At the end of this exercise, your group should have information about sixteen students!
(Answers will vary.)

Name	Question 1	Question 2	Question 3
1.			
2.			
3.			
4.			

LESSON 2

Learning strategies

GOAL ➤ **Identify learning strategies**

A How do you learn English? Make a list. (Answers will vary.)

1. Go to school.
2. _____
3. _____
4. _____
5. _____
6. _____

B Learning a new language takes place inside and outside the classroom. Below is a list of strategies you can use to learn a new language. Read them with your teacher.

Learning Strategies
Learn grammar rules.
Listen to the radio in English.
Read English books, magazines, and newspapers.
Talk to native speakers.
Watch TV in English.
Write in English.

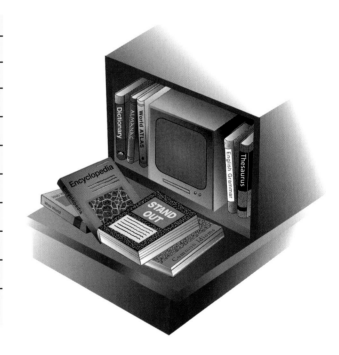

C Think of other learning strategies and add them to the list above.
(Answers will vary.)

Objective: Identify learning strategies
Academic Strategies: Using a bar graph, comparing and contrasting
Vocabulary: *strategy, native speakers, interview, bar graph*

RESOURCES

Activity Bank: Pre-Unit, Lesson 2, Worksheet 1   **Grammar Challenge 4:** Pre-Unit, Challenge 2

■ 1.5 hour classes ■ 2.5 hour classes ■ 3⁺ hour classes

AGENDA

Discuss ways you learn English.
Identify learning strategies.
Discuss personal learning strategies.
Interview your classmates.
Create a bar graph.

Warm-up and Review   10–15 mins. ■■■

Review Lesson 1 by having students stand up and introduce the classmates they met. See if any student in the class can name all of the other students.

Introduction   5–10 mins. ■■■

Ask students how they learn English. Accept any answers they offer.

(A) How do you learn English? Make a list.

As a class, brainstorm ideas and write them on the board. Have students use these ideas as well as their own ideas to make their lists. State the objective: *Today we will identify and discuss different strategies that you can use to learn English.*

Presentation 1   10–15 mins. ■■■

(B) Learning a new language takes place inside and outside the classroom. Below is a list of strategies you can use to learn a new language. Read them with your teacher.

Talk about each strategy with students and ask them to raise their hands if they already use that strategy.

Practice 1   10–15 mins. ■■■

(C) Think of other learning strategies and add them to the list above.

Have students do this activity in pairs or groups.

Evaluation 1   5 mins. ■■■

Make a list on the board of all the strategies that students came up with.

STANDARDS CORRELATIONS

CASAS: 0.1.2, 4.8.1, 6.1.1, 6.7.2, 7.4.1, 7.4.9
(See CASAS Competency List on pages 169–175.)
SCANS: **Resources** Allocate human resources
Information Acquire and evaluate information, organize and maintain information, interpret and communicate information
Interpersonal Participate as a member of a team, teach others, exercise leadership, negotiate to arrive at a decision, work with cultural diversity
Systems Understand systems
Basic Skills Reading, writing, arithmetic, listening, speaking

Thinking Skills Creative thinking, decision making, problem solving, seeing things in the mind's eye
Personal Qualities Responsibility, sociability, self-management
EFF: **Communication** Read with understanding, speak so others can understand, listen actively
Decision Making Use math to solve problems and communicate, plan
Interpersonal Cooperate with others
Lifelong Learning Take responsibility for learning, reflect and evaluate, learn through research, use information and communications technology (optional)

Presentation 2

5 mins. ▪▪▪

Go over the questions in Exercise D and make sure students understand how to answer them.

Practice 2

5-15 mins. ▪▪

(Shorter classes can do Exercise D for homework.)

D Answer the questions about your personal studying strategies.

When students have finished, have them share their answers with a partner.

Evaluation 2

10-20 mins. ▪▪

Review each question and ask volunteers to give their answers to the class.

Presentation 3

5-10 mins. ▪▪▪

Go over the instructions to Exercise E. Demonstrate the activity by asking a few students the questions and writing their answers in your book. Explain to students that they will be walking around the classroom and gathering answers. They do not need to write down the name of the person who gives them the answers.

Practice 3

5-10 mins. ▪

E Interview other students in your class using the questions in Exercise D. Write their answers below. (If more than one student has the same answer, you don't need to write it twice.)

Evaluation 3

10-15 mins. ▪

Walk around the classroom and observe the activity. When students have finished, ask them to share the feedback they got with the class.

D Answer the questions about your personal studying strategies. (Answers will vary.)

1. Where do you usually study? _____

2. What strategies do you use inside the classroom? _____
   _____

3. What strategies do you use outside the classroom? _____
   _____

4. Write two strategies that you don't use now, but that you would like to use in the
   future. _____
   _____

5. What do you think is the best strategy for learning English? _____
   _____

E Interview other students in your class using the questions in Exercise D. Write their answers below. (If more than one student has the same answer, you don't need to write it twice.) (Answers will vary.)

Study Locations	
Classroom Strategies	
Outside Strategies	
New Strategies to Use	
Best Strategies	

GOAL ➤ **Identify learning strategies**

F Look at the bar graph and answer the questions.

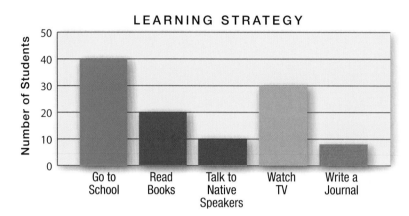

How many students. . .

go to school?	40
read books?	20
talk to native speakers?	10
watch TV?	30
write a journal?	8/9

G With a group, decide on six effective learning strategies. Take a class poll to see how many people use these learning strategies. (Answers will vary.)

Our Class: Effective Learning Strategies

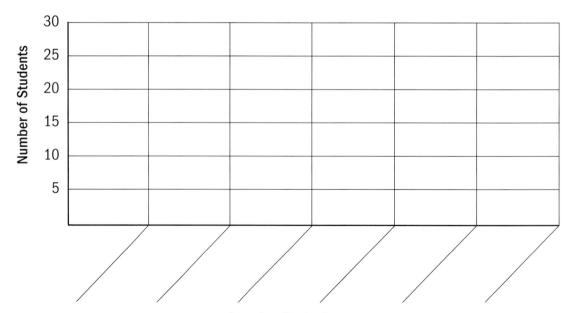

Application   10–20 mins. ▮▮▮▮

F Look at the bar graph and answer the questions.

Go over the bar graph with students, making sure they understand how to read it. As a class, answer the questions.

G With a group, decide on six effective learning strategies. Take a class poll to see how many people use these learning strategies.

Explain the activity to students, helping them come up with a method for completing the class poll. (They will have to decide how to ask each student in the class, once and only once, about the learning strategies so they don't duplicate information.) Ask a volunteer from each group to draw their bar graph on the board and compare and contrast the results.

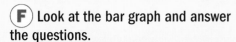

Activity Bank

Lesson 2, Worksheet 1: Learning Strategies

Refer students to *Stand Out 4 Grammar Challenge*, Pre-Unit, Challenge 2 for more practice with information questions.

AT-A-GLANCE PREP

Objective: Write about your goals
Grammar: Editing
Academic Strategies: Writing a paragraph, setting goals
Vocabulary: *word family, noun, verb, adjective, adverb, paragraph, topic sentence, support sentence, conclusion sentence, punctuation, capitalization*

RESOURCES

Activity Bank: Pre-Unit, Lesson 3, Worksheet 1; Templates

Grammar Challenge 4: Pre-Unit, Challenge 3

■ 1.5 hour classes ■ 2.5 hour classes ■ 3⁺ hour classes

AGENDA

Identify word families.
List your goals.
Identify sentence types.
Write a paragraph.
Identify types of errors.
Edit a paragraph.

Warm-up and Review   5 mins.

Review learning strategies with students. Ask students what learning strategies they used the previous day or before class to improve their English. Ask students what strategies they plan to use over the coming weekend.

Introduction   5–10 mins.

Ask students to tell you what a paragraph is. Come up with a definition as a class. (Example definition: A paragraph is a group of sentences about the same topic.) State the objective: *Today we will edit a paragraph and write our own paragraphs about our goals.*

Presentation 1   10–15 mins.

Write the phrase *word family* on the board. Ask students if they know what the term means.

(A) In this book, you will be learning many new strategies to help you learn and remember vocabulary. The first strategy involves word families. What do you think a word family is? Look at the example below.

Have students put the definition of *word family* in their own words. Explain the term if students

are still unsure of its meaning. Go over the example of a word family.

(B) Read the paragraph. There are five words that belong to the same word family. Find and underline them.

Have students do this activity by themselves and then go over the answers as a class. Show students that if they learn one new word and its word-family members, they can learn three or four new words at the same time.

Practice 1   10–15 mins.

(C) Complete the chart with word families. You may need to use a dictionary or ask another student for help.

Have students work in small groups to complete this exercise.

Evaluation 1   5 mins.

Ask volunteers to fill out the word family chart on the board.

(D) The student who wrote the paragraph in Exercise B has a goal—to get organized. What are your goals for the year? List them in the chart below.

Make sure students understand what a goal is. Give them a few examples if necessary.

STANDARDS CORRELATIONS

CASAS: 7.1.1, 7.2.4, 7.4.1, 7.4.3, 7.4.5
(See CASAS Competency List on pages 169–175.)
SCANS: Information Acquire and evaluate information, organize and maintain information, interpret and communicate information, use computers to process information (optional)
Interpersonal Participate as a member of a team, teach others, exercise leadership, negotiate to arrive at a decision, work with cultural diversity
Systems Monitor and correct performance
Technology (optional) Select technology, apply technology to a task, maintain and troubleshoot technology

Basic Skills Reading, writing, listening, speaking
Thinking Skills Creative thinking, decision making, problem solving, seeing things in the mind's eye
Personal Qualities Responsibility, sociability, self-management
EFF: Communication Read with understanding, convey ideas in writing, speak so others can understand, listen actively, observe critically
Decision Making Plan
Interpersonal Guide others, advocate and influence, cooperate with others
Lifelong Learning Take responsibility for learning, reflect and evaluate, use information and communications technology (optional)

LESSON 3

What are your goals?

GOAL ➤ Write about your goals

A In this book, you will be learning many new strategies to help you learn and remember vocabulary. The first strategy involves word families. What do you think a word family is? Look at the example below.

Noun	Verb	Adjective	Adverb
creation	create	creative	creatively

B Read the paragraph. There are five words that belong to the same word family. Find and underline them.

> My goal for the year is to get <u>organized</u>. To learn a new language, you need to study a lot of vocabulary. Good <u>organization</u> requires writing down the new words you learn and finding out their meanings. You should <u>organize</u> the words in a notebook so you can easily find them. Once you learn how to keep a well-<u>organized</u> vocabulary list, you can say, "I have good <u>organizational</u> skills!"

C Complete the chart with word families. You may need to use a dictionary or ask another student for help.

Noun	Verb	Adjective	Adverb
education	educate	educational	educationally
success	succeed	successful	successfully
decision	decide	decisive	decisively
achiever	achieve	achievable	XXXXX

D The student who wrote the paragraph in Exercise B has a goal—to get organized. What are your goals for the year? List them in the chart below. (Answers will vary.)

My Goals

GOAL ➤ Write about your goals

E Takuji has had three goals since he came to the United States. Read his paragraph. What are his three goals? 1. to improve his English 3. buy a new house
(Answers may vary slightly.) 2. get a job that pays more money

My Goals

Ever since I came to the United States, I have had three goals. First, I want to improve my English by going to school every day and studying at night. Then, once my English is better, I will look for a job that pays more money. Finally, when I have saved up enough money, I will buy a new house for my family. These are the three goals that I made when I first came to the United States.

F What is a paragraph? Discuss the words in italics with your teacher.

A paragraph is a group of sentences (usually 5–7 sentences) about the *same topic*. A *topic sentence* is usually the first sentence and it introduces your topic or *main idea*. *Support sentences* are the sentences that follow your topic sentence. They give *details* about your topic. A *conclusion sentence* is the last sentence of your paragraph and it summarizes what you have written.

G Look back at Takuji's paragraph. Can you find each of the three sentence types discussed in Exercise F? Sentence 1: topic sentence; Sentences 2-4: support sentences; Sentence 5: conclusion sentence

H What are your goals? Write a paragraph about your goals on a piece of paper. Make sure your first sentence is a topic sentence. Follow your topic sentence with support sentences and then, finish your paragraph with a conclusion sentence.

Presentation 2   10–15 mins.

E Takuji has had three goals since he came to the United States. Read his paragraph. What are his three goals?

Ask a volunteer to read the paragraph out loud. As a class, discuss Takuji's goals.

F What is a paragraph? Discuss the words in italics with your teacher.

G Look back at Takuji's paragraph. Can you find each of the three sentence types discussed in Exercise F?

Practice 2   20–25 mins.

(Shorter classes can do Exercise H for homework.)

H What are your goals? Write a paragraph about your goals on a piece of paper. Make sure your first sentence is a topic sentence. Follow your topic sentence with support sentences and then, finish your paragraph with a conclusion sentence.

Teaching Tip

Writing a paragraph following a model

If students haven't had much writing practice, it is OK to let them follow a model, copying where they need to and adding in their own information when necessary or possible. By using a model, they will get comfortable with the structure of an English paragraph and will eventually be able to write one on their own.

Evaluation 2   20–25 mins.

Walk around the classroom and help students as necessary as they write their paragraphs.

Instructor's Notes

_____
_____
_____
_____
_____
_____
_____
_____
_____
_____
_____
_____
_____
_____
_____
_____
_____
_____
_____
_____
_____
_____
_____
_____
_____
_____
_____
_____
_____
_____
_____
_____

Presentation 3   5-10 mins.

I Look at the first draft of Takuji's paragraph. There are eight errors. The first one has been done for you. Can you find and correct the rest?

Ask students if they know what an error is. As a class, look at the example error and correction in the first sentence. Then see if students can find the second error and make a correction. Have students find the rest of the errors on their own and then go over the answers as a class.

Practice 3   5-10 mins. ■

(Shorter classes can do Exercise J for homework.)

J Write each of the errors from the paragraph in the chart below. Then, write the correct form and identify the type of error. Use choices from the box.

Go over each error type with students, giving them examples if necessary. Don't give them the example from Takuji's paragraph since this is what they will be doing for the exercise. Have students work with a partner to complete the chart.

Evaluation 3   5 mins. ■

Go over the answers as a class.

Teaching Tip

Error correction

There are many different philosophies about correcting students' errors, but the *Stand Out* authors believe that you, as the teacher, should do as little correcting as possible, allowing students to try to find their own mistakes. It can be overwhelming for a teacher to feel like he or she has to correct every mistake on an assignment, and even more intimidating for a student to be given that assignment back covered in red ink.

To make the task more manageable and less intimidating, it is a good idea to let students know what you will be looking for. Then both of you can focus only on those specific errors, such as verb tenses and subject-verb agreement. As students master new grammar points, they can begin focusing on more types of errors at a time.

Application   15-25 mins. ■■■

K Now exchange the paragraph you wrote in Exercise H with a partner. Check your partner's work for errors using the error types listed in Exercise J.

Refer students to *Stand Out 4 Grammar Challenge*, Pre-Unit, Challenge 3 for more practice with editing.

Activity Bank

Lesson 3, Worksheet 1: Word Family Practice

Instructor's Notes

_____
_____
_____
_____
_____
_____
_____
_____
_____
_____
_____
_____
_____
_____
_____
_____
_____
_____
_____
_____
_____
_____
_____

GOAL ➤ **Write about your goals**

I Look at the first draft of Takuji's paragraph. There are eight errors. The first one has been done for you. Can you find and correct the rest?

My Goals

Ever since I came to the United States, I have had three goal^s. First I need
to improve my English by going at[to] school every day and studying at night. Once my
English are[is] better, I will look for a job that pays more money. Finally, when I have
saved up enough money. I will buy a house new for my family. This[These] are the three goals
that I made when I first come[came] to the united States.

J Write each of the errors from the paragraph in the chart below. Then, write the correct form and identify the type of error. Use choices from the box.

punctuation	capitalization	subject/verb agreement	verb tense
spelling	singular/plural	word choice	word order

Error	Correction	Type of Error
goal	goals	singular/plural
at	to	word choice
are	is	subject/verb agreement
money.	money,	punctuation
house new	new house	word order
This	These	singlular/plural
come	came	verb tense
united	United	capitalization

K Now exchange the paragraph you wrote in Exercise H with a partner. Check your partner's work for errors using the error types listed in Exercise J.

My Dictionary

Find three new words you learned in this unit. Write down the word and the sentence where you found the word. (Answers will vary.)

EXAMPLE: Word: organizational   Page: P7
Sentence: I have good organizational skills!

1. Word: _____   Page: _____
   Sentence: _____

2. Word: _____   Page: _____
   Sentence: _____

3. Word: _____   Page: _____
   Sentence: _____

Learner Log

In this unit, you had a chance to fill out an application, meet your classmates, identify learning strategies, and think about your goals. How comfortable do you feel doing each of the skills listed below? Rate your comfort level on a scale of 1 to 4. (Answers will vary.)

1 = Need more practice   **2** = OK   **3** = Good   **4** = Great!

Life Skill	Comfort Level	Page
I can fill out an application form.	1 2 3 4	_____
I can tell others about myself.	1 2 3 4	_____
I can introduce my friends.	1 2 3 4	_____
I can identify learning strategies.	1 2 3 4	_____
I can create a bar graph.	1 2 3 4	_____
I can complete word families.	1 2 3 4	_____
I can write a paragraph.	1 2 3 4	_____
I can find and identify errors.	1 2 3 4	_____
I can edit a classmate's paragraph.	1 2 3 4	_____

If you circled a 1 or 2, write down the page number where you can review this skill.

Reflection

1. What was the most useful skill you learned in this unit? _____

2. How will this help you in life? _____

Presentation 1   5-15 mins.

My Dictionary

Write the word *Dictionary* on the board. Ask students what the purpose of a dictionary is. Tell them they are going to be creating their own mini-dictionaries for each unit. Ask students to look back through the unit and call out new words that they learned. Write what they say on the board.

Find three new words you learned in this unit. Write down the word and the sentence where you found the word.

Go over the example with students by showing them the word in the book and the example sentence.

Practice 1   10-15 mins.

Have students work by themselves to find 3 new words they learned in this unit. Have them complete the exercise.

Evaluation 1   10-20 mins.

Walk around the classroom and help students as needed. Ask for volunteers to share their words and sentences with other students. Take a few quick polls to see how many students identified the same words.

Presentation 2   5-10 mins.

Learner Log

Write the word *Log* on the board. Ask students if they know what this means. Explain to them that it is a journal, notebook, or place where you keep track of information. In this case, they will be keeping track of what they learned. Tell them that they will be completing a Learner Log at the end of each unit.

In this unit, you had a chance to fill out an application, meet your classmates, identify learning strategies, and think about your goals. How comfortable do you feel doing each of the skills listed below? Rate your comfort level on a scale of 1 to 4.

Go over the instructions with students and make sure they understand what to do. You may want to do the first one or two with the class to make sure they understand.

Teaching Tip

Learner Logs

Learner Logs function to help students in many different ways.

1. They serve as part of the review process.
2. They help students to gain confidence and document what they have learned. In this way, students see that they are progressing and want to move forward in learning.
3. They provide students with a tool that they can use over and over to check and recheck their understanding. In this way, students become independent learners.

Practice 2   5 mins.

Have students complete the Learner Log, describing how they feel about doing each one.

Evaluation 2   5 mins.

Walk around the classroom and help students as needed. Take a poll to see how good students feel about doing each of the skills.

Application   10-20 mins.

Go over the reflection statements with students and have them complete the answers by themselves.

TB Assessment *(optional)*

Use the Stand Out 4 Assessment CD-ROM with Exam*View*® to create a post-test for the Pre-Unit.

AT-A-GLANCE PREP

Objective: Compare past and present using *used to*
Grammar: *Used to*
Academic Strategies: Focused listening, comparing and contrasting
Vocabulary: *Used to, habits, architect*

RESOURCES

Activity Bank: Unit 1, Lesson 1, Worksheet 1
Reading and Writing Challenge: Unit 1

Grammar Challenge: Unit 1, Challenge 1
Audio: CD 1, Tracks 2–3

■ 1.5 hour classes ■ 2.5 hour classes ■ 3⁺ hour classes

Preassessment *(optional)*

Use the Stand Out 4 Assessment CD-ROM with Exam*View*® to create a pretest for Unit 1.

Warm-up and Review   5-10 mins.

Ask students *What did you do as a child that you don't do now? Five years ago? Last year?* (Encourage students to focus on habitual or long-term actions, not one-time events.)

Introduction   5-10 mins.

Restate some student answers orally, using *used to*. For example, if a student said: *When I was a child, I played soccer*, say: *(Jorge) used to play soccer*. Then write some examples on the board so students can see the written form. State the objective: *Today we will be comparing things you did in the past to what you do now using* used to.

Presentation 1   10-15 mins.

A Bita and Minh are new students at Bellingham Adult School. Listen to their conversation on the first day of class.

Before students listen, talk about the pictures. Then have them read the questions in Exercise B and guess the answers.

 Listening Script   CD 1, Track 2

Bita: *Excuse me. Is this Ms. Johnson's ESL class? I'm new here.*
Minh: *I'm pretty sure this is her class. I attended classes at this school five years ago, and this is where her class was.*
Bita: *Oh good. I used to go to school in the daytime before I got a new job. Now that I'm working during the day, I have to go to school in the evening. My other school doesn't offer evening classes so I had to leave there and come here.*

Minh: *I used to go to school during the day too, but sometimes I take care of my grandchildren so evening classes are better for me. What kind of work do you do?*
Bita: *I used to be an architect in Iran, but I don't have the right qualifications to be an architect in the United States. So, I'm doing administrative work for an engineering company until my English is good enough to go back to college and get the right degree.*
Minh: *Wow, I'm impressed.*
Bita: *Do you work?*
Minh: *Not anymore. I used to work for a computer company, assembling computers, but now I just go to school and help my children with their children.*
Bita: *That's nice. I bet your children appreciate that. Why are you studying English?*
Minh: *First of all, I want to help my grandchildren with their homework. But also, I figure since I live in this country, I should be able to speak the language. Don't you agree?*
Bita: *Completely!*

B With a partner, answer the questions about Bita and Minh. You may have to guess some of the answers.

Explain to students that they might have to make inferences based on what they heard in the recording. When they have completed the activity, discuss the answers as a class.

Practice 1   10-15 mins.

C Bita and Minh both talk about things they did in the past and things they do now. Listen again and complete the chart. (CD 1, TR3 is the same as TR 2)

Ask students to write down what they can remember from their first listening. Then have them fill in the chart after they've heard it the second time.

Evaluation 1   5 mins.

Go over the answers as a class.

Note: Standards Correlations are on next page.

UNIT 1

Balancing Your Life

GOALS

➤ Compare past and present
➤ Create a goal chart
➤ Identify obstacles and give advice
➤ Write about an important person
➤ Identify and apply time-management skills

LESSON 1

Where did you use to study?

GOAL ➤ Compare past and present

CD 1
TR 2

A Bita and Minh are new students at Bellingham Adult School. Listen to their conversation on the first day of class.

B With a partner, answer the questions about Bita and Minh. You may have to guess some of the answers.

Minh:
1. Old enough to be a grandfather.
2. He is retired and a student.
3. Vietnam.
4. To help his grandchildren with their homework and to speak the language of the country.

1. How old are they?

2. What do they do?

3. Where are they from?

4. Why are they studying English?

Minh

Bita:
1. Answers will vary.
2. Administrative work for an engineering company.
3. Iran
4. So she can go to college.

Bita

CD 1
TR 3

C Bita and Minh both talk about things they did in the past and things they do now. Listen again and complete the chart. (Answers may vary. Possible answers below.)

	Past	Now
Bita	went to another school in the daytime was an architect	goes to school in the evening does administrative work
Minh	went to school during the day worked for a computer company	takes care of his grandchildren goes to school in the evening

GOAL ➤ **Compare past and present**

D Study the chart with your classmates and teacher.

Used to	
Example	**Rule**
Minh *used to* go to school during the day. Bita *used to* be an architect in Iran.	**Affirmative:** *used to* + base verb
Bita *did not use to* go to school at night. Minh *didn't use to* take care of his grandchildren.	**Negative:** *did* + *not (didn't)* + *use to* + base verb **Incorrect:** ~~I didn't used to go to school.~~
Did Minh *use to* work? *Did* Bita *use to* study English?	**Yes/No Question:** *did* + subject + *use to* + base verb **Incorrect:** ~~Did Bita used to live in Iran?~~
Where *did* Minh *use to* work? What *did* Bita *use to* study?	**Wh- Question:** *wh-* word + *did* + subject + *use to* + base verb
Used to + base verb expresses a past habit or state which is now different.	

E Complete the sentences with the correct form of *used to* and the base form of the verb in parentheses, or the simple present tense form of the verb.

EXAMPLE: Kaitlin _____used to live_____ (live) with her family, but now she

_____lives_____ (live) alone.

1. Armando _____used to go_____ (go) to school in the daytime, but now he

_____goes_____ (go) in the evening.

2. Where did Su _____use to teach_____ (teach)?

3. Heidi _____is_____ (be) an administrative assistant now, but she

_____used to be_____ (be) an architect in Sweden.

4. He _____goes_____ (go) to school and _____helps_____ (help) his

children now, but he _____used to assemble_____ (assemble) computers.

5. Elisa _____used to live_____ (live) near her family, but now she

_____lives_____ (live) far away.

6. Did the two brothers _____use to study_____ (study) together?

Presentation 2   5-10 mins. ■■■□

D Study the chart with your classmates and teacher.

In addition to the examples in the chart, remind students of some of the things they said in the warm-up and go over those examples again.

Go over the example in Exercise E with students, asking them when they should use *used to* and when they should use the present tense.

Practice 2   10-15 mins. ■■□

(Shorter classes can do Exercise E for homework.)

E Complete the sentences with the correct form of *used to* and the base form of the verb in parentheses, or the simple present tense form of the verb.

For extra practice, have students rewrite the sentences in question form. For example: *When did Armando use to go to school?* Students can then practice asking and answering the questions they wrote with a partner.

Evaluation 2   5 mins. ■■□

Go over the answers as a class.

 Activity Bank

Lesson 1, Worksheet 1: *Used to*

 Instructor's Notes

_____

_____

_____

_____

_____

_____

_____

_____

_____

_____

_____

_____

_____

_____

_____

_____

_____

_____

_____

_____

_____

_____

_____

_____

_____

_____

_____

_____

STANDARDS CORRELATIONS

CASAS: 0.2.4 (See CASAS Competency List on pages 169–175.)
SCANS: **Information** Acquire and evaluate information, interpret and communicate information
Interpersonal Participate as a member of a team, teach others, exercise leadership, negotiate to arrive at a decision, work with cultural diversity
Systems Monitor and correct performance
Basic Skills Reading, writing, listening, speaking

Thinking Skills Creative thinking, decision making
Personal Qualities Responsibility, sociability, self-management
EFF: **Communication** Read with understanding, convey ideas in writing, speak so others can understand, listen actively
Interpersonal Guide others, advocate and influence, cooperate with others

Presentation 3   5–10 mins. ■■■

Have students turn back to the chart about Bita and Minh on page 1, Exercise C. Ask them questions such as: *What did Bita use to do?* Encourage them to answer in complete sentences using *used to*.

Practice 3   15–20 mins. ■

F Look back at the things that you wrote about Bita and Minh in Exercise C. With a partner, make sentences about what Bita and Minh *used to* do and what they do now.

G Write three *wh-* questions using *used to*. Then, ask a partner your questions.

 Refer students to *Stand Out 4 Grammar Challenge*, Unit 1, Challenge 1 for more practice with *used to* in affirmative and negative statements.

Evaluation 3   5–10 mins. ■

For Exercise F, ask volunteers to read their sentences out loud.

For Exercise G, ask volunteers to write their questions on the board. Focus on the difference between *used to* in a sentence (I *used to* . . .) and *used to* in a question (*Did* you *use to* . . . ?) Ask volunteers to report on their partners' answers.

Application   10–20 mins. ■■■

H Look at the pictures. With a partner, make sentences comparing the past and the present.

Use this activity as a presentation for the next exercise. Walk around the classroom and listen to students make sentences. Go over the answers as a class before students go on to Exercise I.

I Write two sentences comparing your past and present habits.

Call on individual students to write their sentences on the board. If you have time, erase the sentences and ask questions about what was written on the board to see what the class remembers. For example, assume the following sentence was written on the board: *I used to run in the morning, but now I walk in the evening.* You could ask: *What did (Lisa) use to do in the morning?*

F Look back at the things that you wrote about Bita and Minh in Exercise C. With a partner, make sentences about what Bita and Minh *used to* do and what they do now.

EXAMPLE: Bita used to go to another school in the daytime, but now she goes to school in the evening.

1. (Answers will vary.)

2. _____

3. _____

G Write three *wh-* questions using *used to*. Then, ask a partner your questions.

EXAMPLE: Where did you use to work?

1. (Answers will vary.)

2. _____

3. _____

H Look at the pictures. With a partner, make sentences comparing the past and the present.

Subject / Verb	Past	Present
1. Suzanne / play Suzanne used to play the piano, but now she doesn't.		
2. Eli and Rosa / live Eli and Rosa used to live in New York, but now they don't.		

I Write two sentences comparing your past and present habits. (Answers will vary.)

1. _____

2. _____

LESSON 2 **Reaching your goals**

GOAL ➤ Create a goal chart

 A Read the paragraph about Bita's goals. Use the context (surrounding words) to work out the meanings of the words in *italics*. Do the first one with your teacher.

My name is Bita and I'm from Iran. I've been in the United States for six years. In my country, I was an *architect* and I designed schools and hospitals, but in the United States, I don't have the right *qualifications* to be an architect. I have a plan. I'm going to learn English, go to school for architecture, and become an architect in the U.S. Here is my dream. In nine years, I will be an architect working in a *firm* with three other partners. We will design and build homes in *suburban* neighborhoods. I will live in a nice home that I designed, and I will look for the man of my dreams to share my life with. How does that sound to you?

 B Read the paragraph about Minh. Use the context to work out the meanings of the words in *italics*.

I'm Minh and I've been in the United States since 1975. I came here as a *refugee* from Vietnam. I used to work for a computer company, but now I'm *retired*. I help take care of my grandchildren while their parents are working, but I also do something else on the side. I make jewelry to sell to local jewelers. My father was a jeweler in Vietnam, and he taught me his art. My goal is to help send my grandchildren to college, so I save every penny I make from the jewelry. This is my dream. In five years, my oldest grandchild will teach elementary school in the community where she lives and she will *raise* her own family. My other grandchild will study medicine at one of the best schools in the country because he wants to be a *surgeon*. I hope that all of their dreams come true.

 C Answer the questions with a partner. (Answers are in paragraphs above.)

1. What are Bita's and Minh's goals?

2. What are they doing to make their goals a reality?

3. What are their dreams?

 D What are some examples of goals? Discuss your ideas with your teacher.

E What are your future goals? Write them on a piece of paper.

---

4 Unit 1 Lesson 2

AT-A-GLANCE PREP

Objective: Create a goal chart
Grammar: Future tense using *will*
Academic Strategies: Active reading, using context clues, setting goals, focused listening
Vocabulary: *goals, dreams, reality, qualifications, firm, suburban, refugee, retired, raise, jewelry, medicine, surgeon, intern, partner, context, designed*

RESOURCES

Activity Bank: Unit 1, Lesson 2, Worksheets 1–3
Reading and Writing Challenge: Unit 1

Grammar Challenge: Unit 1, Challenge 2
Audio: CD 1, Track 4

■ 1.5 hour classes ■ 2.5 hour classes ■ 3⁺ hour classes

AGENDA

Read about Bita's and Minh's goals.
Use context to find meaning.
List your goals.
Listen and fill in a goal chart.
Create a personal goal chart.
Use the future tense with will.

Warm-up and Review   5–10 mins.

Review Lesson 1 by asking volunteers to read the sentences they wrote with *used to* in Exercise H on page 3.

Introduction   5 mins.

Write the words *dream* and *goal* on the board. Ask students to help you define these two words. Ask: *Do they have the same meaning? How are their meanings different?* State the objective: *Today we will read about goals, identify our own goals and create charts for goals we would like to achieve.*

Presentation 1   5–10 mins.

Prepare students for the readings in Exercises A and B by asking them what Bita's and Minh's goals might be. As a class, look at the first word in italics, *architect,* in the reading in Exercise A. Show students how to use context to find the meaning of this new vocabulary word. Ask students the following questions: *What does this word mean? What words near this word might help you find its meaning? Is it a noun or a verb?*

Practice 1   10–15 mins.

A Read the paragraph about Bita's goals. Use the context (surrounding words) to work out the meanings of the words in *italics*. Do the first one with your teacher.

B Read the paragraph about Minh. Use the context to work out the meanings of the words in *italics*.

C Answer the questions with a partner.

Evaluation 1   10–15 mins.

As a class, go over the new vocabulary in the readings. Also, review the answers to Exercise C.

D What are some examples of goals? Discuss your ideas with your teacher.

Help students come up with examples of different types of goals including personal, educational, vocational, and professional goals.

E What are your future goals? Write them on a piece of paper.

Ask students to list at least three goals. They will use these goals in the application activity for this lesson.

Presentation 2

10–15 mins.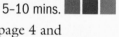

Ask students what steps they think Bita will need to take to achieve her goal. Make a list of their ideas on the board.

Prepare students for focused listening by having them look at the chart in Exercise F. Ask them questions about the chart to familiarize them with the information: *What is Bita's first step? When will she finish studying English?* Ask students what information is missing and what they will need to listen carefully for.

Teaching Tip

Focused listening

The purpose of focused listening is to expose students to real-life listening situations and teach them how to pick out the most important information.

- Make it clear to students that they don't need to understand everything that is spoken to grasp the meaning of the passage.
- Present the context.
- Make sure students understand what they are listening for.
- After they complete the task, ask for a report.

Specific Steps

1. Play the recording with student books closed. Tell students just to listen.
2. Have them open their books and see if they can write anything in the chart that they remember.
3. Play the recording again and have them write what they hear.
4. Have them share their answers with a partner and fill in what they missed.
5. Play the recording one final time.

Practice 2

5–15 mins. ■ ■

 Listen to the conversation that Bita is having with her friend, Yoshiko. Fill in Bita's goal chart with the missing steps and dates.

 Listening Script CD 1, Track 4

Yoshiko: *How long do you think it will take you to become an architect?*
Bita: *My goal is to become a partner in a firm by the year 2017.*

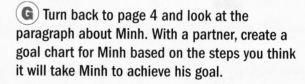

Yoshiko: *What'll you do first?*
Bita: *Well, the first thing I have to do is improve my English, which I plan to study for two more years. Then by the fall of 2011, I'll be ready to register for college.*
Yoshiko: *How long will it take you to finish?*
Bita: *Well, usually a degree in architecture takes five or six years to complete, but some of the classes I took in my country will transfer, so I should be able to do it faster. I plan to get my degree in the spring of 2015.*
Yoshiko: *Then you can become an architect?*
Bita: *Not quite. Then I'll have to become an intern to get some practical experience and prepare for my licensing exams.*
Yoshiko: *Exams?*
Bita: *Yes, I'll have to take a series of tests before I can get my license to be an architect. Once I have my license, which I hope to get in the winter of 2016, I can apply to work as a partner in an architectural firm.*
Yoshiko: *Whew! That sounds like a lot of work!*
Bita: *It will be, but it'll be worth it in the end.*

Evaluation 2

10–20 mins. ■ ■

Go over the completed chart as a class. Ask students if the order of the steps makes sense and if the completion dates are realistic. Help students analyze the chart very carefully so they understand this system of organization.

Presentation 3

5–10 mins. ■ ■ ■

Ask students to turn back to page 4 and look at Minh's paragraph in Exercise B. Ask them to name Minh's goal, which is for his granddaughter to be a teacher and his grandson to be a surgeon. Write his goal on the board.

Practice 3

5–10 mins. ■

Ⓖ Turn back to page 4 and look at the paragraph about Minh. With a partner, create a goal chart for Minh based on the steps you think it will take Minh to achieve his goal.

Evaluation 3

10–15 mins. ■

Ⓗ Share your ideas with another pair of students.

After students have shared their ideas, have a spokesperson from each group share their goal charts with the class. Have students talk about the similarities and differences. Ask questions, such as: *Which chart is the most realistic?*

LESSON 2 **GOAL** ➤ **Create a goal chart**

CD 1
TR 4

F Listen to the conversation that Bita is having with her friend, Yoshiko. Fill in Bita's goal chart with the missing steps and dates.

Goal: To become an architect and a partner in a firm.	
Steps	**Completion Dates**
Step 1: Study English	Spring 2011
Step 2: Register for college	Fall 2011
Step 3: Get degree	Spring 2015
Step 4: Become an intern	Summer 2015
Step 5: Take tests and get license	Winter 2016
Step 6: Become a partner in a firm	2017

G Turn back to page 4 and look at the paragraph about Minh. With a partner, create a goal chart for Minh based on the steps you think it will take Minh to achieve his goal. (Answers will vary. See sample answers below.)

Goal: For my granddaughter to be a teacher and my grandson to be a surgeon.	
Steps	**Completion Dates**
Step 1: Take care of grandchildren	(Answers will vary.)
Step 2: Make jewelry	
Step 3: Save money from the jewelry I sell	
Step 4: Help pay for my grandchildren's college tuition	
Step 5: My granddaughter will be a teacher and my grandson will be a surgeon.	

H Share your ideas with another pair of students.

LESSON **2**   **GOAL** ➤ Create a goal chart

I   Look back at the goals you wrote in Exercise E. Choose the most important goal and write it below. (Answers will vary.)

My goal: _____

By what year do you want to achieve your goal? _____

J   Look at the goal chart below. Write your goal at the top. Write your goal again next to "Step 6," and write the date you will complete this goal. Now fill in the chart with the steps it will take to reach this goal. Estimate your completion dates. (Answers will vary.)

Goal: _____

Steps	Completion Dates
Step 1:	
Step 2:	
Step 3:	
Step 4:	
Step 5:	
Step 6:	

K   Now talk to a partner about your goal and the steps that you will take to achieve it.

EXAMPLE: In the fall of 2010, I will take classes at a community college.

Future Tense Using *Will*	
Example	**Rule**
In the spring of 2009, *I will ask* my boss for a raise. In the summer, *I will look* for a job.	Future tense = *will* + base verb
In spoken English, people often use contractions: I will = *I'll*.	

Application   10-20 mins.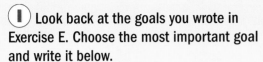

Ⅰ Look back at the goals you wrote in Exercise E. Choose the most important goal and write it below.

Help students clearly define their goals by asking a few volunteers to write their goals on the board. Make sure they are long-term goals that can be achieved by following a number of steps.

Ｊ Look at the goal chart below. Write your goal at the top. Write your goal again next to "Step 6," and write the date you will complete this goal. Now fill in the chart with the steps it will take to reach this goal. Estimate your completion dates.

Ｋ Now talk to a partner about your goal and the steps that you will take to achieve it.

Call students' attention to the grammar box on Future Tense Using *Will*. Go over the two examples and the rule with students and give them a few more examples.

Activity Bank

Lesson 2, Worksheet 1: Goal Practice
Lesson 2, Worksheet 2: Goal Chart
Lesson 2, Worksheet 3: Personal Goal Chart

Refer students to *Stand Out 4 Grammar Challenge*, Unit 1, Challenge 2 for practice with *used to* in *yes/no* and *wh-* questions.

Instructor's Notes

_____

_____

_____

_____

_____

_____

_____

_____

_____

_____

_____

_____

_____

_____

_____

_____

_____

_____

_____

_____

_____

_____

_____

_____

_____

_____

_____

_____

_____

Objective: Identify obstacles and give advice

Grammar: Modals *could, should*; *Why don't you . . . ?*; *How about . . . ?*

Pronunciation: Intonation: giving and responding to advice

Academic Strategies: Brainstorming, focused listening, problem solving

Vocabulary: *obstacle, solution, brainstorm, overcome, reliable, advice, respond, toddler, daycare facility*

RESOURCES

Activity Bank: Unit 1, Lesson 3, Worksheets 1–3
Reading and Writing Challenge: Unit 1

Grammar Challenge: Unit 1, Challenge 3
Audio: CD 1, Track 5

■ 1.5 hour classes   ■ 2.5 hour classes   ■ 3⁺ hour classes

AGENDA

Identify obstacles.
Brainstorm solutions to obstacles.
Give and respond to advice.

Warm-up and Review   5 mins.

Have students take out their goal charts from the previous lesson and share them with a classmate.

Introduction   5-10 mins.   ■ ■ ■

Ask students the following questions: *Are goals easy to achieve? Why or why not? What are some problems that you might have achieving your goals? What can you do about those problems?* Then write the word *advice* on the board and help students define it. State the objective: *Today we will discuss obstacles (problems) that might get in the way of achieving our goals and possible solutions. We will also practice giving and responding to advice.*

Presentation 1   10-15 mins.   ■ ■ ■

Write the words *obstacle* and *solution* on the board. Help students understand their meanings by talking about Bita and her goal. *What problems or obstacles might Bita have? What solutions can she use to overcome the obstacles?*

Write this problem on the board: *Miyoko wants to go to college, but she doesn't have enough money to pay for it.* Put a circle around the statement and ask students to come up to the board and write possible solutions for Miyoko's problem, similar to the cluster diagram on page 7.

Practice 1   10-15 mins.

(A) Sometimes we have problems achieving our goals. These problems are called *obstacles*. In order to overcome these obstacles, it can be a good idea to brainstorm different possible solutions. Look at the diagram below.

(B) Can you think of any other solutions? Add them to the blank circles in the cluster diagram above.

Have students work with a partner or a small group to complete the cluster diagram.

Evaluation 1   5 mins.

Have the groups share their ideas with the class.

STANDARDS CORRELATIONS

CASAS: 7.2.5, 7.2.7, 7.3.2 (See CASAS Competency List on pages 169-175.)
SCANS: **Resources** Allocate time, allocate money, allocate material and facility resources, allocate human resources
Information Acquire and evaluate information, organize and maintain information, interpret and communicate information
Interpersonal Participate as a member of a team, teach others, exercise leadership, negotiate to arrive at a decision, work with cultural diversity
Systems Understand systems, monitor and correct performance

Basic Skills Reading, writing, listening, speaking
Thinking Skills Creative thinking, decision making, problem solving, seeing things in the mind's eye
Personal Qualities Responsibility, sociability, self-management
EFF: **Communication** Read with understanding, convey ideas in writing, speak so others can understand, listen actively, observe critically
Decision Making Solve problems and make decisions, plan
Interpersonal Solve problems and make decisions, guide others, advocate and influence

LESSON 3

What should I do?

GOAL ➤ Identify obstacles and give advice

A Sometimes we have problems achieving our goals. These problems are called *obstacles*. In order to overcome these obstacles, it can be a good idea to brainstorm different possible solutions. Look at the diagram below.

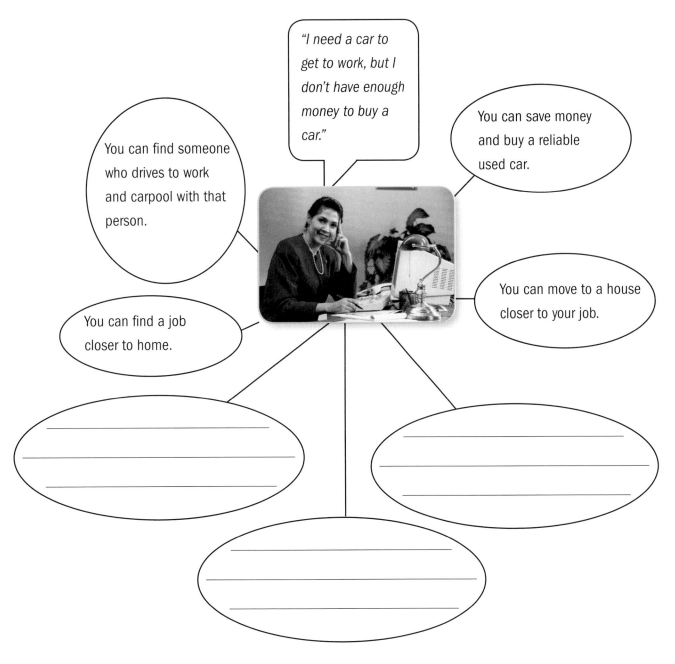

"I need a car to get to work, but I don't have enough money to buy a car."

You can save money and buy a reliable used car.

You can find someone who drives to work and carpool with that person.

You can move to a house closer to your job.

You can find a job closer to home.

B Can you think of any other solutions? Add them to the blank circles in the cluster diagram above. (Answers will vary.)

CD 1
TR 5

C Listen to each person talk to his or her friends about their problems. After you listen to each conversation, write the problem and two pieces of advice that the person receives.

Miyuki	Problem	Advice #1	Advice #2
	Her son is always angry and fights with other students.	talk to the guidance counselor	observe some classes and get to know the teachers
Ron	His landlord wants him to get rid of his dog.	let the landlord meet the dog	look for another apartment
Patty	She needs an operation but doesn't have health insurance.	save up money	find a job that gives health insurance

D Read the ways of giving and responding to advice in the chart below.

Problem	Advice
Magda wants to go back to school, but she has two children that she has to take care of. One of them is a toddler who isn't in school yet.	*Why don't* **you** ask your mother to take care of him?
	How about going to school in the evening?
	You should take some courses at home on the Internet.
	You could find a school with a daycare facility.

Response to advice (positive)	Response to advice (negative)
That's a great idea!	I don't think I can do that because . . .
Why didn't I think of that?	That doesn't sound possible because . . .
That's what I'll do.	That won't work because . . .

Presentation 2   5 mins.

Go over the directions for Exercise C. Ask students to look at the chart and tell you what they will be listening for.

Practice 2   5-10 mins.

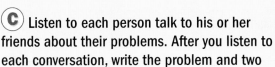 **C** Listen to each person talk to his or her friends about their problems. After you listen to each conversation, write the problem and two pieces of advice that the person receives.

Ask students what they will be listening for. Remind students that they will be listening for specific information so it's not important to understand every word.

 Listening Script   CD 1, Track 5

Conversation 1
Anna: How's Harry doing these days?
Miyuki: I don't know what to do about him. He can't seem to settle down. He's angry all the time and is always fighting with the other students. My husband has to go and talk to the principal almost every week.
Anna: How about talking to the guidance counselor?
Miyuki: I've tried that, but he doesn't have any suggestions.
Anna: Why don't you go and observe some classes and get to know the teachers better? Maybe that would help.
Miyuki: Yes, that's a great idea.

Conversation 2
Ron: What am I going to do? My new landlord doesn't like dogs and he wants me to get rid of Herbie!
Mike: You can't do that! Has he met Herbie? Does he know what a friendly dog he is? Did you try introducing them?
Ron: No, that won't work. I don't think my landlord likes any dogs.
Mike: OK, then why don't you start looking for another apartment?

Conversation 3
Sue: How's your back these days, Patty?
Patty: It's getting worse. I'm going to need an operation, but I don't have any insurance.
Sue: I guess you'll have to save up some money then.
Patty: Yes, it could be expensive.
Sue: Or how about finding a job that gives you health insurance?
Patty: Yes, that's what I'll have to do.

Evaluation 2   3 mins.

Go over the answers as a class.

Presentation 3   10-15 mins.

D Read the ways of giving and responding to advice in the chart below.

Go over the charts with the students. Help students practice the intonation of the phrases in the chart by saying them one at a time and having students repeat after you.

Pronunciation

Intonation: Giving and responding to advice

When giving advice in a question form, such as *Why don't you . . . ?* or *How about . . . ?*, students should use rising and falling intonation. Explain to students that it is like being at the bottom of a hill, going up the hill, and coming back down.

How about going to school in the evening?

When giving advice in a declarative sentence form, such as *You could . . .* , students should speak hesitantly so that they make the suggestion without sounding pushy.

When responding to advice positively, students should sound excited and happy about the advice. When responding negatively, students should speak hesitantly, so as not to offend the person giving the advice.

Lesson Planner: Unit 1, Lesson 3   **8a**

Presentation 3 (continued)

Go over the instructions and first example in Exercise E.

Practice 3   5-10 mins.

(Shorter classes can do Exercise E for homework.)

E Read the situations and come up with two possible solutions for each. Use *could* when writing your solutions.

Have students do this exercise in small groups.

F Work with a partner. Imagine that one of you has one of the problems in Exercise E. Make a conversation like the one below. Use different ways of giving and responding to advice.

Ask two volunteers to perform the example conversation. Ask the class for different ways that Student B could respond to the advice using examples from the charts on page 8. Remind students that more than one response is possible. Remind students to practice their intonation when making conversations.

Evaluation 3   5 mins.

For Exercise E, have students share their answers in groups. For Exercise F, call on students to present their conversations to the class.

Application   15-25 mins.

G Look back at Exercise J on page 6. Think of an obstacle that might get in your way of achieving this goal. Make a cluster diagram like the one on page 7 and brainstorm different solutions with a partner.

When students have finished their cluster diagrams, have them make conversations with their partner about the obstacles and give advice.

Application Extension

Pass out note cards and ask students to write down a problem. Ask them to write it in the first person. For example: *I'm going on vacation next week and I don't have anyone to watch my dog.* As you walk around the classroom to collect each card, check and make sure it is a real problem that can be plausibly solved. Once you've collected all the cards, ask for a volunteer to perform a role-play with you. He or she should read the problem and ask for advice. This would be a good time to introduce the phrase, *What should I do?* Role-play with one more volunteer before calling up two students to role-play for the class. Then pass out the "problem" cards

and explain to students that they must find another student to give them advice. Once they have received it, they switch cards and seek advice from another student about their new "problem."

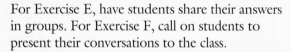

Activity Bank

Lesson 3, Worksheet 1: Obstacles and Solutions
Lesson 3, Worksheet 2: Listening to Advice
Lesson 3, Worksheet 3: A Letter of Advice

Refer students to *Stand Out 4 Grammar Challenge*, Unit 1, Challenge 3 for more practice giving advice with *could, should, how about . . . ?, why don't you . . . ?*

Instructor's Notes

E Read the situations and come up with two possible solutions for each. Use *could* when writing your solutions. (Answers will vary. Sample answers below.)

EXAMPLE: Magda wants to go back to school, but she has two children that she has to take care of. One of her children is a toddler who isn't in school yet.

Solution: <u>She could ask a family member to take care of her toddler</u>

<u>so she can go to school during the day.</u>

1. Frank wants to open up a restaurant in his neighborhood. He can get a loan to buy the property, but he won't have enough money to pay his employees until the restaurant starts making money.

Solution 1: <u>He can apply for a small business loan.</u>

Solution 2: <u>He could try to find a partner to help him finance the restaurant.</u>

2. Sergei works for a computer software company and wants to be promoted to project manager. The problem is that he needs to get more training before he can move up, but he doesn't have time to do training during the day.

Solution 1: <u>He could take classes in the evening.</u>

Solution 2: <u>He could talk to his supervisor about ways to make time for training</u>
<u>in his schedule.</u>

F Work with a partner. Imagine that one of you has one of the problems in Exercise E. Make a conversation like the one below. Use different ways of giving and responding to advice. (Answers will vary.)

EXAMPLE: *Student A:* I want to go back to school, but I have a young child to take care of.
Student B: Why don't you ask your mother to take care of him?
Student A: That won't work because she lives too far away.
Student B: Then how about taking some courses on the Internet?
Student A: That's a good idea!

G Look back at Exercise J on page 6. Think of an obstacle that might get in your way of achieving this goal. Make a cluster diagram like the one on page 7 and brainstorm different solutions with a partner. (Answers will vary.)

LESSON 4 — What is most important to me?

GOAL ➤ Write about an important person

CD 1
TR 6

A Look at the photos and listen to Eliana talk about why they are important to her. Then, read the paragraphs.

This is a picture of the house <u>where</u> I grew up in Argentina. It's very important to me because it holds a lot of memories. This is the garden <u>where</u> I played with my brothers and sisters, and the veranda <u>where</u> I often sat with my parents in the evenings, listening to their stories and watching the stars and dreaming about my future.

This is the person <u>who</u> influenced me the most when I was young. She was my teacher in the first grade and we stayed friends until I left home. She was always so calm and gave me good advice. She was the kind of person <u>who</u> is able to give you another perspective on a problem and make you feel hopeful, no matter how troubled you are.

This is my daily journal. I use it to write about my feelings and hopes. It helps me understand them better. Sometimes I just write about things <u>which</u> happened to me during the day. My journal is something <u>which</u> helps me focus on the important things in my life.

B Read the paragraphs again and underline the words *who, which,* and *where.* When do we use these words? Circle the correct answers below.

1. We use (*which* / (*where*) / *who*) for places.
2. We use (*which* / *where* / (*who*)) for people.
3. We use ((*which*) / *where* / *who*) for things.

AT-A-GLANCE PREP

Objective: Write about an important person
Grammar: Adjective clauses
Academic Strategy: Writing a paragraph
Vocabulary: *veranda, calm, influence, perspective, hopeful, troubled, daily journal, focus, adjective clause, patience, determination, positive influence*

RESOURCES

Activity Bank: Unit 1, Lesson 4, Worksheets 1–2; Templates
Reading and Writing Challenge: Unit 1

Grammar Challenge: Unit 1, Challenge 4
Audio: CD 1, Track 6

■ 1.5 hour classes   ■ 2.5 hour classes   ■ 3⁺ hour classes

AGENDA

Read and listen to a paragraph.
Use which, where, and who correctly.
Use adjective clauses.
Read about an influential person.
Do pre-writing activities.
Write a paragraph.

Warm-up and Review   5-10 mins. ■■■

Have students take out the obstacle(s) and solutions they wrote in Exercise G on page 9. Have them find a partner and practice conversations giving advice.

Introduction   5-10 mins. ■■■

Ask students to tell what is the most important thing in the world to them. Then ask them to tell you why. Write what they say on the board in note form. (Do not erase this information because you will use it in Presentation 2.) State the objective: *Today we will be talking about what is important to you and using adjective clauses to describe those things. Then you will write a paragraph about an important person in your life.*

Presentation 1   10-15 mins. ■■■

Have students open their books and look at the photos. Ask them what they think is important to Eliana and why.

 Look at the photos and listen to Eliana talk about why they are important to her. Then, read the paragraphs.

First, play the recording and have students follow along in their books. Then call on volunteers to read the paragraphs out loud. Ask students some basic comprehension questions about the reading.

> 🎧 **Listening Script**   *CD 1, Track 6*
>
> The listening script matches the paragraphs in Exercise A.

Practice 1   5 mins.

 Read the paragraphs again and underline the words *who, which,* and *where*. When do we use these words? Circle the correct answers below.

Evaluation 1   5 mins.

Go over the answers as a class.

STANDARDS CORRELATIONS

CASAS: 7.2.1, 7.2.2, 7.2.6 (See CASAS Competency List on pages 169–175.)
SCANS: **Information** Acquire and evaluate information, organize and maintain information, interpret and communicate information, use computers to process information (optional)
Systems Monitor and correct performance
Technology Select technology, apply technology to a task, maintain and troubleshoot technology

Basic Skills Reading, writing, listening, speaking
Thinking Skills Creative thinking, decision making, problem solving, seeing things in the mind's eye
Personal Qualities Responsibility, sociability, self-management
EFF: **Communication** Read with understanding, convey ideas in writing, speak so others can understand, listen actively
Interpersonal Cooperate with others
Lifelong Learning Reflect and evaluate

Presentation 2   10-15 mins.

C Study the chart with your teacher.

Have students go back to the reading on page 10 and underline examples of adjective clauses. Go over them as a class. Now go back to the information that you wrote on the board during the introduction and help students make adjective clauses about what they regard as important.

Practice 2   10-15 mins.

(Shorter classes can do these exercises for homework.)

D Combine the sentences using adjective clauses. In which sentence can you leave out the relative pronoun?

Go over the example as a class. Have students complete this exercise on their own and then share their answers with a partner.

E Look at the pictures with a partner, and make sentence about them using adjective clauses.

Evaluation 2   5-10 mins.

Ask volunteers to write their answers on the board. Go over them as a class.

Activity Bank

Lesson 4, Worksheet 1: Adjective Clauses

 Study the chart with your teacher.

Adjective Clauses		
Main clause (Subject clause)	**Relative pronoun**	**Adjective clause**
This is the place	where	I grew up.
She is the person	who (that)	influenced me most.
A journal is something	which (that)	can help you focus on important things.
Main clause (Object clause)	**Relative pronoun**	**Adjective clause**
This is the woman	who (whom)	I met yesterday.
Here is the book	which	you gave me this morning.
Adjectival clauses describe a preceding noun. They can describe a subject noun or an object noun. If the noun is an object, you can leave out the relative pronoun.		

 Combine the sentences using adjective clauses. In which sentence can you leave out the relative pronoun?

EXAMPLE: This is the house. I grew up there.
This is the house where I grew up.

1. That is the city. I was born there.
That is the city where I was born.

2. I have a friend. She helps me when I am sick.
I have a friend who helps me when I am sick.

3. We have some neighbors. They are very friendly.
We have some neighbors who are very friendly.

*4. This is the gold ring. My mother bought it for me.
This is the gold ring (which) my mother bought for me.
* Relative pronoun can be left out.

E Look at the pictures with a partner, and make sentences about them using adjective clauses. (Answers will vary.)

LESSON 4   **GOAL** ➤ **Write about an important person**

F Bita wrote a paragraph about her brother. Read the paragraph. With a partner, discuss the questions that follow.
(Answers may vary. Possible answers below.)

Someone Who Has Influenced Me

The person who has influenced me most in my life is my brother, Karim. I admire my brother for three reasons. First, he has patience and determination. Second, he does a fantastic job helping the community. Third, he is the type of person who always has time for his friends and family, no matter how busy he is. He has had a very positive influence on my life.

1. What type of person is Bita's brother? Bita's brother is patient and determined.
2. Why does Bita admire him? Bita admires him because he helps the community, his friends, and his family.
3. How has he influenced Bita? He has influenced Bita positively.

G Now it's your turn to write about a person who has influenced you. Complete these pre-writing activities before you begin. (Answers will vary.)

➤ **Brainstorm** (Think about your ideas before you write.)

Who has influenced you most in your life? _____

Why is this person so important to you? List three reasons.

1. _____

2. _____

3. _____

➤ **Introduce** (Tell your readers what you are writing about.) Write your topic sentence.

_____

➤ **Conclude** (Remind your reader of the main idea, but don't restate your topic sentence.) Write your conclusion sentence.

_____

H Now write a paragraph about an important person in your life. Start with your topic sentence. Put your reasons (support sentences) in the middle of your paragraph and finish with your conclusion sentence.

Presentation 3

15–20 mins.

Ask students to think of an important person in their lives. Now ask them to think about why this person is important to them. Give them a few minutes to think about this. At this stage, they do not need to tell you who it is or their reasons why it is this person.

F Bita wrote a paragraph about her brother. Read the paragraph. With a partner, discuss the questions that follow.

After answering the questions in the book, ask students to help you define what a paragraph is. Remind students about the parts of a paragraph. Have them turn back to page P8 if they need help. Make a list on the board of the parts of a paragraph: *topic sentence, support sentences, conclusion sentence.* Have students read Bita's paragraph again and look for each of the parts you listed. Ask them to label the sentences in their books accordingly.

Activity Bank

Lesson 4, Worksheet 2: Parts of a Paragraph

Practice 3

10–15 mins.

(Shorter classes can do these exercises for homework. Go over the instructions with students and have them complete exercise G at home. If you have time in the next class, have them write their paragraphs. If not, have them do Exercises G and H at home.)

G Now it's your turn to write about a person who has influenced you. Complete these pre-writing activities before you begin.

Have students complete the activity on their own, and then share what they have written with a partner.

Evaluation 3

10–15 mins.

Walk around the classroom and help students as they work.

Refer students to *Stand Out 4 Grammar Challenge*, Unit 1, Challenge 4 for more practice with adjective clauses.

Application

20–25 mins.

H Now write a paragraph about an important person in your life. Start with your topic sentence. Put your reasons (support sentences) in the middle of your paragraph and finish with your conclusion sentence.

Activity Bank

Templates: Editing
On the Activity Bank CD-ROM in the Templates folder, there are several editing worksheets that give students more practice with personal editing and peer-editing. Some worksheets focus on content and others on mechanics.

Instructor's Notes

Objective: Identify and apply time-management strategies

Academic Strategies: Using context clues, active reading, using an outline

Vocabulary: *organized, time management, last-minute changes, in advance, to the last minute, accomplish, sacrifice, allocate, realistic, prioritize, simultaneously, deadlines*

RESOURCES

Activity Bank: Unit 1, Lesson 5, Worksheet 1
Reading and Writing Challenge: Unit 1

Grammar Challenge: Unit 1, Challenge 5; Extension Challenges 1–2

■ 1.5 hour classes   ■ 2.5 hour classes   ■ 3⁺ hour classes

AGENDA

List time-management strategies.
Read about time management.
Use context to find meaning.
Complete an outline.
Identify personal time-management strategies.

Warm-up and Review   5-10 mins.

Have students take out the paragraphs they wrote in the previous lesson and share them with a partner.

Introduction   5-10 mins. ■■■

Write the phrase *time management* on the board. Ask students to help you define the term. State the objective: *Today you will read about time management and think about your own time-management strategies. Hopefully, you will find some new strategies to incorporate into your life.*

Presentation 1   10-15 mins. ■■■

 Are you an organized person? Do you . . .

Have students read these sentence endings silently and put a check next to each one that describes them. Take an informal poll of the class for each item.

Practice 1   10-15 mins.

B Work with a partner to list time-management strategies that you know.

C Talk to other pairs in your class. What are some strategies they came up with that are not on your list? Write them below.

Evaluation 1   10-15 mins.

Compile a complete list of time-management strategies on the board from all of the students.

STANDARDS CORRELATIONS

CASAS: 7.1.2, 7.2.1, 7.2.4 (See CASAS Competency List on pages 169–175.)
SCANS: **Information** Acquire and evaluate information, organize and maintain information, interpret and communicate information
Interpersonal Participate as a member of a team, teach others, exercise leadership, negotiate to arrive at a decision, work with cultural diversity

Systems Understand systems, monitor and correct performance
Basic Skills Reading, writing, listening, speaking
Thinking Skills Creative thinking, decision making, problem solving, seeing things in the mind's eye
Personal Qualities Responsibility, sociability, self-management
EFF: **Communication** Read with understanding

Time management

GOAL ➤ **Identify and apply time-management skills**

A Are you an organized person? Do you . . . (Answers will vary.)

- ❏ try to do everything but run out of time?
- ❏ always plan everything far in advance?
- ❏ dislike planning things too far ahead?
- ❏ tend to leave things to the last minute?
- ❏ get upset by last-minute changes to your schedule?
- ❏ only plan for important tasks like exams and job interviews?

Important	Very Important	URGENT!

B Work with a partner to list time-management strategies that you know. (Answers will vary.)

Time-Management Strategies

1. keep a schedule

C Talk to other pairs in your class. What are some strategies they came up with that are not on your list? Write them below. (Answers will vary.)

More Time-Management Strategies

GOAL ➤ Identify and apply time-management skills

Vocabulary | Grammar
Life Skills
Academic | Pronunciation

D Read the paragraphs about time management. Write the number of the corresponding paragraph next to each topic below.

_4_ How can I get everything done?

_5_ Why is good health important to time management?

_2_ How can I be organized?

_1_ How can I manage my time? Why is it important?

_3_ How can I get important tasks done first?

Time-Management Skills

(1) Finding enough time to study is very important for all students. There are a number of time-management strategies that can help you to manage your time wisely. You can use them to *accomplish* the goals you have set for yourself without *sacrificing* the time you spend with your family and friends.

(2) One of the best ways to stay organized is to keep a schedule. First, write down everything you need to do in a week. This includes work, study, taking care of children, shopping, and other tasks. Next, *allocate* a time slot to complete each of these tasks. Be *realistic* about the time you will need for each task. Mark these *deadlines* on your schedule. Finally, check off each task when you have completed it.

(3) It is a good idea to *prioritize* your tasks in order of importance. First, make a "To Do" list of all your tasks. Second, divide your list into three groups: A, B, and C. The A list is for tasks you need to do today. The B list is for tasks you need to do tomorrow. The C list is for tasks you need to do sometime this week. Dividing your list will help you get your most important tasks done first. You can also list tasks according to urgency: tasks you have to do, tasks you should do, and tasks you'd like to do if you have time.

(4) Another time-management strategy is to combine two or more tasks and do them *simultaneously*. You can listen to audio study tapes while you are driving, for example. Or, you can review verb tenses while you are eating lunch.

(5) Lastly, remember that good health is also important to managing your time effectively. If you are burned out or overtired, you cannot do your best. First, you need to allow time for rest and exercise. Also, you need to have time to spend with family, friends, and people who are important to you.

In conclusion, don't get upset if you cannot accomplish all your goals. Be positive about your *achievements* and reward yourself for goals that you have accomplished.

Presentation 2   5 mins.

Prepare students for Exercise D by going over each of the questions listed above the reading. Explain the directions if necessary.

Teaching Tip

Active reading

The purpose of active reading is to help students engage their reading comprehension skills so they can tackle any reading with confidence. Explain that they may not understand the passage on the first reading. Help them realize that to understand a reading, they may need to read it more than once—maybe even three or four times.

Pre-reading: Teach students that anticipating the content of a reading and recalling information they already know about the topic will help make the reading easier to understand.

First reading: Focus on the main ideas by asking students to find the topic sentence in each paragraph, or to summarize the main point of each paragraph.

Second reading: Show students how to scan the reading quickly to find details that support the main ideas or that answer the post-reading questions.

Guessing from context: Encourage students to guess the meaning of new words from context by analyzing the words surrounding the vocabulary item. They should not let unknown words slow down their reading and should use a dictionary only after they are familiar with the context.

Practice 2   10-15 mins.

(Shorter classes can do Exercise D for homework.)

D Read the paragraphs about time management. Write the number of the corresponding paragraph next to each topic below.

Tell students not to worry about the meaning of every single word. Instead, they should focus on getting the general idea of the reading so that they can complete the exercise.

Evaluation 2   5-10 mins.

Go over the answers as a class. Ask students to tell you how they came up with their decisions.

Instructor's Notes

_____
_____
_____
_____
_____
_____
_____
_____
_____
_____
_____
_____
_____
_____
_____
_____
_____
_____

Presentation 3   15–20 mins.

E Find the following words in the reading and use the context to work out their meanings: *accomplish, sacrificing, allocate, realistic, deadlines, prioritize, simultaneously, achievements.*

Do this exercise together as a class. If you have extra time, ask students to write a sentence or two using a few of the words. Have them share their sentences with the class.

Academic Skill

Find the meaning using context clues

Students will not understand all of the words they come across as they read, but it's important to teach them skills that will help them better understand the meaning of unknown words without having to look them up in a dictionary. Looking every word up in a dictionary will slow students down and discourage them from wanting to read more.

Show students how to use clues around the unknown word to help discover its meaning. Look at the example below:

It is a good idea to *prioritize* your tasks in <u>order</u> of <u>importance</u>. Show students that the key words in this sentence are *order* and *importance*, both of which they probably know. So, with this knowledge and awareness, they can then figure out that *to prioritize tasks* means to put them in a certain order, in this case by importance.

This is not an easy skill and may take your students weeks, months, or even years to master. But, if you practice it with them every time there is a reading, they will become more confident in their vocabulary-building skills.

Explain the diagram in Exercise F. Show students how it goes from the main topic to more specific topics to smaller details. Go over the first set of smaller details with students, going back to the reading to show them where the answers came from. Remind them to look for transitions (*first, second, next, also*) to signal key points.

Practice 3   10–15 mins. ■

(Shorter classes can do Exercises F and G for homework.)

F Use the diagram below to record the main points of the reading.

Have students complete this task by themselves.

Evaluation 3   10–15 mins. ■

Have students share their answers with a partner and then go over the outline as a class.

Application   10–15 mins. ■■■

G Think about what you learned today and complete the chart.

 Refer students to *Stand Out 4 Grammar Challenge*, Unit 1, Challenge 5 for more practice with modals and related expressions for suggestions, advice, and necessity.

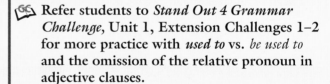

Activity Bank

Lesson 5, Worksheet 1: Time Management

Refer students to *Stand Out 4 Grammar Challenge*, Unit 1, Extension Challenges 1–2 for more practice with *used to* vs. *be used to* and the omission of the relative pronoun in adjective clauses.

GOAL ➤ **Identify and apply time-management skills**

E Find the following words in the reading and use the context to work out their meanings: *accomplish, sacrificing, allocate, realistic, deadlines, prioritize, simultaneously, achievements.*

F Use the diagram below to record the main points of the reading.

Time-Management Strategies	Keep a schedule.	Write down everything you need to do in a week.
		Allocate a time slot to complete each task.
		Check off each task when completed.
	Prioritize tasks.	Make a "To Do" list for all your tasks.
		Organize tasks for day, week, and month.
		Organize tasks according to urgency.
	Combine two or more tasks.	Listen to audio tapes while driving.
		Review verb tenses during lunch.
	Good health is important.	Allow time for rest and exercise.
		Spend time with family and friends.

G Think about what you learned today and complete the chart. (Answers will vary.)

My Time-Management Strategies	
Strategies I Use Now	**New Strategies I Will Start Using**

Review

A Make sentences to contrast past and present habits. (Lesson 1)

EXAMPLE:

Past: I ate meat.   Present: I don't eat meat now.

<u>I used to eat meat, but now I don't.</u>

1. Past: Paolo didn't have a computer.   Present: He has a computer.

   Paolo didn't use to have a computer, but now he does.

2. Past: Maria swam every day.   Present: She doesn't swim now.

   Maria used to swim everyday, but now she doesn't.

3. Past: My children didn't like vegetables.   Present: They like vegetables now.

   My children didn't use to like vegetables, but now they do.

4. Past: I didn't study full time.   Present: Now I study full time.

   I didn't use to study full time, but now I do.

B Write four questions using the correct form of *used to* that you can ask your partner. Leave the answer lines blank for now. (Lesson 1) (Answers will vary.)

EXAMPLE: <u>Where did you use to live?</u>

ANSWER: _____

1. _____

Answer: _____

2. _____

Answer: _____

3. _____

Answer: _____

4. _____

Answer: _____

Now ask your partner the questions and write down his or her answers.

Objectives: All Unit 1 objectives
Grammar: All Unit 1 grammar
Academic Strategy: Reviewing
Vocabulary: All Unit 1 vocabulary

AGENDA

Unit objectives.
Review exercises.
My Dictionary.
Learner Log.

RESOURCES

Activity Bank: Unit 1, Lessons 1–5; Templates
Reading and Writing Challenge: Unit 1

Grammar Challenge: Unit 1, Challenges 1–5; Extension Challenges 1–2

■ 1.5 hour classes   ■ 2.5 hour classes   ■ 3⁺ hour classes

Warm-up and Review   5-10 mins. ■■■

In groups, have students come up with a list of time-management strategies that they have used since the last lesson.

Introduction   5-10 mins. ■■■

Ask students as a class to try to recall (in general) all the goals of this unit without looking at their books. Then remind them which goals they omitted, if any. (Unit Goals: Compare past and present, create a goal chart, identify obstacles and give advice, write about an important person, identify and apply time-management skills.) Write all the objectives on the board from Unit 1. Show students the first page of the unit and mention the five objectives. State the objective for the review: *Today we will be reviewing everything we have learned in this unit.*

Presentation 1   10-15 mins. ■■■

This presentation will cover the first three pages of the review. Quickly go to the first page of each lesson. Discuss the objective of each. Ask simple questions to remind students of what they have learned.

Note: Since there is little presentation in the review, you can assign the review exercises that don't require collaboration with a partner or group for homework and go over them in class the following day.

Practice 1   20-25 mins. ■■■

Note: There are two ways to do the review: (1) Go through each exercise one at a time and, as students complete each one, go over the answers. (2) Briefly go through the instructions of each exercise, allow students to complete all of the exercises at once, and then go over the answers. Stop and evaluate whenever it is appropriate for the class. (*See Evaluation 1 on pg. 18a.*)

(A) Make sentences to contrast past and present habits. (Lesson 1)

(B) Write four questions using the correct form of *used to* that you can ask your partner. Leave the answer lines blank for now. (Lesson 1)

Make sure that students understand there are two stages to this activity. They will fill in the answers after they write the questions and interview a partner.

Now ask your partner the questions and write down his or her answers.

STANDARDS CORRELATIONS

CASAS: 7.2.1 (See CASAS Competency List on pages 169–175.)
SCANS: **Resources** Allocate time
Information Acquire and evaluate information
Interpersonal Participate as a member of a team, teach others, negotiate to arrive at a decision, work with cultural diversity
Systems Monitor and correct performance
Basic Skills Reading, writing, listening, speaking
Thinking Skills Creative thinking, decision making, problem solving, seeing things in the mind's eye

Personal Qualities Responsibility, sociability, self-management
EFF: **Communication** Convey ideas in writing, speak so others can understand, listen actively
Decision Making Solve problems and make decisions
Interpersonal Guide others, cooperate with others
Lifelong Learning Take responsibility for learning, reflect and evaluate, learn through research

Practice 1 (*continued*)   25–30 mins.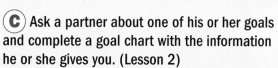

C Ask a partner about one of his or her goals and complete a goal chart with the information he or she gives you. (Lesson 2)

D Dave wants to study at college, but he needs to work full time while he is going to school in order to pay for his education and support his family. Dave asks his friend, Camille, for advice. With a partner, create a conversation between two friends. Make sure Camille suggests two or three different solutions to Dave's problem. Use expressions from this unit for giving and responding to advice. (Lesson 3)

E Combine the sentences using adjective clauses. (Lesson 4)

Teaching Tip

Recycling/Review

The review process and the project that follows are part of the recycling/review process. Students at this level often need to be reintroduced to concepts to solidify what they have learned. Many concepts are learned and forgotten while learning other new concepts. This is because students learn but are not necessarily ready to acquire language concepts.

Therefore, it becomes very important to review and to show students how to review on their own. It is also important to recycle the new concepts in different contexts.

Instructor's Notes

C Ask a partner about one of his or her goals and complete a goal chart with the information he or she gives you. (Lesson 2) (Answers will vary.)

Goal: _____

Steps	Completion Dates
Step 1:	
Step 2:	
Step 3:	
Step 4:	

D Dave wants to study at college, but he needs to work full time while he is going to school in order to pay for his education and support his family. Dave asks his friend, Camille, for advice. With a partner, create a conversation between the two friends. Make sure Camille suggests two or three different solutions to Dave's problem. Use expressions from this unit for giving and responding to advice. (Lesson 3) (Answers will vary.)

Dave: _____

Camille: _____

Dave: _____

Camille: _____

Dave: _____

Camille: _____

Dave: _____

E Combine the sentences using adjective clauses. (Lesson 4)

1. Esra has many brothers and sisters. They live in Argentina.

   Esra has many brothers and sisters who live in Argentina.

2. This is a good grammar book. It can help you improve your writing.

   This is a good grammar book that/which can help you improve your writing.

3. I am trying to find a school. I can study computers.

   I am trying to find a school where I can study computers.

4. E-mail is a type of communication. We use it at home and at work.

   E-mail is a type of communication that/which we use at home and at work.

Review

F Read the list of statements below. Write *TM* next to the ones that are time-management strategies. (Lesson 5)

___ Become an architect.

___ Buy new clothes.

TM Check off your tasks when you have finished them.

TM Combine two tasks.

___ Give advice.

TM Keep a schedule.

___ Make jewelry.

TM Prioritize your tasks.

___ Send your children to college.

TM Set realistic deadlines.

TM Stay healthy.

___ Write about your teacher.

G Use the words from the box to complete the sentences. (Lessons 1-5)

| deadline | prioritize | simultaneously |
| raising | refugee | retired |

1. Someone who stops work because they are old is _____ retired _____.

2. Someone who escapes from a country because of danger is a _____ refugee _____.

3. If you have young children, you are _____ raising _____ a family.

4. If you are doing two things at the same time, you are doing them _____ simultaneously _____.

5. If you have to complete a task by a certain time, that is your _____ deadline _____.

6. When you put things in order of importance, you _____ prioritize _____ them.

Practice 1 (*continued*)   25-30 mins.

F Read the list of statements below. Write *TM* next to the ones that are time-management strategies. (Lesson 5)

G Use the words from the box to complete the sentences. (Lessons 1–5)

Evaluation 1   45-60 mins.

Go around the classroom and check on students' progress. Help individuals as needed. If you see consistent errors among several students, interrupt the class and give a mini-lesson or review to help students feel comfortable with the concept.

Instructor's Notes

Presentation 2

5-10 mins.

My Dictionary

Ask students to brainstorm new vocabulary they have learned in this unit. Have them do this without looking in their books.

It is useful to make vocabulary cards to help you practice new vocabulary words and phrases. Look at the sample card below.

Practice 2

15-20 mins.

(Shorter classes can do this exercise for homework.)

Choose five new words you learned in this unit and make vocabulary cards using 4-by-6 index cards. If you don't have index cards, use pieces of paper.

Evaluation 2

5-10 mins.

Ask students to look at each others' cards in small groups.

Presentation 3

5-10 mins.

Learner Log

If students completed Learner Logs in the Pre-Unit, briefly go over the instructions with them. If this is the first time students have done a Learner Log, write the word *log* on the board. Ask students if they know what this word means. Explain to them that it is a journal, notebook, or place where you keep track of information. In this case, they will be keeping track of what they have learned. Tell them that they will do a learner log at the end of each unit.

In this unit, you learned many things about balancing your life. How comfortable do you feel doing each of the skills listed below? Rate your comfort level on a scale of 1 to 4.

Go over the instructions with students and make sure they understand what to do. You may want to do the first one or two items with the class to make sure students understand.

Practice 3

5-10 mins.

Have students complete the Learner Log.

Evaluation 3

5-10 mins.

Walk around the classroom and help students as needed.

Application

5-10 mins.

Go over the reflection statements with students and have them complete the answers by themselves.

TB Assessment *(optional)*

Use the Stand Out 4 Assessment CD-ROM with Exam*View*® to create a post-test for Unit 1.

My Dictionary

It is useful to make vocabulary cards to help you practice new vocabulary words and phrases. Look at the sample card below.

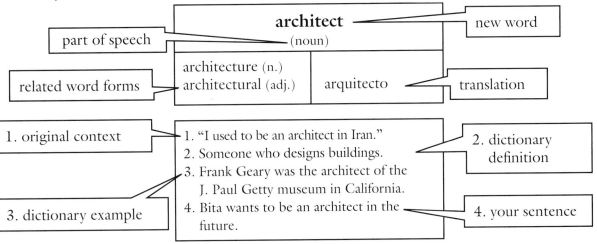

Choose five new words you learned in this unit and make vocabulary cards using 4-by-6 index cards. If you don't have cards, use pieces of paper.

Learner Log

In this unit, you learned many things about balancing your life. How comfortable do you feel doing each of the skills listed below? Rate your comfort level on a scale of 1 to 4.
(Answers will vary.)

1 = Need more practice   **2** = OK   **3** = Good   **4** = Great!

Life Skill	Comfort Level				Page
I can compare the past and present.	1	2	3	4	_____
I can create a goal chart.	1	2	3	4	_____
I can identify obstacles and solutions.	1	2	3	4	_____
I can give and respond to advice.	1	2	3	4	_____
I can write about an important person.	1	2	3	4	_____
I can identify time-management skills.	1	2	3	4	_____
I can use context clues to discover word meaning.	1	2	3	4	_____
I can analyze time-management techniques.	1	2	3	4	_____

If you circled 1 or 2, write down the page number where you can review this skill.

Reflection

1. I learned _____.

2. I would like to find out more about _____.

3. I am still confused about _____.

Team Project

Create a goal chart.

With a team, you will create a goal chart for goals you want to accomplish in this class.

1. Form a team with four or five students. Choose positions for each member of your team.

GOAL CHART

STEPS	COMPLETION DATE
STEP 1:	
STEP 2:	
STEP 3:	
STEP 4:	
STEP 5:	
STEP 6:	

POSITION	JOB DESCRIPTION	STUDENT NAME
Student 1: **Team Leader**	See that everyone speaks English and participates.	
Student 2: **Secretary**	Take notes.	
Student 3: **Designer**	Design the goal chart.	
Student 4: **Spokesperson**	Prepare team for presentation.	
Student 5: **Assistant**	Help team members with their jobs.	

2. Decide on one goal that your team would like to accomplish by the end of this class. Make it specific. ("Learn English" is not a very specific goal, but "improve our reading skills" and "learn more vocabulary" are.)

3. Write down the steps it will take to reach this goal. Write down a completion date for each step.

4. Write down two obstacles that might get in the way of achieving your goal and possible solutions for each one.

5. Make a list of three time-management techniques that will help you reach your goal.

6. Design a goal chart that includes all of the information from Steps 2–5.

7. Present your chart to the class.

Create a goal chart.

Each team will create a goal chart with one goal they would like to achieve by the end of the semester. The chart will include their goal, the steps it will take to reach the goal, completion dates for the steps, a list of obstacles and possible solutions, and a list of time-management strategies.

The team project is the final application for the unit. It gives students a chance to show that they have mastered all of the Unit 1 objectives.

Note: Shorter classes can extend this project over two class meetings.

Stage 1   5 mins.

Form a team with four or five students. Choose positions for each member of your team.

Have students decide who will lead each step as described on the student page. Provide well-defined directions on the board for how teams should proceed. Explain that all the students do every step as a team. Teams shouldn't go to the next stage until the previous one is complete.

Stage 2   15-20 mins.

Decide on one goal that your team would like to accomplish by the end of this class. Make it specific. ("Learn English" is not a very specific goal, but "improve our reading skills" and "learn more vocabulary" are.)

When students have come up with their goal, ask each team's spokesperson to report it to the class. This will give other teams a chance to see what their classmates are doing as well as give you a chance to make sure each team has chosen a goal that is specific enough.

Stage 3   10-15 mins.

Write down the steps it will take to reach this goal. Write down a completion date for each step.

You may wish to give the class an end date for their goal, such as the end of the semester. That way they can actually follow their steps and see their progression as a group. If you decide to do this, the completion dates will be weeks or months, instead of seasons or years. For example: Goal: *Improve our reading* Step 1: Learn new reading skills (January), Read English newspapers (February), Read English books (March), and so on.

Stage 4   10-15 mins.

Write down two obstacles that might get in the way of achieving your goal and possible solutions for each one.

Stage 5   5 mins.

Make a list of three time-management techniques that will help you reach your goal.

Make sure students make the techniques specific to their goals.

Stage 6   15-20 mins.

Design a goal chart that includes all of the information from Steps 2–5.

Stage 7   15-20 mins.

Present your chart to the class.

Help teams prepare for their presentations. Suggest that each member choose a different part of the poster to present.

STANDARDS CORRELATIONS

CASAS: 4.8.1, 4.8.5, 4.8.6. (See CASAS Competency List on pages 169–175.)
SCANS: **Resources** Allocate time
Information Acquire and evaluate information, organize and maintain information, interpret and communicate information, use computers to process information
Systems Understand systems, improve and design systems
Technology (optional) Select technology, apply technology to exercise
Basic Skills Reading, writing, listening, speaking
Thinking Skills Creative thinking, decision making, problem solving, seeing things in the mind's eye, reasoning

Personal Qualities Responsibility, self-esteem, self-management, integrity/honesty
EFF: **Communication** Read with understanding, convey ideas in writing, speak so others can understand, listen actively, observe critically
Decision Making Solve problems and make decisions, plan
Interpersonal Guide others, resolve conflict and negotiate, advocate and influence, cooperate with others
Lifelong Learning Take responsibility for learning, reflect and evaluate, learn through research, use information and communications technology (optional)

Objective: Calculate monthly expenses
Academic Strategies: Focused listening, calculating budgets
Vocabulary: *personal finances, monthly expenses, budgeted amount, budget*

RESOURCES

Activity Bank: Unit 2, Lesson 1, Worksheets 1–2
Reading and Writing Challenge: Unit 2

Grammar Challenge: Unit 2, Challenge 1
Audio: CD 1, Tracks 7–8

■ 1.5 hour classes   ■ 2.5 hour classes   ■ 3⁺ hour classes

AGENDA

Analyze expenses.
Listen and fill in a budget.
Calculate a budget.
Create a personal budget.

Preassessment *(optional)*

Use the Stand Out 4 Assessment CD-ROM with Exam*View*® to create a pretest for Unit 2.

Warm-up and Review   5-10 mins.

Write *budget* on the board and elicit its meaning. Ask: *How many of you budget your money? What are the benefits of budgeting?*

Introduction   5-10 mins.

A Think about your personal finances. What do you spend money on every month? Make a list.

Ask students to work individually. Then ask students to share items on their lists with the class, and make a list on the board. State the objective: *Today we will be looking at how one family spends its money. Then we will practice calculating monthly expenses, and creating budgets.*

Presentation 1   10-15 mins. ■■■

Have students look at the Masons' chart in Exercise B and guess how much money the family spends in each category.

Practice 1   10-15 mins. ■■■

B Listen to Sara and Todd Mason talk about their finances. Fill in the missing numbers.

🎧 **Listening Script**   CD 1, Track 7

Todd: *I think it's time we sat down and made a family budget. As the kids grow older, we're going to need to budget our money more wisely.*
Sara: *Good idea. How should we start?*
Todd: *Well, let's make a list of everything we spend money on, and then let's guess at how much we spend in each category. Then we'll save our receipts for next month and see how much we actually spent.*

Sara: *OK, why don't we start with the cars? Since both of them are paid off, we don't have any loan payments, but we do have to pay for gas, insurance, and maintenance. I'd say we spend $300 a month on gas, $150 a month on insurance, and I don't know about maintenance, but it might come to $550 a month for everything.*
Todd: *That sounds right. Now let's talk about rent. We know it's going to be $1,500.*
Sara: *Right. In the utilities category, I'd say we spend about $40 on gas, $100 on electricity, and $20 on water. That adds up to $160.*
Todd: *Don't forget cable, phone, and Internet. Cable is $50, phone is $95, and Internet is $45. That's $190 right there.*
Sara: *Wow, we spend money on a lot of things!*
Todd: *And we're not even finished! How much do you think we spend on food each month?*
Sara: *I spend about $400 a month on groceries, and I'd say we spend about $200 going out to dinner.*
Todd: *What about school supplies and clothing?*
Sara: *School supplies are about $60 a month and clothing about $200.*
Todd: *Are we forgetting anything? . . . Oh, medical expenses. It's a good thing we have insurance, but it doesn't pay for everything. I'd say we spend about $50 a month.*
Sara: *That sounds about right. And don't forget entertainment. Movies and taking the kids on trips adds up! I'd be willing to bet we spend at least $150 a month on those kinds of thing—I'm afraid to add all this up!*

Evaluation 1   5 mins. ■■■

Go over the answers as a class.

C Compare your list of expenses from Exercise A to the Masons' list. What are the similarities? What are the differences?

Have students add any missing categories to the lists they made in Exercise A.

Note: Standards Correlations are on next page.

Personal Finance

GOALS

➤ Calculate monthly expenses
➤ Identify ways to be a smart consumer

➤ Interpret credit card and loan information
➤ Analyze advertising techniques
➤ Write a business letter

LESSON **1**

Money in, money out

GOAL ➤ Calculate monthly expenses

A Think about your personal finances. What do you spend money on every month? Make a list. (Answers will vary.)

CD 1
TR 7

B Listen to Sara and Todd Mason talk about their finances. Fill in the missing numbers.

Monthly Expenses	
Auto	$550
Cable/Phone/Internet	$190
Clothing	$200
Entertainment	$150
Food	$600
Medical	$50
Rent	$1,500
School Supplies	$60
Utilities (gas, electricity, water)	$160

C Compare your list of expenses from Exercise A to the Masons' list. What are the similarities? What are the differences? (Answers will vary.)

D Look at the chart below. The first column, "Monthly Expenses," lists all the things that the Masons spend money on. The second column, "Budgeted Amount," is how much they think they will spend this month on each expense. Look at the numbers you wrote on page 21 and transfer them to the second column.

Monthly Expenses	Budgeted Amount	Actual Amount Spent in May	Difference
Auto	$550	$445.50	$104.50
Cable/Phone/Internet	$190	$235.72	$-45.72
Clothing	$200	$102.14	$97.86
Entertainment	$150	$132.96	$17.04
Food	$600	$659.81	$-59.81
Medical	$50	$45.28	$4.72
Rent	$1,500	$1,500	$0
School Supplies	$60	$30	$30.00
Utilities	$160	$208.12	$-48.12
TOTAL	$3,460.00	$3,359.53	$100.47

CD 1
TR 8

E Now listen to Sara and Todd talk about what they actually spent in the month of May. Write their actual expenses in the third column.

F The last row in the chart is for the total amount. This is where the Masons write their total budgeted amount and the total amount they actually spent. To get each total, you must add the numbers in the column together. The items below are for practice. Look at the first example and then complete the other totals on your own.

1.
$1,500.00
+$550.00
$2,050.00

2.
$1,300.00
+$475.60
$1,775.60

3.
$875.42
$165.00
+$45.70
$1,086.12

4.
$900.00
$32.75
$450.00
+$76.22
$1,458.97

5.
$234.56
$987.23
$39.00
+$75.11
$1,335.90

 G Look back at the chart and calculate the totals of the first two columns in the Masons' budget. Write the answers in the chart.

Presentation 2   5-10 mins.

Have students look at the Masons' budget in Exercise B. Explain each column to them. Ask why it is important to keep track of such information.

D Look at the chart below. The first column, "Monthly Expenses," lists all the things that the Masons spend money on. The second column, "Budgeted Amount," is how much they think they will spend this month on each expense. Look at the numbers you wrote on page 21 and transfer them to the second column.

Ask students the following questions: *Did the Masons spend more or less money than they thought they would on auto expenses? Why were their budgeted amount for rent and the actual amount they spent exactly the same?* Explain the difference between fixed and variable expenses.

Practice 2   10-15 mins.

E Now listen to Sara and Todd talk about what they actually spent in the month of May. Write their actual expenses in the third column.

 Listening Script   *CD 1, Track 8*

Sara: *I can't believe it's been a month since we sat down and wrote our budget. Time flies!*
Todd: *Yep, it sure does. OK, since we've already totaled up the receipts, let's write down the total amount of money we spent last month in each category.*
Sara: *OK, I've got the auto expenses. We spent $295.50 on gas, $150 on insurance, and nothing on maintenance. So, that's $445.50 total. That's less than what we thought.*
Todd: *OK, rent and utilities. Obviously, rent is what we thought—$1,500. Gas was $35.76, electricity was $150.02, and water was $22.34. That comes to $208.12. We were close on gas and water, but we were way off on the electricity.*
Sara: *I guess we're not used to that rate increase yet.*

Todd: *I don't think I'll ever get used to it. OK, cable was $50, phone was $155.72, and Internet was $30. That adds up to $235.72.*
Sara: *Not bad. I guess the bigger phone bill was because of all those calls you made to your mother last month. Maybe we can make her pay for it!*
Todd: *Oh, she'd love that! OK, what else?*
Sara: *I spent $359.81 last month on groceries, and we spent about $300 going out to dinner. I guess we underestimated on that one.*
Todd: *What about school supplies and clothing?*
Sara: *School supplies were about $30 and clothing was $102.14, but I still think we should leave the clothing budget at $200. The boys are still growing and they need new clothes quite often.*
Todd: *Good idea. We spent $45.28 on medical expenses and $132.96 on entertainment.*
Sara: *All right. Let's add it up!*

Evaluation 2   10-15 mins.

Go over the answers to Exercise E together.

Presentation 3   5-10 mins.

The next five exercises deal with calculations. Presentation will depend on the math skills of your students. Go through the directions and examples. Help students as needed. Decide if they can use calculators or not.

Practice 3   15-20 mins.

(Shorter classes can do these exercises for homework.)

F The last row in the chart is for the total amount. This is where the Masons write their total budgeted amount and the total amount they actually spent. To get each total, you must add the numbers in the column together. The items below are for practice. Look at the first example and then complete the other totals on your own.

G Look back at the chart and calculate the totals of the first two columns in the Masons' budget. Write the answers in the chart.

STANDARDS CORRELATIONS

CASAS: 1.5.1, 6.1.1, 6.1.2 (See CASAS Competency List on pages 169–175.)
SCANS: Resources Allocate money
Information Acquire and evaluate information, organize and maintain information, interpret and communicate information, use computers to process information (optional)
Interpersonal Participate as a member of a team, teach others, exercise leadership, negotiate to arrive at a decision, work with cultural diversity
Systems Understand systems, monitor and correct performance
Technology (optional) Select technology, apply technology to a task, maintain and troubleshoot technology

Basic Skills Reading, writing, arithmetic, listening, speaking
Thinking Skills Creative thinking, decision making, problem solving, seeing things in the mind's eye
Personal Qualities Responsibility, sociability, self-management
EFF: **Communication** Speak so others can understand, listen actively
Decision Making Use math to solve problems and communicate, solve problems and make decisions, plan
Lifelong Learning Use information and communication technology (optional)

H The last *column* of the chart is for the difference between the amount of money the Masons budgeted for each expense and what they actually spent. To make this calculation, you must use subtraction. The items below are for practice. Look at the first example and then complete the other differences on your own.

I Sometimes the Masons budgeted *less* than they spent. (For example, they spent more on utilities than they budgeted.) In this case, you still do the subtraction with the larger number on top, but the end result is a negative number.

The items below are for practice. Look at the first example and then complete the other differences on your own.

Evaluation 3   5-10 mins. ▪

Go over the answers to all of the exercises on the board, making sure students did the calculations correctly. Offer help with addition and subtraction as needed.

Refer students to *Stand Out 4 Grammar Challenge*, Unit 2, Challenge 1 for practice with *How much . . . ?*

J Calculate the differences between the first two columns in the Mason's budget. Write the answers in the chart.

Go over the completed chart in Exercise D as a class. You may want to reproduce this on the board, so that students can see what the finished chart should look like.

Application   10-20 mins. ▪▪▪

K Make a budget of your own, estimating the amount of all of your expenses. Then, keep track of how much money you actually spend over the next month. Finally, calculate the difference between the amount you budgeted and the amount you actually spent.

Instructor's Notes

GOAL ➤ **Calculate monthly expenses**

 The last *column* of the chart is for the difference between the amount of money the Masons budgeted for each expense and what they actually spent. To make this calculation, you must use subtraction. The items below are for practice. Look at the first example and then complete the other differences on your own.

1.	2.	3.	4.	5.
$550.00	$1,300.00	$875.42	$450.00	$987.23
−$445.50	−$475.60	−$165.00	−$76.22	−$75.11
$104.50	$824.40	$710.42	$373.78	$912.12

*Note: When doing subtraction, the larger number must be on top.

 Sometimes the Masons budgeted *less* than they spent. (For example, they spent more on utilities than they budgeted.) In this case, you still do the subtraction with the larger number on top, but the end result is a negative number.

The items below are for practice. Look at the first example and then complete the other differences on your own.

They budgeted:	$160.00	$85.00	$200.00
They spent:	$208.12	$100.10	$213.45
	1.	2.	3.
	$208.12	$100.10	$213.45
	−$160.00	−$85.00	−$200.00
	$48.12	151.00	13.45

 Calculate the differences between the first two columns in the Masons' budget. Write the answers in the chart. (For answers, see the completed chart on pg. 22, Exercise D.)

K Make a budget of your own, estimating the amount of all of your expenses. Then, keep track of how much money you actually spend over the next month. Finally, calculate the difference between the amount you budgeted and the amount you actually spent.

(Answers will vary.)

Savvy shopper

GOAL ➤ **Identify ways to be a smart consumer**

 A The Masons have decided to buy a new couch for their home. They want a good-quality piece of furniture that will last a long time. What do you think they will do before buying the couch? Discuss your ideas with your classmates. (Answers will vary.)

B Sara did some research on the Internet. Read the web page below to see what information she found.

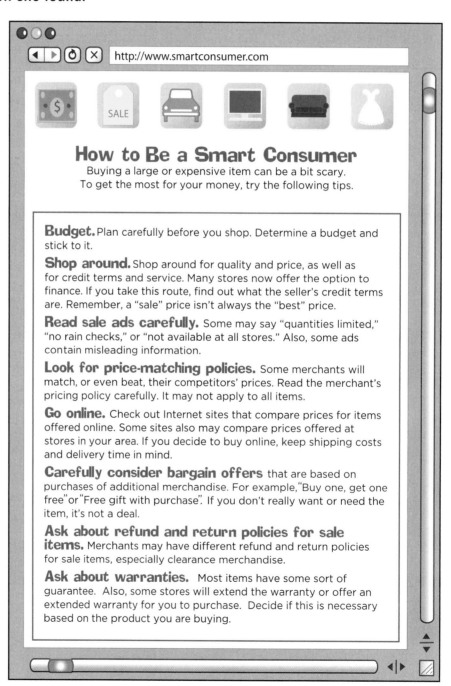

http://www.smartconsumer.com

How to Be a Smart Consumer

Buying a large or expensive item can be a bit scary.
To get the most for your money, try the following tips.

Budget. Plan carefully before you shop. Determine a budget and stick to it.

Shop around. Shop around for quality and price, as well as for credit terms and service. Many stores now offer the option to finance. If you take this route, find out what the seller's credit terms are. Remember, a "sale" price isn't always the "best" price.

Read sale ads carefully. Some may say "quantities limited," "no rain checks," or "not available at all stores." Also, some ads contain misleading information.

Look for price-matching policies. Some merchants will match, or even beat, their competitors' prices. Read the merchant's pricing policy carefully. It may not apply to all items.

Go online. Check out Internet sites that compare prices for items offered online. Some sites also may compare prices offered at stores in your area. If you decide to buy online, keep shipping costs and delivery time in mind.

Carefully consider bargain offers that are based on purchases of additional merchandise. For example, "Buy one, get one free" or "Free gift with purchase". If you don't really want or need the item, it's not a deal.

Ask about refund and return policies for sale items. Merchants may have different refund and return policies for sale items, especially clearance merchandise.

Ask about warranties. Most items have some sort of guarantee. Also, some stores will extend the warranty or offer an extended warranty for you to purchase. Decide if this is necessary based on the product you are buying.

AT-A-GLANCE PREP

Objective: Identify ways to be a smart consumer
Grammar: Contrary-to-fact conditionals
Academic Strategies: Active reading, using context clues, comparing and contrasting
Vocabulary: *shop around, price matching, shipping costs, delivery time, bargain, warranty*

RESOURCES

Activity Bank: Unit 2, Lesson 2: Worksheets 1–2
Reading and Writing Challenge: Unit 2

Grammar Challenge: Unit 2, Challenge 2

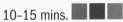 1.5 hour classes   2.5 hour classes   3+ hour classes

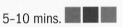

AGENDA
Plan and research large purchases.
Make a smart purchase.
Use contrary-to-fact conditionals.

Warm-up and Review   5-10 mins.

Have students take out their budgets from the previous lesson. Review the concepts by asking them some questions about their categories, budgeted amount, and actual amount.

Introduction   5-10 mins.

Ask students to think of something expensive they've bought within the last year. Make a list of their answers on the board. Ask them what they did before they bought the expensive item, such as researching the item, comparison shopping, and saving money. Make another list of these ideas on the board. State the objective: *Today we will identify ways to be a smart consumer.*

Presentation 1   10-15 mins.

A The Masons have decided to buy a new couch for their home. They want a good-quality piece of furniture that will last a long time. What do you think they will do before buying the couch? Discuss your ideas with your classmates.

Have students get into small groups and discuss the question. Give them five or ten minutes for their discussions and then ask the groups to report to the class. Make a list of everything that is said on the board.

Have students look at the web page in their books. Ask them what sort of information they think they will read about.

Practice 1   10-15 mins.

B Sara did some research on the Internet. Read the web page below to see what information she found.

Tell students to read the web page and then go on to Exercise C on the next page. Remind them not to worry about the vocabulary from the reading that they can't understand. Instead, they should focus on the main ideas.

Note: (Practice 1 continues on the next page.)

STANDARDS CORRELATIONS

CASAS: 1.2.5, 7.2.2, 7.2.7 (See CASAS Competency List on pages 169–175.)
SCANS: **Information** Acquire and evaluate information, organize and maintain information, interpret and communicate information
Interpersonal Participate as a member of a team, teach others, exercise leadership, negotiate to arrive at a decision, work with cultural diversity
Systems Monitor and correct performance
Basic Skills Reading, writing, listening, speaking
Thinking Skills Creative thinking, decision making, problem solving, seeing things in the mind's eye

Personal Qualities Responsibility, sociability, self-management
EFF: **Communication** Read with understanding, convey ideas in writing, speak so others can understand, listen actively
Decision Making Solve problems and make decisions, plan
Interpersonal Resolve conflict and negotiate, cooperate with others
Lifelong Learning Learn through research, use information and communication technology (optional)

Practice 1 *(continued)*

C Based on the reading in Exercise B, list six things you should do before you make a large purchase.

Have students do this exercise by themselves.

Evaluation 1   5 mins. ■■■■

Have students share their lists in small groups and decide on the best six from all of their lists. Then ask for a volunteer to come to the board to write and have students call out the things they should do before making a large purchase.

Go back to the reading and ask students if they have any questions about what they read. If they don't understand some vocabulary words, help them use context clues to work out the meaning.

Take a class poll to see how many students are thinking about making an expensive purchase. Ask them what things would be most important to them to do before making this purchase.

Presentation 2   5-10 mins. ■■■■

Ask students the following questions:

> *What would you do if you had a million dollars?*
>
> *What would you do if you won the lottery?*
>
> *What would you do if you could speak English perfectly?*

Don't expect grammatically correct answers. The point is to get them thinking about the use of *if*.

D Sometimes being a smart consumer means not buying something even when you want it. If you had all the money in the world, what two items would you buy?

Have students write down their answers and then ask for volunteers to share what they wrote with the class.

E Study the chart with your teacher.

LESSON 2   **GOAL** ➤ **Identify ways to be a smart consumer**

C Based on the reading in Exercise B, list six things you should do before you make a large purchase. (Answers may vary. Possible answers below.)

1. Plan your budget.

2. Compare prices and terms at different stores.

3. Read ads carefully for misleading information.

4. Look for price-matching policies.

5. Carefully consider bargain offers.

6. Ask about warranty policies.

D Sometimes being a smart consumer means not buying something even when you want it. If you had all the money in the world, what two items would you buy? (Answers will vary.)

1. _____   2. _____

Now look at these examples:

1. If I were rich, I would buy a new car. (I'm not really rich, so I can't buy a new car.)
2. If they had a million dollars, they would move to Beverly Hills. (They don't have a million dollars, so they can't move to Beverly Hills.)

These statements are called *contrary-to-fact conditionals*. They express a condition and a result that are not true at this point in time.

E Study the chart with your teacher.

Contrary-to-Fact Conditionals	
Condition (*if* + past tense verb)	**Result (*would* + base verb)**
If she *got* a raise,	she *would buy* a new house.
If they *didn't spend* so much money on rent,	they *would have* more money for entertainment.
If I *were* a millionaire,	I *would give* all my money to charity.
If John *weren't* so busy at work,	he *would spend* more time with his children.

- *Contrary-to-fact* (or *unreal*) *conditional statements* are sentences that are not true.
- The *if*-clause can come in the first or second part of the sentence. Notice how commas are used in the examples. (If you reverse the order of the condition and result clauses, omit the comma.)
- In written English, use *were* (instead of *was*) for *if*-clauses with first and third person singular forms of *be*.
- In spoken English, people often use contractions: I would = *I'd*; she would = *she'd*, etc.

LESSON 2

GOAL ➤ **Identify ways to be a smart consumer**

F Complete the sentences with the correct form of the verbs in parentheses.

1. If Bita _____ were _____ (be) an architect in the United States, she
_____ would design _____ (design) beautiful homes.

2. Van's parents _____ would purchase _____ (purchase) a new computer if they
_____ had _____ (have) some extra money.

3. If my husband _____ were _____ (be) rich, he _____ would buy _____ (buy) me
an expensive diamond ring.

4. George _____ would save _____ (save) more money if he _____ didn't spend _____ (not
spend) so much on eating out.

5. You _____ wouldn't be _____ (not be) so tired if you _____ had _____ (have)
more time to relax.

G Study the chart with your teacher.

Contrary-to-Fact Questions	
Wh-Question	**Yes/No Question**
What + *would* + subject + base verb + *if* + subject + past tense	*Would* + subject + base verb + *if* + subject + past tense
What would you do *if* you won the lottery?	*Would* you give up your job *if* you won the lottery?

H Work in groups. Take turns asking your group the questions below. Each person must answer with a conditional statement.

EXAMPLE: *Student A:* What would you do if you won the lottery?
Student B: If I won the lottery, I'd buy a house.
Student C: If I won the lottery, I'd travel around the world.

What would you do if . . .

1. you had a million dollars?
2. you lived in a mansion?
3. you had your own airplane?
4. you were the boss of a huge company?
5. you owned an island in the Pacific?
6. (your own idea)?

I Write three statements about what *you* would do if you won the lottery. (Answers will vary.)

1. _____

2. _____

3. _____

Practice 2 · 5-10 mins.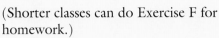

(Shorter classes can do Exercise F for homework.)

F Complete the sentences with the correct form of the verbs in parentheses.

Evaluation 2 · 10-15 mins.

Ask volunteers to write the completed sentences on the board. Go over the answers as a class.

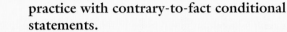 Refer students to *Stand Out 4 Grammar Challenge*, Unit 2, Challenge 2 for more practice with contrary-to-fact conditional statements.

Presentation 3 · 5-10 mins.

G Study the chart with your teacher.

Prepare students for Exercise H by going over the example conversation. Have students get into groups and show them how the activity will work by demonstrating with one group.

Practice 3 · 15-20 mins.

H Work in groups. Take turns asking your group the questions below. Each person must answer with a conditional statement.

Evaluation 3 · 5-10 mins.

Observe students as they work. Call on groups to perform the exercise for the class.

Application · 5-10 mins.

I Write three statements about what *you* would do if you won the lottery.

Ask students to stay with their groups but write the statements individually. After they have written their statements, have students share them with their group members. When students have finished, have each group choose and then share its three best statements with the class. If you have time, have each group also write its best statements on the board or on poster paper to place around the classroom.

Extended Application: Have students in groups create a list of important points for consumers to consider. They can use information that they read on the web page on page 24, but tell them they must put the ideas into their own words. They can add some of their own ideas and exclude ideas that they think are not important.

Activity Bank

Lesson 2, Worksheet 1: Being a Smart Consumer
Lesson 2, Worksheet 2: Contrary-to-Fact Conditionals

Instructor's Notes

Objective: Interpret credit card and loan information

Academic Strategies: Using context clues, comparing and contrasting

Vocabulary: *credit card, debit card, annual fee, APR, introductory rate, grace period, late fee, creditworthiness, credit limit, capacity, character, collateral, loan, down payment*

AGENDA

Discuss credit cards.
Read and talk about the advantages and disadvantages of credit cards.
Use context to find meaning.
Read about loans.
Choose the best purchasing option.

RESOURCES

Activity Bank: Unit 2, Lesson 3, Worksheets 1–2
Reading and Writing Challenge: Unit 2

Grammar Challenge: Unit 2, Challenge 3

■ 1.5 hour classes   ■ 2.5 hour classes   ■ 3⁺ hour classes

Warm-up and Review   5-10 mins. ■■■

Write this question on the board: *What would you do if you owned your own business?* Have students get into small groups and come up with answers. Ask for volunteers to write their ideas on the board in complete sentences. Go over the ideas and the grammar.

Introduction   5-10 mins. ■■■

Write a list of items that can be purchased on the board. Include small purchases like books or CDs; medium purchases like groceries and clothing; and large purchases like furniture, cars, and houses. Ask students what purchasing methods they use for each. State the objective: *Today we will be interpreting credit card and loan information and talking about the advantages and disadvantages of each.*

Presentation 1   10-15 mins. ■■■

(A) Do you have a credit card? What kind of card is it? What is the interest rate? What do you use it for? Discuss these questions with your group.

Have students discuss these questions in small groups.

Have students first look at the bold headings in the article. Ask them what kind of information they think they will be reading about.

(B) Read the information below about credit cards.

Ask volunteers to read one paragraph each out loud. As you go through the reading, answer any questions that come up about the article's content. Then ask students to reread the entire article silently.

STANDARDS CORRELATIONS

CASAS: 1.2.5, 1.3.1, 1.3.2, 1.3.3 (See CASAS Competency List on pages 169-175.)
SCANS: **Information** Acquire and evaluate information, organize and maintain information, interpret and communicate information
Interpersonal Participate as a member of a team, teach others, exercise leadership, negotiate to arrive at a decision, work with cultural diversity
Systems Monitor and correct performance
Basic Skills Reading, writing, arithmetic, listening, speaking
Thinking Skills Creative thinking, decision making, problem solving, seeing things in the mind's eye

Personal Qualities Responsibility, sociability, self-management
EFF: **Communication** Read with understanding, convey ideas in writing, speak so others can understand, listen actively, observe critically
Decision Making Use math to solve problems and communicate, solve problems and make decisions, plan
Interpersonal Cooperate with others
Lifelong Learning Learn through research, use information and communication technology (optional)

Charge it!

GOAL ➤ Interpret credit card and loan information

A Do you have a credit card? What kind of card is it? What is the interest rate? What do you use it for? Discuss these questions with your group. (Answers will vary.)

B Read the information below about credit cards.

What do I need to know before applying for a credit card?

What is a credit card and how is it different from a debit card? A credit card is a flexible way of borrowing money to make a purchase and paying back the money later. A debit card is a way of taking money directly from your bank account.

Annual fee: Many issuers charge an *annual* fee for using their card—typically between $15 and $50. If you do not plan to pay your bill within a month or two from the date you make a purchase, you should probably look for a card with no annual fee.

Annual percentage rate (APR): APR can be either "fixed" or "variable." Fixed rate APRs are usually a little higher, but you know exactly how much you will be charged each month.

Introductory rate: Some credit cards offer a low *introductory rate* that switches to a higher rate later. Make sure that you know how long the introductory rate is applicable and what APR the card will carry after the introductory period. Be aware that the introductory rate for some cards will be terminated if you are late with a payment.

Grace period: The *grace period* is the time between the day you make a purchase and the day when interest begins to be charged. For most cards, it is 25 days from the billing date. Many cards have no grace period and you will pay interest from the date you make a purchase.

Other fees: How much is the penalty for being late? How much do you pay if you go over the *credit limit*? How much does

your bank charge you for an ATM withdrawal (cash advance fee)? Is the interest rate for cash advances the same or is it higher than the card's "regular" APR? What is your cash advance limit? Answers to all these questions may influence your choice of credit card.

Benefits: A number of issuers offer additional benefits to card members. Rebate cards allow you to earn cash back and discounts on goods and services based on card usage. Frequent flyer cards allow you to earn miles for each dollar charged.

How do issuers evaluate if I am creditworthy?
Issuers determine *creditworthiness* by what are called the three Cs of credit (capacity, collateral, and character). **Capacity** refers to your ability to pay based on your income and existing debt. **Collateral** refers to any assets you have that can secure payment (e.g., your savings or home ownership). **Character** refers to factors such as your payment history and length of employment. The criteria for accepting applicants vary between issuers and credit card products.

LESSON **3** **GOAL** ➤ Interpret credit card and loan information

C What do you think these words mean? Use context clues from the reading in Exercise B to figure out their meanings. Discuss the words with a partner.

annual fee	annual percentage rate (APR)	introductory rate
grace period	late fee credit limit	creditworthiness

D Read the chart and decide which credit card is the best deal for you.

	Verso	Maincard	Explore Card (must pay in full each month)	iCard
Annual Fee	$20	$15	$55	$0
APR	15%	14.9%	NA	21%
Introductory Rate (6 months)	2.9%	0%	3.8%	9.9%
Late Fee	$20	$10	$50	$25
Benefits	none	airline miles (one mile for each dollar you spend)	none	cash back (1% of purchases)

E Which card did you choose? (Answers will vary.)

_____

Why? (Answers will vary.)

_____

F What are the advantages and disadvantages of having a credit card? Work in a group to list them. (Answers will vary.)

Practice 1 15-20 mins. ■■■

Ask students to look back in the reading and find the word *debit card*. Ask them if they know what the term refers to. Ask them if the article explains its meaning.

 What do you think these words mean? Use context clues from the reading in Exercise B to figure out their meanings. Discuss the words with a partner.

Ask students to go back to the article and find each of the words in the box. Have them make a note of what each word means or what they think it means based on the reading.

 Read the chart and decide which credit card is the best deal for you.

Have students look at the chart in Exercise D. Ask them what sort of information it contains. Ask them basic comprehension questions, such as: *What is Verso's annual fee? Does Maincard charge a late fee? How much is it?*

 Which card did you choose? Why?

Evaluation 1 5 mins. ■■■

Have students share their choices and reasons for making those choices with the class.

Presentation 2 5-10 mins. ■■□

Write the words *advantages* and *disadvantages* on the board. Ask students what these words mean. Have them help you come up with a list of *advantages* and *disadvantages* of a debit card.

Practice 2 10-15 mins. ■■□

 What are the advantages and disadvantages of having a credit card? Work in a group to list them.

Have students work in small groups to complete this exercise.

Evaluation 2 5-10 mins. ■■□

Have each group share their ideas by making a list of the advantages and disadvantages of having a credit card on the board.

Presentation 3   5-10 mins.

G Read the information about loans.

Read this information out loud to your students. Ask the class to help you make a list on the board of information about loans.

Practice 3   10-15 mins. ■

You may want to erase the board before beginning Exercise H.

H With a partner, discuss the differences between these purchasing options. Make notes in the chart.

Evaluation 3   5-10 mins. ■

Ask students to share their answers with the class. Make a list on the board.

Application   5-10 mins. ■■■

I Look at the list of items. For each item, decide if you should get a loan or put it on a credit card. Discuss your answers with a group.

When students have finished, take a class poll to see if there is a consensus on how to pay for each item.

 Refer students to *Stand Out 4 Grammar Challenge*, Unit 2, Challenge 3 for practice with contrary-to-fact conditional *yes/no* questions.

Activity Bank

Lesson 3, Worksheet 1: Credit Card Application
Lesson 3, Worksheet 2: Credit Card Team Project

Instructor's Notes

LESSON **3** GOAL ➤ **Interpret credit card and loan information**

G Read the information about loans.

When you decide to purchase something that costs more than you can pay right now, you can put it on your credit card or you can get a loan. A loan from a bank or lending institution is something you have to apply for. You usually have to specify the amount you want to borrow and what kind of purchase you want to make. For large purchases, you usually need collateral, such as your house, your business, or a down payment. The interest rate will vary according to the amount you borrow, where you borrow the money from, and your creditworthiness.

H With a partner, discuss the differences between these purchasing options. **Make notes in the chart.** (Answers may vary. Possible answers below.)

Loan	Credit Card
must apply for	may charge up to limit without approval
need collateral	no collateral needed
interest rates vary	interest rates vary
may or may not be approved	

I Look at the list of items. For each item, decide if you should get a loan or put it on a credit card. Discuss your answers with a group. (Answers will vary.)

	Car	College Course	TV	Computer	Airline Ticket	Small Business
loan						
credit card						

How they pull you in

GOAL ➤ **Analyze advertising techniques**

A Look at the ads for digital camcorders.

1 JUST ARRIVED!

SONIC RS-200 MINIDV

30x optical zoom • 1000x digital zoom
2.5" LCD screen • built-in light
color viewfinder • image stabilization
$329 (with 20% off coupon)

2 ◆ One-touch recording! ◆

$399

Canyon ZT500 miniDV

25x optical zoom
1000x digital zoom
digital still mode
sleep button
2.7" LCD screen

3 *Great for the professional!*

Tihachi miniDVD

weighs *less than a pound!*

$799
(after $100 rebate)

★ digital still mode
★ 25x optical zoom
★ 1200x digital zoom
★ includes **FREE** camera bag

4 Perfect family camcorder!

$299

Niken miniDV

20x optical zoom

2.5" LCD screen • digital still mode • includes extra battery

---

miniDV: records video to small cassette tapes

miniDVD: records video to small DVDs

optical zoom: uses the lens of the camera to bring the subject closer without sacrificing quality

digital zoom: crops the image and then digitally enlarges it on your screen. This process does sacrifice quality.

B Discuss these questions with a group. (Answers will vary.)

1. Which ad is the most attractive to you? Why?
2. What kind of information do the ads give?
3. What information is not included?
4. How do the ads try to persuade you to buy the products?

AT-A-GLANCE PREP

Objective: Analyze advertising techniques
Grammar: Passive voice
Academic Strategies: Comparing and contrasting
Vocabulary: *digital camcorder, miniDV, digital zoom, optical zoom, LCD, viewfinder, image, stabilization, still mode, miniDVD, attractive, persuade, trust*

RESOURCES

Activity Bank: Unit 2, Lesson 4, Worksheet 1
Reading and Writing Challenge: Unit 2

Grammar Challenge: Unit 2, Challenge 4

■ 1.5 hour classes   ■ 2.5 hour classes   ■ 3⁺ hour classes

Warm-up and Review   5-10 mins.

Write *car, computer, TV,* and *airline ticket* on the board. Ask students if they would pay for these items by taking out a loan or using a credit card. Also, ask if they would buy on impulse or do some research beforehand? How would they do such research?

Introduction   5-10 mins. ■■■

Ask students the following questions:
How are advertisements good for you, the buyer?
How are they good for the seller?
Do you look at advertisements? For what products? Why?

State the objective: *Today we will be looking at advertisements and interpreting them. Then you will create your own advertisement for a product.*

Presentation 1   10-15 mins.

A **Look at the ads for digital camcorders.**

Have students read the ads. If they don't know very much about camcorders, you may need to briefly explain the features of each of the four featured in the ads.

B **Discuss these questions with a group.**

Have students work in small groups to answer the questions.

Prepare students for the practice by going over the instructions and the chart on the next page.

STANDARDS CORRELATIONS

CASAS: 1.2.1, 1.2.2 (See CASAS Competency List on pages 169–175.)
SCANS: **Information** Acquire and evaluate information, organize and maintain information, interpret and communicate information
Interpersonal Participate as a member of a team, teach others, serve clients and customers, exercise leadership, negotiate to arrive at a decision, work with cultural diversity
Systems Understand systems, monitor and correct performance, improve and design systems
Basic Skills Reading, writing, listening, speaking
Thinking Skills Creative thinking, decision making, problem solving, seeing things in the mind's eye

Personal Qualities Responsibility, sociability, self-management
EFF: **Communication** Read with understanding, convey ideas in writing, speak so others can understand, listen actively, observe critically
Decision Making Solve problems and make decisions, plan
Interpersonal Guide others, advocate and influence, cooperate with others
Lifelong Learning Take responsibility for learning, reflect and evaluate, learn through research, use information and communication technology (optional)

Practice 1   10-15 mins. ▪▪▪

C Look at the ads on page 30 to complete the table. If the information is missing from the ad, write *doesn't say*.

Evaluation 1   5 mins. ▪▪▪

Go over the answers as a class.

Note: On the Activity Bank CD-ROM, there is a template of this table so that you can make a transparency for students to fill out in class. (Unit 2, Lesson 4)

Presentation 2   5 mins. ▪▪▪

Go over the instructions for Exercises D and E.

Practice 2   10-15 mins. ▪▪

D Is there anything else that you would like to know about the camcorders? Write three questions that you might ask a salesperson.

E Based on the advertisements, which camera would you buy?

F Discuss these questions with a group.

Evaluation 2   10-15 mins. ▪▪

Have each group prepare a short class presentation based on the questions in Exercise F. Remind them to answer each question. Help the groups as needed.

GOAL ➤ Analyze advertising techniques

C Look at the ads on page 30 to complete the chart. If the information is missing from the ad, write *doesn't say*.

	Sonic	Canyon	Tihachi	Niken
Price	$329	$399	$799	$299
Coupon or rebate needed?	20% off coupon for above price	no	$100 rebate for above price	no
Digital zoom	1000x	1000x	1200x	doesn't say
Optical zoom	30x	25x	25x	20x
Digital still mode	doesn't say	yes	yes	yes
LCD screen size	2.5"	2.7"	doesn't say	2.5"
Recording media	miniDV	miniDV	miniDVD	miniDV
Other	built-in light, color viewfinder, image stabilization	sleep button	doesn't say	
Special offers	no	no	free camera bag	includes extra battery

D Is there anything else that you would like to know about the camcorders? Write three questions that you might ask a salesperson. (Answers will vary.)

1. _____

2. _____

3. _____

E Based on the advertisements, which camera would you buy? (Answers will vary.)

F Discuss these questions with a group. (Answers will vary.)

1. What do advertisers do to get you interested in their products?
2. Can you always trust advertisements?
3. What's the best way to find out the truth about a product?

LESSON **GOAL** ➤ **Analyze advertising techniques**

G Study the chart with your classmates and teacher.

Passive Voice: Present Tense				
Subject	**be**	**Past Participle**		**Explanation**
Ads	are	written	to sell products.	Since we know that ads are written by advertisers, the information "by advertisers" is not important.
The camera	is	advertised	on television.	Since we know that the store is advertising the camera, the information "by the store" is not important.
We use the passive voice to emphasize the object of the action or when the doer is not important.				

H Complete each sentence with the passive voice form of the verbs in parentheses. Make sure you use the correct form of the verb **be**.

1. Special offers _____are made_____ (make) to consumers.

2. Some advertising techniques _____are used_____ (use) in order to confuse the buyer.

3. Many products _____are sold_____ (sell) because of ads.

4. The truth about a product _____is discovered_____ (discover) by doing research and talking to other people who have bought the same product.

5. Often, consumers _____are tricked_____ (trick) into buying a product that they don't really need.

I With a small group, discuss the statements above.

J Imagine that you and a group of students are part of an advertising firm. Choose a product to write an ad for. Try to persuade people to buy your product. Use some passive voice sentences in your ad! Share your ad with the class.

Presentation 3   5-10 mins.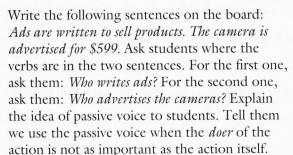

Write the following sentences on the board: *Ads are written to sell products. The camera is advertised for $599.* Ask students where the verbs are in the two sentences. For the first one, ask them: *Who writes ads?* For the second one, ask them: *Who advertises the cameras?* Explain the idea of passive voice to students. Tell them we use the passive voice when the *doer* of the action is not as important as the action itself.

(G) Study the chart with your classmates and teacher.

Practice 3   5-10 mins. ▣

(Shorter classes can do Exercise G for homework.)

(H) Complete each sentence with the passive voice form of the verbs in parentheses. Make sure you use the correct form of the verb *be*.

(I) With a small group, discuss the statements above.

Ask students if they agree or disagree with the statements and why. Model the exercise by going over the first sentence with a volunteer, asking them to give their opinion and then an example.

 Refer students to *Stand Out 4 Grammar Challenge*, Unit 2, Challenge 4 for more practice with the passive voice, present tense.

Evaluation 3   5-10 mins. ▣

Ask volunteers to write the sentences on the board. Answer any questions students have about the passive voice. If time allows, ask the groups whether they agreed or disagreed with the statements.

Application   10-20 mins. ▣▣▣

(J) Imagine that you and a group of students are part of an advertising firm. Choose a product to write an ad for. Try to persuade people to buy your product. Use some passive voice sentences in your ad! Share your ad with the class.

Activity Bank

Lesson 4, Worksheet 1: Analyze an Ad

Objective: Write a business letter
Academic Strategies: Active reading, writing a business letter
Vocabulary: *complain, complaint, return address, address, greeting, salutation, body, closing, signature*

RESOURCES

Activity Bank: Unit 2, Lesson 5, Worksheet 1
Reading and Writing Challenge: Unit 2

Grammar Challenge: Unit 2, Challenge 5; Extension Challenges 1-2

▪ 1.5 hour classes   ▪ 2.5 hour classes   ▪ 3⁺ hour classes

AGENDA

Discuss complaints.
Complain about a product or service.
Study the parts of a business letter.
Write a business letter of complaint.

Warm-up and Review   5–10 mins.

Have the groups take out the ads they created in the previous lesson and share them with the class. Ask each group what sort of techniques they used to persuade the buyer.

Introduction   5–10 mins. ▪▪▪

Tell a short story about a time when you complained about a product or service; for example when you purchased an item that didn't work properly or received poor service at a restaurant. Explain that you had a *complaint*. Elicit ways you could have handled your situation. State the objective: *Today we will practice complaining about products and services. Then we will write a business letter expressing a complaint.*

(A) Tell your classmates about a time when you complained about a product or service.

Presentation 1   5 mins. ▪▪▪

Go over the instructions and first example for Exercise B.

Practice 1   15–20 mins. ▪▪▪

(B) Read each situation below. Answer the questions with a partner.

(C) With a partner, choose one of the situations in Exercise B and write a conversation between the customer and the representative of the business. Practice your conversation and present it to the class.

Evaluation 1   5 mins.

Have each pair present their conversation to the class.

STANDARDS CORRELATIONS

CASAS: 1.6.3 (See CASAS Competency List on pages 169–175.)
SCANS: **Information** Acquire and evaluate information, organize and maintain information, interpret and communicate information, use computers to process information (optional)
Interpersonal Participate as a member of a team, teach others, serve clients and customers, exercise leadership, negotiate to arrive at a decision, work with cultural diversity
Systems Monitor and correct performance
Technology (optional) Select technology, apply technology to a task, maintain and troubleshoot technology

Basic Skills Reading, writing, listening, speaking
Thinking Skills Creative thinking, decision making, problem solving, seeing things in the mind's eye
Personal Qualities Responsibility, sociability, self-management
EFF: **Communication** Read with understanding, convey ideas in writing, speak so others can understand, listen actively
Decision Making Solve problems and make decisions
Interpersonal Resolve conflict and negotiate, advocate and influence, cooperate with others

Express yourself

GOAL ➤ Write a business letter

A Tell your classmates about a time when you complained about a product or service.

B Read each situation below. Answer the questions with a partner.
(Answers may vary. Possible answers below.)

1. You got home from the grocery store and realized the milk is sour. Who would you talk to? _the grocery store manager_

   What would you say? _I just got home and realized this milk is sour._

   What would you like to see happen? _I would like a new carton of milk._

2. You took a suit to the dry cleaners and it came back with a stain on it. Who would you talk to?

   the manager

   What would you say?

   Excuse me, this suit has a stain on it.

   What would you like to see happen?

   I would like the stain removed or get a refund.

3. You paid cash for your meal in a restaurant, but the server did not bring back your change. Who would you talk to?

   the server

   What would you say?

   Excuse me, but you haven't brought me my change (yet).

   What would you like to see happen? _Please bring me my change._

4. There is a charge on your credit card bill for something that you didn't buy. Who would you talk to?

   customer service representative

   What would you say?

   Excuse me, but I didn't purchase this item.

   What would you like to see happen?

   I would like the item removed from my bill.

C With a partner, choose one of the situations in Exercise B and write a conversation between the customer and the representative of the business. Practice your conversation and present it to the class.

D One of the most effective ways to complain about a product or service is to write a business letter. Read the letter below.

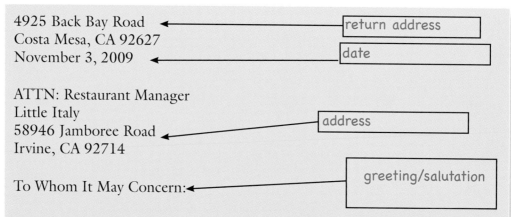

4925 Back Bay Road ← | return address
Costa Mesa, CA 92627
November 3, 2009 ← | date

ATTN: Restaurant Manager
Little Italy
58946 Jamboree Road ← | address
Irvine, CA 92714

To Whom It May Concern: ← | greeting/salutation

    I have been a customer at your restaurant many times and usually the food and service are wonderful. However, last night I was there having dinner with my husband and we had a terrible experience. First of all, our server, Kimberly, greeted us, took our order, and then never returned. When we finally tracked her down, forty minutes later, she was bringing our food, which was cold because it had been sitting in the kitchen too long. We never did get our drinks. When we were finished, we had to find another food server to get our check. We spent two hours at your restaurant and had bad service and a bad meal.

    We have really enjoyed eating at your restaurant in the past so I hope you will take this letter seriously and do more training with your staff.

Sincerely, ← | closing

Sara Lindgren ← | signature
Sara Lindgren ← | typed/printed name

E Answer the questions about the letter.

1. Who is Sara complaining to? _the restaurant manager_

2. What is she complaining about? _bad service_

3. What do you think will happen? _The manager may offer a complimentary meal._

Presentation 2

5-10 mins. ■■■

Have students look at the letter on page 34. Ask them some basic questions that they can answer by skimming the letter, such as: *Who wrote the letter? Whom did she write it to? Where is the restaurant located? Why would you write a letter to a restaurant?*

Practice 2

10-15 mins. ■■

(Shorter classes can do these exercises for homework.)

(D) One of the most effective ways to complain about a product or service is to write a business letter. Read the letter below.

Have students read the letter silently and then go on to Exercise E. (The parts of the letter will be covered in the next practice.)

(E) Answer the questions about the letter.

Evaluation 2

10-15 mins. ■■

Go over the answers to Exercise E. Ask students what makes this letter more formal than a personal letter they might write to a friend. Some of the things students might include are addresses at the top, the formal greeting, and the tone.

Presentation 3   5–10 mins. ■ ■ ■

Prepare students for the practice by going over the directions to Exercises F and G.

Practice 3   15–20 mins. ■

(Shorter classes can do these exercises for homework.)

(F) Use these words to label the parts of the business letter on page 34.

(G) A business letter should contain certain information. Look at Sara's letter again. Did she mention all of these pieces of information in her letter?

Evaluation 3   5–10 mins. ■

Go over the exercises as a class.

Application   10–20 mins. ■ ■ ■

(H) Choose one of these situations and write a business letter to make a complaint. Don't forget to format the letter correctly and include all of the necessary information.

Refer students to *Stand Out 4 Grammar Challenge,* Unit 2, Challenge 5 for practice with contrary-to-fact conditional *wh*-questions.

Activity Bank

Lesson 5, Worksheet 1: Complaints

Refer students to *Stand Out 4 Grammar Challenge*, Unit 2, Extension Challenges 1-2 for practice with future conditionals and wishes for desired changes.

Instructor's Notes

LESSON 5   **GOAL** ➤ **Write a business letter**

 F Use these words to label the parts of the business letter on page 34. (See answers on page 34.)

- return address
- date
- address
- greeting/salutation

- body
- closing
- typed/printed name
- signature

G A business letter should contain certain information. Look at Sara's letter again. Did she mention all of these pieces of information in her letter?

- who she is Yes.
- why she is writing Yes.
- an explanation of the problem or situation Yes.
- a satisfactory resolution Yes.

 H Choose one of these situations and write a business letter to make a complaint. Don't forget to format the letter correctly and include all of the necessary information.

Company	Reason for Letter
1. Lane's Accessories 8695 Tiguk Ave. Sioux Falls, SD 57104	The purse you bought is falling apart after one month.
2. Media Vision 4679 Lolly Lane Long Beach, CA 90745	You were charged for two months of cable instead of one.
3. Riverview Bank 47986 Washington Ave. Grand Rapids, MI 49503	There is a charge on your credit card statement that doesn't belong to you.
4. Produce World 875 7th Ave. New York, NY 10011	You were treated poorly by an employee.
5. (your own idea)	(your own idea)

A Imagine that your family of four has $3,000 to live on per month. Realistically, how would you budget your money? Fill in the chart. (Lesson 1) (Answers will vary. Sample answers below.)

Monthly Expense	Budgeted Amount
Rent / Mortgage Payment	$1,350
Utilities	$150
Auto: Car Payment /Gas/ Insurance	$600
Food	$400
Medical	$100
Clothing	$200
Entertainment	$200
TOTAL	$3,000

 B Look at the budget below. Calculate the differences and totals. (Lesson 1)

Monthly Expense		Budgeted Amount	Actual Amount Spent	Difference
Auto	Car Payment	$404.00	$404.00	$0
	Insurance	$72.39	$72.39	$0
	Gas	$180.00	$179.90	$.10
	Maintenance	$100.00	$29.99	$70.01
Housing	House Payment	$1,490.00	$1,490.00	$0
	Utilities	$122.00	$110.75	$11.25
	Phone (home, cell)	$150.00	$230.00	$-80.00
Food	Groceries	$350.00	$345.00	$5.00
	Eating Out	$200.00	$215.00	$-15.00
Other	Clothing	$350.00	$224.59	$125.41
	Entertainment	$300.00	$315.03	$-15.03
	Medical	$100.00	$40.00	$60.00
	TOTAL	$3,818.39	$3,656.65	$161.74

 C What are three things you can do to be a smart consumer? (Lesson 2) (Answers may vary. Possible answers below.)

1. compare prices at different stores

2. look for price matching policies

3. read ads carefully for misleading information

AT-A-GLANCE PREP

Objectives: All Unit 2 objectives
Grammar: All Unit 2 grammar
Academic Strategy: Reviewing
Vocabulary: All Unit 2 vocabulary

RESOURCES

Activity Bank: Unit 2, Lessons 1–5
Reading and Writing Challenge: Unit 2

Grammar Challenge: Unit 2, Challenges 1–5; Extension Challenges 1-2

■ 1.5 hour classes   ■ 2.5 hour classes   ■ 3+ hour classes

AGENDA

Unit objectives.
Review exercises.
My Dictionary.
Learner Log.

Warm-up and Review   5-10 mins. ■■■

In groups, have students share their letters of complaint from the previous lesson.

Introduction   5-10 mins. ■■■

Ask students to try to recall (in general) all the goals of this unit without looking at their books. Then remind them of the goals they omitted, if any. (Unit Goals: Calculate monthly expenses, identify ways to be a smart consumer, interpret credit card and loan information, analyze advertising techniques, and write a business letter.) Write all the objectives on the board from Unit 2. Show the students the first page of the unit and mention the five objectives. State the objective: *Today we will be reviewing everything you have learned in this unit.*

Presentation 1   10-15 mins. ■■■

This presentation will cover the first three pages of the review. Quickly go to the first page of each lesson. Discuss the objective of each. Ask simple questions to remind students of what they have learned.

Note: Since there is little presentation in the review, you can assign the review exercises that don't involve pair work or group work for homework and go over them in class the following day.

Practice 1   20-25 mins. ■■■

Note: There are two ways to do the review: (1) Go through the exercises one at a time and, as students complete each one, go over the answers. (2) Briefly go through the instructions of each exercise, allow students to complete all of the exercises at once, and then go over the answers. Stop and evaluate whenever it is appropriate for the class. *(See Evaluation 1 on pg. 38a.)*

 Imagine that your family of four has $3,000 to live on per month. Realistically, how would you budget your money? Fill in the chart. (Lesson 1)

 Look at the budget below. Calculate the differences and totals. (Lesson 1)

C What are three things you can do to be a smart consumer? (Lesson 2)

STANDARDS CORRELATIONS

CASAS: 7.2.1 (See CASAS Competency List on pages 169–175.)
SCANS: **Resources** Allocate time
Information Acquire and evaluate information
Interpersonal Participate as a member of a team, teach others, negotiate to arrive at a decision, work with cultural diversity
Systems Monitor and correct performance
Basic Skills Reading, writing, arithmetic, listening, speaking
Thinking Skills Creative thinking, decision making, problem solving, seeing things in the mind's eye

Personal Qualities Responsibility, sociability, self-management
EFF: **Communication** Convey ideas in writing, speak so others can understand, listen actively
Decision Making Solve problems and make decisions
Interpersonal Guide others, cooperate with others
Lifelong Learning Take responsibility for learning, reflect and evaluate, learn through research

Practice 1 (continued)   25–30 mins. ■■■

(D) Imagine that you have just inherited $100,000 from a relative. What would you do with it? Write three conditional statements about the possibilities. Then, share your answers with the class. (Lesson 2)

(E) Write *credit card, loan,* or *both* for each statement. (Lesson 3)

(F) List three advertising techniques that are used to get you to buy a product. (Lesson 4)

(G) Imagine that you are writing an advertisement for a product. What information should be included in your ad? Make a list and share it with the class. (Lesson 4)

Teaching Tip

Recycling/Review

The review and the project that follows are part of the recycling/review process. Students at this level often need to be reintroduced to concepts to solidify what they have learned. Many concepts are learned and forgotten while learning other new concepts. This is because students learn but are not necessarily ready to acquire language concepts.

Therefore, it becomes very important to review and to show students how to review on their own. It is also important to recycle the new concepts in different contexts.

Instructor's Notes

D Imagine that you have just inherited $100,000 from a relative. What would you do with it? Write three conditional statements about the possibilities. Then, share your answers with the class. (Lesson 2) (Answers will vary. Possible answers below.)

1. If I inherited $100,000, I would _buy a car._ _____

   _____

2. _If I inherited $100,000, I would take a trip around the world._ _____

   _____

3. _If I inherited $100,000, I would save it for my children's college education._ ___

   _____

E Write *credit card*, *loan*, or *both* for each statement. (Lesson 3)

1. You need to apply for this. _____ both _____

2. This can be used to buy an expensive item. _____ both _____

3. You need collateral for this. _____ loan _____

4. This often has an annual fee. _____ credit card _____

5. Sometimes this has an introductory offer. _____ credit card _____

6. You will pay a penalty if your payment is late. _____ both _____

7. This has an interest rate that affects your payments. _____ both _____

8. You can get this from the bank. _____ loan _____

F List three advertising techniques that are used to get you to buy a product. (Lesson 4)
(Answers will vary. Possible answers below.)

1. _special offers_ _____

2. _coupons_ _____

3. _rebates_ _____

G Imagine that you are writing an advertisement for a product. What information should be included in your ad? Make a list and share it with the class. (Lesson 4)

(Answers will vary.)

Review

H Complete each sentence with the passive form of the verb in parentheses. (Lesson 4)

1. Camcorders _____are sold_____ (sell) at electronics stores.

2. Advertisements _____are created_____ (create) to sell products.

3. Advertisers _____are paid_____ (pay) to convince you to buy certain products.

4. Sometimes an ad _____is written_____ (write) to confuse you.

I What four things should be included in a business letter that expresses a complaint? (Lesson 5)

1. who you are

2. why you are writing

3. an explanation of the problem or situation

4. a (satisfactory) resolution

J Decide if each statement is true or false, based on what you learned in this unit. If the statement is false, rewrite it to make it true. (Lessons 1-5)

__T__ 1. A smart consumer asks a lot of questions about a product before buying it.

__F__ 2. Advertisements always tell you everything about the product.

Advertisements don't always tell you everything about the product.

__F__ 3. Budgets are only for people with a lot of money.

Budgets are helpful for everyone.

__T__ 4. It is better to pay cash for something if you can.

__T__ 5. Sometimes credit cards carry high interest rates.

__T__ 6. Writing a business letter is a good way to express a complaint.

__F__ 7. You must have a credit card to buy an expensive item.

You could use a credit card to buy an expensive item.

Practice 1 *(continued)*   25–30 mins. ■■■

(H) Complete each sentence with the passive form of the verb in parentheses. (Lesson 4)

(I) What four things should be included in a business letter that expresses a complaint? (Lesson 5)

(J) Decide if each statement is true or false based on what you learned in this unit. If the statement is false, rewrite it to make it true. (Lessons 1–5)

Evaluation 1   45–60 mins. ■■■

Go around the classroom and check on students' progress. Help individuals when needed. If you see consistent errors among several students, interrupt the class and give a mini-lesson or review to help students feel comfortable with the concept.

Instructor's Notes

_____
_____
_____
_____
_____
_____
_____
_____
_____
_____
_____
_____
_____
_____
_____
_____
_____
_____
_____
_____
_____
_____
_____
_____
_____
_____

Presentation 2   5-10 mins.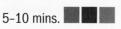

My Dictionary

Note: You may want to tell students a few days before this lesson to bring in a notebook, so they can complete the My Dictionary activity in class.

Without looking through their books, ask students to brainstorm the new vocabulary they learned in this unit. Ask them for ideas on how they can keep track of all the new words they are learning. Brainstorm a list of ideas on the board.

Practice 2   15-20 mins.

(Shorter classes can do these exercises for homework.)

Make your own dictionary of the new words you are learning in this class.

Go through the instructions with students and, if they already have notebooks, you can have them start making their dictionaries.

Go through Pre-Unit, Unit 1, and Unit 2. Make a list of twelve words that were new to you. Put them in alphabetical order below.

Now add these words to your dictionary.

Evaluation 2   5-10 mins.

Walk around the classroom and help students. Ask two or three volunteers to write the twelve words on their list on the board.

Presentation 3   5-10 mins.

Learner Log

In this unit, you learned many things about personal finance. How comfortable do you feel doing each of the skills listed below? Rate your comfort level on a scale of 1 to 4.

Go over the instructions with students and make sure they understand what to do. You may want to do the first one or two with the class to make sure they understand.

Teaching Tip

Learner Logs

Learner Logs function to help students in many different ways.

1. They serve as part of the review process.
2. They help students to gain confidence and document what they have learned. Consequently, students see that they are making progress and want to move forward in learning.
3. They provide students with a tool that they can use over and over to check and recheck their understanding. In this way, students become independent learners.

Practice 3   5-10 mins.

Have students complete the Learner Log.

Evaluation 3   5-10 mins.

Walk around the classroom and help students as needed.

Application   5-10 mins.

Go over the reflection statements with students and have them complete the answers by themselves.

Assessment (optional)

Use the Stand Out 4 Assessment CD-ROM with Exam*View*® to create a post-test for Unit 2.

My Dictionary

Make your own dictionary of the new words that you are learning in this class.

1. Buy a ruled notebook.
2. Divide the notebook into 26 sections—one for each letter of the alphabet.
3. As you learn new words, write them in your dictionary in the correct section.
4. After each word, write the page number where the word appears in your book, the definition, and an example sentence.

Go through Pre-Unit, Unit 1, and Unit 2. Make a list of twelve words that were new to you. Put them in alphabetical order below. (Answers will vary.)

1. _____   5. _____   9. _____

2. _____   6. _____   10. _____

3. _____   7. _____   11. _____

4. _____   8. _____   12. _____

Now add these words to your dictionary.

Learner Log

In this unit, you learned many things about personal finance. How comfortable do you feel doing each of the skills listed below? Rate your comfort level on a scale of 1 to 4. (Answers will vary.)

1 = Need more practice   **2** = OK   **3** = Good   **4** = Great!

Life Skill	Comfort Level				Page
I can calculate monthly expenses.	1	2	3	4	_____
I can plan a monthly budget.	1	2	3	4	_____
I know how to be a smart consumer.	1	2	3	4	_____
I can discuss purchasing options.	1	2	3	4	_____
I can interpret credit card and loan information.	1	2	3	4	_____
I can analyze advertising techniques.	1	2	3	4	_____
I can express consumer complaints.	1	2	3	4	_____
I can write a business letter.	1	2	3	4	_____

If you circled 1 or 2, write down the page number where you can review this skill.

Reflection

1. I learned _____.

2. I would like to find out more about _____.

Create a purchase plan.

With a team, you will create a purchase plan for a large item.

1. Form a team with four or five students. Choose positions for each member of your team.

POSITION	JOB DESCRIPTION	STUDENT NAME
Student 1: **Team Leader**	See that everyone speaks English and participates.	
Student 2: **Secretary**	Take notes. Write down purchase plan.	
Student 3: **Designer**	Design ad for product and purchase plan layout.	
Student 4: **Spokesperson**	Report information to the class. Prepare team for the presentation.	
Student 5: **Assistant**	Help the secretary and designer with their work.	

2. Decide on a large item that your team would like to purchase.

3. Create an advertisement for this product.

4. Write down all the steps you will need to take to purchase this item. (*Hint:* think about a budget, comparison shopping, ads, loan information)

5. Write a brief description of how you will complete each step.

6. Design a purchase plan poster that has a space for the ad, each step in your purchase plan, and artwork.

7. Present your purchase plan to the class.

Team Project

Create a purchase plan.

Each team will decide on a large item to purchase. Then they will create an ad and purchasing plan to buy the product.

The team project is the final application for the unit. It gives students a chance to show that they have mastered all of the Unit 2 objectives.

Note: Shorter classes can extend this project over two class meetings.

Stage 1   5 mins.

Form a team with four or five students. Choose positions for each member of your team.

Have students decide who will lead each step as described on the student page. Provide well-defined directions on the board for how teams should proceed. Explain that all the students do every step as a team. Teams shouldn't go to the next stage until the previous one is complete.

Stage 2   5 mins.

Decide on a large item that your team would like to purchase.

When students have come up with the large item, ask for the spokesperson from each group to report their decisions to the class.

Stage 3   15–20 mins.

Create an advertisement for this product.

Before students begin, brainstorm a list of things they might include in their ads.

Optional Computer Activity: Students may want to use the computer to design their ads.

Stage 4   5–10 mins.

Write down all the steps you will need to take to purchase this item. (*Hint:* think about a budget, comparison shopping, ads, loan information)

Stage 5   10–15 mins.

Write a brief description of how you will complete each step.

Stage 6   20–25 mins.

Design a purchase plan poster that has a space for the ad, each step in your purchase plan, and artwork.

Stage 7   15–20 mins.

Present your purchase plan to the class.

Help teams prepare for their presentations. Suggest that each member choose a different part of the poster to present.

AT-A-GLANCE PREP

Objective: Interpret housing advertisements
Academic Strategies: Using context clues, focused listening, reading a bar graph
Vocabulary: *offer, closing, detached, market, negotiate, cozy, nightlife, secluded, needs loving care, seasonal views, brand-new, master suite, amenities, asking price*

RESOURCES

Activity Bank: Unit 3, Lesson 1, Worksheet 1
Reading and Writing Challenge: Unit 3

Grammar Challenge: Unit 3, Challenge 1
Audio: CD 1, Track 9

■ 1.5 hour classes　■ 2.5 hour classes　■ 3⁺ hour classes

AGENDA

Read housing advertisements.
Understand housing ad vocabulary.
Listen for information.
Write a housing advertisement.

 Preassessment *(optional)* ■■■

Use the Stand Out 4 Assessment CD-ROM with Exam*View*® to create a pretest for Unit 3.

Warm-up and Review　5-10 mins. ■■■

Write the following words on the board and ask students the difference between these types of housing: *house, condo, apartment, townhouse,* and *mobile home.*

Introduction　5-10 mins. ■■■

Take a class poll of the types of housing students live in. Make a quick bar graph on the board based on the poll. Ask the following questions: *What type of housing do most of our students live in? What type of housing does no one in our class live in?*

Take another poll, asking students where they would like to live if they could live in a different type of housing. Make a quick bar graph of the results of this poll and compare the two graphs. State the objective: *Today we will be interpreting housing advertisements.*

Presentation 1　10-15 mins. ■■■

Have students look at the three houses pictured in their books. Ask them where they think each one is located.

A **Read the advertisements of homes for sale. Which name goes with which description? Write the names from the box above the correct description.**

Ask volunteers to read each ad out loud and then ask the class which house fits each ad.

Write *asking price* on the board and ask students what they think this means. If they can't come up with a definition, point out the words in the second ad and help them figure out the meaning using context.

STANDARDS CORRELATIONS

CASAS: 1.4.1, 1.4.2 (See CASAS Competency List on pages 169–175.)
SCANS: **Information** Acquire and evaluate information, organize and maintain information, interpret and communicate information
Interpersonal Participate as a member of a team, teach others, exercise leadership, negotiate to arrive at a decision, work with cultural diversity
Systems Monitor and correct performance
Basic Skills Reading, writing, arithmetic, listening, speaking
Thinking Skills Creative thinking, decision making, problem solving

Personal Qualities Responsibility, sociability, self-management
EFF: **Communication** Read with understanding, convey ideas in writing, speak so others can understand, listen actively
Decision Making Solve problems and make decisions, plan
Interpersonal Advocate and influence, cooperate with others
Lifelong Learning Use information and communications technology (optional)

41a　Lesson Planner: Unit 3, Lesson 1

Buying a Home

GOALS

➤ **Interpret housing advertisements**

➤ **Compare types of housing**

➤ **Identify housing preferences**

➤ **Identify the steps to buying a home**

➤ **Interpret mortgage information**

The American dream

GOAL ➤ **Interpret housing advertisements**

Vocabulary · Grammar
Life Skills
Academic · Pronunciation

 A Read the advertisements of homes for sale. Which name goes with which description? Write the names from the box above the correct description.

Suburban Dream	Country Cottage	Downtown Condominium

HOMES FOR SALE

Country Cottage

Cozy two-bedroom, two-bath, single-family home. Located in a secluded neighborhood, far from city life.

You won't believe this price for a house in this area.
Working fireplace.
Big yard.
Excellent seasonal views.
Must sell. Come see and make an offer now!
$240,000

★★★★★★★★★★

Suburban Dream

Single-family, 4-bedroom, 3-bath, 2500 sq. ft. home with an added family room. Needs some loving care.

Location is great!

Near jobs, bus, and schools. You must see this home and area.

Amenities: pool, fireplace, central a/c, built-in master suite and big yard!

Let's negotiate!
Asking price
$325,000

RENTAL SALES

Downtown Condominium

This 1000-square-foot condo is owned by the original owner and you'd think it was brand-new! Located in the heart of Los Angeles near all the nightlife you could imagine. Seller just added new carpet, new paint, new faucets and sinks, and beautiful ceramic tile flooring. Two master suites, indoor laundry room, detached two-car garage and large patio area. This condo will not last long on the market, so hurry!
$300,000

GOAL ➤ Interpret housing advertisements

B Real estate agents write advertisements to get you excited about a property. What do you think the following phrases from the ads could mean? Write your own definitions.
(Answers will vary. Possible answers below.)

asking price	a starting price, the price that the sellers want for their house
brand-new	built very recently, newly renovated, new fixtures
cozy	small but comfortable
master suite	a large bedroom with a bathroom attached
near nightlife	close to bars and restaurants, noisy, on a busy street
needs loving care	house/yard needs work
seasonal views	lots of trees, not too close to other houses
secluded	far from stores, services, other houses, main roads

C The words in the box below describe the process of buying a home. Find each word in the ads on page 41 and try to work out the meaning by using the context. Then, discuss the meanings with a partner.

offer	market	negotiate	amenities

D Look back at the ads on page 41 and complete the chart.

	Type of Property	Size	Asking Price	Number of Bedrooms	Number of Bathrooms	Location	Amenities
Country Cottage	single-family home	cozy (small)	$240,000	2	2	country/ secluded neighborhood	big yard, fireplace, view
Suburban Dream	single-family home	2,500 sq.ft	$325,000	4	3	suburb	pool, fireplace, a/c, yard, master suite
Downtown Condominium	condo	1,000 sq. ft.	$300,000	2	not given	city/L.A., near nightlife	new carpet, new faucets, laundry room parking, patio

Practice 1   10-15 mins.

 **B** **Real estate agents write advertisements to get you excited about a property. What do you think the following phrases from the ads could mean? Write your own definitions.**

Have students work with a partner or small group to come up with their own definitions.

C **The words in the box below describe the process of buying a home. Find each word in the ads on page 41 and try to work out the meaning by using the context. Then, discuss the meanings with a partner.**

Have students work with a partner or small group to figure out the meanings of these words using context clues.

Evaluation 1   5 mins.

Go over the answers as a class.

Presentation 2   5-10 mins.

Ask students what information is usually given in a housing ad. Make a list of students' ideas on the board. Students may include price, size, number of bedrooms, and so on.

Ask students questions about the housing ads, such as: *What type of property is the suburban dream? How big is the downtown condo? What amenities does the country cottage have?* (The answers to these questions have already been filled in in the chart in Exercise D.)

Show students the chart and explain to them how to fill it in.

Practice 2   10-15 mins.

(Shorter classes can do Exercise D for homework.)

D **Look back at the ads on page 41 and complete the chart.**

Have students complete the chart on their own.

Evaluation 2   5 mins.

Go over the answers as a class.

Presentation 3
5–10 mins.

Prepare students for the listening exercise by discussing the pictures in Exercise E. Ask them questions, such as: *How big do you think the fixer-upper is? How much do you think the Prince's Palace costs?*

Practice 3
15–20 mins.

E Listen to the advertisements of homes for sale and fill in the information you hear.

Play the recording once. Have students share the information they heard with their classmates. Play the recording several more times until students have all the information.

🎧 Listening Script
CD 1, Track 9

1. *Wanna live like a king? Then you can't pass up the Prince's Palace. Offered at a mere $1.2 million, this sprawling 15,000-square-foot palace is located at the top of a hill far away from other residences. Not only does it have every appliance you can think of, but all the rooms have beautiful hardwood floors. Wanna find out more about this princely estate? Call today!*

2. *Always wanted to take a house and make it your own? Here's your chance! Settle into this four-bedroom, 2,000-square-foot fixer-upper for only $150,000. Located in a busy neighborhood with lots of other families, this place is perfect for a young family.*

3. *Move out of the slow life and into the fast lane! A beautifully spacious 1,000-square-foot studio apartment at the top of one of the city's newest high-rises is just what you're looking for. The building has 24-hour security. Utility room with washers and dryers is in the basement. The owner wants to lease it for $2,000 a month but is willing to sell. Hurry! This one will go fast!*

4. *You've finally decided it's time to move out of the city and into the country. Well, we've got the place for you. This three-bedroom rural residence is just what you need. It's a spacious 3,500-square-foot, ranch-style home with a huge backyard and a pool. It's located at the end of a cul-de-sac where there are only five other homes. It is now being offered at $325,000.*

Evaluation 3
5–10 mins.

Go over the answers as a class.

Application
15–20 mins.

F Using the vocabulary you have learned in this lesson, write an advertisement for the place where you live now. Draw or paste in a picture.

As a model, write an ad for your own home on the board. Make sure you include all the necessary details as well as some of the new vocabulary items learned in this lesson.

Have students write their ads and then encourage volunteers to share their ads with the class by writing them on the board.

 Refer students to *Stand Out 4 Grammar Challenge*, Unit 3, Challenge 1 for more practice with comparative and superlative adjectives.

Activity Bank 📀

Lesson 1, Worksheet 1: Homes for Sale

Instructor's Notes

LESSON 1

GOAL ➤ Interpret housing advertisements

  E Listen to the advertisements of homes for sale and fill in the information you hear.

CD 1
TR 9

Prince's Palace

Price: 1.2 million

Size: 15,000 sq.ft.

Neighborhood:
hill-top neighborhood

Amenities: all
appliances,
hardwood floors

Fixer-Upper

Price: $150,000

Size: 4 bdrm,
2,000 sq. ft.

Neighborhood:
busy neighborhood

Amenities: none
stated

City High-Rise

Price: $2,000/mnth

Size: 1,000 sq.ft.

Neighborhood:
city, new high-rise

Amenities: washer
and dryer,
24-hour security

Rural Residence

Price: $325,000

Size: 3 bdrm
3,500 sq.ft.

Neighborhood:
country, cul de sac

Amenities: big
backyard, pool

F Using the vocabulary you have learned in this lesson, write an advertisement for the place where you live now. Draw or paste in a picture.

(Answers will vary.)

LESSON **2**

Bigger? Better?

GOAL ➤ **Compare types of housing**

CD 1
TR 10

A Listen to Joey and Courtney discuss two properties that Courtney looked at. As you listen, take notes about the advantages and disadvantages of each place.

House	Advantages	Disadvantages
	closer to job no association fees bigger	higher price not as nice neighborhood
Condominium		
	nicer neighborhood less expensive safe because of gate friendly neighbors	association fees

B With a partner, compare the house and the condominium.

EXAMPLE: *Student A:* What's an advantage of living in the house?
            Student B: The house is larger than the condo.

C Which one would you rather live in? Why? Explain your reasons to a partner.

D Complete the chart with a partner.

Adjective	Comparative	Superlative
beautiful	more beautiful	the most beautiful
noisy	noisier	the noisiest
safe	safer	the safest
comfortable	more comfortable	the most comfortable
far	farther	the farthest
friendly	friendlier/more friendly	the friendliest
cheap	cheaper	the cheapest
big	bigger	the biggest

* Note: Some two-syllable adjectives have two forms; for example, *quieter* or *more quiet.*

AT-A-GLANCE PREP

Objective: Compare types of housing
Grammar: Comparative and superlative adjectives, questions using comparative and superlative adjectives, long and short answers
Academic Strategies: Comparing and contrasting, focused listening
Vocabulary: *properties, advantages, disadvantages, comparative, superlative, noisy, floor plan, expensive taste*

RESOURCES

Activity Bank: Unit 3, Lesson 2, Worksheets 1–3
Reading and Writing Challenge: Unit 3

Grammar Challenge: Unit 3, Challenge 2
Audio: CD 1, Tracks 10–11

■ 1.5 hour classes   ■ 2.5 hour classes   ■ 3⁺ hour classes

AGENDA

Compare two places to live.
Identify comparative and superlative adjectives.
Write questions using comparative and superlative adjectives.
Compare homes you have lived in.

Warm-up and Review   5-10 mins.

Ask for volunteers to share the ads they wrote in the previous lesson. Encourage the rest of the class to ask questions about the ads.

Introduction   5 mins.

Describe two properties to students, one really nice and one not so nice. Ask students which one they would rather live in and why. State the objective: *Today we will be comparing types of housing and houses that we have lived in.*

Presentation 1   5 mins.

Prepare students for focused listening by having them look at the two pictures in the book. Ask them what they think the differences are. Discuss the meanings of *advantages* and *disadvantages*.

Practice 1   10-15 mins.

(A) Listen to Joey and Courtney discuss two properties that Courtney looked at. As you listen, take notes about the advantages and disadvantages of each place.

🎧 Listening Script   CD 1, Track 10

The listening script for Exercise A is on page 45a.

Evaluation 1   10-15 mins.

Go over the answers as a class.

(B) With a partner, compare the house and the condominium.

Go over the example with students before they talk to a partner. **Note:** The focus of this activity should not be grammar at this point.

(C) Which one would you rather live in? Why? Explain your reasons to a partner.

Presentation 2   5 mins.

Go over the first example in the chart with students. Comparative and superlative forms should be familiar to students at this level.

Practice 2   10-15 mins.

(Shorter classes can do Exercises D and E for homework.)

(D) Complete the chart with a partner.

STANDARDS CORRELATIONS

CASAS: 1.4.2 (See CASAS Competency List on pages 169–175.)
SCANS: **Information** Acquire and evaluate information, organize and maintain information, interpret and communicate information
Interpersonal Participate as a member of a team, exercise leadership, negotiate to arrive at a decision, work with cultural diversity
Systems Monitor and correct performance
Basic Skills Reading, writing, listening, speaking

Thinking Skills Creative thinking, decision making
Personal Qualities Responsibility, sociability, self-management
EFF: **Communication** Convey ideas in writing, speak so others can understand, listen actively
Interpersonal Cooperate with others
Lifelong Learning Reflect and evaluate

Listening Script CD 1, Track 10

Courtney: *I went and looked at houses yesterday.*
Joey: *You did? How did it go?*
Courtney: *Well, I found two that I really liked. One was a three-bedroom house and the other was a two-bedroom condominium.*
Joey: *Which one did you like better?*
Courtney: *Well, they both have their plusses and minuses. The house is closer to my job than the condo, but the condo is in a much nicer neighborhood.*
Joey: *What about price?*
Courtney: *The condo is cheaper than the house, but the condo has association fees.*
Joey: *Did you talk to any of the people who live in the area?*
Courtney: *Yep. I met one of the women who lives in the condominium complex, and she looked in both neighborhoods as well when she was buying her place. She said the condominium complex is safer than the housing neighborhood because of the gate at the front. She also said that there are more children in the complex and that the neighbors seem to be friendlier because everyone lives so close together.*

Activity Bank

Lesson 2, Worksheet 1: Comparative and Superlative Adjectives

Evaluation 2   10–15 mins. ■ ■

Go over the answers to Exercise D by doing Exercise E as a class. Students can then go back and check their answers in Exercise D. (Shorter classes can do Exercise E for homework.)

E Write the adjective(s) from Exercise D that corresponds to each rule.

F Describe the place you live in now and compare it to a place that you used to live in. Use the adjectives from Exercise D.

Have students use what they've just reviewed as they talk to a partner.

Presentation 3   10–20 mins. ■ ■ ■

As students are describing their former and current homes, ask them questions, such as: *Which one is bigger? Which one is more comfortable? Which one is cheaper?*

G Listen to Sara and Courtney talk about homes that Sara has looked at recently.

 Listening Script   CD 1, Track 11

The listening script matches the conversation in Exercise G.

H What questions does Courtney ask? How does Sara answer her? Practice the conversation with a partner.

Ask students for the questions and answers and write them on the board as they give them to you.

Instructor's Notes

_____
_____
_____
_____
_____
_____
_____
_____
_____
_____
_____
_____
_____
_____
_____
_____
_____

LESSON **2** **GOAL** ➤ **Compare types of housing**

 E Write the adjective(s) from Exercise D that corresponds to each rule.

1. Add *-er* or *-est* to one-syllable adjectives.   *cheap*

2. Use *more* or *the most* before two-syllable adjectives.   *beautiful, comfortable*

3. Add *-r* or *-st* to one-syllable adjectives that end in *e*.   *safe*

4. Change *y* to *i* and add *-er* or *-est*.   *noisy, friendly*

5. Some adjectives have irregular forms.   *far*

6. Double the final consonant of adjectives ending in the pattern

   of consonant-vowel-consonant and add *-er* or *-est*.   *big*

 F Describe the place you live in now and compare it to a place that you used to live in. Use the adjectives from Exercise D.

EXAMPLE: I used to live in a small, one-bedroom apartment with uncomfortable furniture. Now I live in a bigger apartment with the most comfortable couch in the world!

  G Listen to Sara and Courtney talk about homes that Sara has looked at recently.

CD 1
TR 11

Courtney: Have you looked at any new houses this week?
Sara: Yes, I looked at three places the other day. Look at this brochure!
Courtney: The *Country Cottage*, the *Suburban Dream*, and the *Downtown Condominium*. I like the sound of the *Country Cottage* best. It sounds more comfortable than the others.
Sara: Yeah, and it's the closest to where we live now.
Courtney: Oh really? Which place is the safest?
Sara: Actually, I think the *Suburban Dream* is the safest.
Courtney: Which one has the biggest floor plan?
Sara: The *Suburban Dream*. It would be ideal for our family.
Courtney: Is it the most expensive?
Sara: Why, of course! I have expensive taste.

 H What questions does Courtney ask? How does Sara answer her? Practice the conversation with a partner.

LESSON **2** **GOAL** ➤ **Compare types of housing**

 Study the charts with your teacher.

Questions Using Comparative and Superlative Adjectives				
Question word	Subject	Verb	Adjective or Noun	Rule
Which	one place house	is	bigger? closer to work? the safest?	Use *be* when following the verb with an adjective.
		has	more rooms? the biggest floor plan?	Use *have* before a noun.

Long and Short Answers				
Question	Short answer	Long answer	Rules
Which one is bigger, the condominium or the house?	The condominium.	The condominium is bigger. The condominium is bigger than the house.	• When talking about two things and mentioning both of them, use *than*. • When talking about two things, but only mentioning one of them, do not use *than*.
Which place has more rooms?	The house.	The house has more rooms. The house has more rooms than the condominium.	

 Write four comparative questions about the homes Joey and Courtney talked about in Exercise A. (Answers will vary. Possible answers below.)

EXAMPLE: Which place is closer to Courtney's job?

1. Which one is more expensive?

2. Which one is safer?

3. Which place has friendlier neighbors?

4. Which place is in a nicer neighborhood?

 With a partner, practice asking and answering the questions you wrote in Exercise J.

 Write sentences on a piece of paper comparing a place you used to live in to the place you live in now.

EXAMPLE: My old house had more bedrooms than the house I live in now.

Presentation 3 *(continued)*

I Study the charts with your teacher.

After explaining the charts, go back to Exercise H and show students how Sara and Courtney followed the same rules.

Practice 3   10-15 mins. ■

J Write four comparative questions about the homes Joey and Courtney talked about in Exercise A.

K With a partner, practice asking and answering the questions you wrote in Exercise J.

Refer students to *Stand Out 4 Grammar Challenge*, Unit 3, Challenge 2 for practice with comparative and superlative questions.

Evaluation 3   5-10 mins. ■

Ask volunteers to write their questions on the board. Review with the class by asking students the questions written on the board.

Application   10-20 mins. ■■■

L Write sentences on a piece of paper comparing a place you used to live in to the place you live in now.

Expansion activity or homework: Have students write a paragraph comparing the place they live in now to a place where they used to live.

Activity Bank

Lesson 3, Worksheet 2: Compare the Homes
Lesson 3, Worksheet 3: Comparative and Superlative
              Questions

Instructor's Notes

AT-A-GLANCE PREP

Objective: Identify housing preferences
Grammar: *Yes/No* questions and answers, information questions
Pronunciation: Rising and falling intonation
Academic Strategy: Using context clues
Vocabulary: *preferences, down payment, on the way, outgrown, pile into, putting away, realtor, within walking distance, attached garage, works out of the home, ideal, survive, thought long and hard, location, price range*

RESOURCES

Activity Bank: Unit 3, Lesson 3, Worksheets 1–2
Reading and Writing Challenge: Unit 3

Grammar Challenge: Unit 3, Challenge 3
Audio: CD 1, Track 12

 1.5 hour classes   ■ 2.5 hour classes   ■ 3⁺ hour classes

AGENDA

Listen and read about one family's housing preferences.
Use context to find meaning of housing vocabulary.
Ask and answer yes/no questions.
Ask and answer information questions.
Identify your own housing preferences.

Warm-up and Review   5-10 mins.

Have students find a partner and talk about the homes they live in. Ask them to compare their homes using comparatives and superlatives.

Introduction   5 mins. ■■□

Have students open their books and look at the picture of the Bwarie family. Write the two questions from Exercise A on the board. Ask students to predict possible answers. State the objective: *Today we will identify housing preferences.*

Presentation 1   10-15 mins. ■■□

(A) Think about these questions as you listen to the story about the Bwarie family.

> 🎧 **Listening Script**   CD 1, Track 12
>
> The listening script matches the story on page 47.

Ask students to close their books while they listen to the recording. Ask them the questions on the board afterward. Then, let them read the story as they listen to the recording a second time.

Practice 1   10-15 mins.

(B) Read the story again. Try to work out the meanings of these words and expressions by using the context.

Use the first expression, *down payment*, as an example. Find it in the story and show students how to use context clues to discover its meaning.

Evaluation 1   10-15 mins.

(C) Go over the meanings of the words and expressions with your teacher. Then, choose three of the words or expressions and use them in sentences.

Ask a few volunteers to write their sentences on the board. Evaluate them as a class.

Housing preferences

GOAL ➤ Identify housing preferences

CD 1
TR 12

A Think about these questions as you listen to the story about the Bwarie family.

1. Why is the Bwarie family looking for a new home?

2. What are they looking for in a new home?

The Bwarie family has outgrown their apartment. They have three children and a baby on the way, and they are now renting a two-bedroom house. They've been putting away money every month from their paychecks, and they finally have enough money for a down payment on a house. Every Sunday, the whole family piles into the car and goes to look at properties for sale. So far, they have been doing this on their own, but now it's time to find a realtor.

However, before they meet with a realtor, they need to decide exactly what they want. Courtney and Joey Bwarie have thought long and hard about what they want to purchase. First of all, they want a house in a safe neighborhood that is within walking distance to the school that their children attend. Second of all, they want four bedrooms, one for Courtney and Joey, one for the two boys, and another for their daughter and the baby girl who will be born next month. The fourth room will be used as an office for Courtney, who works out of the home. As far as bathrooms, four would be ideal, but they could survive with three if they had to. Some other things they would like are a big backyard for the children to play in and an attached two-car garage. Other amenities, such as air-conditioning or a pool, are not important to them.

Now they know what they are looking for in a new home. That was the easy part. Finding the home . . . that's a different story!

B Read the story again. Try to work out the meanings of these words and expressions by using the context.

down payment	on the way	outgrown
pile into	putting away	realtor
within walking distance	works out of the home	ideal
survive	thought long and hard	

C Go over the meanings of the words and expressions with your teacher. Then, choose three of the words or expressions and use them in sentences. (Answers will vary.)

GOAL ➤ **Identify housing preferences**

D What are the Bwaries looking for in a home? Complete the checklist with as much information as you can based on the story in Exercise A.

Housing Preferences Checklist				
Features	**Yes**	**No**	**Features**	**Preference**
air-conditioning	☐	☒	type of property	house
backyard	☒	☐	number of bathrooms	four
balcony	☐	☒	number of bedrooms	four
garage	☒	☐	location	safe neighborhood, close to children's school
heating	☐	☐	price range	none
pool	☐	☒	down payment (percentage)	none

E What information on the checklist did the Bwaries not talk about? What do you think their preferences might be regarding these items? (Answers may vary. Possible answers below.)

Price range (something they can afford), down payment % (what they have saved). Heating (yes?)

F When asking someone about their preferences, you can use *yes/no* questions. Study the chart below.

Yes/No Questions and Answers		
Do you want	air-conditioning?	Yes, I do.
	a backyard?	No, I don't.
Do they need	a balcony?	Yes, they do.
	a garage?	No, they don't.
Does the house have	heating?	Yes, it does.
	a pool?	No, it doesn't.

Pronunciation

Yes/No Questions:

Rising Intonation

➤ Do you want a yard?

➤ Do you want five bedrooms?

➤ Does the house have a pool?

➤ Does it have a balcony?

G Practice asking and answering *yes/no* questions with a partner. Use the information in Exercise D.

EXAMPLE: *Student A:* Do they want air-conditioning?
Student B: No, they don't.

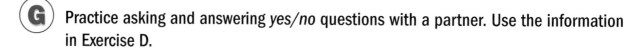

Presentation 2   5-10 mins.

D **What are the Bwaries looking for in a home? Complete the checklist with as much information as you can based on the story in Exercise A.**

Use this exercise to check that students understand what they have read. Then go over the answers with them.

E **What information on the checklist did the Bwaries not talk about? What do you think their preferences might be regarding these items?**

F **When asking someone about their preferences, you can use** *yes/no* **questions. Study the chart below.**

Go over the chart with students by reading the questions and having them practice answering with the answers provided. The questions and answers are more important than the grammar structure here so just make sure students understand the concepts. Then go over the pronunciation box.

Pronunciation

Rising intonation

Ask students some *yes/no* questions. (Examples from the book are fine.) Ask them if your voice goes up or down at the end of each question. Students should be able to recognize the rising intonation in your voice. Explain that this rising intonation helps the listener know that you are asking a *yes/no* question that requires an answer.

Go over the examples in the box in the student's book and show with your voice how to create rising intonation. Have the students practice by repeating after you. Have students repeat as a class and then call on individuals to demonstrate rising intonation.

Practice 2   10-15 mins.

G **Practice asking and answering** *yes/no* **questions with a partner. Use the information in Exercise D.**

Go over the example with students before they begin to practice. Don't forget to use rising intonation!

Evaluation 2   10-15 mins.

Observe students while they practice. Offer feedback and instruction as necessary.

Instructor's Notes

Presentation 3

5-10 mins.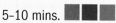

H Information questions start with *who, what, where, when, why,* or *how.* Study the chart.

Pronunciation

Rising and falling intonation

Ask students some information questions. (The examples from the book are fine.) Ask them if your voice goes up or down at the end of each question. Students should be able to recognize the rising and falling intonation in your voice. Explain that this rising and falling intonation helps the listener know that you are asking an information question that requires an answer.

Go over the examples in the box in the student's book and show with your voice how to create rising and falling intonation. Have the students practice by repeating after you. Have them repeat as a class and then call on individuals to demonstrate.

Practice 3

5-10 mins. ■

I Practice asking and answering information questions with a partner. Use the information from the chart in Exercise D.

Go over the example with students before they begin to practice.

 Refer students to *Stand Out 4 Grammar Challenge*, Unit 3, Challenge 3 for more practice with *yes/no* and information questions.

Evaluation 3

4-10 mins. ■

Observe students as they practice. Offer feedback and instruction as needed.

Activity Bank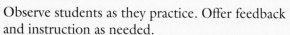

Lesson 3, Worksheet 2: Information Questions

Application

10-20 mins. ■■■

J What would *you* like in a new home? Look back at the checklist in Exercise D and make your own list of housing preferences. You might want to add some extra things that are not on the list. Compare your list with a partner.

After students have completed their lists, have them interview a partner using *yes/no* and information questions. Ask some students to report to the class what they learned from their partners.

Instructor's Notes

_____

_____

_____

_____

_____

_____

_____

_____

_____

_____

_____

_____

_____

_____

_____

_____

_____

_____

_____

_____

_____

_____

_____

H Information questions start with *who, what, where, when, why,* or *how*. Study the chart.

Information Questions			
Information	**Example questions**		
type of property	What type	of property	do you want? is it?
number of bathrooms number of bedrooms	How many	bedrooms bathrooms	do you want? does it have?
location	Where		is it?
price range	What		is your price range?
down payment (percentage)	How much		can you put down?

 I Practice asking and answering information questions with a partner. Use the information from the chart in Exercise D.

EXAMPLE:
Student A: What type of property do they want?
Student B: They want a house.

Pronunciation

Information Questions:
Rising and Falling Intonation

➤ What type of property do you want?

➤ How much can you put down?

➤ When will you be moving?

J What would *you* like in a new home? Look back at the checklist in Exercise D and make your own list of housing preferences. You might want to add some extra things that are not on the list. Compare your list with a partner. (Answers will vary.)

 LESSON **4**

Step-by-step

GOAL ➤ **Identify the steps to buying a home**

A What are some ways to find a house? With a group, list your ideas.

B Read the letter that Joey wrote to Paradise Realty.

15236 Dahlia Avenue
Costa Mesa, CA 92627
February 13, 2008

Paradise Realty
9875 Timber Lane
Costa Mesa, CA 92627

Dear Paradise Realty:

My family has decided to purchase a new home, and we would appreciate any information you can send us about homes for sale.

We are looking for a four-bedroom home. We would like to live in a safe neighborhood, close to our children's school. We would prefer a home with a big enclosed yard that our children can play in. We might want to build a pool in the future, but right now it is not a priority. Other amenities, such as air-conditioning, central heating, and closet space would be nice, but they are not essential.

Our price range is between $300,000 and $350,000, and we are prepared to put down 10%. Please contact me at the address above or you may call me or my wife, Courtney, at (949) 555-2408. Thank you for your time.

Sincerely,

Joseph Bwarie
Joseph Bwarie

AT-A-GLANCE PREP

Objective: Identify the steps to buying a home

Academic Strategies: Using context clues, sequencing, active reading, summarizing a process

Vocabulary: *enclosed, priority, central heating, closet space, real estate agent, closing, contract, cost comparison, lender, motivation*

RESOURCES

Activity Bank: Unit 3, Lesson 4, Worksheet 1
Reading and Writing Challenge: Unit 3

■ 1.5 hour classes ■ 2.5 hour classes ■ 3⁺ hour classes

AGENDA

Read a letter to a realtor.
Order the steps to buying a home.
Use context to find meaning.
Write a paragraph about buying a home.

Grammar Challenge 4: Unit 3, Challenge 4

Warm-up and Review   5-10 mins. ■■■

Have students find a partner and ask each other questions about the housing preferences checklist they completed in the previous lesson.

Introduction   5-10 mins. ■■■

(A) What are some ways to find a house? With a group, list your ideas.

Allow ample time for this activity. When groups have finished, have them share their lists with the class. State the objective: *Today we will identify the steps to buying a home.*

Presentation 1   5-10 mins. ■■■

Have students look at the letter as you review the parts of a business letter that they learned in the previous unit. (It may be helpful to show a transparency of this book page on an overhead projector.) Ask students letter-format questions, such as: *What is the greeting? What is the first word of the body? What is the closing?*

Ask students if they've ever dealt with a real estate agent before. Ask: *What does a real estate agent need to know to help you look for a house that is right for you?*

Practice 1   5 mins. ■■■

(B) Read the letter that Joey wrote to Paradise Realty.

Evaluation 1   5 mins. ■■■

Ask students basic comprehension questions about the letter to make sure they have understood what they read.

Presentation 2   5-10 mins.

Ask how many students own their own homes. Ask how many students would like to own homes. Ask students if they or anyone they know has ever bought a home. Ask them to share their experiences.

Go through each of the steps in Exercise C and make sure students understand them.

Practice 2   10-15 mins.

(Shorter classes can do these exercises for homework.)

C Read the steps for buying a home and put them in the correct order. Write a number next to each sentence.

Put up a transparency of the home-buying steps or have a student write them on the board. As a class, put the steps in order. At this point, don't tell students if the order is correct.

Ask students what they think the article on the student page will be about. What specific information do they think they might find?

D Now read the article about home buying and check your answers.

Teaching Tip

Active reading

The purpose of active reading is to help students engage their reading comprehension skills so they can tackle any reading with confidence. Explain that they may not understand the passage on the first reading. Help them realize that to understand a reading, they may need to read it more than once—maybe even three or four times.

Pre-reading: Teach students that anticipating the content of a reading and recalling information they already know about the topic will help make the reading easier to understand.

First reading: Focus on the main ideas by asking students to find the topic sentence in each paragraph, or to summarize the main point of each paragraph.

Second reading: Show students how to scan the reading quickly to find details that support the main ideas or that answer the post-reading questions.

Guessing from context: Encourage students to guess the meaning of new words from context by analyzing the words surrounding the vocabulary item. They should not let unknown words slow down their reading and should use a dictionary only after they are familiar with the context.

Instructor's Notes

_____

_____

_____

_____

_____

_____

_____

_____

_____

_____

_____

_____

_____

_____

_____

_____

_____

_____

_____

_____

_____

_____

C Read the steps for buying a home and put them in the correct order.
Write a number next to each sentence.

_3_ Apply for a loan.
_5_ Choose a home you'd like to buy.
_2_ Decide how much money you can spend.
_1_ Decide what you are looking for.
_7_ Have the home inspected.
_6_ Make an offer on the home.
_9_ Move in.
_8_ Negotiate until both parties come to an agreement.
_4_ Start looking for homes in a neighborhood you'd like to live in.

D Now read the article about home buying and check your answers.

BUYING A HOME

Home buyers can spend up to three months, and possibly more, looking for and purchasing a home. Their search begins by looking at housing ads, driving through neighborhoods they are interested in, and walking through open houses. Many first-time buyers will meet with a real estate agent to get help finding and buying a home.

Home buyers should know how much they can afford before they start looking for a home. It isn't worth your time to look for a new home if you can't really afford to buy one. So, it's a good idea to look at your financial situation first. You might be surprised how much money you can borrow, especially if the interest rates are good. Also, if you have some money for a down payment, your monthly payments may be lower than you think.

You should never make an offer on a home without looking at other houses in the same neighborhood. Just as you would comparison shop for a car or computer, you should do a cost comparison on different homes for sale. You can do this by asking about the recent sales of similar properties, which any real estate agent can tell you. Also, if you can find something out about the seller and his or her motivation for selling, it will put you in a better position to negotiate. For instance, maybe the seller needs to sell quickly and would accept a low offer.

Once you have found the property that you want and can afford, you are ready to make an offer. A low-ball offer is an offer that is much lower than the asking price. Unless the house is really overpriced or the seller needs to sell it quickly, he or she will probably not accept a low-ball offer. Once you make an offer that is reasonable to the seller, he or she will either accept it or make a counter offer. If he or she makes a counteroffer, the negotiating process has begun. You may have to go back three or four times before an agreement is reached.

Being a good negotiator can be tricky. Take your time when making your decision. This is a very important decision and you don't want to be rushed. Sometimes you can negotiate for repairs to be done to the home before you move in, or you can ask the seller to pay for some of your closing costs. As soon as a written offer is made and accepted by both parties, the document becomes a legally binding contract.

One of the first things you do after the contract is agreed upon is to get a home inspection. You need to hire a paid professional inspector to inspect the home, searching for defects or other problems.

The inspector usually represents the buyer and is paid for by the buyer. The contract that you sign with the seller protects you as a buyer by allowing you to cancel closing on the deal if an inspector finds problems with the property that the seller is unwilling to have fixed or give the buyer credit for.

Once the contract has been signed, the lender (usually a bank) starts processing the loan. Once all the inspections are done and any repairs are completed, the final papers for the transfer of the title are prepared. Finally, the closing takes place on the date agreed upon in the offer. On that date, the title comes to you and you can begin enjoying your new home!

E Find these words in the article and match them with the correct meaning.

_g_ 1. afford

_a_ 2. contract

_c_ 3. cost comparison

_h_ 4. negotiate

_d_ 5. lender

_e_ 6. motivation

_b_ 7. offer

_f_ 8. closing

a. a legal document

b. amount of money that buyer is willing to pay for a house

c. looking at different prices of homes

d. person or company that loans money

e. the desire to do something

f. when all papers are signed and titles are transferred

g. to have enough money to purchase something

h. discuss until you reach an agreement

F What are the benefits of owning your own home? What are the drawbacks? Discuss them with a partner.

G Write a paragraph summarizing the process of buying a home.

Evaluation 2   10-15 mins. ■ ■

Have students compare the steps numbered in the article to those the class numbered in Exercise C.

Go over the article with students and help them with any ideas they don't understand.

Presentation 3   5-10 mins. ■ ■ ■

Go over the instructions and do the first item in Exercise E with students.

Practice 3   10-15 mins. ■

(Shorter classes can do Exercise E for homework.)

E Find these words in the article and match them with the correct meaning.

Evaluation 3   5-10 mins. ■

Observe students as they work independently. When students are finished, have them share their answers with a partner. Then, go over the answers as a class. To make sure students understand the meanings, ask for volunteers to come up with new sentences using each word. If you have time, ask for students to write their new sentences on the board.

Application   10-20 mins. ■ ■ ■

F What are the benefits of owning your own home? What are the drawbacks? Discuss them with a partner.

G Write a paragraph summarizing the process of buying a home.

This is a good chance for students to practice using transitions. Use the writing and editing templates on the Activity Bank CD-ROM to help students with their paragraphs.

Refer students to *Stand Out 4 Grammar Challenge*, Unit 3, Challenge 4 for practice with irregular comparative and superlative adjectives.

Activity Bank

Lesson 4, Worksheet 1: Buying a House

Instructor's Notes

AT-A-GLANCE PREP

Objective: Interpret mortgage information
Academic Strategies: Focused listening, writing about preferences, sequencing, reading a graph, comparing and contrasting
Vocabulary: *down payment, determine, make an offer, long-term financial commitment, afford, credit check, get approved for a loan, recent pay stubs, put down a deposit, price range, purchase price, mortgage*

RESOURCES

Activity Bank: Unit 3, Lesson 5, Worksheet 1
Reading and Writing Challenge: Unit 3

 1.5 hour classes   2.5 hour classes   3+ hour classes

Grammar Challenge 4: Unit 3, Challenge 5; Extension Challenges 1-2
Audio: CD 1, Tracks 13–16

AGENDA

Discuss financial planning.
Learn mortgage vocabulary.
Identify the steps to getting a mortgage.
Analyze types of mortgages.
Write a paragraph.

Warm-up and Review   5 mins.

Review the benefits and drawbacks of owning your own home. Ask students if they think the benefits outweigh the drawbacks or vice versa.

Introduction   5–10 mins.

Remind students that in the previous unit they learned about credit cards and loans. Ask them if they know what a loan for a house is called (a mortgage). State the objective: *In this lesson, we will be interpreting mortgage information by listening to a talk with a financial planner and then comparing different types of mortgages.*

Presentation 1   10–15 mins.

A Todd and Sara Mason are thinking of buying a house. Todd is worried about money, so he made an appointment with a financial planner to talk about a mortgage. Discuss the questions below with a partner.

Talk about financial planners and what they do. Ask the class if anyone has a financial planner. If so, ask the student what sort of advice a financial planner gives.

Have students work in small groups to make a list of what they think the financial planner will tell Todd and Sara about getting a mortgage. Discuss the groups' lists as a class.

Practice 1   5–10 mins.

B Listen to Todd talk to the financial planner. What does the financial planner say? Is anything he says on the list you made?

> **Listening Script**   CD 1, Track 13
>
> See the listening script on the next page.

Evaluation 1   5 mins.

Discuss the listening as a class.

Presentation 2   5–10 mins.

C Do you know what these words and expressions mean? Discuss them with your classmates and teacher.

STANDARDS CORRELATIONS

CASAS: 1.3.1, 1.4.6, 1.5.2 (See CASAS Competency List on pages 169–175.)
SCANS: Information Acquire and evaluate information, organize and maintain information, interpret and communicate information
Interpersonal Participate as a member of a team, teach others, negotiate to arrive at a decision, work with cultural diversity
Systems Monitor and correct performance
Basic Skills Reading, writing, arithmetic, listening, speaking

Thinking Skills Creative thinking, decision making, problem solving
Personal Qualities Responsibility, sociability, self-management
EFF: Communication Read with understanding, convey ideas in writing, speak so others can understand, listen actively
Decision Making Solve problems and make decisions
Interpersonal Resolve conflict and negotiate, cooperate with others
Lifelong Learning Reflect and evaluate, learn through research, use information and communication technology (optional)

Financial planning

GOAL ➤ Interpret mortgage information

A Todd and Sara Mason are thinking of buying a house. Todd is worried about money, so he made an appointment with a financial planner to talk about a mortgage. Discuss the questions below with a partner.

1. What is a financial planner?

2. What do you think the financial planner will tell Todd and Sara about getting a mortgage? Make a list with a partner. (Answers will vary.)

1. _____
2. _____
3. _____
4. _____
5. _____

CD 1
TR 13

B Listen to Todd talk to the financial planner. What does the financial planner say? Is anything he says on the list you made?

C Do you know what these words and expressions mean? Discuss them with your classmates and teacher.

mortgage	financial commitment	afford
get approved for a loan	price range	credit check
down payment	deposit	purchase price

LESSON 5 **GOAL** ➤ Interpret mortgage information

CD 1
TR 14

D Listen to the first part of the conversation again. What are the three questions Todd must ask himself? Write them below.

1. Do you have money set aside for a down payment?

2. Do you have enough money each month to make a loan payment?

3. Are you ready to make a long-term financial commitment?

CD 1
TR 15

E What are the next steps Todd must take? Listen to what the financial planner says and write the four steps below.

1. determine how much you can afford to spend on a house

2. get approved for a loan for that amount

3. start looking for a home in that price range

4. make an offer on the house you want

CD 1
TR 16

F Todd will need to give the financial planner six things. Do you remember what they are? Write them below. If you can't remember, listen again.

1. Social Security number

2. tax statements from the past two years

3. two most recent pay stubs

4. most recent statements from all bank accounts

5. most recent credit card statements

6. statements from any other loans you have

G Imagine that you are trying to get a mortgage and you have to gather all of the items listed in Exercise F. Put a check mark (✓) next to each one that you have at home right now.

Teaching Tip

Focused listening

The purpose of focused listening is to expose students to real-life listening situations and teach them how to pick out the most important information.

1. Make it clear to students that they don't need to understand everything that is spoken to grasp the meaning of the passage or conversation.
2. Present the context.
3. Make sure students understand what they are listening for.
4. Start with a few examples and allow students to be successful before you expect them to complete the whole task.
5. After they complete the task, ask for a report.

Practice 2   15-20 mins.

For each of the exercises below, play each segment once. Then have students share their answers with a partner. Play the segment again if students want. Then go over the answers as a class.

D Listen to the first part of the conversation again. What are the three questions Todd must ask himself? Write them below.

E What are the next steps Todd must take? Listen to what the financial planner says and write the four steps below.

F Todd will need to give the financial planner six things. Do you remember what they are? Write them below. If you can't remember, listen again.

Evaluation 2   10-15 mins.

Go over the answers as a class.

G Imagine that you are trying to get a mortgage and you have to gather all of the items listed in Exercise F. Put a check mark (✓) next to each one that you have at home right now.

 Listening Script   CD 1, Track 13–16

Track 13 contains the entire script as follows.
(Track 14)

Todd: *I really appreciate your taking time to talk to me.*
Financial Planner: *No problem, Todd. I always have time for an old friend.*
Todd: *Well, as I told you over the phone, the boys are starting to grow up and Sara and I would like to move into a permanent place of our own. We're just a little worried about how we're going to pay for it.*
Financial Planner: *I think it's great that you and Sara are ready to take the next step, but only you can decide if you're ready to buy a house. Here's what I tell all my clients. First, you have to ask yourself three questions. Do you have money set aside for a down payment? Do you have enough money each month to make a loan payment? And are you ready to make a long-term financial commitment? If you can answer "yes" to all three of those questions, you are ready to buy a home.*
Todd: *How much will we need for a down payment?*
Financial Planner: *Well, that all depends on how much the house is that you want to buy. Also, you have to decide how much you want to put down. It's best if you can put 20% down, but some people can only put 5% down. The more you put down, the lower your monthly payments will be.*

(Track 15)
Todd: *OK, so if we can answer yes to all of those questions, what's the next step?*
Financial Planner: *First, you need to determine how much you can afford to spend on a house. Next, you get approved for a loan for that amount. Third, start looking for a home in your price range. And fourth, make an offer on the house you want.*
Todd: *Looking for a home and making an offer are easy, but how do we figure out how much we can afford?*
Financial Planner: *The best thing to do is gather all the necessary paperwork, and then we can determine how much you can spend.*

(Listening script continues on page 55a.)

(Track 16)
Todd: *What's the necessary paperwork?*
Financial Planner: *I'll need six things. I'll need your Social Security number to run a credit check, tax statements from the past two years, two of your most recent pay stubs, the most recent statements from all your bank accounts, your most recent credit card statements, and statements from any other loans that you have. Once I have those things, I should be able to determine what your purchase price can be. If not, I'll ask you for more information.*
Todd: *Is there anything else I need to know?*
Financial Planner: *That's it for now. Why don't you and Sara sit down and discuss the three questions we talked about. If the answer is yes to all three, start gathering that paperwork and give me a call.*
Todd: *Great! Thanks for all your help.*

Presentation 3   5-10 mins. ■■■

Ask students if any of them have mortgages. If so, ask them what type of mortgage they have? Make a list on the board, if possible. Tell students there are three main types of mortgages.

Practice 3   10-15 mins. ■

(Shorter classes can do these exercises for homework.)

(H) Now that Todd knows how to get a mortgage, he needs to learn about the different types of mortgages. Read about each type below.

(I) Using the information from Exercise H, put a check mark (✓) in the correct column(s).

Evaluation 3   5-10 mins. ■

Review the reading with students to make sure they understand its main points. Then go over the answers to Exercise I.

Application   10-20 mins. ■■■

(J) If you were going to buy a house, which type of loan would you get? Why? Write a short paragraph about your preference.

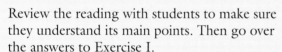
Activity Bank

Lesson 5, Worksheet 1: Getting a Mortgage

 Refer students to *Stand Out 4 Grammar Challenge*, Unit 3, Challenge 5 for practice with *should* and *should have*.

 Refer students to *Stand Out 4 Grammar Challenge*, Extension Challenges 1-2 for more practice with compound adjectives and *as many . . . as, as much . . . as.*

Instructor's Notes

H   Now that Todd knows how to get a mortgage, he needs to learn about the different types of mortgages. Read about each type below.

Fixed-Rate Mortgages

A fixed-rate mortgage has a fixed interest rate for the life of the loan, which could be 10, 20, or 30 years. You will make the same payment every month for the life of the loan and, at the end of the term, your loan will be paid off. The advantage of this type of loan is the interest rate never changes and the monthly payment is always the same.

Adjustable Rate Mortgages

An adjustable rate mortgage (ARM) begins like a fixed-rate mortgage with a fixed interest and a constant monthly payment, but this mortgage will adjust after a certain amount of time, anywhere from six months to five years. At this point, the interest rate and your monthly payment will change based on the market at the time. Furthermore, every month the rate and payment could change based on how the market changes.

Balloon Mortgages

A balloon mortgage has a fixed interest rate and a fixed monthly payment, but after a certain amount of time, for example five years, the entire balance of the loan is due. This is a short-term loan, usually for people who can't qualify for a fixed-rate mortgage or an ARM.

I   Using the information from Exercise H, put a check mark (✓) in the correct column(s).

	Fixed-Rate	ARM	Balloon
1. The monthly payment is always the same.	✓		✓
2. The interest rate changes after a certain period of time.		✓	
3. The interest rate is fixed.	✓		✓
4. The monthly payment will change based on the market.		✓	
5. This type of loan is short term.			✓

J   If you were going to buy a house, which type of loan would you get? Why? Write a short paragraph about your preference.

A Read the housing advertisements and complete the chart below. (Lesson 1)

1. Always wanted to take a house and make it your own? Here's your chance! Settle into this 4-bedroom, 3.5 bath, 2,000-square-foot fixer-upper: $250,000. Located in a busy neighborhood with lots of other families, this place is perfect for a young family.

2. Move out of the slow life and into the fast lane! A beautifully spacious, 1,200-square-foot studio apartment at the top of one of the city's newest sky-rises is just what you're looking for. The building has 24-hour security. Utility room with washers and dryers is in the basement. The owner wants to lease it for $2,000 a month but will sell for $700,000. Hurry! This one will go fast!

3. You've finally decided it's time to move out of the city and into the country. Well, we've got just the place for you. This 3-bedroom, 3-bathroom rural residence is just what you need. It's a spacious, 5,000-square-foot, ranch-style home with a huge backyard and pool. It's located at the end of a cul-de-sac with only five other homes. It is now being offered at $600,000.

	Type of Property	Size	Asking Price	Number of Bedrooms	Number of Bathrooms	Location	Amenities
Home 1	House	2,000 sq. ft.	$250,000	4	3.5	busy neighborhood, near other families	(not given)
Home 2	Studio apt.	1,200 sq. ft.	Lease $2,000 Sell $700,000	Studio	1 (not given)	city, sky-rise	24-hr security, washer/dryer in basement
Home 3	House	5,000 sq. ft.	$600,000	3	3	country, cul-de-sac	huge backyard, pool

Objectives: All Unit 3 objectives
Grammar: All Unit 3 grammar
Academic Strategy: Reviewing
Vocabulary: All Unit 3 vocabulary

RESOURCES

Activity Bank: Unit 3, Lessons 1–5
Reading and Writing Challenge: Unit 3

Grammar Challenge: Unit 3, Challenges 1–5; Extension Challenges 1-2

■ 1.5 hour classes   ■ 2.5 hour classes   ■ 3⁺ hour classes

AGENDA

Unit objectives.
Review exercises.
My Dictionary.
Learner Log.

Warm-up and Review   5-10 mins.

In groups, have students come up with a list of the steps it takes to get a mortgage.

Introduction   5-10 mins.

Ask students as a class to try to recall (in general) all the goals of this unit without looking at their books. Then remind them which goals they omitted, if any. (Unit Goals: Interpret housing advertisements, compare types of housing, identify housing preferences, identify the steps to buying a home, and interpret mortgage information.) Write all the objectives on the board from Unit 3. Show students the first page of the unit and mention the five objectives. State the objective: *Today we will be reviewing everything you have learned in this unit.*

Presentation 1   10-15 mins.

This presentation will cover the first three pages of the review. Quickly go to the first page of each lesson. Discuss the objective of each one. Ask simple questions to remind students of what they have learned.

Note: Since there is little presentation in the review, you can assign the review exercises that don't involve pair work or group work for homework and go over them in class the following day.

Practice 1   20-25 mins.

Note: There are two ways to do the review: (1) Go through the exercises one at a time and, as students complete each one, go over the answers. (2) Briefly go through the instructions of each exercise, allow students to complete all of the exercises at once, and then go over the answers.

Stop and evaluate whenever it is appropriate for the class. *(See Evaluation 1 on pg. 58a.)*

A Read the housing advertisements and complete the chart below. (Lesson 1)

STANDARDS CORRELATIONS

CASAS: 7.2.1 (See CASAS Competency List on pages 169–175.)
SCANS: **Resources** Allocate time
Information Acquire and evaluate information
Interpersonal Participate as a member of a team, teach others, negotiate to arrive at a decision, work with cultural diversity
Systems Monitor and correct performance
Basic Skills Reading, writing, arithmetic, listening, speaking
Thinking Skills Creative thinking, decision making, problem solving, seeing things in the mind's eye

Personal Qualities Responsibility, sociability, self-management
EFF: **Communication** Read with understanding, convey ideas in writing, speak so others can understand, listen actively
Decision Making Solve problems and make decisions
Interpersonal Guide others, cooperate with others
Lifelong Learning Take responsibility for learning, reflect and evaluate, learn through research

Practice 1 (*continued*)   25-30 mins.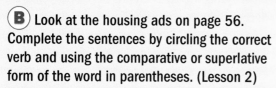

B Look at the housing ads on page 56.
Complete the sentences by circling the correct
verb and using the comparative or superlative
form of the word in parentheses. (Lesson 2)

C Complete the housing preferences checklist
based on what you would want in a home.
(Lesson 3)

D Write four *yes/no* questions you could ask
someone about his or her housing preferences.
(Lesson 3)

Teaching Tip

Recycling/Review

The review process and the project that follows
are part of the recycling/review process. Students
at this level often need to be reintroduced to
concepts to solidify what they have learned.
Many concepts are learned and forgotten while
learning other new concepts. This is because
students learn but are not necessarily ready to
acquire language concepts.

Therefore, it becomes very important to review
and to show students how to review on their
own. It is also important to recycle the new
concepts in different contexts.

Instructor's Notes

B Look at the housing ads on page 56. Complete the sentences by circling the correct verb and using the comparative or superlative form of the word in parentheses. (Lesson 2)

1. Home #3 (is /(has)) _____more space_____ than Home #2. (space)
2. Home #2 ((is)/ has) ____the most expensive____. (expensive)
3. Home #2 (is /(has)) ____has more amenities____ than Home #1. (amenities)
4. Home #1 ((is)/ has) _____is bigger_____ than Home #2. (big)
5. Home #3 ((is)/ has) ____is the largest____. (large)
6. Home #1 (is /(has)) ____has more bathrooms____ than Home #3. (bathrooms)
7. Home #2 (is /(has)) ____the most security____. (security)
8. Home #3 ((is)/ has) ____is more spacious____ than Home #2. (spacious)
9. Home #2 ((is)/ has) _____is smaller_____ than Home #1. (small)
10. Home #1 (is /(has)) ____has more bedrooms____ than Home #3. (bedrooms)

C Complete the housing preferences checklist based on what you would want in a home. (Lesson 3) (Answers will vary.)

Housing Preferences Checklist				
Features	Yes	No	Features	Preference
air-conditioning	❏	❏	type of property	
backyard	❏	❏	number of bathrooms	
garage	❏	❏	number of bedrooms	
heating	❏	❏	location	
pool	❏	❏	price range	

D Write four *yes/no* questions you could ask someone about his or her housing preferences. (Lesson 3) (Answers will vary.)

1. _____
2. _____
3. _____
4. _____

Review

E Write four information questions you could ask someone about his or her housing preferences. (Lesson 3) (Answers will vary.)

1. _____

2. _____

3. _____

4. _____

F Now ask a partner the questions you wrote in Exercises D and E and complete the checklist below based on his or her answers. (Lesson 3) (Answers will vary.)

Housing Preferences Checklist				
Features	**Yes**	**No**	**Features**	**Preference**
air-conditioning	❏	❏	type of property	
backyard	❏	❏	number of bathrooms	
garage	❏	❏	number of bedrooms	
heating	❏	❏	location	
pool	❏	❏	price range	

G Put the steps to buying a home in the correct order (1–10). (Lesson 4)

_4_ Start looking at ads in the newspaper and looking in neighborhoods you'd like to live in.

_8_ Negotiate with the seller until you come to an agreement.

_10_ Move in.

_6_ Make an offer on a home.

_9_ Get the title to the house transferred into your name.

_7_ Get a home inspection.

_5_ Find the home you want to buy.

_2_ Figure out how much money you can spend.

_1_ Decide on your housing preferences.

_3_ Apply for a loan.

H Take turns describing the process of getting a mortgage with a partner. Then, discuss the three different types of mortgages. (Lesson 5)

Practice 1 *(continued)*   25–30 mins. ■■■

E Write four information questions you could ask someone about his or her housing preferences. (Lesson 3)

F Now ask a partner the questions you wrote in Exercises D and E and complete the checklist below based on his or her answers. (Lesson 3)

G Put the steps to buying a home in the correct order (1–10). (Lesson 4)

H Take turns describing the process of getting a mortgage with a partner. Then, discuss the three different types of mortgages. (Lesson 5)

Evaluation 1   45-60 mins. ■■■

Go around the classroom and check on students' progress. Help individuals when needed. If you see consistent errors among several students, interrupt the class and give a mini-lesson or review to help students feel comfortable with the concept.

Instructor's Notes

Presentation 2   5-10 mins.

My Dictionary

Ask students to brainstorm new vocabulary they have learned in this unit. Have them do this without looking in their books.

Practice 2   15-20 mins.

(Shorter classes can do these exercises for homework.)

Making lists of words that are related to each other can help you recall them when you need them. For example, in this unit you learned new words related to buying a home. Complete the lists below with related words from this unit.

Add these lists to the back of the dictionary that you started in Unit 2. (Save some pages in the back for more vocabulary lists.) Add the words that are new to you to your dictionary with definitions and examples.

Evaluation 2   5-10 mins.

Walk around the classroom and help students as needed. Ask volunteers to write their word lists on the board.

Presentation 3   5-10 mins.

Learner Log

In this unit, you learned many things about buying a home. How comfortable do you feel doing each of the skills listed below? Rate your comfort level on a scale of 1 to 4.

Teaching Tip

Learner Logs

Learner Logs function to help students in many different ways.

1. They serve as part of the review process.
2. They help students to gain confidence and document what they have learned. Consequently, students see that they are making progress and want to move forward in learning.
3. They provide students with a tool that they can use over and over to check and recheck their understanding. In this way, students become independent learners.

Practice 3   5-10 mins. ▪

Have students complete the Learner Log.

Evaluation 3   5-10 mins. ▪

Walk around the classroom and help students as needed.

Application   5-10 mins.

Go over the reflection statements with students and have them complete the answers by themselves.

TB ### Assessment *(optional)*   ▪▪▪

Use the Stand Out 4 Assessment CD-ROM with Exam*View®* to create a post-test for Unit 3.

Instructor's Notes

_____

_____

_____

_____

_____

_____

_____

_____

_____

_____

_____

_____

_____

_____

_____

_____

_____

_____

My Dictionary

Making lists of words that are related to each other can help you recall them when you need them. For example, in this unit you learned new words related to buying a home. Complete the lists below with related words from this unit.

(Answers will vary. Possible answers are given.)

Housing Ads	Buying a Home	Mortgages
cozy	home inspection	fixed-rate
secluded	lender	credit check
amenities	contract	interest rate

Add these lists to the back of the dictionary that you started in Unit 2. (Save some pages in the back for more vocabulary lists.) Add the words that are new to you to your dictionary with definitions and examples.

Learner Log

In this unit, you learned many things about buying a home. How comfortable do you feel doing each of the skills listed below? Rate your comfort level on a scale of 1 to 4. *(Answers will vary.)*

1 = Need more practice   **2** = OK   **3** = Good   **4** = Great!

Life Skill	Comfort Level	Page
I can interpret housing advertisements.	1 2 3 4	_____
I can use context clues to understand vocabulary.	1 2 3 4	_____
I can write an advertisement.	1 2 3 4	_____
I can compare properties.	1 2 3 4	_____
I can complete a housing preferences checklist.	1 2 3 4	_____
I can explain the steps to buying a home.	1 2 3 4	_____
I can interpret mortgage information.	1 2 3 4	_____

If you circled 1 or 2 of the skills, write down the page number where you can review these skills.

Reflection

1. I learned _____.

2. I would like to find out more about _____.

Team Project

Create a real estate brochure and decide on a property to buy.

Form a team with four or five students. Choose positions for each member of your team.

HOMES FOR SALE

Let's Negotiate! Asking price just $225,000
Single-family 4-bedroom, 3-bath, 1500 sq. ft., home with an added family room. Near jobs, bus, and schools. You must see this home and area. Amenities: pool, fireplace, central a/c, master suite and big yard!

Cozy, two-bedroom, two-bath, single-family home. Located in select neighborhood, far from city life.

You won't believe this price for a house in this area. Working fireplace, big yard, excellent seasonal views. Must sell. Come see and make an offer now! $120,000

You'd think this 1,000-square foot condo was brand new! Located in the heart of Los Angeles, near all the nightlife you can imagine. Seller just added new carpet, paint, new faucets and sinks, and beautiful ceramic tile flooring. Two master suites, laundry room, underground parking, balcony with spectacular views. This condo will not last long on the market, so hurry! $200,000

POSITION	JOB DESCRIPTION	STUDENT NAME
Student 1: **Team Leader**	See that everyone speaks English and partcipates.	
Student 2: **Writer**	Write advertisements. Write list of preferences and questions.	
Student 3: **Designer**	Design a brochure.	
Students 4/5: **Realtors**	Represent the real estate agency.	

Part 1: With an advertising team, you will create a real estate brochure.

1. Create an imaginary real estate agency. What is the name of your agency?
2. Come up with three houses that your agency is trying to sell. Make a brochure for these properties, including pictures and brief advertisements. Display your brochure in the classroom.

Part 2: As a family, you will choose which properties you are interested in, meet with a realtor and decide which property to purchase.

1. As a family, decide what your housing preferences are and make a list.
2. From the brochures posted around the room, choose two properties that you are interested in, each one from a different agency.
3. Prepare a list of questions that you'd like to ask about each property.
4. In teams of two or three, set up appointments with the realtor and meet with them about the properties you are interested in purchasing.
5. Report back to your group and make a decision about which property you'd like to make an offer on.
6. Make an offer on the property.

Create a real estate brochure and decide on a property to buy.

Each team will create a real estate brochure. Then each team will become a family and decide on their housing preferences. They will look at all of the brochures and find two properties they are interested in. After interviewing realtors, each family will make an offer on a home.

The team project is the final application for the unit. It gives students a chance to show that they have mastered all of the Unit 3 objectives.

Note: Shorter classes can extend this project over two class meetings.

Stage 1   5 mins.

Form a team with four or five students. Choose positions for each member of your team.

Have students decide who will lead each step as described on the student page. Show students how in this project they will take on two different roles in the course of this project. Provide well-defined directions on the board for how teams should proceed. Explain that all the students do every step as a team. Teams shouldn't go to the next stage until the previous one is complete.

Stage 2   5 mins.

Create an imaginary real estate agency. What is the name of your agency?

When teams have come up with their agencies' names, ask for a representative of each team to report the name to the class.

Stage 3   20-30 mins.

Come up with three houses that your agency is trying to sell. Make a brochure for these

properties, including pictures and brief advertisements. Display your brochure in the classroom.

Optional Computer Activity: Design the brochure on the computer.

Stage 4   10-15 mins.

As a family, decide what your housing preferences are and make a list.

Remind students that they are now a family and have to decide what they are looking for in a home. Some of the things they should consider include size, price, and location.

Stage 5   5-10 mins.

From the brochures posted around the room, choose two properties that you are interested in, each one from a different agency.

Stage 6   10-15 mins.

Prepare a list of questions that you'd like to ask about each property.

Stage 7   15-20 mins.

In teams of two or three, set up appointments with the realtor and meet with them about the properties you are interested in purchasing.

Stage 8   5 mins.

Report back to your group and make a decision about which property you'd like to make an offer on.

Stage 9   10-15 mins.

Make an offer on the property.

Ask each team to write their family name and offer on a post-it note, and to put their notes on the home that they want to purchase. Ask each realtor if they will accept any of the offers. Sometimes, two teams will want the same house, and you can let them negotiate.

STANDARDS CORRELATIONS

CASAS: 4.8.1, 4.8.5, 4.8.6. (See CASAS Competency List on pages 169-175.)
SCANS: **Resources** Allocate Time
Information Acquire and evaluate information, organize and maintain information, interpret and communicate information, use computers to process information
Systems Understand systems, improve and design systems
Technology (optional) Select technology, apply technology to exercise
Basic Skills Reading, writing, listening, speaking
Thinking Skills Creative thinking, decision making, problem solving, seeing things in the mind's eye, reasoning

Personal Qualities Responsibility, self-esteem, self-management, integrity/honesty
EFF: **Communication** Read with understanding, convey ideas in writing, speak so others can understand, listen actively, observe critically
Decision Making Solve problems and make decisions, plan
Interpersonal Guide others, resolve conflict and negotiate, advocate and influence, cooperate with others
Lifelong Learning Take responsibility for learning, reflect and evaluate, learn through research, use information and communications technology (optional)

Objective: Locate community resources
Grammar: Embedded questions
Vocabulary: *locate, resources, sign-up*

RESOURCES

Activity Bank: Unit 4, Lesson 1, Worksheets 1–2
Reading and Writing Challenge: Unit 4

Grammar Challenge 4: Unit 4, Challenge 1

 1.5 hour classes   ■ 2.5 hour classes   ■ 3· hour classes

AGENDA

Ask for information.
Use embedded questions.
Write questions.

 Preassessment *(optional)* ■■■
Use the Stand Out 4 Assessment CD-ROM with Exam*View*® to create a pretest for Unit 4.

Warm-up and Review   5 mins. ■■■
Write the word *community* on the board. Ask students what the word means to them.

Introduction   5 mins. ■■■
Tell students that *Community* is the title of this unit. Ask them what they think they will be learning about. State the objective: *Today we will be learning how to locate resources in your community by asking for information.*

Presentation 1   10-15 mins. ■■■

 Consuela Sanchez is at the Loronado Welcome Center. She needs some help. Read the conversation.

Modeling

Before students do any dialog or conversation practice, it is a good idea to model it in a few different ways until they understand what to do.

1. Read the example conversation.
2. Have the class repeat each line of the conversation after you.
3. Divide the class in half. Have one half be one person and the other half be the other person in the dialog.
4. Ask for a volunteer to practice with you.
5. Ask for two volunteers to demonstrate the conversation for the class.

Practice 1   10-15 mins. ■■■

 With a partner, practice the conversation in Exercise A, but change the underlined information. Use the expressions below and the information you know about your community.

Evaluation 1   5 mins. ■■■
Ask volunteers to present conversations to the class.

UNIT 4

Community

GOALS
➤ Locate community resources
➤ Use the telephone
➤ Give suggestions

➤ Interpret a road map
➤ Identify ways to volunteer
   in the community

LESSON 1

Your community

GOAL ➤ Locate community resources

> Where is Consuela?
> What information can she find here?

(A) Consuela Sanchez is at the Loronado Welcome Center. She needs some help. Read the conversation.

Consuela: Hi. We just moved to <u>Loronado</u> and I'm looking for a place to <u>get a job</u>. Can you help me?
Receptionist: Of course. Why don't you try the <u>Employment Development Department</u>? It's located on <u>Orange Avenue</u>.
Consuela: Great! Thanks.

(B) With a partner, practice the conversation in Exercise A, but change the <u>underlined</u> information. Use the expressions below and information you know about your community.

1. take some English classes
2. get a bus schedule
3. use a computer
4. volunteer
5. check out some books

6. get medical help
7. register my little boy for school
8. go swimming
9. look at some art
10. sign up for baseball

GOAL ➤ **Locate community resources**

Do you know if there is a library near here?
Can you show me where Orange Avenue is?
Can you tell me when the post office opens?

C In each question in the box above, there are actually two questions. Can you find them? Write them below.

EXAMPLE: Do you know if there is a library near here?

1st question: **Do you know?**

2nd question: **Is there a library near here?**

1. Can you show me where Orange Avenue is?

1st question: Can you show me?

2nd question: Where is Orange Avenue?

2. Can you tell me when the post office opens?

1st question: Can you tell me?

2nd question: When does the post office open?

D When two questions are combined into one, it is called an *embedded question*. One question is embedded in the other. Study the chart.

Embedded Questions		
Introductory question	**Embedded question**	**Rules**
Can you show me	where *Orange Avenue is?*	In an embedded information question, the subject comes before the verb.
Do you know	if there is a library near here?	For *yes/no* questions, use *if* before the embedded question.
Can you tell me	when the library opens?	For questions with *do* or *does*, take out *do/does* and use the base form of the verb.
Why do we use embedded questions? They sound more polite than direct questions.		

Presentation 2   5-10 mins.

Ask students the following embedded questions: *Do you know if there's a library near here? Can you tell me when the post office opens?*

Practice 2   5-10 mins.

(Shorter classes can do Exercise C for homework.)

 In each question in the box above, there are actually two questions. Can you find them? Write them below.

Go over the example with students. Have them complete the exercise alone and then go over the answers as a class. As a follow-up, ask students to come up with three examples on their own, similar to the models in Exercise C.

Evaluation 2   5-10 mins.

Give students a few minutes to complete the exercise and then ask volunteers to write the embedded questions they came up with on the board. Ask the class to find the two questions in each embedded question just as they did in Exercise C.

Presentation 3   5-10 mins.

 When two questions are combined into one, it is called an *embedded question*. One question is embedded in the other. Study the chart.

Activity Bank 🔵

Lesson 1, Worksheet 1: Embedded Questions
Lesson 1, Worksheet 2: Read for Information

Instructor's Notes

Practice 3 — 15-20 mins.

(Shorter classes can do Exercise E for homework.)

E Change these questions to embedded questions using the expressions from the box.

Go over the example with students and then have them complete the exercise on their own.

 Refer students to *Stand Out 4 Grammar Challenge*, Unit 4, Challenge 1 for more practice with embedded *wh-* questions.

Evaluation 3 — 5-10 mins.

Ask volunteers to write their embedded questions from Exercise E on the board.

Teaching Tip

Evaluating by having students write on the board

A very useful way to evaluate student work is to ask for volunteers to write the answers on the board.

1. Ask volunteers to write a completed exercise item on the board.
2. Ask the class to check the volunteers' work. If students think an item contains an error, have them come up to the board and make the necessary corrections.
3. Go through each example and indicate whether it is right or wrong. (You may wish to circle or underline the mistake or just indicate that something in the entire phrase is wrong.)
4. Repeat this procedure until all of the sentences are correct.

Application — 10-20 mins.

F On a piece of paper, write five embedded questions that you could ask a school counselor.

Ask students what a school counselor does in a school, and have a quick discussion on the topic. Go over the example on the board, and then ask students to write their own questions. Make sure students write embedded questions. When they have finished, have them share their questions with a group. If you have time, ask students to write their questions on the board.

Instructor's Notes

_____

_____

_____

_____

_____

_____

_____

_____

_____

_____

_____

_____

_____

_____

_____

_____

_____

_____

_____

_____

_____

LESSON 1

GOAL ➤ **Locate community resources**

Common Expressions Used to Introduce Embedded Questions	
Would you tell me . . . ?	Will you show me . . . ?
Can you explain . . . ?	Do you know . . . ?

 E Change these questions to embedded questions using the expressions from the box.

EXAMPLE: What is the name of the local adult school?

Do you know what the name of the local adult school is?

(Answers may vary. Possible answers below.)

1. What is the address of the public pool?

   Would you tell me the address of the public school?

2. Where is Loronado?

   Will you show me where Loronado is?

3. Do you sell running shoes?

   Would you tell me if you sell running shoes?

4. What time does the library close?

   Do you know what time the library closes?

5. Is Orange Adult School on this street?

   Do you know if Orange Adult school is on this street?

6. When do classes begin?

   Would you tell me when classes begin?

7. Where do you take your cans and papers for recycling?

   Can you explain where you take your cans and papers for recycling?

8. Is your restaurant open on Sunday evenings?

   Would you tell me if your restaurant is open on Sunday evenings?

 F On a piece of paper, write five embedded questions that you could ask a school counselor.

EXAMPLE: Can you explain how to get a high school diploma?
(Answers will vary.)

Can you tell me . . . ?

GOAL ➤ Use the telephone

A What phone number would you call if you wanted information about the following items? Look at the directory below and write the correct number on the line.

1. getting a driver's license	555-0013
2. a bus schedule	555-2678
3. a place to borrow books	555-0507
4. medical help	555-8473/7623
5. school registration for your teenage son	555-1238
6. swim lessons	555-4499
7. looking at some art	555-2939
8. a place for your daughter to skate after school	555-6482
9. contesting your parking ticket	555-1796
10. activities for your grandparents	555-7342

Community Resources

Balboa Park Museum
555-2939   71852 Orange Ave

Bus Transit
555-2678   35984 First Street

Chamber of Commerce
555-4671   72064 Orange Ave

City Clerk
555-8403   63246 Fifth Street #1

Department of Motor Vehicles
555-0013   54679 Fourth Street

Employment Development Department
555-5334   94678 Orange Avenue

Health Clinic
555-8473   26489 First Street

High School
555-1238   34658 Loro Road

Hospital
555-7623   79346 Orange Ave

Little League Baseball
555-7300   66554 Third Street

Orange Adult School
555-9134   46589 Fourth Street

Public Library
555-0507   34661 Loro Road

Public Pool
555-4499   56321 Third Street

Senior Center
555-7342   97685 Sixth Street

Skate Park
555-6482   35211 Fourth Street

Superior Court
555-1796   96345 Orange Avenue

Village Elementary School
555-8462   34660 Loro Road

AT-A-GLANCE PREP

Objective: Use the telephone
Pronunciation: Annunciation and intonation
Academic Strategy: Focused listening
Vocabulary: *registration, contesting a ticket, annunciation, reservations, dress code*

AGENDA

Use a phone directory.
Listen to phone conversations for information.
Plan for a phone conversation.
Practice using the telephone.

RESOURCES

Activity Bank: Unit 4, Lesson 2, Worksheet 1
Reading and Writing Challenge: Unit 4

Grammar Challenge 4: Unit 4, Challenge 2
Audio: CD 1, Tracks 17–18

■ 1.5 hour classes   ■ 2.5 hour classes   ■ 3· hour classes

Warm-up and Review   5-10 mins.

Have students take out the questions they wrote for a school counselor in the previous lesson. Have them work in small groups to come up with answers they think the counselor might give.

Introduction   5-10 mins.

Ask students what they use the telephone for. Most likely, they will say that they use the phone to call friends and family. If they don't bring it up, ask students if they use the phone to call local businesses to ask questions. Once you lead them to this idea, ask them what they might call local businesses for, such as hours of operation and address. State the objective: *Today we will practice conversations using the telephone.*

Presentation 1   10-15 mins.

Ask students to come up with specific names of businesses in their community that they have called and asked for information. Ask students to share their experiences. For many students, using the telephone to speak to someone in English is very difficult.

Ask students how they would get the phone number of a place they wanted to call. They might suggest referring to a phone book, using the Internet, or calling 411.

Practice 1   10-15 mins.

(A) What phone number would you call if you wanted information about the following items? Look at the directory below and write the correct number on the line.

Evaluation 1   5 mins.

Go over the answers as a class.

STANDARDS CORRELATIONS

CASAS: 0.1.2, 0.1.4, 2.1.1, 2.1.8 (See CASAS Competency List on pages 169–175.)
SCANS: Information Acquire and evaluate information, interpret and communicate information
Interpersonal Participate as a member of a team, teach others, work with cultural diversity
Systems Monitor and correct performance

Basic Skills Reading, writing, listening, speaking
Thinking Skills Creative thinking, decision making, problem solving
Personal Qualities Responsibility, sociability, self-management
EFF: **Communication** Read with understanding, convey ideas in writing, speak so others can understand, listen actively, observe critically
Interpersonal Cooperate with others

Presentation 2   1 min.

Prepare students for the listening exercise by looking at the example in Exercise B.

Practice 2   10–15 mins.

B Listen to the phone conversations. Who did each person call? What information did he or she want?

 Listening Script   CD 1, Track 17

1.
Clerk: *Bay Books, how can I help you?*
Caller: *Um, yes, I was wondering what your store hours are?*
Clerk: *We're open Monday to Friday from 10 to 9 and Saturday and Sunday from 11 to 2.*
Caller: *Great! I think I'll stop by this afternoon.*
Clerk: *Is there anything in particular you're looking for?*
Caller: *Nope. Just want to do some browsing.*
Clerk: *OK! We look forward to seeing you.*
Caller: *Thanks. Goodbye.*
Clerk: *Bye.*

2.
Clerk 1: *Department of Motor Vehicles, this is Clarissa. How may I be of service?*
Caller: *I'd like to make an appointment to take a driving test.*
Clerk 1: *Let me transfer you to our appointment desk.*
Clerk 2: *Appointment desk, how can I help you?*
Caller: *Yes, I'd like to make an appointment to take a driving test.*
Clerk 2: *The next available appointment I have is on Tuesday at 3:10 P.M.*
Caller: *That's fine.*
Clerk 2: *Your name?*
Caller: *Peter Jones.*
Clerk 2: *OK, Peter. I have you down for next Tuesday the 8th at 3:10 P.M.*
Caller: *Thanks! See you then.*

3. *Thank you for calling the Loronado Public Library. Please listen carefully to the following menu options. For our hours, press 1. For our address, press 2. For questions about our reading room, press 3. For times and dates of Children's Story Hour, press 4. For all other questions, please press 0 and you'll be connected to a librarian. Our address is 34661 Loro Road. Thank you for calling.*

4.
Clerk: *Computer Warehouse.*
Caller: *Um, yes, I was wondering if you had a certain computer in stock?*
Clerk: *Let me transfer you.*

5.
Clerk: *Hi, this is Village Elementary School. Can you please hold?*
Caller: *Sure.*
Clerk: *Thank you for holding. How may I help you?*
Caller: *Yes, my name is Veronica and we just moved to Loronado from Texas.*
Clerk: *Wow! That's a long way!*
Caller: *Yes, my husband's job transferred him here.*
Clerk: *Well, I think you'll love Loronado.*
Caller: *Well, we do so far. Anyway, my son is going to be in the third grade in the fall and I need some information on how to get him registered.*
Clerk: *Why don't you come down to the school tomorrow morning and I'll give you all the information you need.*
Caller: *That would be great. Thanks!*
Clerk: *See you tomorrow!*

Evaluation 2   5 mins.

Go over the answers as a class.

 **Activity Bank**

Lesson 2, Worksheet 1: Practice Telephone Conversations

Presentation 3   5–10 mins.

Go over the instructions to Exercises C and D. Model Exercise D with a volunteer if necessary.

Practice 3   15–20 mins.

(Shorter classes can do Exercise C for homework.)

C Sometimes it is helpful to write down what you want to say before you make a phone call. For each of the examples above, write what you might say when the person answers the phone.

D Using the questions you wrote above, practice short conversations with a partner. Change the underlined information for each item you wrote in Exercise C. Take turns being the clerk who answers the phone.

Evaluation 3   5–10 mins.

For Exercise C, ask volunteers to read their answers out loud. Observe Exercise D.

CD 1
TR 17

B Listen to the phone conversations. Who did each person call? What information did he or she want?

1. Place: <u>Bay Books</u>

   Information: <u>store hours</u>

2. Place: <u>Department of Motor Vehicles, appt desk</u>

   Information: <u>to schedule a driving test</u>

3. Place: <u>Loronado Public Library</u>

   Information: <u>library address</u>

4. Place: <u>Computer Warehouse</u>

   Information: <u>a certain computer in stock</u>

5. Place: <u>Village Elementary School</u>

   Information: <u>registration of son</u>

C Sometimes it is helpful to write down what you want to say before you make a phone call. For each of the examples above, write what you might say when the person answers the phone. (Answers may vary slightly.)

1. <u>Hi. Could you please tell me your store hours?</u>

2. <u>Hello. I'd like to schedule a driving test.</u>

3. <u>Hi. Could you please tell me the address of the library?</u>

4. <u>Hi. I would like to know if you have a certain computer in stock?</u>

5. <u>Hello. Could you please explain what I need to do to register my son?</u>

D Using the questions you wrote above, practice short conversations with a partner. Change the underlined information for each item you wrote in Exercise C. Take turns being the clerk who answers the phone.

EXAMPLE: *Clerk:* Thank you for calling <u>*Bay Books.*</u> How can I help you?

   You: <u>*Hi. Could you please tell me your store hours?*</u>

 E   **Read and listen to the conversation.**

CD 1
TR 18

Host: Thank you for calling Scott's Steakhouse. How can I help you?
Caller: Yes, I was wondering if you are open for lunch.
Host: Yes, we are open for lunch from 11 A.M. to 3 P.M., Monday through Friday.
Caller: Do I need reservations?
Host: Reservations are not necessary, but we recommend them during the busy lunch hours.
Caller: Great. Thanks for your help!
Host: You're welcome. Goodbye.
Caller: Bye.

 F   **Practice the conversation in Exercise E with a partner.**

Pronunciation

Annunciation and Intonation

➤ When you are talking on the telephone, it is important that you pronounce every word very clearly (annunciate) and speak with rising and falling intonation. This is important because the person on the other end of the line can't see your mouth or your facial expressions. Try to remember this tip as you do the exercises below.

 G   **Walk around the classroom and talk to four different classmates. Using the information below, have conversations like the one in Exercise E.**

Calling	Information Needed	Response
Paris French Bistro	if reservations are needed and if there is a dress code	yes yes—coat and tie for men; no jeans for women
Loronado High School	location of the school's talent show	Coast Community Church at 11341 Fifth Street
Community Center	days and times of concerts in the park	every Sunday from 1–4 P.M.
Loronado Public Library	age required to get a library card	age five with parent's signature

Application   10–20 mins. ■■□

 E Read and listen to the conversation.

 Listening Script   CD 1, Track 18

Host: *Thank you for calling Scott's Steakhouse. How can I help you?*
Caller: *Yes, I was wondering if you are open for lunch.*
Host: *Yes, we are open for lunch from 11 A.M. to 3 P.M., Monday through Friday.*
Caller: *Do I need reservations?*
Host: *Reservations are not necessary, but we recommend them during the busy lunch hours.*
Caller: *Great. Thanks for your help!*
Host: *You're welcome. Goodbye.*
Caller: *Bye.*

Pronunciation

Annunciation and intonation

At this level, many students are pronouncing their words correctly but still have trouble being understood. Therefore, on a daily basis, it's important to work on annunciation (speaking clearly) and intonation (the rising and falling of the voice in different sentence patterns). Some ways to practice these aspects of language production include the following ideas:

1. Read a sentence out loud and have students repeat after you.
2. Ask for individual students to read a sentence out loud and ask the class to repeat what they have said.
3. Work individually with students, critiquing their annunciation and intonation.

In this lesson, it is especially important to focus on these two concepts because when students are using the phone, the other person will not be able to read their lips or see their facial expressions and body language.

F Practice the conversation in Exercise E with a partner.

G Walk around the classroom and talk to four different classmates. Using the information below, have conversations like the one in Exercise E.

Tell students to talk to a different person for each conversation. Ask them to switch roles so they each get a chance to play the caller and the person receiving the call.

Refer students to *Stand Out 4 Grammar Challenge*, Unit 4, Challenge 2 for practice with embedded *yes/no* questions.

Instructor's Notes

_____
_____
_____
_____
_____
_____
_____
_____
_____
_____
_____
_____
_____
_____
_____
_____
_____
_____
_____
_____
_____
_____
_____
_____

Objective: Give suggestions
Grammar: Making suggestions
Academic Strategy: Focused listening
Vocabulary: *bulletin board, suggestion, local hangout, notices, flyers, marathon, bingo*

RESOURCES

Activity Bank: Unit 4, Lesson 3, Worksheet 1
Reading and Writing Challenge: Unit 4

Grammar Challenge 4: Unit 4, Challenge 3
Audio: CD 1, Track 19

■ 1.5 hour classes ■ 2.5 hour classes ■ 3⁺ hour classes

AGENDA
Make and respond to suggestions.
Read a bulletin board.
Make a bulletin board.

Warm-up and Review   10–15 mins.

Write the following items on the board:

> *Garden Center: store hours*
> *Post Office: address*
> *Community Center: swimming classes*

Have students find a partner and create telephone conversations they might have using this information. Ask volunteers to present their conversations for the class.

Introduction   5–10 mins.

Write *bulletin board* on the board. Ask students what this term refers to and then elicit what sort of information they might find on a bulletin board. Ask students where they have seen bulletin boards in their community.

State the objective: *Today we will practice giving suggestions.*

Presentation 1   5–10 mins.

(A) Consuela and her husband, Ricardo, are talking to their next-door neighbors. Read their conversation.

Ask students what suggestions Jim and Marie make. Go over the phrases used to make and respond to suggestions giving students examples of each one.

Practice 1   10–15 mins.

(B) With a partner, make new conversations. Use the topics below and the suggestions from the chart. Talk about places in your community.

Do the first item with a volunteer as an example.

Evaluation 1   5 mins.

Ask volunteers to present their conversations.

STANDARDS CORRELATIONS

CASAS: 2.5.4, 2.5.5 (See CASAS Competency List on pages 169–175.)
SCANS: **Resources** Allocate time, allocate human resources
Information Acquire and evaluate information, organize and maintain information, interpret and communicate information, use computers to process information (optional)
Interpersonal Participate as a member of a team, teach others, exercise leadership, negotiate to arrive at a decision, work with cultural diversity
Systems Understand systems, monitor and correct performance, improve and design systems
Technology Select technology, apply technology to a task, maintain and troubleshoot technology (optional)

Basic Skills Reading, listening, speaking
Thinking Skills Creative thinking, decision making, problem solving
Personal Qualities Responsibility, sociability, self-management
EFF: **Communication** Read with understanding, convey ideas in writing, speak so others can understand, listen actively, observe critically
Decision Making Solve problems and make decisions, plan
Interpersonal Guide others, resolve conflict and negotiate, advocate and influence, cooperate with others
Lifelong Learning Learn through research, use information and communications technology (optional)

LESSON 3

Why don't we . . . ?

GOAL ➤ Give suggestions

Where are Consuela and her husband?
Who are they talking to?

A Consuela and her husband, Ricardo, are talking to their next-door neighbors. Read their conversation.

Ricardo: Let's find a good Italian restaurant. Can you think of where we could go?
Jim: Why don't we try this great little place called Island Pasta? It's a local hangout and I've heard the food is great!
Marie: I think they're closed tonight. How about going to Laredo's for a Mexican meal instead?
Consuela: Great idea!

Making Suggestions	Responding to Suggestions
Why don't we . . . ? We could . . . How about . . . ? Do you want to . . . ? Let's . . .	Great idea! Yes, let's do that! Sure! How about . . . instead.

B With a partner, make new conversations. Use the topics below and the suggestions from the chart. Talk about places in your community.

1. a good shoe store
2. a good movie for kids
3. a nice restaurant for your best friend's birthday dinner
4. a bookstore with a large selection of books
5. a good place to find really fresh fruit and vegetables
6. a place to eat Mexican food
7. a place to listen to good music
8. a bookstore to buy the required book for class

LESSON **3**   **GOAL** ➤ Give suggestions

C Read the notices on the community bulletin board. Which notice is the most interesting to you? Why?

COMMUNITY BULLETIN BOARD

3

Summer Day Camp!
Ages 3-6, 7-10, 11-14
Morning session 9-12pm,
Afternoon Session 1-4pm
June 25-August 24
$60 a week per child.
Discounts available for more than one child.
Discounts available for morning and afternoon session.
See Activities Director to sign up.
Or call (777) 555-6211

9

Lost Black Cat
Answers to the name
Blackie
Reward!
If found, please call:
(619) 555-9617

4

Have you ever wanted to
run a marathon?
Now's your chance!
Run with a group of people just like yourself, get advice from a group leader on fitness, health, and nutrition, and **HAVE FUN!**
Call **(858) 555-9768**
for more info.

1

Intro to
T'ai Chi Chih
Discover a wonderful form of exercise and meditation that is centuries old. Involve your mind, body, and spirit. All ages welcome.
Begins September 4th
Instructor: Mary Walker
Class Site: Room 209
Day: Thursday
Time: 6pm
Cost: $49/8 weeks

2

Guitar Lessons
All levels
Must have a guitar
Music will be provided
Call to set up lessons
$20 a half hour
(858)719-8697
(858)719-8697
(858)719-8697
(858)719-8697
(858)719-8697

CD 1
TR 19

D Listen to the community members. Where can they find the information they need? Write the correct number next to each notice.

(Answers set in bulletin above.)

Presentation 2   5-10 mins. ■■□

 Read the notices on the community bulletin board. Which notice is the most interesting to you? Why?

Give students a chance to read the bulletin board on their own and then ask them basic comprehension questions about the notices and flyers.

Prepare students for the listening activity by telling them they will be listening to different community members make statements about activities and information that can be found on the bulletin board. They will have to write the correct number in the circle next to each bulletin board item.

Practice 2   5-10 mins. ■■□

 Listen to the community members. Where can they find the information they need? Write the correct number next to each notice.

 Listening Script   *CD 1, Track 19*

1. *I want to do individual exercises that will help me relax.*
2. *I've always wanted to learn how to play an instrument.*
3. *I need a place to send my kids for the summer while I'm at work.*
4. *Wouldn't it be fun to play on a team with other people?*
5. *There's gotta be something my grandmother can do Sunday nights to keep herself busy.*
6. *I need to find a place to live.*
7. *Is there a gym around here where I can play basketball?*
8. *I've always wanted to learn some crafts.*
9. *I found a lost cat in my neighborhood.*

Evaluation 2   5 mins. ■■□

Go over the answers to Exercise D.

Presentation 3   5–10 mins. ▪▪▪

Demonstrate how to do Exercise E with a volunteer by making a statement about something on the bulletin board and asking the volunteer to give you a suggestion. Then have two students demonstrate the activity.

Practice 3   15–20 mins. ▪

(E) Work in pairs. Student A: Make a statement about one of the notices on the community bulletin board. Student B: Respond with a suggestion.

Refer students to *Stand Out 4 Grammar Challenge*, Unit 4, Challenge 3 for more practice with making suggestions.

Evaluation 3   5–10 mins. ▪

Walk around and observe students acting out the activity.

Application   10–20 mins. ▪▪▪

(F) Make a community bulletin board in your classroom. Think of things you could offer and make flyers.

Encourage students to offer their own talents (musical, athletic, etc.) or items they want to sell.

Have students work in teams to create flyers. Make sure each team has a leader, a writer, and a designer.

Once students have completed their bulletin boards, post them around the classroom. In pairs, have students go around and make suggestions for things to do in the community.

Activity Bank

Lesson 3, Worksheet 1: Making Suggestions

Instructor's Notes

COMMUNITY BULLETIN BOARD

8 **Arts and Crafts**

Ever wanted to
learn how to knit?
Do needlepoint?
Make gifts for friends?
Help your children with art projects?
Come join our craft group on Saturday mornings. There is a $5 material fee each day you attend.
Come this Saturday!
For more information, call Rick (858) 555-8693

4 **Summer Volleyball League**

Got a group of people who want to play volleyball?
Want to join a team that needs another player?
Sign up for our summer volleyball league!
All league games are on Tuesday nights.
For more information, call (777)555-7809

5 **B22**

Did you hear your number?
Bingo Sunday nights starting 4pm.
Call Charlene for more info
(619) 438-9728

7 **Basketball-Open Gym**

The new downtown
Recreation Center
is where the action is!
Come on down Mondays and Wednesdays afternoon from 5-7pm and join a game.
Recreation Center
4350 Third Street, (777)555-6211

Roommate wanted **6**

Female, non-smoker
1 bed, 1 bath, kitchen, garage
$400 + sec. deposit.
Call Laura (619) 555-9475.

(619) 555-9475
(619) 555-9475
(619) 555-9475
(619) 555-9475
(619) 555-9475

BOOK CLUB
Do you like mysteries? Fiction? Romance? Non-fiction? Suspense?
Come down to the Book Barn and join one of our book clubs! Read a book every month and meet with others who share your passion to discuss it!
Book Barn,
4212 Loro Road,
Tel. (777) 555-5630

E Work in pairs. Student A: Make a statement about one of the notices on the community bulletin board. Student B: Respond with a suggestion.

EXAMPLE: *Student A:* I need a place to send my kids for the summer while I'm at work.
                 Student B: Why don't you phone the Summer Day Camp?
                 Student A: That's a good idea.

F Make a community bulletin board in your classroom. Think of things you could offer and make flyers.

LESSON 4 **How far is it?**

GOAL ➤ Interpret a road map

A A legend helps you read the symbols on a road map. Write the correct words from the box next to the symbols.

✈ _____airport_____   🛡3 _____interstate_____

H _____hospital_____   5 _____freeway_____

A _____campground_____   8 _____exit_____

▮▮▮ _state scenic highway_   🛏 _____hotel/motel_____

5 _____state highway_____   R _____rest area_____

> airport
> hospital
> campground
> exit
> freeway
> interstate
> state highway
> state scenic highway
> hotel/motel
> rest area

B Look at the map on page 71 and answer these questions with a partner.

1. Is there a hospital in Rose? No
2. What interstate has rest areas? 315
3. Where is the nearest campground to Grandville? Mountain State Park
4. Which highways are scenic? 13 & 15
5. Is there an airport near Lake Ellie? No

C Look at the highway map scale and estimate the road distances on the map on page 71.

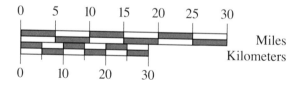

1. How far is it from Grandville to Rose? ≈ 60 miles
2. How far is it from Poppington to Lake Ellie? ≈ 120 miles
3. How far is it from Loronado to Poppington? ≈ 30 miles
4. How far is it from Lake Ellie to Rose? ≈ 90 miles
5. How far is it from Grandville to Poppington? ≈ 90 miles
6. How far is it from Rose to Loronado? ≈0 miles

AT-A-GLANCE PREP

Objective: Interpret a road map
Grammar: Imperatives
Academic Strategy: Focused listening
Vocabulary: *legend, freeway, interstate, airport, campground, exit, rest area, scenic, map scale, speed limit*

RESOURCES

Activity Bank: Unit 4, Lesson 4, Worksheet 1
Reading and Writing Challenge: Unit 4

Grammar Challenge 4: Unit 4, Challenge 4
Audio: CD 1, Track 20

■ 1.5 hour classes   ■ 2.5 hour classes   ■ 3⁺ hour classes

AGENDA
Read a map legend.
Estimate distances using a map scale.
Listen to directions.
Give and receive directions.

Warm-up and Review   5-10 mins.

Ask students to look at the bulletin boards they made in the previous lesson. Have them ask other students which notices were most interesting to them.

Introduction   5-10 mins.

Find out how many students drive. Ask how many of those who drive drive on the highway. Ask them how they know how to get where they need to go. State the objective: *Today we will read a road map and practice giving and receiving directions from one place to another.*

Presentation 1   10-15 mins.

 A *legend* helps you read the symbols on a road map. Write the correct words from the box next to the symbols.

Do this activity together as a class.

Practice 1   5-10 mins.

 Look at the map on page 71 and answer these questions with a partner.

Evaluation 1   5 mins.

Go over the answers as a class to Exercise B. Check comprehension by asking a few extra questions.

Presentation 2   5-10 mins.

Explain map scales and their purpose.

Practice 2   10-15 mins. ■■

(Shorter classes can do Exercise C for homework.)

 Look at the highway map scale and estimate the road distances on the map on page 71.

Evaluation 2   10-15 mins. ■■

Go over the answers.

STANDARDS CORRELATIONS

CASAS: 1.9.1, 1.9.3, 1.9.4 (See CASAS Competency List on pages 169–175.)
SCANS: **Information** Acquire and evaluate information, interpret and communicate information
Interpersonal Participate as a member of a team, teach others, exercise leadership, work with cultural diversity
Systems Monitor and correct performance
Basic Skills Reading, writing, arithmetic, listening, speaking
Thinking Skills Decision making, problem solving, seeing things in the mind's eye

Personal Qualities Responsibility, sociability, self-management
EFF: **Communication** Read with understanding, convey ideas in writing, speak so others can understand, listen actively, observe critically
Decision Making Solve problems and make decisions, plan
Interpersonal Guide others, cooperate with others
Lifelong Learning Reflect and evaluate, learn through research, use information and communications technology (optional)

Presentation 3 5-10 mins.

Go over the directions to Exercise D with students.

Practice 3 15-20 mins. ■

 Listen to the people giving directions. Where will the driver end up? Fill in the circle next to the correct answer.

🎧 **Listening Script**   *CD 1, Track 20*

1. *Since you'll be coming from Rose, get on 24 going west. Then take 315 South. You'll drive for a while and then get off at the first exit.*
2. *From Grandville, get on 315 South. Then take 24 East. You'll pass the airport. Get off right before 24 and 89 intersect.*
3. *If you're coming from Poppington, take 315 North. Then get on 13 West, the scenic route, and go on to 15 North. You'll pass by Lake Ellie, which might be a nice place to stop and have lunch. Then continue on 15 North till you get to 315 North. Take the first exit.*
4. *From Rose, take 89 South until you get to the first exit. Keep going until you get to the hospital.*

Evaluation 3 5-10 mins. ■

Go over the answers to Exercise D with students.

Instructor's Notes

**CD 1
TR 20**

D Listen to the people giving directions. Where will the driver end up? Fill in the circle next to the correct answer.

1. ○ Grandville   ○ Rose   ○ Lake Ellie   ● Loronado   ○ Poppington
2. ○ Grandville   ● Rose   ○ Lake Ellie   ○ Loronado   ○ Poppington
3. ● Grandville   ○ Rose   ○ Lake Ellie   ○ Loronado   ○ Poppington
4. ○ Grandville   ○ Rose   ○ Lake Ellie   ● Loronado   ○ Poppington

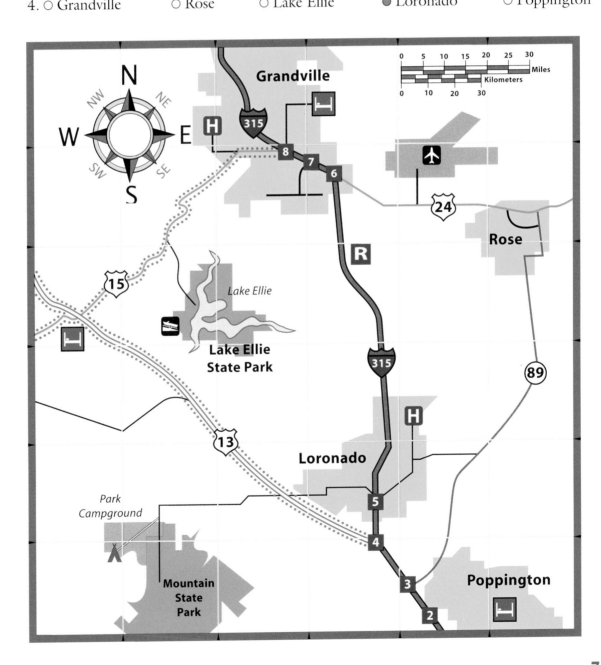

LESSON 4 **GOAL** ➤ Interpret a road map

Conversation Strategy: Repeat for Clarification

When you are getting important information from someone, such as directions, it is always a good idea to ask for clarification. Asking for clarification means repeating back what was said or asking the other person to repeat it so you can double-check what you wrote down. One way to do this is to repeat just the part of the sentence that you are unsure of.

EXAMPLES: *A:* Take the freeway exit and veer left.
 B: Veer left?
 A: Yes.

 A: Take 605 to 405 to 22.
 B: Did you say 605 to 405 to 22?
 A: Yes.

 Now practice giving and receiving directions with a partner. Student A: Look at the map on page 71 to give directions. Student B: Write down what your partner says. If you get confused, ask your partner to slow down or repeat for clarification. Then, change roles.

EXAMPLE: From Rose to Grandville
 Student A: I live in Rose and I need to get to Grandville. What's the best way to get there?
 Student B: Take 24 East to 315 North. Follow 315 North to the third exit.
 Student A: About how far is it?
 Student B: Sixty miles.
 Student A: Thank you so much.

1. Poppington to Lake Ellie
2. Loronado to Poppington
3. Lake Ellie to Rose
4. Rose to Loronado
5. Grandville to Poppington

(Answers may vary. Possible answers below.)
1. Take 315 North to exit 4. Go north on route 13 for about 80 miles, then take 15 East. In about 25 miles you'll make a right turn onto the road to Lake Ellie.
2. Take 315 South and get off at exit 2.
3. Take 15 North to Grandville. Then take 315 South until exit 6 for 24 East. Follow 24 East for about 45 miles to Rose.
4. Take 89 South until it ends at route 315. Take 315 North to exit 5 for Loronado.
5. Take 315 South to exit 2 for Poppington.

 Now look at the directions you wrote down when you were Student B. Compare them to the map. Are they correct?

Application

10-20 mins. ██ ■ ██ ▨

E Now practice giving and receiving directions with a partner. Student A: Look at the map on page 71 to give directions. Student B: Write down what your partner says. If you get confused, ask your partner to slow down or repeat for clarification. Then, change roles.

Go over the example with students and show them how to take notes by writing the directions on the board: Take 24 East to 315 North. Follow 315 North to the third exit. (60 miles) Ask a few volunteer students to help you demonstrate the conversation.

Refer students to *Stand Out 4 Grammar Challenge*, Unit 4, Challenge 4 for more practice with imperatives.

Teaching Tip

Conversation strategies

Throughout *Stand Out 4*, students will be given many opportunities to have conversations. It is always a good idea to give them one or two new strategies every time they have a conversation to help them improve their conversation skills. Encourage them to build on what they know by using the strategies you have already taught them as well as implementing a new one.

F Now look at the directions you wrote down when you were Student B. Compare them to the map. Are they correct?

Activity Bank

Lesson 4, Worksheet 1: Calling for Directions

Instructor's Notes

AT-A-GLANCE PREP

Objective: Identify ways to volunteer in the community
Academic Strategy: Making inferences
Vocabulary: *volunteer, community organizations, keep track of, structures , decorations*

AGENDA

Identify places to volunteer.
Identify your skills.
Find out about your partner's skills.
Identify specific places that you could volunteer.
Write questions.

RESOURCES

Activity Bank: Unit 4, Lesson 5, Worksheet 1
Reading and Writing Challenge: Unit 4

Grammar Challenge 4: Unit 4, Challenge 5; Extension Challenges 1-2

■ 1.5 hour classes ■ 2.5 hour classes ■ 3⁺ hour classes

Warm-up and Review   5-10 mins.

Have students review giving directions by turning to page 72 and doing Exercise E again. This time, just have them give the directions to their partners, not write them down.

Introduction   5-10 mins. ■■■

State the objective: *Today we will be identifying ways to volunteer in the community.*

Ask students the questions in Exercise A and go over the concept of volunteering. Ask students to share any volunteer experience they have had.

Ⓐ Have you ever offered to help a friend or family member do something? Have you ever done something for your neighbor? Do you belong to any local community organizations where you help out in some way? If you answered *yes* to any of these questions, you are a volunteer!

Presentation 1   10-15 mins.

As a class, come up with a list of places to volunteer. Write all the student responses on the board. Then go through each one and ask students what type of volunteer work could be done there. For example: *retirement home—read to residents, teach a class to residents, help serve meals to residents, etc.*

Practice 1   10-15 mins. ■■■

Ⓑ Look at the pictures. Where do you think these people are volunteering? Write your ideas on the line below each picture.

Have students do this activity with a partner or in small groups. Tell them there is more than one possible place for each picture.

Evaluation 1   5 mins.

Go over students' ideas as a class.

LESSON 5 Volunteering

Vocabulary   Grammar
Life Skills
Academic   Pronunciation

GOAL ➤ Identify ways to volunteer in the community

 Have you ever offered to help a friend or family member do something? Have you ever done something for your neighbor? Do you belong to any local community organizations where you help out in some way? If you answered *yes* to any of these questions, you are a volunteer!

 Look at the pictures. Where do you think these people are volunteering? Write your ideas on the line below each picture.   (Answers may vary. Possible answers below.)

1.

art gallery

2.

senior center

3.

soccer camp

4.

soup kitchen

5.

library

6.
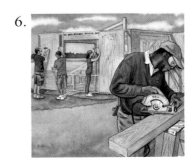
Habitat for Humanity

7.

community theater

8.

animal shelter

9.

political campaign

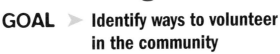

GOAL ➤ **Identify ways to volunteer in the community**

Ⓒ Before you volunteer, you need to think about what you would like to do or what you are good at. Look at the list below and check (✓) the things that you like to do and are good at. Add your own ideas to the bottom of the list.
(Answers will vary.)

Skills	I can . . .	I like to . . .	My partner can . . .	My partner likes to . . .
ask for money				
build structures				
clean				
cook				
give a speech				
keep track of money				
make decorations				
make phone calls				
organize				
plan a meeting				
plan a party				
put books in alphabetical order				
spend time with children				
talk to people				
teach someone English				
teach someone to read				
teach someone math				
use the computer				

Ⓓ Now interview a partner. Ask him or her what he or she likes to do and put check marks (✓) in the appropriate columns. Use these question beginnings: *Can you . . . ? Do you like to . . . ?*

Presentation 2   10-15 mins.

C Before you volunteer, you need to think about what you would like to do or what you are good at. Look at the list below and check (✓) the things that you like to do and are good at. Add your own ideas to the bottom of the list.

Do this exercise as a class. Go through each item on the list and make sure students understand what it entails. Have them put checks in the first two columns based on their preferences and abilities. Help them come up with some ideas of things they might write on the last three lines.

Practice 2   10-15 mins.

D Now interview your partner. Ask him or her what he or she likes to do and put check marks (✓) in the appropriate columns. Use these question beginnings: *Can you . . . ? Do you like to . . . ?*

Ask a few students questions using the question beginnings and the information from the chart in Exercise C.

Evaluation 2   10-15 mins.

Ask students to report what they learned about their partners. Ask: *(John), what does (Sara) like to do? (Emilio), what can (Flavio) do?*

Presentation 3   5-10 mins. ■■■

Ask: *Who likes to spend time with children?* Have students raise their hands if this is true for them. Ask: *Where are some places you might be able to work as a volunteer?* Make a list of places on the board.

(E) What are some places in your community you might be able to volunteer? With a group, make a list. Share your list with the class.

Practice 3   5-10 mins. ■

(F) Now look back at the checklist on page 74. Come up with two places where you and your partner might like to volunteer based on your skills and preferences.

Ask students to work with a partner, and give their partner suggestions.

Evaluation 3   5-10 mins. ■

Ask pairs to report their decisions for Exercise F to the class.

Application   10-20 mins. ■■■

(G) Now that you have two places where you can volunteer, what's the next step? With your partner, come up with four questions you might ask when you visit or call the location.

When students have finished, ask them to write some of their questions on the board. This will give other students more ideas of what else they could ask.

(H) Now practice asking your questions to a partner. Imagine that your partner works at the place where you want to volunteer. Your partner will have to be creative and come up with answers to your questions.

Encourage students to actually contact an organization and ask them to report back to the class if they do.

Activity Bank

Lesson 5, Worksheet 1: Volunteer at the Animal Shelter

 Refer students to *Stand Out 4 Grammar Challenge*, Unit 4, Challenge 5 for more practice with *can, could* and *should*.

Refer students to *Stand Out 4 Grammar Challenge*, Unit 4, Extension Challenges 1–2 for practice with embedded questions in statements and embedded questions with infinitive phrases.

Instructor's Notes

_____
_____
_____
_____
_____
_____
_____
_____
_____
_____
_____
_____
_____
_____
_____
_____
_____
_____
_____
_____

GOAL ➤ **Identify ways to volunteer in the community**

E What are some places in your community you might be able to volunteer? With a group, make a list. Share your list with the class. (Answers may vary. Possible answers below.)

Places to Volunteer
library, school, hospital, animal shelter, senior center,
homeless shelter, soup kitchen

F Now look back at the checklist on page 74. Come up with two places where you and your partner might like to volunteer based on your skills and preferences.
(Answers will vary.)

Places Where I Can Volunteer	Places Where My Partner Can Volunteer
1.	1.
2.	2.

G Now that you have two places where you can volunteer, what's the next step? With your partner, come up with four questions you might ask when you visit or call the location.
(Answers will vary. Possible answers below.)

1. Can I speak to the person in charge of volunteering?

2. Do you need volunteers?

3. What kind of skills do you need?

4. Is there a training program?

H Now practice asking your questions to a partner. Imagine that your partner works at the place where you want to volunteer. Your partner will have to be creative and come up with answers to your questions.

A In your community, where would you go to do the following things? Write one idea on each line. (Lessons 1–2) (Answers may vary. Possible answers below.)

1. get a bus schedule — transit authority

2. borrow books — library

3. get a flu vaccine — health clinic

4. take an art class — museum

5. use a computer for free — library/school

B Change the questions below to embedded questions. (Lesson 1)
(Answers may vary.)

1. What is the address of the library?

   Can you tell me the address of the library?

2. Do you sell vitamins?

   Can you tell me if you sell vitamins?

3. What time does the museum close?

   Do you know what time the museum closes?

4. Is the Adult School on this street?

   Do you know if the Adult School is on this street?

5. When do classes begin?

   Do you know when classes begin?

C Imagine you are calling the places that you wrote down in Exercise A. With a partner, practice having telephone conversations about each of the topics listed. (Lesson 2)

EXAMPLE: get a bus schedule

Receptionist: Transit Authority, can I help you?
Caller: Yes, I was wondering how I can get a bus schedule.
Receptionist: Well, you can come down to our office and pick one up or you can go online and print out a schedule of any route you want.
Caller: Really? Oh, that's a great idea. I'll use my computer to print out a schedule. Thanks!
Receptionist: You're welcome.

AT-A-GLANCE PREP

Objectives: All Unit 4 objectives
Grammar: All Unit 4 grammar
Academic Strategy: Reviewing
Vocabulary: All Unit 4 vocabulary

RESOURCES

Activity Bank: Unit 4, Lessons 1–5
Reading and Writing Challenge: Unit 4

Grammar Challenge: Unit 4, Challenges 1–5

■ 1.5 hour classes ■ 2.5 hour classes ■ 3⁺ hour classes

AGENDA

Unit objectives.
Review exercises.
My Dictionary.
Learner Log.

Warm-up and Review 5-10 mins.

In groups, have students come up with a list of places to volunteer.

Introduction 5-10 mins.

Ask students to try to recall (in general) all the goals of this unit without looking at their books. Then remind them which goals they omitted, if any. (Unit Goals: Locate community resources, use the telephone, give suggestions, interpret a road map, and identify ways to volunteer in the community.) Write all the objectives on the board from Unit 4. Show students the first page of the unit and mention the five objectives. State the objective: *Today we will be reviewing everything you have learned in this unit.*

Presentation 1 10-15 mins.

This presentation will cover the first three pages of the review. Quickly go to the first page of each lesson. Discuss the objective of each. Ask simple questions to remind students of what they have learned.

Note: Since there is little presentation in the review, you can assign the review exercises that don't involve pair work or group work for homework and go over them in class the following day.

Practice 1 20-25 mins.

Note: There are two ways to do the review: (1) Go through the exercises one at a time and, as students complete each one, go over the answers. (2) Briefly go through the instructions of each exercise, allow students to complete all of the exercises at once, and then go over the answers.

Stop and evaluate whenever it is appropriate for the class. (*See Evaluation 1 on pg. 78a.*)

A In your community, where would you go to do the following things? Write one idea on each line. (Lessons 1-2)

B Change the questions below to embedded questions. (Lesson 1)

C Imagine you are calling the places that you wrote down in Exercise A. With a partner, practice having telephone conversations about each of the topics listed. (Lesson 2)

STANDARDS CORRELATIONS

CASAS: 7.2.1 (See CASAS Competency List on pages 169–175.)
SCANS: **Resources** Allocate time
Information Acquire and evaluate information
Interpersonal Participate as a member of a team, teach others, negotiate to arrive at a decision, work with cultural diversity
Systems Monitor and correct performance
Basic Skills Reading, writing, arithmetic, listening, speaking
Thinking Skills Creative thinking, decision making, problem solving, seeing things in the mind's eye

Personal Qualities Responsibility, sociability, self-management
EFF: **Communication** Convey ideas in writing, speak so others can understand, listen actively
Decision Making Solve problems and make decisions
Interpersonal Guide others, cooperate with others
Lifelong Learning Take responsibility for learning, reflect and evaluate, learn through research

Practice 1 *(continued)*   25–30 mins.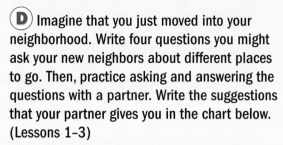

D Imagine that you just moved into your neighborhood. Write four questions you might ask your new neighbors about different places to go. Then, practice asking and answering the questions with a partner. Write the suggestions that your partner gives you in the chart below. (Lessons 1–3)

E Now ask your partner to give you directions from the school to the four places he or she suggested. Write down the directions. Ask for clarifications to double-check them with your partner. (Lesson 4)

Teaching Tip

Recycling/Review

The review process and the project that follows are part of the recycling/review process. Students at this level often need to be reintroduced to concepts to solidify what they have learned. Many concepts are learned and forgotten while learning other new concepts. This is because students learn but are not necessarily ready to acquire language concepts.

Therefore, it becomes very important to review and to show students how to review on their own. It is also important to recycle the new concepts in different contexts.

Instructor's Notes

D Imagine that you just moved into your neighborhood. Write four questions you might ask your new neighbors about different places to go. Then, practice asking and answering the questions with a partner. Write the suggestions that your partner gives you in the chart below. **(Lessons 1–3)** (Answers will vary.)

Questions	Suggestions
1. Do you know of a good coffee shop?	1. Why don't you try the Happy Kettle on 4th street?
2.	2.
3.	3.
4.	4.
5.	5.

E Now ask your partner to give you directions from the school to the four places he or she suggested. Write down the directions. Ask for clarification to double check them with your partner. **(Lesson 4)** (Answers will vary.)

1.

2.

3.

4.

Review

 F Read the map and answer the questions. (Lesson 4)

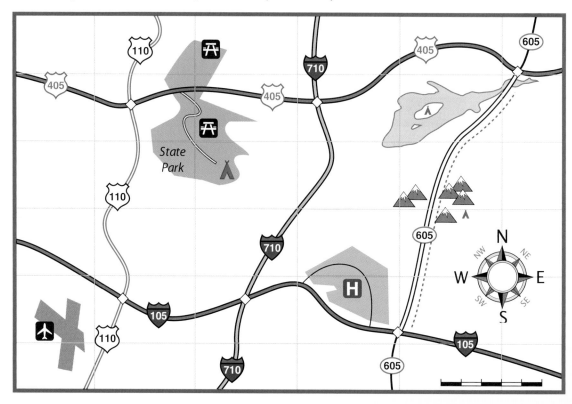

1. What highway would you take to get to the hospital? <u>Interstate 105</u>

2. What highway would you take to get to the state park? <u>State highway 405</u>

3. Which highways run north-south? <u>State highway 110, Interstate 710, Freeway 605</u>

4. How would you get from the lake to the hospital? <u>Coming from the lake, take 605</u>
   <u>South (scenic highway), then take Interstate 105 West to get to the hospital.</u>

G List three things you like to do. For each thing you like to do, write two places where you could volunteer. (Lesson 5) (Answers will vary.)

Things That I Like To Do	Places Where I Could Volunteer
1.	1. 2.
2.	1. 2.
3.	1. 2.

Practice 1 *(continued)*   25–30 mins. ■■■

F Read the map and answer the questions. (Lesson 4)

G List three things you like to do. For each thing you like to do, write two places where you could volunteer. (Lesson 5)

Evaluation 1   45–60 mins. ■■■

Go around the classroom and check on students' progress. Help individuals when needed. If you see consistent errors among several students, interrupt the class and give a mini-lesson or review to help students feel comfortable with the concept.

Presentation 2

5-10 mins.

My Dictionary

Ask students to brainstorm new vocabulary they learned in this unit. Have them do this without looking in their books.

Practice 2

15-20 mins.

(Shorter classes can do these exercises for homework.)

Brainstorm a list of new words that you learned in this unit.

Sometimes one of the easiest ways for you to learn a new word is to write down the translation from your native language. For each word you wrote above, write the translation.

Now look back through the dictionary that you started in Unit 2. Write translations for all the words and expressions that are in there.

Evaluation 2   5 mins.

Walk around the classroom and help students as needed.

Presentation 3

5-10 mins.

Learner Log

In this unit, you learned many things about community. How comfortable do you feel doing each of the skills listed below? Rate your comfort level on a scale of 1 to 4.

Go over the instructions with students and make sure they understand what to do. You may want to go over the first one or two skills with the class to make sure students understand.

Practice 3

5-10 mins.

Have students complete the Learner Log.

Evaluation 3

5-10 mins.

Walk around the classroom and help students.

Application

5-10 mins.

Go over the reflection statements with students and have them complete the answers by themselves.

TB
Assessment *(optional)*

Use the Stand Out 4 Assessment CD-ROM with Exam*View*® to create a post-test for Unit 4.

My Dictionary

Brainstorm a list of new words that you learned in this unit. (Answers will vary.)

_____   _____

_____   _____

_____   _____

_____   _____

Sometimes one of the easiest ways for you to learn a new word is to write down the translation from your native language. For each word you wrote above, write its translation.

Now look back through the dictionary that you started in Unit 2. Write translations for all the words and expressions that are in there.

Learner Log

In this unit, you learned many things about community. How comfortable do you feel doing each of the skills listed below? Rate your comfort level on a scale of 1 to 4. (Answers will vary.)

1 = Need more practice   **2** = OK   **3** = Good   **4** = Great!

Life Skill	Comfort Level				Page
I can identify resources in a community.	1	2	3	4	_____
I can ask about resources in a community.	1	2	3	4	_____
I can use the telephone.	1	2	3	4	_____
I can use embedded questions to ask for information.	1	2	3	4	_____
I can read a community bulletin board.	1	2	3	4	_____
I can make suggestions.	1	2	3	4	_____
I can interpret a road map.	1	2	3	4	_____
I can give and understand driving directions.	1	2	3	4	_____
I can volunteer in my community.	1	2	3	4	_____

If you circled 1 or 2, write down the page number where you can review this skill.

Reflection

1. I learned _____.

2. I would like to find out more about _____.

Create a community resource guide.

With a team, you will create a community resource guide. This project can be done in two ways:

1. Each team creates its own guide.
2. Each team creates a portion of a guide and all parts are combined at the end to make a class guide.

1. Form a team with four or five students. Choose positions for each member of your team.

POSITION	JOB DESCRIPTION	STUDENT NAME
Student 1: **Team Leader**	See that everyone speaks English and participates.	
Student 2: **Writer**	Take notes and write information for guide	
Student 3: **Designer**	Design and add art to guide.	
Students 4/5: **Spokespeople**	Report information to the class. Prepare team for the presentation	

2. As a class, decide what information should go in your guide(s), such as the names of local services, medical facilities, restaurants, events, and places to volunteer. Make a list on the board.

3. Decide if each team will create its own guide or if each team will work on a portion of a class guide. (If the second option is chosen, decide what section each team will work on.)

4. Create your guide or portion of the class guide. Each portion should include addresses, phone numbers, basic information, and a map. (Use the phone book or the Internet if you need to.)

5. Put your guide together.

6. Present your guide or portion of your guide to the class.

Create a community resource guide.

With a team, you will create a community resource guide. This project can be done in two ways:

1. Each team creates its own guide.
2. Each team creates a portion of a guide and all parts are combined at the end to make a class guide.

The team project is the final application for the unit. It gives students a chance to show that they have mastered all of the Unit 4 objectives.

Note: Shorter classes can extend this project over class meetings.

Stage 1   5 mins.

Form a team with four or five students. Choose positions for each member of your team.

Have students decide who will lead each step as described on the student page. Provide well-defined directions on the board for how teams should proceed. Explain that all the students do every step as a team. Teams shouldn't go to the next stage until the previous one is complete.

Stage 2   15–20 mins.

As a class, decide what information should go in your guide(s), such as the names of local services, medical facilities, restaurants, events, and places to volunteer. Make a list on the board.

Stage 3   10–15 mins.

Decide if each team will create its own guide or if each team will work on a portion of the guide. (If the second option is chosen, decide what section each team will work on.)

Stage 4   10–15 mins.

Create your guide or portion of the class guide. Each portion should include addresses, phone numbers, basic information, and a map. (Use the phone book or the Internet if you need to.)

Optional Computer Activity: Students may want to use the computer to design their ads.

Stage 5   5 mins.

Put your guide together.

Stage 6   15–20 mins.

Present your guide or portion of your guide to the class.

Help teams prepare for their presentations. Suggest that each member choose a different part of the guide to present.

STANDARDS CORRELATIONS

CASAS: 4.8.1, 4.8.5, 4.8.6. (See CASAS Competency List on pages 169–175.)
SCANS: **Resources** Allocate time
Information Acquire and evaluate information, organize and maintain information, interpret and communicate information, use computers to process information
Systems Understand systems, improve and design systems
Technology (optional) Select technology, apply technology to exercise
Basic Skills Reading, writing, listening, speaking
Thinking Skills Creative thinking, decision making, problem solving, seeing things in the mind's eye, reasoning

Personal Qualities Responsibility, self-esteem, self-management, integrity/honesty
EFF: **Communication** Read with understanding, convey ideas in writing, speak so others can understand, listen actively, observe critically
Decision Making Solve problems and make decisions, plan
Interpersonal Guide others, resolve conflict and negotiate, advocate and influence, cooperate with others
Lifelong Learning Take responsibility for learning, reflect and evaluate, learn through research, use information and communication technologies (optional)

Objective: Identify health habits
Academic Strategies: Making a bar graph, calculating percentages
Vocabulary: *healthy, unhealthy, puzzles, meditating, mental health, calculate, percentage, poll*

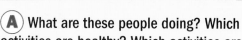

AGENDA

Identify healthy and unhealthy activities.
Understand mental health and physical health.
Read a bar graph.
Take a poll.
Make a bar graph calculating percentages.

RESOURCES

Activity Bank: Unit 5, Lesson 1, Worksheets 1–2
Reading and Writing Challenge: Unit 5

Grammar Challenge 4: Unit 5, Challenge 1

 1.5 hour classes　　2.5 hour classes　　3+ hour classes

  Preassessment *(optional)*

Use the Stand Out 4 Assessment CD-ROM with Exam*View*® to create a pretest for Unit 5.

Warm-up and Review　　5 mins.

Write *health* on the board. Ask students what the word means to them.

Introduction　　5-10 mins.

Write *healthy* and *unhealthy* on the board. Ask students the difference between these two adjectives. Have them give you some examples of healthy and unhealthy foods to check their understanding. State the objective: *Today we will identify healthy and unhealthy habits, calculate percentages, and make a bar graph of the healthy habits of students in this class.*

Presentation 1　　5 mins.

(A) What are these people doing? Which activities are healthy? Which activities are unhealthy? Make two lists below.

Do this exercise as a class.

Practice 1　　10-15 mins.

(B) Can you think of other healthy or unhealthy habits? Add them to your lists.

Have students do this activity in small groups.

Evaluation 1　　5 mins.

Have each group report to the class by writing their answers on the board in two columns.

STANDARDS CORRELATIONS

CASAS: 3.5.8, 3.5.9, 6.4.3, 6.7.2 (See CASAS Competency List on pages 169-175.)
SCANS: **Resources** Allocate human resources
Information Acquire and evaluate information, organize and maintain information, interpret and communicate information
Interpersonal Participate as a member of a team, teach others, exercise leadership, negotiate to arrive at a decision, work with cultural diversity
Systems Monitor and correct performance
Basic Skills Reading, writing, arithmetic, listening, speaking

Thinking Skills Creative thinking, decision making, problem solving;
Personal Qualities Responsibility, sociability, self-management
EFF: **Communication** Read with understanding, speak so others can understand, listen actively
Decision Making Use math to solve problems and communicate, solve problems and make decisions, plan
Interpersonal Cooperate with others
Lifelong Learning Learn through research, reflect and evaluate, use information and communications technology (optional)

UNIT 5 — Health

GOALS

- ➤ Identify health habits
- ➤ Describe symptoms of illnesses
- ➤ Interpret doctor's instructions
- ➤ Interpret nutrition information
- ➤ Complete a health insurance form

Vocabulary · Grammar
Life Skills
Academic · Pronunciation

LESSON 1 — Health habits

GOAL ➤ Identify health habits

A What are these people doing? Which activities are healthy? Which activities are unhealthy? Make two lists below. (Answers may vary slightly.)

Healthy Habits	Unhealthy Habits
walking/jogging/exercising	eating junk food
eating fruit	smoking

B Can you think of other healthy and unhealthy habits? Add them to your lists.

GOAL ➤ **Identify health habits**

 C Look at each health habit in the chart below and decide if it is healthy or unhealthy. Put a check mark (✓) in the correct column.

Health Habit	Healthy	Unhealthy
watching a lot of TV		✓
doing puzzles	✓	
drinking too much alcohol		✓
drinking water	✓	
eating fruits and vegetables	✓	
eating junk food		✓
lifting weights	✓	
meditating	✓	
playing sports	✓	
reading	✓	
sleeping	✓	
smoking		✓
spending time with friends and family	✓	
taking illegal drugs		✓
walking	✓	

D There are two different types of health—mental health and physical health. Mental health is anything related to your mind and psychological well-being. Physical health is anything related to your body, both from a fitness and nutritional standpoint.

Look at the health habits you checked as healthy in the chart above. Decide which type of health each one benefits and write it in the correct column in the chart below.

Mental Health	Physical Health
doing puzzles	drinking water
meditating	eating fruits and vegetables
reading	lifting weights
sleeping	playing sports
spending time with friends and family	sleeping
	walking

Presentation 2   10-15 mins. ▪▪▪

C **Look at each health habit in the chart below and decide if it is healthy or unhealthy. Put a check mark (✓) in the correct column.**

Do this exercise as a class, making sure students understand the vocabulary. As you go through each habit, have students check if it is healthy or unhealthy.

Practice 2   10-15 mins. ▪▪

D **There are two different types of health— mental health and physical health. Mental health is anything related to your mind and psychological well-being. Physical health is anything related to your body, both from a fitness and nutritional standpoint.**

Make sure students understand the difference between the two types of health.

Look at the habits you checked as healthy in the chart above. Decide which type of health each one benefits and write it in the correct column in the chart below.

Have students work in small groups to complete this chart. You might do one or two examples as a class to get them started.

Evaluation 2   5-10 mins. ▪▪

Have each group report its answers to the class by asking a representative from each group to come to the board and work together to compile the two lists.

Activity Bank 💿

Lesson 1, Worksheet 1: Healthy vs. Unhealthy

Instructor's Notes

Presentation 3

5-15 mins. ■■■

Ask students to raise their hands if they eat junk food. Ask a volunteer to count the total number of students in the class and the number of students who eat junk food. Now ask students what percentage of them eats junk food. See if anyone can figure this calculation out. Then show students how to calculate percentages using the steps in the book.

> ### Teaching Tip
>
> **Calculating percentages**
>
> This concept may be very simple for your students who have studied math but difficult for those who haven't. Spend as much time as you feel necessary teaching how to calculate percentages. (If your students seem to be getting frustrated, you may want to move on to another activity.) It's up to you if you want students to work out the calculations on paper or if you want to show them how to use a calculator to compute percentages.
>
> For the application activity (which will be done as group work), students will need to calculate percentages. You may want to carefully select the groups so you can be sure that at least one person in each group can calculate the percentages.

Ask students to scan the bar graph in Exercise E and make guesses/observations about the information that is presented.

Practice 3

5-10 mins. ■

(Shorter classes can do Exercise E for homework.)

E Ms. Tracy's students took a poll in their class to find out what bad health habits they have. They presented their results in a bar graph. Read the bar graph and answer the questions.

Evaluation 3

5 mins. ■

Go over the answers as a class.

Application

10-20 mins. ■■■

F With a group of students, list four good health habits. Take a poll in your class to see who practices these health habits. Make sure you ask everyone. Make a bar graph of your findings.

Explain to students how this activity will work:

1. Students will come up with four health habits they want to ask about.
2. They will need to ask all the students in the class their questions. First, they will need to know how many students are in the class so they don't miss anyone, and, second, they will need to come up with a way to make sure they don't ask the same person twice.
3. Once they have all their data, they will calculate the percentages and make their graphs.
4. When they finish, they will report their findings to the class.

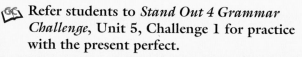 **Refer students to *Stand Out 4 Grammar Challenge*, Unit 5, Challenge 1 for practice with the present perfect.**

> ### Activity Bank
>
> Lesson 1, Worksheet 2: My Health Habits

E Ms. Tracy's students took a poll in their class to find out what bad health habits they have. They presented their results in a bar graph. Read the bar graph and answer the questions.

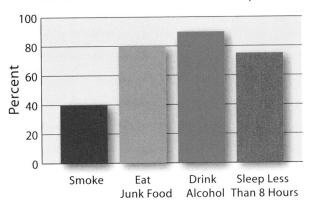

The Bad Health Habits of Ms. Tracy's Class

How to Calculate Percentage
1. First, find out the total number of students in your class.
2. Then divide the total number of students into the number of students who answered the question yes.
EXAMPLE: In a class of 25 students, 15 students exercise.

$$25\overline{)15.00}$$
$$\begin{array}{r}.60\\ \underline{15.00}\\ 0\end{array}$$

3. Move the decimal over two places to the right to get the percentage.
    .60 = 60%

1. What percentage of students eats junk food? <u>80%</u>

2. What percentage of students sleeps less than eight hours? <u>75%</u>

3. What percentage of students *doesn't* smoke? <u>60%</u>

4. What percentage of students *doesn't* drink alcohol? <u>10%</u>

5. What is the worst health habit Ms. Tracy's class has? <u>drinking alcohol</u>

F With a group of students, list four good health habits. Take a poll in your class to see who practices these health habits. Make sure you ask everyone. Make a bar graph of your findings.

EXAMPLE: health habits—exercise poll question: Do you exercise?

(Answers will vary.)

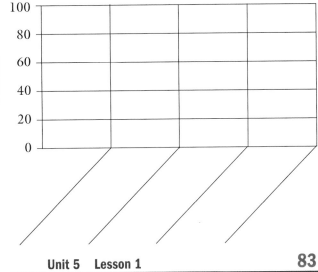

The Good Health Habits of My Class

What's the problem?

GOAL ➤ **Describe symptoms of illnesses**

Who are the people in the picture?
What are they saying?

 Read the conversation between the doctor and the patient.

Doctor: Hello, John. What seems to be the problem?
John: <u>I've been coughing a lot</u>.
Doctor: Anything else?
John: Yes, <u>my chest has been hurting</u>, too.
Doctor: It sounds like you might have <u>bronchitis</u>. I'd like to do some tests to be sure, and then I'll give you a prescription to relieve your symptoms.
John: Thanks, Doc.

 Practice the conversation with a partner. Then, practice the conversation several more times, replacing the underlined parts with the information below.

Symptom 1	Symptom 2	Diagnosis
1. I've been blowing my nose a lot.	My body has been aching.	common cold
2. My leg's been hurting.	I haven't been walking properly.	muscle spasm
3. I've been throwing up.	I've been feeling faint and dizzy.	flu

AT-A-GLANCE PREP

Objective: Describe symptoms of illnesses
Grammar: Present perfect simple and present perfect
continuous
Pronunciation: Word linking
Vocabulary: *cough, ache, common cold, muscle spasm,
flu, throwing up, examine*

AGENDA

*Read and practice conversations
between a doctor and patient.
Read about symptoms and diagnoses.
Use the present perfect continuous.
Review the present perfect simple tense.
Ask and answer questions with "How long
have you ... ?"*

RESOURCES

Activity Bank: Unit 5, Lesson 2, Worksheet 1
Reading and Writing Challenge: Unit 5

Grammar Challenge 4: Unit 5, Challenge 2

■ 1.5 hour classes ■ 2.5 hour classes ■ 3+ hour classes

Warm-up and Review   5–10 mins. ■■■

Ask students about their friends' and family's
healthy and unhealthy habits.

Introduction   5–10 mins. ■■■

Tell students about a family member or
friend who has been sick recently. (If you are
uncomfortable sharing this information, you can
ask a volunteer to tell about someone he or she
knows.) Ask students: *Who should this person see
to get help?* (the doctor) *What should this person
tell the doctor?* (his or her symptoms) State the
objective: *Today we will learn how to describe
symptoms of an illness.*

Presentation 1   5–10 mins. ■■■

 **Read the conversation between the doctor
and the patient.**

Ask volunteers to role-play the conversation.
Show students how to do Exercise B by
role-playing the conversation with a volunteer
and then having two students role-play the
conversation with the substituted information.

Practice 1   10–15 mins. ■■■

 **Practice the conversation with a partner.
Then, practice the conversation several more
times, replacing the underlined parts with the
information below.**

Have each student complete this exercise with
a partner. Have partners take turns being the
doctor and patient. If students finish early,
encourage them to come up with additional
symptoms and diagnoses.

Evaluation 1   5 mins. ■■■

Ask volunteers to perform conversations
for the class.

Presentation 2   5-10 mins. ■■■

C **Study the chart with your teacher.**

Go over the examples with students. Explain when we use present perfect continuous and have them come up with more examples. Then go over the form and make sure students understand the three parts.

Practice 2   10-15 mins. ■■□

(Shorter classes can do Exercise D for homework.)

D **Complete the sentences using the present perfect continuous form of the verbs in parentheses and suitable time expressions.**

Point out the *for/since* chart to students and go over the examples that can be used after each.

Evaluation 2   10-15 mins. ■■□

Go over the answers as a class by asking volunteers to write the sentences on the board.

Pronunciation

Word linking

(**Note:** This pronunciation aspect is not covered explicitly in the student book, but this may be a good time to teach your students word linking.)

Word linking: In spoken English, the pronoun *he* often loses its initial /h/ sound when it is linked to the previous word. Write some of these examples on the board and have students repeat after you.

1. Is he taking any medication? (izzy)
2. Has he been ill for a long time? (hazzy)
3. Does he often go to the doctor? (duzzy)
4. Did he give you some advice? (diddy)
5. Isn't he going to take sick leave? (izzeny)
6. Hasn't he phoned yet? (hazzeny)
7. Doesn't he have insurance? (duzzeny)
8. Didn't he tell you about the pills? (diddeny)

LESSON **2** **GOAL** ▶ **Describe symptoms of illnesses**

C Study the chart with your teacher.

Present Perfect Continuous	
Example	**Form**
I *have been resting* for three hours.	*Affirmative sentence*: has/have + been + present participle
He *hasn't been sleeping* well recently.	*Negative sentence*: has/have + not + been + present participle
How *long have they lived/have they been living* here?	*Question*: has/have + subject + been + present participle

- To emphasize the duration of an activity or state that started in the past and continues in the present. Example: The president *has been sleeping* since 9 A.M.
- To show that an activity has been in progress recently. Example: You've *been going* to the doctor a lot lately.
- With some verbs (*work, live, teach*), there is no difference in meaning between the present perfect simple and the present perfect continuous. Example: They *have lived/have been living* here since 2000.

Note: Some verbs are not usually used in the continuous form. These include *be, believe, hate, have, know, like,* and *want*.

D Complete the sentences using the present perfect continuous form of the verbs in parentheses and suitable time expressions. (Time expressions will vary slightly.)

for + period of time	*since* + point in time
two weeks	Tuesday
five days	5:30 P.M.
a month	1964
a long time	last night
a while	I was a child

1. We <u>have been going</u> (go) to our family doctor for <u>a long time</u>.

2. The kids <u>have been sleeping</u> (sleep) since <u>last night</u>.

3. The couple <u>has been practicing</u> (practice) medicine in Mexico for <u>a long time</u>.

4. I <u>have been working</u> (work) at the same job for <u>a while</u>.

5. How long <u>have you been studying</u> (you, study) to be an optometrist?

6. Satomi <u>has not been feeling well</u> (feel well / not) since <u>Tuesday</u>.

7. The boy <u>has been coughing</u> (cough) since <u>5:30 p.m.</u>.

8. Enrico <u>has been taking</u> (take) his medicine for <u>five days</u>.

9. Minh <u>has been thinking</u> (think) about changing jobs for <u>two weeks</u>.

10. They <u>have been going</u> (go) to the gym together for <u>a month</u>.

E Now review the present perfect simple with your teacher.

Present Perfect Simple	
Example	**Form**
He *has seen* the doctor. I *have moved* four times in my life.	*Affirmative sentence:* has/have + past participle
They *haven't been* to the hospital to see her.	*Negative sentence:* has/have + not + past participle OR has/have + never + past participle
Have you *written* to your mother?	*Question:* has/have + subject + past participle

- When something happened (or didn't happen) at an unspecified time in the past.
  Example: She *has* never *broken* her arm.
- When something happened more than once in the past (and could possibly happen again in the future). Example: I *have moved* four times in my life.
- When something started at a specific time in the past and continues in the present.
  Example: They *have lived* here for ten years.

F Choose the present perfect simple or the present perfect continuous form of the verbs in parentheses. In some sentences, you will also need to decide if *for* or *since* should be used.

1. They _____have been_____ (be) to their new doctor several times.

2. Marco _____has had_____ (have) asthma ___since___ 1995.

3. She __has given/has been giving__ (give) me a lot of help ___since___ I moved here.

4. I _____have not seen_____ (see / not) the dentist ___for___ a year.

5. _____Have you seen_____ (you / see) the new hospital downtown?

6. _____Have you been waiting_____ (you / wait) ___for___ a long time?

7. Santiago _____has missed_____ (miss) two appointments this week.

8. We _____have been cooking_____ (cook) ___for___ three hours.

9. He _____has not examined_____ (examine / not) her ___since___ she was a child.

10. How long _____have you known_____ (you / know) Maria?

G Work in groups of three or four. Ask and answer questions beginning with *How long*. Use the present perfect simple or present perfect continuous.

EXAMPLES: How long have you been going to the same doctor?
How long have you had a headache?

Presentation 3   5–10 mins.

E Now review the present perfect simple with your teacher.

Practice 3   10–15 mins.

(Shorter classes can do Exercise F for homework.)

F Choose the present perfect simple or the present perfect continuous form of the verbs in parentheses. In some sentences, you will also need to decide if *for* or *since* should be used.

Remind students that they can look back at the *for/since* chart on the previous page for help.

📖 **Refer students to *Stand Out 4 Grammar Challenge*, Unit 5, Challenge 2 for more practice with present perfect continuous statements.**

Evaluation 3   5–10 mins.

Go over the completed sentences as a class.

Application   10–20 mins.

G Work in groups of three or four. Ask and answer questions beginning with *How long*. Use the present perfect simple or present perfect continuous.

To help students get started, you may want to brainstorm some ideas on the board first, for example, what situations *How long* could be used for. Once you have some topics on the board, have the class help you write one or two *How long* questions. Then ask for a volunteer to practice asking and answering the questions with you.

Activity Bank

Lesson 2, Worksheet 1: Present Perfect and Present Perfect Continuous

---

Instructor's Notes

Objectives: Interpret doctor's instructions
Grammar: Direct vs. Indirect speech
Academic Strategy: Focused listening
Vocabulary: *cholesterol, obstetrician, podiatrist, chiropractor, dentist, pediatrician, nutritionist, announce, advise, warn, state*

AGENDA

Listen to a doctor's advice.
Understand and use indirect speech.
Identify types of doctors.
Retell doctor's advice.

RESOURCES

Activity Bank: Unit 5, Lesson 3, Worksheet 1
Reading and Writing Challenge: Unit 5

Grammar Challenge 4: Unit 5, Challenge 3
Audio: CD 1, Tracks 21–22

■ 1.5 hour classes   ■ 2.5 hour classes   ■ 3⁺ hour classes

Warm-up and Review   5-10 mins. ■■■

Review present perfect simple and present perfect continuous with students by asking some basic information questions. For example: *How long have you been studying English?* Briefly review the rules of the two tenses.

Introduction   5-10 mins. ■■■

Ask students to recall the poll that they took about health habits. Ask a student *What did you say about your good health habits?* Rephrase the student's answer using indirect speech. This will introduce students to the structure and concept of indirect speech. State the objective: *Today we will learn how to interpret a doctor's instructions and tell someone else what a doctor told you.*

Presentation 1   10-15 mins. ■■■

Have students look at the picture on page 87. Ask students: *Who are the people in the picture? What do you think they are saying?*

Practice 1   10-15 mins. ■■■

 **A** The doctor tells Rosa several important things about her health at her checkup. Listen and number the sentences in the correct order (1–5).

 Listening Script   CD 1, Track 21

Doctor: *Rosa, I can give you some more tests, but you'll have to come back in two weeks to get the results. Here's an information leaflet that tells you about exercises that will be good for your back and for your knees. If you start exercising more, your cholesterol level should go down. The fact is, if you don't stop eating junk food, you will have serious health problems. The most important thing is to stay active.*

 B Now listen to Rosa reporting her conversation to her friend. Fill in the missing words.

 Listening Script   CD 1, Track 22

Friend: *What did the doctor tell you, Rosa?*
Rosa: *She said she would give me some more tests.*
Friend: *Why? Are you very sick?*
Rosa: *Not now, but I might get sick. The doctor told me the most important thing was to stay active. She told me if I started exercising more, my cholesterol should go down. She said if I didn't stop eating junk food, I would have serious health problems. She said I had to come back in two weeks.*

Evaluation 1   5 mins. ■■■

Go over the answers to both exercises by playing the recording again, pausing the CD so that students can check their work.

 C What differences do you notice between the sentences in Exercise A and Exercise B? Study the chart with your teacher.

STANDARDS CORRELATIONS

CASAS: 3.1.1 (See CASAS Competency List on pages 169–175.)
SCANS: **Information** Acquire and evaluate information, organize and maintain information, interpret and communicate information
Interpersonal Participate as a member of a team, teach others, work with cultural diversity
Systems Monitor and correct performance

Basic Skills Reading, writing, listening, speaking
Thinking Skills Creative thinking, decision making
Personal Qualities Responsibility, sociability, self-management
EFF: **Communication** Read with understanding, convey ideas in writing, speak so others can understand, listen actively
Interpersonal Cooperate with others

LESSON 3

What did she say?

GOAL ➤ Interpret doctor's instructions

What are these people talking about? What do you think they are saying?

CD 1
TR 21

A The doctor tells Rosa several important things about her health at her checkup. Listen and number the sentences in the correct order (1–5).

_1_ "I can give you some more tests."

_5_ "The most important thing is to stay active."

_2_ "You'll have to come back in two weeks."

_3_ "If you start exercising more, your cholesterol should go down."

_4_ "If you don't stop eating junk food, you will have serious health problems."

CD 1
TR 22

B Now listen to Rosa reporting her conversation to her friend. Fill in the missing words.

1. She said she __would__ give __me__ some more tests.

2. The doctor told me the most important thing __was__ to stay active.

3. She told me if __I__ __started__ exercising more, __my__ cholesterol should go down.

4. She said if __I__ __didn't__ stop eating junk food, __I__ __would__ have serious health problems.

5. She said __I__ __had__ to come back in two weeks.

C What differences do you notice between the sentences in Exercise A and Exercise B? Study the chart with your teacher.

Direct Speech	Indirect Speech	Rule
"You have to exercise more."	The doctor *explained* (that) I had to exercise more.	• Change pronoun. • Change present tense to past tense.
"The most important thing is your health."	The doctor *said* (that) the most important thing was my health.	

GOAL ➤ Interpret doctor's instructions

D Match the kinds of doctors with the type of treatment they provide.

| dentist | chiropractor | pediatrician | obstetrician | podiatrist |

  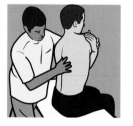  

obstetrician   podiatrist   chiropractor   dentist   pediatrician

E Read the statements and decide what kind of doctor said each one. Use indirect speech to tell your partner what each person said.

EXAMPLE: "Your child is in perfect health!"
The pediatrician said my child was in perfect health.

 The indirect speech verbs may vary slightly.

Indirect Speech Verbs

announced	stated
answered	said
complained	explained
replied	agreed

1. "You need to brush your gums and floss your teeth every day." The dentist explained that I needed to brush my gums and floss my teeth every day.
2. "Your children are eating too many sweets and sugary foods. They need to eat more fruits and vegetables." The pediatrician complained that my children were eating too many sweets and sugary foods and that they need to eat more fruits and vegetables.
3. "It is a good idea to go to prenatal classes for at least three weeks." The obstetrician agreed that it was a good idea to go to prenatal classes for at least three weeks.
4. "The shoes you are wearing aren't good for your feet." The podiatrist said the shoes I was wearing weren't good for my feet.
5. "You'll hurt your back if you don't bend your knees to lift heavy objects." The chiropractor explained that I'd hurt my back if I didn't bend my knees to lift heavy objects.
6. "You need to make an appointment to have those cavities filled." The dentist stated that I'd have to make an appointment to have my cavities filled.
7. "You need to make sure you take your vitamins every day." The obstetrician/pediatrician said that I needed to make sure I took my vitamins every day.

Presentation 2   5–10 mins.

Ask students to brainstorm a list with you of different types of doctors. Get them started by asking: *What doctor would you see if you had a problem with your teeth?*

D Match the kinds of doctors with the type of treatment they provide.

Do this exercise as a class.

Prepare students for Exercise E by going over the example and demonstrating with a few volunteers. Remind students they can look back at the chart on page 87 if they need help. Before students begin, go over the list of indirect speech verbs.

Practice 2   10–15 mins.

(Shorter classes can do Exercise E for homework.)

E Read the statements and decide what kind of doctor said each one. Use indirect speech to tell your partner what each person said.

Evaluation 2   10–15 mins.

Observe the activity. When finished, ask volunteers to demonstrate.

If you think students need more practice, ask them to take each of the statements and write an indirect speech statement on a piece of paper. Put these statements on the board so you can evaluate them as a class.

Activity Bank

Lesson 3, Worksheet 1: Indirect Speech

Instructor's Notes

Teaching Tip

Grammar presentation

It is often useful to have students try to figure out the grammar rules for themselves. One way to do this is to give them a list of sentences, questions, phrases, and so forth, that follow a specific rule. After they have studied the list, have them deduce the rule.

Dictate the following sentences to students.

1. I told *you* (that) I wanted to lose weight.
2. He notified *me* (that) my test results were negative.
3. My personal trainer said (that) it was important to check my heart rate.
4. She complained (that) she felt sick.

Ask students if they can find what is different between the first two sentences and the last two sentences. (The pronoun is after the main verb.)

Teaching Tip

Dictation

The purpose of dictation is to help students improve their listening skills. One objective of dictation is to get students to understand what you've said before they write it down.

1. Write the following steps on the board for students and go over them until students have them memorized.
   Listen first. (the most important part!)
   Repeat it to yourself.
   Write.
2. Tell students that you will only be reading the statements one time. This will encourage them to listen more carefully.
3. Tell students to listen to the whole sentence before they begin writing. Remind them that if they start writing before you've finished talking, they won't hear the end of what you say.

4. Dictate the sentences (one time each) at a normal pace, pausing between each one to allow students time to write.
5. Once you've finished dictating, have students check their answers with a partner or group. Encourage them to write down what they missed or fix what they think they got wrong.
6. Read the dictation one more time at normal speed. This time, don't pause between sentences.
7. Ask for volunteers to come and write each statement on the board.
8. Ask the class to check the volunteers' statements. If students think there is an error, ask them to come up to the board and make changes.
9. Repeat this procedure until all of the sentences are correct.

F Study the chart.

Practice 3   15–20 mins. ■
(Shorter classes can do Exercise G for homework.)

G Rewrite each quote using indirect speech with the subject and verb in parentheses.

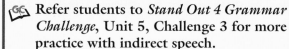 Refer students to *Stand Out 4 Grammar Challenge*, Unit 5, Challenge 3 for more practice with indirect speech.

Evaluation 3   5–10 mins. ■
Ask volunteers to write the sentences on the board. Evaluate the sentences as a class.

Application   5–10 mins. ■■■

 **H** Think of a conversation you had with a doctor or health care professional. Tell your partner what the person said to you.

LESSON 3 **GOAL** ➤ **Interpret doctor's instructions**

 F Study the chart.

Direct Speech	Indirect Speech
I want to lose weight.	I told *you* (that) I wanted to lose weight.
My test results are negative.	He notified *me* (that) my test results were negative.
It is important to check your heart rate.	My personal trainer said (that) it was important to check my heart rate.
I feel sick.	She complained (that) she felt sick.

- Some verbs are usually followed by an indirect object or pronoun. (*tell, assure, advise, convince, notify, promise, remind, teach, warn*)

- Some verbs are NOT followed by an indirect object or pronoun. (*say, agree, announce, answer, complain, explain, reply, state*)

 G Rewrite each quote using indirect speech with the subject and verb in parentheses.

EXAMPLE: "You need to walk for 30 minutes every day." (the doctor, remind)

  The doctor reminded me that I needed to walk for 30 minutes every day.

1. "He needs to stop smoking." (the cardiologist, warn)

  The cardiologist warned him that he needed to stop smoking.

2. "You have a very balanced diet." (the nutritionist, assure)

  The nutritionist assured me that I had a very balanced diet.

3. "She is very healthy." (the pediatrician, agree)

  The pediatrician agreed that she was very healthy.

4. "You eat too much junk food." (the doctor, convince)

  The doctor convinced me that I ate too much junk food.

5. "I read nutrition labels for every food I eat." (I, tell, the doctor)

  I told the doctor that I read nutrition labels for every food I ate.

6. "We want to start exercising together." (our parents, announce)

  Our parents announced that they wanted to start exercising together.

H Think of a conversation you had with a doctor or health care professional. Tell your partner what the person said to you.

Unit 5   Lesson 3   **89**

Nutrition labels

GOAL ➤ Interpret nutrition information

A Do you read the nutrition labels on the food that you buy? What do you look for? Why?

B Scan the nutrition label and answer the questions.

Nutrition Facts
Serving Size 2 oz. (56gm)
Servings Per Container 8

Amount Per Serving

Calories 200	Calories from Fat 10

% Daily Value*

Total Fat 1g	2%
Saturated Fat 0g	
Cholesterol 0mg	
Sodium 0mg	
Total Carbohydrate 42g	14%
Dietary Fiber 2g	8%
Sugars 1g	
Protein 7g	

Vitamin A	0%
Calcium	0%
Thiamin	35%
Niacin	15%
Vitamin C	0%
Iron	10%
Riboflavin	15%
Folate	30%

*Percent Davily Values are based on a 2,000-calorie diet. Your daily values may be higher or lower depending on your caloric needs:

Calories		2,000	2,500
Total Fat	Less than	65g	80g
Sat Fat	Less than	20g	25g
Cholesterol	Less than	300mg	300mg
Sodium	Less than	2,400mg	2,400mg
Total Carbohydrate		300g	375g
Dietary Fiber		25g	30g

Calories per gram:
Fat 9   Carbohydrate 4   Protein   4

Ingredients: Semolina, Niacin, Iron, Thiamin Mononitrate, Riboflavin, Folic Acid

1. How much protein is in one serving of this product? ____7g____

2. How many calories are in one serving of this product? ____200____ How many of those calories are from fat? ____10____

3. What vitamins and/or minerals does this product contain per serving?

   ____Riboflavin____   ____Iron____

   ____Folate____   ____Vitamin A____

   ____Thiamin____   ____Vitamin C____

   ____Niacin____   ____Calcium____

4. How many carbohydrates are in one serving of this product? ____42g____

5. How much fat is in one serving of this product? ____1g____ How much of the fat is saturated? ____0g____

6. How much of this product is one serving? ____2 oz. (56 gm)____

7. How many servings are in the box? ____8____

AT-A-GLANCE PREP

Objective: Interpret nutrition information
Academic Strategy: Active reading
Vocabulary: *fat, sodium, calories, carbohydrates, serving size, protein, ingredients, cholesterol, fiber*

AGENDA
Read and interpret a nutrition label.
Learn nutrition vocabulary.
Share information about nutrition.
Read about nutrition.

RESOURCES

Activity Bank: Unit 5, Lesson 4, Worksheet 1
Reading and Writing Challenge: Unit 5

Grammar Challenge 4: Unit 5, Challenge 4

 1.5 hour classes   2.5 hour classes   3+ hour classes

---

Warm-up and Review   5–10 mins.

Review indirect speech by asking some students to tell you about conversations they had with people before class.

Introduction   5–10 mins.

Write *nutrition* on the board. Ask students what this means to them. Ask them how they can find the nutritional information of certain foods. (*Optional:* Pass around some cans or food packages to show them examples.) State the objective: *Today we will learn about the nutritional information found on product labels.*

Presentation 1   5–10 mins.

(A) Do you read the nutrition labels on the food that you buy? What do you look for? Why?

Discuss these questions as a class.

Practice 1   10–15 mins.

(B) Scan the nutrition label and answer the questions.

Evaluation 1   5 mins.

Go over the answers as a class.

STANDARDS CORRELATIONS

CASAS: 3.5.1 (See CASAS Competency List on pages 169–175.)
SCANS: **Information** Acquire and evaluate information, organize and maintain information, interpret and communicate information
Interpersonal Participate as a member of a team, teach others, work with cultural diversity
Systems Monitor and correct performance
Basic Skills Reading, writing, arithmetic, listening, speaking

Thinking Skills Creative thinking, decision making, problem solving
Personal Qualities Responsibility, sociability, self-management
EFF: **Communication** Read with understanding, speak so others can understand, listen actively
Decision Making Solve problems and make decisions
Lifelong Learning Take responsibility for learning, learn through research, use information and communications technology (optional)

Presentation 2   5-10 mins.

Write the following words on the board and see if students can help you define them: *fat, sodium, calories,* and *protein*. Accept all answers at this point and don't correct students.

Practice 2   10-15 mins.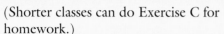

(Shorter classes can do Exercise C for homework.)

C These words can be found on a nutrition label. (See the highlighted words on the nutrition label on page 90.) Write the correct letter next to each definition. Use each letter only once.

Evaluation 2   10-15 mins.

Have students check their answers with a partner when they have finished. Then go over the answers as a class.

Presentation 3   5-10 mins.

D How much do you know about the nutrients on food labels? Discuss the questions below with a small group.

Teaching Tip

Discussion

Many exercises at this level involve students discussing something in groups. As the instructor, it's important for you to decide if students can choose their own groups or if you should group students together. Some ways to group students are: by level, by language group, by sex, or mixed levels and/or language groups. You may also want to assign or have students self-select certain positions, such as leader, secretary, reporter, timekeeper, etc.

Make sure that students clearly understand the task by modeling a discussion. Let students know what you expect the outcome of their discussion to be. Give students a certain amount of time for the discussion, and then ask each group to report to the class.

Instructor's Notes

C   These words can be found on a nutrition label. (See the highlighted words on the nutrition label on page 90.) Write the correct letter next to each definition. Use each letter only once.

a. saturated fat   e. serving size   h. cholesterol
b. sodium   f. protein   i. vitamins
c. calories   g. ingredients   j. fiber
d. carbohydrates

_e_ 1. This is the amount of food that a person actually eats at one time.

_c_ 2. This is the amount of energy supplied by a kind of food.

_a_ 3. This is a type of fat. It can contribute to heart disease.

_j_ 4. This ingredient of food is not digested but it aids digestion.

_b_ 5. This type of nutrient indicates the salt content of food.

_f_ 6. This helps to build and repair muscles. It is found mainly in meat, fish, eggs, beans, and cheese.

_g_ 7. These are whatever is contained in a type of food. On a nutrition label, they are presented in order of weight from most to least.

_d_ 8. These are the best source of energy and can be found in breads, grains, fruits, and vegetables.

_h_ 9. Eating too much of this can cause you to have heart disease and to be overweight.

_i_ 10. These nutrients are found in food and help to keep your body healthy.

D   How much do you know about the nutrients on food labels? Discuss the questions below with a small group. (Answers will vary.)

1. Why is it good to read nutrition labels?

2. What do complex carbohydrates do for your body?

3. What does saturated fat do to your body?

4. What type of person should watch his or her sodium intake?

5. How much protein should you eat per day?

6. Why are simple carbohydrates good?

7. Why is it good to eat fiber?

E Read the information about food labels.

Reading Nutritional Information on Food Labels

Knowing how to read the food label on packaged foods can help you build better eating habits. Here's a rundown of the basics you'll find on a food label and how you can use the information to improve your daily diet:

1. Serving Size The serving size on the label is supposed to be close to a "real-life" serving size—no more listing a teaspoon of salad dressing when most of us use a tablespoon. The information on the rest of the label is based on data for one serving. Remember, a package may contain more than one serving.

2. Calories The number of calories tells you how many calories are in one serving. The number of calories from fat tells you how many of those calories come from fat. Try to find foods with low amounts of calories from fat.

3. Fat This is where you look if you are trying to count fat grams. Total fat is important to watch, but saturated fat is particularly bad for you. Saturated fat raises your blood cholesterol level, which could lead to heart trouble.

4. Cholesterol Along with the saturated-fat information above, cholesterol amounts are important for anyone concerned about heart disease. High levels of cholesterol can lead to serious heart problems later in life.

5. Sodium Sodium (or salt) levels are important to monitor if you have high blood pressure.

6. Carbohydrates These fit into two categories—complex carbohydrates (dietary fiber) and simple carbohydrates (sugars). You want to eat more complex carbohydrates and fewer simple carbohydrates. Diets high in complex carbohydrates have been shown to fight cancer and heart disease. Simple carbohydrates are good for energy, but if you eat too many of them, you can expect your waistline to grow.

7. Fiber Fiber consists of complex carbohydrates that cannot be absorbed by the body. It aids digestion and can help lower blood cholesterol. High fiber foods include fruits, vegetables, brown rice, and whole-grain products.

8. Protein The food label doesn't specify a daily percentage or guideline for protein consumption because so much depends on individual needs. An athlete needs more than an office worker, but in a typical 2,000-calorie diet, most people need no more than 50 grams of protein per day.

9. Vitamins and Minerals The FDA requires only Vitamin A, Vitamin C, iron, and calcium amounts to be on food labels although food companies can voluntarily list others. Try and get 100 % of each of these essential vitamins and minerals every day.

10. Ingredients Ingredients are listed on food labels by weight from the most to the least. This section can alert you to any ingredients you may want to avoid because of food allergies.

F How much do you know about nutrition now? Decide if each statement is true or false. Fill in the correct circle.

	True	False
1. Reading food labels can improve your eating habits.	●	○
2. Diets high in complex carbohydrates can help fight cancer and heart disease.	●	○
3. Saturated fat lowers your blood cholesterol level.	○	●
4. You should watch your sodium intake if you have high blood pressure.	●	○
5. Most people need at least 100 grams of protein per day.	○	●
6. Simple carbohydrates are good for energy.	●	○
7. Foods with fiber can help lower cholesterol.	●	○

Practice 3   15–20 mins.

(E) **Read the information about food labels.**

Put students in small groups. First, have them read the article to themselves. Then assign each group a number (1–10). Have them find the term in the reading that corresponds to their number and have them prepare to explain the term to the class. Go around the classroom and help each group make sure the information they are going to present to the class is accurate.

Evaluation 3   5–10 mins. ▪

Discuss each part of the reading after the groups have presented.

Application   5–10 mins. ▪▪▪

(F) **How much do you know about nutrition now? Decide if each statement is true or false. Fill in the correct circle.**

Activity Bank

Lesson 4, Worksheet 1: Nutrition Label Practice

Refer students to *Stand Out 4 Grammar Challenge*, Unit 5, Challenge 4 for more practice with indirect speech and modals.

AT-A-GLANCE PREP

Objective: Complete a health insurance form
Academic Strategies: Skimming, active reading
Vocabulary: *coverage, prescription plan, vision, premium, deductible, co-pay, providers, reputation, spouse, dependants, stroke, intestinal, colon, kidney, muscular, circulatory, cancer, diabetes, respiratory, mental, emotional, liver, hernia, thyroid, allergy, digestive system, joint, asthma, reproductive organs, ulcer, arthritis, high blood pressure*

AGENDA

Talk about health insurance.
Compare types of insurance—
HMO vs. PPO.
Read a health insurance form.
Fill out a health insurance form.

RESOURCES

Activity Bank: Unit 5, Lesson 5, Worksheet 1, and Extension

Reading and Writing Challenge: Unit 5

Grammar Challenge 4: Unit 5, Challenge 5; Extension Challenges 1–2

█ 1.5 hour classes █ 2.5 hour classes █ 3⁺ hour classes

Warm-up and Review   5-10 mins.

Ask students if they went home after the previous lesson and looked at any food labels. Ask them to share any interesting information that they found.

Introduction   5-10 mins. ■■■

Ask students to raise their hands if they have health insurance. Ask how many have it through their work and how many pay for it out of pocket. Ask students who don't have health insurance why they don't. Talk about why health insurance is important. State the objective: *Today we will talk about health insurance options and learn how to complete a health insurance form.*

Presentation 1   10-15 mins. ■■■

Ask students what qualities they would look for in a health insurance company. Make a list on the board.

(A) If you were looking for a good health insurance company, what things would you look for? Check (✓) the items below that would be most important for you. Share your answers with the class.

(B) Most insurance companies offer two types of coverage—HMO and PPO. What do these two terms stand for?

Briefly discuss the differences between these two types of coverage.

Practice 1   5-10 mins.

(C) What are the differences between an *HMO* and *PPO*? Work with a small group and write *HMO* or *PPO* on the line before each statement.

Evaluation 1   5 mins. ■■■

Go over the answers as a class.

STANDARDS CORRELATIONS

CASAS: 3.2.3 (See CASAS Competency List on pages 169–175.)
SCANS: **Information** Acquire and evaluate information, organize and maintain information, interpret and communicate information
Interpersonal Participate as a member of a team, teach others, exercise leadership, negotiate to arrive at a decision, work with cultural diversity
Systems Understand systems, monitor and correct performance
Basic Skills Reading, writing, listening, speaking

Thinking Skills Decision making, problem solving
Personal Qualities Responsibility, sociability, self-management
EFF: **Communication** Read with understanding, speak so others can understand, listen actively
Interpersonal Guide others, cooperate with others
Lifelong Learning Take responsibility for learning, learn through research, use information and communications technology (optional)

Do you want dental coverage?

GOAL ➤ **Complete a health insurance form**

A If you were looking for a good health insurance company, what things would you look for? Check (✓) the items below that would be most important for you. Share your answers with the class. (Answers will vary.)

❏ dental coverage   ❏ low deductible

❏ prescription plan   ❏ low co-pay

❏ vision plan   ❏ good choice of providers

❏ low premium   ❏ good reputation

B Most insurance companies offer two types of coverage—HMO and PPO. What do these two terms stand for?

HMO: ___Health___   ___Maintenance___   ___Organization___

PPO: ___Preferred___   ___Provider___   ___Organization___

C What are the differences between an *HMO* and *PPO*? Work with a small group and write *HMO* or *PPO* on the line before each statement.

1. __PPO__ higher out-of-pocket expenses

2. __HMO__ low or sometimes free co-pay

3. __PPO__ you can see any doctor you want to at any time

4. __HMO__ you must choose one primary-care physician

5. __PPO__ higher monthly premium

6. __HMO__ lower monthly premium

7. __HMO__ you must get a referral from your primary-care physician to see another doctor

8. __HMO__ low or sometimes no out-of-pocket expenses

D Skim the health insurance application on this page and the next page. Put a check (✓) next to every part you can answer. Underline the parts you are not sure about.

Employee Applicant Information

First Name: _____ Middle Name: _____ Last Name: _____

Home Address:

Street: _____ City: _____ State: _____ Zip Code: _____

Sex: Male Female

Social Security Number: _____-_____-_____

Date of Birth: (mm / dd / yyyy) _____ / _____ / _____

Marital Status: ____ Married ____ Single

Work Phone: (_____) _____-_____ Home Phone: (_____) _____-_____

Job Title: _____

Hours Worked Per Week: _____

Annual Salary: _____

Tobacco: Have you or your spouse used any tobacco products in the past 12 months?

         Employee: ____Yes ____No   Spouse: ____Yes ____No

Dental: Do you want dental coverage? ____Yes ____No

Prescription Card: Do you want a prescription card? ____Yes ____No

Dependants: Dependants you want covered on this policy.

Spouse: _____

Date of Birth: (mm / dd / yyyy) _____ / _____ / _____ Sex: ____Male ____Female

Child #1 : _____

Date of Birth: (mm / dd / yyyy) _____ / _____ / _____ Sex: ____Male ____Female

Child #2: _____

Date of Birth: (mm / dd / yyyy) _____ / _____ / _____ Sex: ____Male ____Female

Presentation 2

5-10 mins. ■■□

Ask students what information they might find on a health insurance application. Make a list on the board.

Practice 2

10-15 mins. ■■

(Shorter classes can do Exercise D for homework.)

(D) Skim the health insurance application on this page and the next page. Put a check (✓) next to every part you can answer. Underline the parts you are not sure about.

Evaluation 2

10-15 mins. ■■

Walk around the classroom and observe students as they work.

Presentation 3   5 mins.

Prepare students for the practice by putting them in pairs and explaining the directions to Exercise E. Tell them if they can't figure something out, they can ask another pair sitting next to them. The purpose of this exercise is to get students to work together, rely on one another, and figure out how to learn things without the teacher's help.

Practice 3   15-20 mins. ▪

E Work in pairs. Use a dictionary to help you understand the parts of the form that you underlined.

Evaluation 3   10-15 mins. ▪

Go over the application as a class, explaining any parts that students couldn't figure out.

F Work with a small group to answer the following questions.

Discuss these questions as a class once students have had a chance to work in groups.

Application   10-15 mins. ■■■

G Now that you understand all the parts of the application, fill it out.
Note: If any information is too personal, just think about the answer and don't write it in your book.

 Refer students to *Stand Out 4 Grammar Challenge 4*, Unit 5, Challenge 5 for more practice with present perfect continuous questions.

 Refer students to *Stand Out 4 Grammar Challenge 4*, Unit 5, Extension Challenges 1-2 for practice with present perfect versus present perfect continuous, and the sequence of tenses in indirect speech.

Activity Bank

Lesson 5, Worksheet 1: Volunteer at the Animal Shelter;
Lesson 5, Extension: Class Telephone Directory

Instructor's Notes

GOAL ➤ **Complete a health insurance form**

A-1: Within the last four (4) years, have you or any dependant received or been recommended to have treatment for any disorders or conditions of the following? Please check all that apply.

❏ Back   ❏ Stroke   ❏ Intestinal   ❏ Colon   ❏ Kidney   ❏ Muscular   ❏ Heart or Circulatory

❏ Cancer   ❏ Diabetes   ❏ Respiratory   ❏ Mental or Emotional   ❏ Liver

A-2: Within the last four (4) years, have you or any dependant used drugs not prescribed by a physician, been advised to have treatment or been treated for drug abuse, alcoholism or been a member of Alcoholics Anonymous?   Yes   No

A-3: Have you or any dependant ever had a positive blood test indicating HIV antibodies or been treated and/or advised by a medical practitioner as having Acquired Immune Deficiency Syndrome (AIDS), AIDS Related Complex (ARC), or any other immune system deficiency?   Yes   No

A-4: Have you or any dependant been hospitalized, had surgery, or had more than $5,000 in medical expenses in the last twelve (12) months? ____Yes ____No

A-5: Are you or any dependant pregnant? ____Yes ____No

　　　If "Yes," what is your estimated due date? _____

A-6: Within the last four (4) years, have you or any dependant received or been recommended to have treatment for any disorders or conditions of the following? Please check all that apply.

❏ Ear   ❏ Hernia   ❏ Thyroid   ❏ Breast

❏ Eye   ❏ Allergy   ❏ Digestive System

❏ Joint   ❏ Asthma   ❏ Reproductive Organs

❏ Ulcer   ❏ Arthritis   ❏ High Blood Pressure

A-7: Within the last four (4) years, have you or any dependant received treatment or been advised to seek treatment for any reason not already mentioned? ____Yes ____No

Employee Name: _____

Date: (mm/dd/yyyy)_____ /____ /_____

E Work in pairs. Use a dictionary to help you understand the parts of the form that you underlined.

F Work with a small group to answer the following questions.

1. Why do you think health insurance companies need all of this information?
2. Why is it important to have health insurance?

G Now that you understand all the parts of the application, fill it out.
Note: If any information is too personal, just think about the answer and don't write it in your book.

Review

A In your opinion, what are the three most important good health habits to have? (Lesson 1) (Answers will vary.)

1. _____

2. _____

3. _____

B In your opinion, what are the three worst health habits to have? (Lesson 1)

1. (Answers will vary.) _____

2. _____

3. _____

C Complete the sentences using the present perfect simple or present perfect continuous form of the verb in parentheses. (Lesson 2)

1. I (not/eat) _____ haven't eaten _____ meat for three years.

2. Sara (go) _____ has been going _____ to yoga classes since September.

3. Andres (drink) _____ has drunk _____ two liters of water today.

4. I (not / sleep) _____ haven't been sleeping _____ well recently.

5. I (never / smoke) _____ have never smoked _____ a cigarette.

6. Why (you / choose) _____ have you chosen _____ such a stressful job?

7. Marna (wheeze) _____ has been wheezing _____ since last night.

8. We (see) _____ have seen _____ the same doctor for over ten years.

9. My father (have) _____ has had _____ diabetes since he was a child.

10. The children (not / brush) _____ have not been brushing _____ their teeth very well.

Objectives: All Unit 5 objectives
Grammar: All Unit 5 grammar
Academic Strategy: Reviewing
Vocabulary: All Unit 5 vocabulary

AGENDA

Unit objectives.
Review exercises.
My Dictionary.
Learner Log.

RESOURCES

Activity Bank: Unit 5, Lessons 1–5
Reading and Writing Challenge: Unit 5

Grammar Challenge: Unit 5, Challenges 1–5

 1.5 hour classes    2.5 hour classes   3ᵗ hour classes

Warm-up and Review   5-10 mins.

In groups, have students come up with a list of how HMOs are different from PPOs. Ask them which one they prefer and why.

Introduction   5-10 mins.

Ask students to try to recall (in general) all the goals of this unit without looking at their books. Then remind them which goals they omitted, if any. (Unit Goals: Identify health habits, describe symptoms of illnesses, interpret doctor's directions, interpret nutrition information, and complete a health insurance form.) Write all the goals from Unit 5 on the board. Show students the first page of the unit and mention the five objectives. State the objective: *Today we will be reviewing everything you have learned in this unit.*

Presentation 1   10-15 mins.

This presentation will cover the first three pages of the review. Quickly go to the first page of each lesson. Discuss the objective of each one. Ask simple questions to remind students of what they have learned.

Note: Since there is little presentation in the review, you can assign the review exercises that don't involve pair work or group work for homework and go over them in class the following day.

Practice 1   20-25 mins.

Note: There are two ways to do the review: (1) Go through the exercises one at a time and, as students complete each one, go over the answers. (2) Briefly go through the instructions of each exercise, allow students to complete all of the exercises at once, and then go over the answers.

Stop and evaluate whenever it is appropriate for the class. *(See Evaluation 1 on pg. 98a.)*

(A) In your opinion, what are the three most important good health habits to have? (Lesson 1)

(B) In your opinion, what are the three worst health habits to have? (Lesson 2)

(C) Complete the sentences using the present perfect simple or present perfect continuous form of the verb in parentheses. (Lesson 2)

STANDARDS CORRELATIONS

CASAS: 7.2.1 (See CASAS Competency List on pages 169–175.)
SCANS: **Resources** Allocate time
Information Acquire and evaluate information
Interpersonal Participate as a member of a team, teach others, negotiate to arrive at a decision, work with cultural diversity
Systems Monitor and correct performance
Basic Skills Reading, writing, arithmetic, listening, speaking
Thinking Skills Creative thinking, decision making, problem solving, seeing things in the mind's eye

Personal Qualities Responsibility, sociability, self-management
EFF: **Communication** Convey ideas in writing, speak so others can understand, listen actively
Decision Making Solve problems and make decisions
Interpersonal Guide others, cooperate with others
Lifelong Learning Take responsibility for learning, reflect and evaluate, learn through research

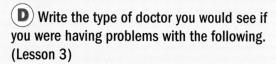
D Write the type of doctor you would see if you were having problems with the following. (Lesson 3)

E Change the sentences from direct speech to indirect speech. (Lesson 3)

Teaching Tip

Recycling/Review

The review process and the project that follows are part of the recycling/review process. Students at this level often need to be reintroduced to concepts to solidify what they have learned. Many concepts are learned and forgotten while learning other new concepts. This is because students learn but are not necessarily ready to acquire language concepts.

Therefore, it becomes very important to review and to show students how to review on their own. It is also important to recycle the new concepts in different contexts.

D Write the type of doctor you would see if you were having problems with the following. (Lesson 3)

1. feet   podiatrist

2. back   chiropractor

3. pregnancy   obstetrician

4. baby's ears   pediatrician

5. teeth   dentist

E Change the sentences from direct speech to indirect speech. (Lesson 3)

1. "My daughter is sick."

   Maria said that _her daughter was sick_.

2. "We won't be able to come to the meeting."

   Luis and Ricardo told me _they wouldn't be able to come to the meeting_.

3. "They don't have time to go out."

   Hanif said _they didn't have time to go out_.

4. "You need to take the medicine on an empty stomach."

   The doctor explained that _I needed to take the medicine on an empty stomach_.

5. "Your son is eating too much sugar."

   The pediatrician said _my son was eating too much sugar_.

6. "My back has been hurting for two months."

   I told the chiropractor _my back had been hurting for two months_.

7. "You need to take your prenatal vitamins every day."

   The obstetrician told me _I needed to take my prenatal vitamins every day_.

8. "Your husband needs to stay off his feet for a few hours a day."

   The podiatrist warned me _my husband needed to stay off his feet for a few hours a day_.

Review

F Match the descriptions to the nutrition items. (Lesson 4)

1. _f_ calories

2. _d_ carbohydrates

3. _j_ cholesterol

4. _g_ saturated fat

5. _b_ fiber

6. _a_ ingredients

7. _i_ protein

8. _h_ serving size

9. _c_ sodium

10. _e_ vitamins

a. listed on a food label by weight

b. complex carbohydrates that cannot be absorbed by the body

c. salt

d. dietary fiber and sugar

e. try to get 100% of each every day

f. energy supplied by food

g. a type of fat that can contribute to heart disease

h. the amount of food a person eats at one time

i. helps build and repair muscles

j. too much of this could lead to heart disease

G What is important to you when looking for health insurance? Make a list. (Lesson 5)

(Answers will vary.)

_____

_____

_____

_____

_____

_____

_____

Practice 1 (*continued*)   25–30 mins. ■ ■ ■

F Match the descriptions to the nutrition items. (Lesson 4)

G What is important to you when looking for health insurance? Make a list. (Lesson 5)

Evaluation 1   45–60 mins. ■ ■ ■

Go around the classroom and check on students' progress. Help individuals when needed. If you see consistent errors among several students, interrupt the class and give a mini-lesson or review to help students feel comfortable with the concept.

Presentation 2   5-10 mins.

My Dictionary

Ask students to brainstorm new vocabulary they learned in this unit. Have them do this without looking in their books.

Practice 2   15-20 mins.

(Shorter classes can do these exercises for homework.)

Do you remember what you learned about word families in the Pre-Unit? If not, look back at page P7 in Lesson 3 of the Pre-Unit.

Complete as much of the chart as you can with words from this unit. Then, complete the word families using your dictionary.

Look in your dictionary and see if any new words you have written down have other "family members." Add them to your dictionary.

Evaluation 2

Walk around and help students use their dictionaries to find word families. If you have time, ask for volunteers to share any new word families they have come up with.

Teaching Tip

Learner Logs

Learner Logs function to help students in many different ways.

1. They serve as part of the review process.
2. They help students to gain confidence and document what they have learned. Consequently, students see that they are making progress and want to move forward in learning.
3. They provide students with a tool that they can use over and over to check and recheck their understanding. In this way, students become independent learners.

Presentation 3   5-10 mins.

Learner Log

In this unit, you learned many things about health. How comfortable do you feel doing each of the skills listed below? Rate your comfort level on a scale of 1 to 4.

Practice 3   5-10 mins.

Have students complete the Learner Log.

Evaluation 3   5-10 mins.

Walk around the classroom and help students as needed.

Application   5-10 mins.

Go over the reflection statements with students and have them complete the answers by themselves.

TB Assessment *(optional)*

Use the Stand Out 4 Assessment CD-ROM with Exam*View*® to create a post-test for Unit 5.

My Dictionary

Do you remember what you learned about word families in the Pre-Unit? If not, look back at page P7 in Lesson 3 of the Pre-Unit.

Complete as much of the chart as you can with words from this unit. Then, complete the word families using your dictionary. (Answers will vary.)

Noun	Verb	Adjective	Adverb
advice	advise	advisable	advisably
insurance	insure	insurable	XXXXX
habit	XXXXX	habitual	habitually
medicine	medicate	medicinal	medicinally

Look in your dictionary and see if any new words you have written down have other "family members." Add them to your dictionary.

Learner Log

In this unit, you learned many things about health. How comfortable do you feel doing each of the skills listed below? Rate your comfort level on a scale of 1 to 4. (Answers will vary.)

1 = Need more practice   **2** = OK   **3** = Good   **4** = Great!

Life Skill	Comfort Level	Page
I can identify good and bad health habits.	1 2 3 4	____
I can report illnesses and symptoms to a doctor.	1 2 3 4	____
I can identify different types of doctors.	1 2 3 4	____
I can tell someone what the doctor told me.	1 2 3 4	____
I can identify vitamins and the nutritional content of foods.	1 2 3 4	____
I can interpret and fill out health insurance forms.	1 2 3 4	____

If you circled 1 or 2, write down the page number where you can review this skill.

Reflection

1. I learned _____.

2. I would like to find out more about _____.

Team Project

Create a community health pamphlet.

With a team, you will create a pamphlet to distribute to the community about good health practices.

1. Form a team with four or five students. Choose positions for each member of your team.

POSITION	JOB DESCRIPTION	STUDENT NAME
Student 1: **Team Leader**	See that everyone speaks English and participates.	
Student 2: **Writer**	Take notes and write information for pamphlet.	
Student 3: **Designer**	Design and add art to pamphlet.	
Students 4/5: **Spokespeople**	Prepare the team for presentation. Present pamphlet to the class.	

2. With your group, decide what information should go in your pamphlet, such as good health habits, types of doctors, nutrition, insurance information, etc.

3. Write the text and decide on the art to use in your pamphlet.

4. Put your pamphlet together.

5. Present your pamphlet to the class.

Team Project

Create a community health pamphlet.

Each team will create a pamphlet providing information about good health practices.

The team project is the final application for the unit. It gives students a chance to show that they have mastered all of the Unit 5 objectives.

Note: Shorter classes can extend this project over two class meetings.

Stage 1   5 mins.

Form a team with four or five students. Choose positions for each member of your team.

Have students decide who will lead each step as described on the student page. Provide well-defined directions on the board for how teams should proceed. Explain that all the students do every step as a team. Teams shouldn't go to the next stage until the previous one is complete.

Stage 2   5-10 mins.

With your group, decide what information should go in your pamphlet, such as good health habits, types of doctors, nutrition, insurance information, etc.

Have each team tell the class which topics they have decided to put in their pamphlets.

Stage 3   20-30 mins.

Write the text and decide on the art to use in your pamphlet.

Optional Computer Activity: Students may want to use the computer to design their pamphlets.

Stage 4   20-30 mins.

Put your pamphlet together.

Stage 5   15-20 mins.

Present your pamphlet to the class.

Help teams prepare for their presentations. Suggest that each member choose a different part of the pamphlet to present.

STANDARDS CORRELATIONS

CASAS: 4.8.1, 4.8.5, 4.8.6 (See CASAS Competency List on pages 169–175.)
SCANS: **Resources** Allocate time
Information Acquire and evaluate information, organize and maintain information, interpret and communicate information, use computers to process information
Systems Understand systems, improve and design systems
Technology (optional) Select technology, apply technology to exercise
Basic Skills Reading, writing, listening, speaking
Thinking Skills Creative thinking, decision making, problem solving, seeing things in the mind's eye, reasoning

Personal Qualities Responsibility, self-esteem, self-management, integrity/honesty
EFF: **Communication** Read with understanding, convey ideas in writing, speak so others can understand, listen actively, observe critically
Decision Making Solve problems and make decisions, plan
Interpersonal Guide others, resolve conflict and negotiate, advocate and influence, cooperate with others
Lifelong Learning Take responsibility for learning, reflect and evaluate, learn through research, use information and communication technologies (optional)

AT-A-GLANCE PREP

Objective: Identify skills and characteristics
Grammar: Simple present tense
Academic Strategy: Focused listening
Vocabulary: *job titles, skills, characteristics, interests*

RESOURCES

Activity Bank: Unit 6, Lesson 1, Worksheet 1
Reading and Writing Challenge: Unit 6

Grammar Challenge 4: Unit 6, Challenge 1
Audio: CD 1, Track 23

■ 1.5 hour classes   ■ 2.5 hour classes   ■ 3⁺ hour classes

 Preassessment *(optional)*

Use the Stand Out 4 Assessment CD-ROM with
Exam*View*® to create a pretest for Unit 6.

Warm-up and Review   5–10 mins.

Have students get into small groups and discuss
their current jobs or those they have held in
the past. Groups should make a list of all jobs
mentioned. Ask a volunteer to come up to the
board and write down the list of job titles that
his or her group came up with.

Introduction   5–10 mins.

Write the word *skills* on the board. Explain that
many jobs require certain skills. For example, an
administrative assistant must be able to type and
use a computer. Ask students what skills they
think a teacher needs. Help them make a list on
the board. Now ask students to form groups. Have
them discuss a few of the jobs they wrote down
in the warm-up. Make sure they talk about what skills
might be needed to do each of the jobs.

State the objective: *Today we will be talking
about skills and characteristics, especially those
that you need for jobs.*

Presentation 1   5–10 mins.

(A) Look at the pictures. What jobs are these
people doing? Discuss them with a partner.

When students have finished discussing the
pictures, go over the answers as a class. Then,
ask the class what skills the first two jobs require.

Practice 1   10–15 mins.

(B) A *skill* is something you can do, such as
use a computer or write a report. What skills are
required for each job above? Discuss your ideas
with a small group.

Evaluation 1   5 mins.

Go over the answers to Exercise B as a class.

STANDARDS CORRELATIONS

CASAS: 4.1.8, 4.1.9, 4.4.2 (See CASAS Competency
List on pages 169–175.)
SCANS: Information Acquire and evaluate information, organize and
maintain information, interpret and communicate information
Interpersonal Participate as a member of a team,
teach others, exercise leadership, negotiate to arrive
at a decision, work with cultural diversity
Systems Monitor and correct performance

Basic Skills Reading, writing, listening, speaking
Thinking Skills Creative thinking, decision making
Personal Qualities Responsibility, sociability, self-management
EFF: Communication Read with understanding, speak so others can
understand, listen actively
Decision Making Solve problems and make decisions
Lifelong Learning Reflect and evaluate

UNIT 6

Getting Hired

GOALS

➤ Identify skills and characteristics

➤ Conduct a job search

➤ Write a resume

➤ Write a cover letter

➤ Prepare for a job interview

LESSON 1

What skills do you have?

GOAL ➤ Identify skills and characteristics

A Look at the pictures. What jobs are these people doing? Discuss them with a partner.

B A *skill* is something you can do, such as use a computer or write a report. What skills are required for each job above? Discuss your ideas with a small group.

LESSON **1**   **GOAL** ➤ Identify skills and characteristics

Vocabulary   Grammar
Life Skills
Academic   Pronunciation

C Below is a list of job titles. Work in groups to write the job responsibilities that go with each job. Then, add two more job titles to the list. (Answers may vary. Possible answers below.)

Job Title	Job Responsibilities
accountant	manages finances
administrative assistant	writes correspondence, schedules appointments
assembler	puts things together
business owner	oversees the creation of products/sales to clients
cashier	handles customer payment for goods
computer technician	repairs computers
delivery person	drives truck, makes deliveries
dental assistant	assists dentist, cleans teeth
electrician	connects/fixes electricity in houses, offices
fire fighter	puts out fires
garment worker	sews clothing
hairstylist	cuts/styles hair
homemaker	cooks meals, takes care of children and house
landscape architect	designs and plans gardens and/or parks
mail carrier	sorts and delivers mail
receptionist	answers telephones, takes messages, greets people
reporter	reports news, writes articles
salesperson	sells merchandise to customers
security guard	protects store or bank from theft

D Practice the conversation below, using the information that you wrote in Exercise C.

Student A: What does a computer technician do?
Student B: A computer technician repairs computers.

E In groups, discuss the difference between skills and characteristics. A *skill* is something you can do, such as deliver mail or type a letter. A *characteristic* describes your personality and work habits, such as hardworking or well-organized. What are some other examples of characteristics?

Presentation 2   5-10 mins. ■■■

Go over the list of job titles in Exercise C. If you have to explain what some of them are, try not to include the skills required for the job. Students will be identifying the skills for the practice. Go over the two examples.

Practice 2   15-20 mins. ■■

(Shorter classes can do Exercise C for homework.)

C Below is a list of job titles. Work in groups to write the job responsibilities that go with each job. Then, add two more job titles to the list.

Evaluation 2   15-25 mins. ■■

Go over the answers as a class.

D Practice the conversation below, using the information you wrote in Exercise C.

Prepare students for Exercise D by doing the conversation with a few volunteers.

Presentation 3   10-20 mins. ■■■

E In groups, discuss the difference between skills and characteristics. A *skill* is something you can do, such as deliver mail or type a letter. A *characteristic* describes your personality and work habits, such as hardworking or well-organized. What are some other examples of characteristics?

Discuss the terms as a class.

Presentation 3 *(continued)* 10-20 mins.

F Read some characteristics that employers look for in employees. Discuss the characteristics with your classmates and check (✓) the ones that describe you.

Do this activity as a class. Then, go back to page 101 and discuss which characteristics would be good for each job in Exercise A.

Practice 3 15-20 mins.

G Read the descriptions and choose a characteristic to describe each person.

H Listen to four people describe their skills, characteristics, and interests. Take notes in the first column. Then, suggest a job for each in the second column.

Prepare students for the listening task by asking them what they think the four people will say.

🎧 Listening Script CD 1, Track 23

1. *My name is Lam and I love to be outdoors. I'm a hard worker and I like to work with my hands. I don't like to tell other people what to do, but I don't mind taking orders from my boss.*
2. *Hello, I'm Lilia and I love working with people. I'm very customer-service oriented and I like to help people. I wouldn't make a good cashier because I'm not very good with numbers, but I'm willing to work hard and I learn quickly.*
3. *My name is Morteza and I was an engineer in my country. Unfortunately, I don't have the right qualifications to be one here, but I'm very good at technical things. I know a lot about computers and really like working with them. I prefer to work alone because I'm not very good with people.*
4. *Hi, I'm Hilda. I've never had a job before, but I'm very organized and good with details. I've always taken care of the finances at our house so I'm good with numbers. Also, I'm creative and like to come up with new ideas.*

 Refer students to *Stand Out 4 Grammar Challenge*, Unit 6, Challenge 1 for a review of restrictive adjective clauses.

Evaluation 3 5-10 mins.

Go over the answers as a class.

Application 10-20 mins.

I Make a list of your skills and interests on a piece of paper. What are some jobs that you think you might enjoy and be good at? List at least three jobs. Then, list the characteristics you have that would make you good for each job.

Write the following chart on the board for students to copy down and complete.

My skills	My interests	Good jobs for me	My characteristics

Activity Bank

Lesson 1, Worksheet 1: Characteristics

GOAL ➤ **Identify skills and characteristics**

F Read some characteristics that employers look for in employees. Discuss the characteristics with your classmates and check (✓) the ones that describe you.

❏ a quick learner   ❏ creative   ❏ dependable
❏ detail-oriented   ❏ efficient   ❏ flexible
❏ good with numbers   ❏ great with people   ❏ hardworking
❏ well-organized   ❏ willing to accept responsibility   ❏ works well under pressure

G Read the descriptions and choose a characteristic to describe each person.

1. Suzanne works long hours and never takes any breaks. ___hardworking___

2. You can always rely on Linh. ___dependable___

3. Li is always calm, even when it's very stressful. ___works well under pressure___

4. You never have to explain anything to Vlasta twice. ___a quick learner___

H Listen to four people describe their skills, characteristics, and interests. Take notes in the first column. Then, suggest a job for each person in the second column.

CD 1
TR 23

(Answers may vary.)

Lam	Skills, characteristics, interests	Most suitable job
	loves being outdoors hard worker likes to use hands doesn't mind taking orders	landscape architect
Lilia	loves working with people likes to help people not good with numbers works hard learns quickly	receptionist
Morteza	engineering skills good at technical things knows a lot about computers prefers to work alone	computer technician
Hilda	well-organized detail-oriented good with numbers creative	accountant

I Make a list of your skills and interests on a piece of paper. What are some jobs that you think you might enjoy and be good at? List at least three jobs. Then, list the characteristics you have that would make you good for each job.

Looking for a job

GOAL ➤ **Conduct a job search**

A What is the best way to look for a job? What are some different ways to look for a job? **Make a list.** (Answers will vary. Possible answers below)

> Ways to Look for a Job
>
> read newspaper 'want' ads
>
> search online
>
> go to a job placement agency
>
> ask friends

B What are some things you need to think about before you begin your job search? **Make a list.** (Answers will vary. Possible answers below.)

1. hours available to work
2. how far I can commute
3. what my skills are
4. the salary I want
5. if I want a temporary or permanent position
6. the benefits I want/need

C When you find a job opportunity in a newspaper or on the Internet, what information is usually included? What information do you usually need to ask about? Look at the list below. Put each piece of information in the correct column. (Answers may vary slightly.)

benefits	job location	required skills
contact information	job title	salary/pay
how to apply	possibility of overtime	vacation
job hours	required qualifications	

Information Found in the Ad	Information I Need to Ask About
contact information job title job location required skills job hours required qualifications how to apply	vacation benefits possibility of overtime salary/pay

AT-A-GLANCE PREP

Objective: Conduct a job search
Vocabulary: *benefits, overtime, required, qualifications, overtime, contact information, salary*

AGENDA
List ways to find a job.
Interpret job advertisements.
Interview your classmates.
Find out company information.
Create a company.

RESOURCES

Activity Bank: Unit 6, Lesson 2, Worksheet 1
Reading and Writing Challenge: Unit 6

Grammar Challenge 4: Unit 6, Challenge 2

■ 1.5 hour classes ■ 2.5 hour classes ■ 3⁺ hour classes

Warm-up and Review   5-10 mins. ■■■

Ask a student what he or she does for a living. Ask another student to make a statement about that person using an adjective clause. For example, (Jen) says: *I'm a seamstress. I sew clothes.* The other student says: *(Jen) is a seamstress who sews clothes.* If students have trouble with the adjective clauses, direct them to Unit 1, page 10 of the student book to review.

Introduction   10-15 mins. ■■■

Call on individual students whom you know have jobs and ask them how they found their jobs. State the objective: *Today we will learn how to conduct a job search and how to learn more about different companies.*

Presentation 1   15-20 mins. ■■■

 What is the best way to look for a job? What are some different ways to look for a job? Make a list.

Do this exercise as a class. Once you have a list on the board, ask for a show of hands of how many students found their jobs in each different way. Review percentages by having students calculate the percentage of students who found their job in each different way. If students have trouble calculating percentages, direct them to Unit 5, page 83 of the student book to review.

B What are some things you need to think about before you begin your job search? Make a list.

Have students work in small groups to make a list.

Practice 1   5-10 mins. ■■■

C When you find a job opportunity in a newspaper or on the Internet, what information is usually included? What information do you usually need to ask about? Look at the list below. Put each piece of information in the correct column.

Evaluation 1   5 mins. ■■■

Go over the answers as a class.

STANDARDS CORRELATIONS

CASAS: 4.1.3, 4.1.9 (See CASAS Competency List on pages 169–175.)
SCANS: **Information** Acquire and evaluate information, organize and maintain information, interpret and communicate information
Interpersonal Participate as a member of a team, teach others, exercise leadership, negotiate to arrive at a decision, work with cultural diversity
Systems Monitor and correct performance
Basic Skills Reading, writing, arithmetic, listening, speaking
Thinking Skills Creative thinking, decision making

Personal Qualities Responsibility, sociability, self-management
EFF: **Communication** Read with understanding, convey ideas in writing, speak so others can understand, listen actively
Decision Making Use math to solve problems and communicate, solve problems and make decisions
Interpersonal Cooperate with others
Lifelong Learning Take responsibility for learning, learn through research, use information and communication technologies (optional)

Presentation 2   15–20 mins.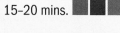

D Think about the job you have now. (Some of you may be students or homemakers. If you are, these are your jobs. If you are retired, think about your last job.) Fill in the chart with information about your job.

Go over this exercise as a class, giving students ideas when necessary. Have them fill in the charts with their own information.

Prepare students for Exercise E by helping them write the first few questions. Then, do an interview with a few volunteers to show students how to fill in the chart.

Practice 2   10-15 mins.

E Interview your classmates about their jobs. Write questions for each piece of information, then ask your classmates the questions and complete the chart.

Evaluation 2   10-15 mins.

Ask volunteers to share what they learned about their classmates.

LESSON 2

GOAL ➤ Conduct a job search

D Think about the job you have now. (Some of you may be students or homemakers. If you are, these are your jobs. If you are retired, think about your last job.) Fill in the chart with information about your job. (Answers will vary.)

	Information About Your Job
Job title	
Job location	
Job skills	
Qualifications	
Hours	
Salary	
Benefits	

E Interview your classmates about their jobs. Write questions for each piece of information, then ask your classmates the questions and complete the chart. (Answers will vary.)

Interview Questions	**Classmate 1**	**Classmate 2**	**Classmate 3**
Title: What is your job title?			
Location:			
Skills:			
Qualifications:			
Hours:			
Benefits:			

GOAL ➤ **Conduct a job search**

 F Imagine that you want to work for a company. It is important to find out some information about the company or business ahead of time. Fill in the chart.

(Answers will vary. Possible answers below.)

What kind of information is useful to know?	Where can you find this information?
1. the number of employees who work for the company	1. in the company brochure or the company's website
2. the kind of business it is	2. in the company brochure or the company's website
3. how long the company has been in business	3. in the company brochure or the company's website
4. if there are branch offices in other locations	4. in the company brochure or the company's website
5. what the company's mission is	5. in the company brochure or the company's website
6. how the company compares to its competition	6. an Internet search for the type of business

G With a group of students, create your own company. Answer the questions below.

(Answers will vary.)

1. What does your company make or do?

2. Where is your company located?

3. How many people work for your company?

4. What are some of the job titles of people who work at your company?

5. What characteristics do you want your employees to have?

6. What do you pay your employees?

7. What hours do your employees work?

8. What benefits do you give your employees?

Presentation 3

5-10 mins.

Ask students to come up with the names of some big companies that they have heard of. Make a list of their ideas on the board. Pick one of the companies and tell students to imagine they will be applying for a job at this company. Ask them what they might want to know about this company, such as the number of employees it has, the number of years it has been in business, and so on.

Practice 3

10-15 mins. ■

(Shorter classes can do Exercise F for homework.)

(F) Imagine that you want to work for a company. It is important to find out some information about the company or business ahead of time. Fill in the chart.

Go over the example with students. Have students work in small groups to complete the chart.

Evaluation 3

5-10 mins. ■

Have the groups share their ideas with the class.

Application

15-25 mins. ■■■

(G) With a group of students, create your own company. Answer the questions below.

Put students in groups and go over the list of questions before they get started.

When students have finished, have them share information about their companies with the class.

 Refer students to *Stand Out 4 Grammar Challenge*, Unit 6, Challenge 2 for an introduction to making generalizations.

Activity Bank

Lesson 2, Worksheet 1: Job Search

Objective: Write a resume
Academic Strategies: Active reading, writing a resume
Vocabulary: *certificate, degree, job responsibilities*

AGENDA
Read and answer questions.
Give your job history.
Read a resume.
Identify the parts of a resume.
Detail information for your resume.
Write a resume.

RESOURCES

Activity Bank: Unit 6, Lesson 3, Worksheets 1–2
Reading and Writing Challenge: Unit 6

Grammar Challenge 4: Unit 6, Challenge 3

 1.5 hour classes   2.5 hour classes   3⁺ hour classes

Warm-up and Review   5-10 mins.

In groups, have students make a list of ways to find a job and things to look for in a good company.

Introduction   5-10 mins.

Ask students what a *resume* is. Ask them what the difference is between a job application and a resume. Pass around sample resumes if you have them. State the objective: *Today we will read and study a resume, then we will write our own resume.*

Presentation 1   10-15 mins.

Have students look in their books at the picture of Ranjit. Ask them to guess what he does.

(A) Read about Ranjit.

Have students read the passage first by themselves. Then read it together as a class.

Practice 1   10-15 mins.

(B) Answer the questions about Ranjit.

Evaluation 1   5 mins.

Go over the answers as a class.

Presentation 2   5-10 mins.

Ask a few volunteer students to share information about different jobs they have had.

Practice 2   10-15 mins.

(Shorter classes can do Exercise C for homework.)

(C) Think about your job history. List your jobs starting with the most recent first.

Evaluation 2   10-15 mins.

Ask two volunteers to come to the board and list their job history.

STANDARDS CORRELATIONS

CASAS: 4.1.2 (See CASAS Competency List on pages 169–175.)
SCANS: **Information** Acquire and evaluate information, organize and maintain information, interpret and communicate information, use computers to process information (optional)
Interpersonal Participate as a member of a team, teach others, exercise leadership, negotiate to arrive at a decision, work with cultural diversity
Systems Monitor and correct performance
Technology Select technology, apply technology to a task, maintain and troubleshoot technology (optional)
Basic Skills Reading, writing, listening, speaking

Thinking Skills Creative thinking, decision making, seeing things in the mind's eye
Personal Qualities Responsibility, sociability, self-management
EFF: **Communication** Read with understanding, convey ideas in writing, speak so others can understand, listen actively
Decision Making Solve problems and make decisions, plan
Interpersonal Cooperate with others
Lifelong Learning Reflect and evaluate, use information and communication technologies (optional)

LESSON 3 **Resumes**

GOAL ➤ Write a resume

A Read about Ranjit.

Ranjit Ghosh is from India. He moved to the United States seven years ago. In India, he attended the National Computer School and received a certificate in computer repair. His first job was troubleshooting computer repairs for a financial company. After he moved to the United States, he started assembling computers and was able to use the skills he had learned in his course in India. Although he loved his job, he needed another job to pay the bills. In addition to assembling computers, now he also repairs computers in the evenings for another company. Ranjit is busy, but he is doing what he loves.

B Answer the questions about Ranjit.

1. Ranjit has had three jobs. List them with the most recent first.

   a. He repairs computers.

   b. He assembles computers.

   c. He was troubleshooting computer repairs in India.

2. Where did he go to school and what did he receive? He received a certificate in computer repair from the National Computer School in India.

3. Why does Ranjit have two jobs in the United States? He has two jobs to be able to earn enough money to pay the bills.

C Think about your job history. List your jobs starting with the most recent first.

1. (Answers will vary.)   4. _____

2. _____   5. _____

3. _____   6. _____

GOAL ➤ Write a resume

D Read Ranjit's resume.

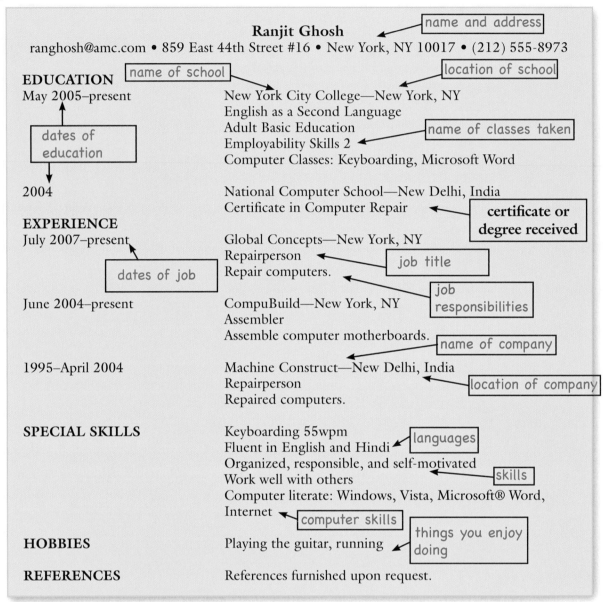

Ranjit Ghosh

ranghosh@amc.com • 859 East 44th Street #16 • New York, NY 10017 • (212) 555-8973

name and address

EDUCATION   name of school   location of school

May 2005–present   New York City College—New York, NY
                          English as a Second Language
dates of   Adult Basic Education   name of classes taken
education   Employability Skills 2
                          Computer Classes: Keyboarding, Microsoft Word

2004   National Computer School—New Delhi, India
                          Certificate in Computer Repair   certificate or degree received

EXPERIENCE
July 2007–present   Global Concepts—New York, NY
                          Repairperson   job title
dates of job   Repair computers.   job responsibilities

June 2004–present   CompuBuild—New York, NY
                          Assembler
                          Assemble computer motherboards.   name of company

1995–April 2004   Machine Construct—New Delhi, India
                          Repairperson   location of company
                          Repaired computers.

SPECIAL SKILLS   Keyboarding 55wpm
                          Fluent in English and Hindi   languages
                          Organized, responsible, and self-motivated
                          Work well with others   skills
                          Computer literate: Windows, Vista, Microsoft® Word,
                          Internet   computer skills

HOBBIES   Playing the guitar, running   things you enjoy doing

REFERENCES   References furnished upon request.

E Can you identify the parts of a resume? Use the words below to label Ranjit's resume.

certificate or degree received	job title	name of company
computer skills	languages	name of school
dates of education	location of company	names of classes taken
dates of job	location of school	skills
job responsibilities	name and address	things you enjoy doing

Presentation 3   5–10 mins. ■■■

D Read Ranjit's resume.

E Can you identify the parts of a resume? Use the words below to label Ranjit's resume.

Go over the different parts of Ranjit's resume as a class. Check students' comprehension by asking them information questions about the resume.

Practice 3   10–15 mins.

F Look at the words in the box in Exercise E. Why is it important to put each of the pieces of information on your resume? Discuss the reasons with a group and make notes about each item.

Evaluation 3   5–10 mins. ■

Have representatives from each group share why they think each part of the resume is important.

Application   20–30 mins. ■■■

G Think about your own resume. Fill in your information.

Walk around the classroom and help students complete the information.

H Using the information you wrote in Exercise G, write your resume on a piece of paper.

If possible, have students type their resumes on a computer and print it out.

 Refer students to *Stand Out 4 Grammar Challenge*, Unit 6, Challenge 3 for an introduction to the past perfect tense forms.

Activity Bank

Lesson 3, Worksheet 1: Write a Resume

Lesson 3, Worksheet 2: Resume

GOAL ➤ Write a resume

F Look at the words in the box in Exercise E. Why is it important to put each of the pieces of information on your resume? Discuss the reasons with a group and make notes about each item.

G Think about your own resume. Fill in your information. (Answers will vary.)

1. Schools you have attended: _____

_____

_____

2. Classes you have taken: _____

_____

_____

3. Certificates or degrees you have received: _____

_____

4. Awards you have received: _____

_____

5. Names and locations of companies you have worked for: _____

_____

_____

6. Job titles and responsibilities you have had: _____

_____

_____

7. Special characteristics you have: _____

_____

_____

8. Things you enjoy doing: _____

_____

_____

H Using the information you wrote in Exercise G, write your resume on a piece of paper.

Cover letters

GOAL ➤ **Write a cover letter**

A What is the purpose of a cover letter? Read the cover letter that Ranjit sent in with his resume.

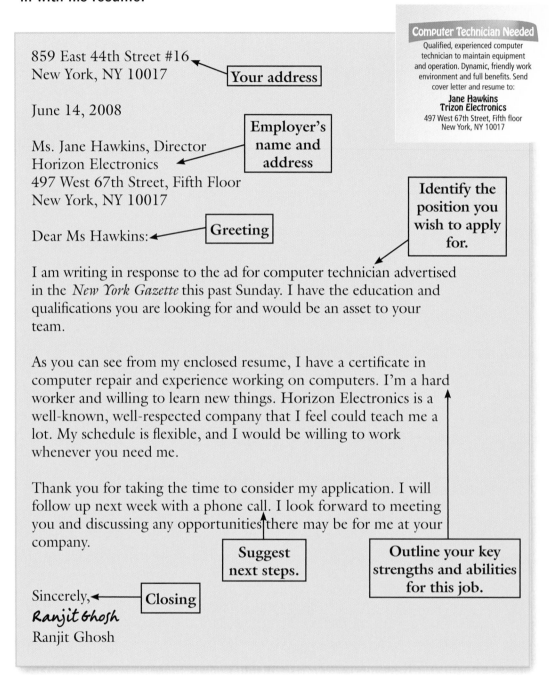

859 East 44th Street #16 — **Your address**
New York, NY 10017

June 14, 2008

Ms. Jane Hawkins, Director — **Employer's name and address**
Horizon Electronics
497 West 67th Street, Fifth Floor
New York, NY 10017

Dear Ms Hawkins: — **Greeting**

Identify the position you wish to apply for.

I am writing in response to the ad for computer technician advertised in the *New York Gazette* this past Sunday. I have the education and qualifications you are looking for and would be an asset to your team.

As you can see from my enclosed resume, I have a certificate in computer repair and experience working on computers. I'm a hard worker and willing to learn new things. Horizon Electronics is a well-known, well-respected company that I feel could teach me a lot. My schedule is flexible, and I would be willing to work whenever you need me.

Thank you for taking the time to consider my application. I will follow up next week with a phone call. I look forward to meeting you and discussing any opportunities there may be for me at your company.

Suggest next steps.

Outline your key strengths and abilities for this job.

Sincerely, — **Closing**
Ranjit Ghosh
Ranjit Ghosh

Computer Technician Needed
Qualified, experienced computer technician to maintain equipment and operation. Dynamic, friendly work environment and full benefits. Send cover letter and resume to:
Jane Hawkins
Trizon Electronics
497 West 67th Street, Fifth floor
New York, NY 10017

AGENDA

Study a cover letter.
Choose a job that you would like to have.
Write a cover letter.

Objective: Write a cover letter
Academic Strategies: Active reading, writing a cover letter
Vocabulary: *cover letter, enclosed, asset, key strengths, identify*

RESOURCES

Activity Bank: Unit 6, Lesson 4, Worksheet 1   **Grammar Challenge 4:** Unit 6, Challenge 4
Reading and Writing Challenge: Unit 6

■ 1.5 hour classes   ■ 2.5 hour classes   ■ 3+ hour classes

Warm-up and Review   5–10 mins.   ■■■

Ask students to share their resumes that they wrote in Lesson 3 with the person sitting next to them.

Introduction   5–10 mins.   ■■■

Write the term *cover letter* on the board. Ask if students know what a cover letter is and what its purpose is. Ask if any of the students have written cover letters before. State the objective: *Today we will write a cover letter to accompany our resume.*

Presentation 1   10–15 mins.   ■■■

Have students look at the cover letter in their books. Ask them some basic comprehension questions, such as: *Who wrote the letter? Whom did he write the letter to? When did he write the letter? Where is Horizon Electronics located?*

Practice 1   10–15 mins.   ■■■

 What is the purpose of a cover letter? Read the cover letter that Ranjit sent in with his resume.

Have students read the letter silently and then discuss it as a class.

Evaluation 1   5 mins.   ■■■

Answer any questions students might have about the cover letter. Ask students what things Ranjit said in his letter that are important.

STANDARDS CORRELATIONS

CASAS: 4.1.2 (See CASAS Competency List on pages 169–175.)
SCANS: **Information** Acquire and evaluate information, organize and maintain information, interpret and communicate information, use computers to process information (optional)
Interpersonal Participate as a member of a team, teach others, exercise leadership, work with cultural diversity
Systems Monitor and correct performance
Technology (optional) Select technology, apply technology to a task, maintain and troubleshoot technology

Basic Skills Reading, writing, listening, speaking
Thinking Skills Creative thinking, decision making, seeing things in the mind's eye
Personal Qualities Responsibility, sociability, self-management
EFF: **Communication** Read with understanding, convey ideas in writing, speak so others can understand, observe critically
Decision Making Solve problems and make decisions, plan
Lifelong Learning Reflect and evaluate, use information and communication technologies (optional)

Presentation 2   5–10 mins. ■■■

Ask volunteers to read each of the job descriptions out loud.

Practice 2   15–20 mins. ■■

B Read the following job descriptions.

Have students work in small groups to talk about each of the jobs. After analyzing all of the job descriptions, students should choose a job that they would like to apply for.

C Choose one job that you would like to apply for from the descriptions in Exercise B. Tell your partner why you would be good for this job.

Evaluation 2   10–15 mins. ■■

Have students report their choices to the class. Ask them why they chose the job they did. Ask them if they think they have the necessary skills for that job.

B Read the following job descriptions.

Company Name: Healthy Living (61835 Valley Road, Grand Rapids, MI 96837)
Company Description: A company that produces and sells vitamins.
Job Title: Warehouse Supervisor
Job Description: In charge of packaging orders in the warehouse. Must be able to supervise 20 employees. No experience with vitamins necessary, but warehouse experience would be helpful.

Company Name: Medical Valley Hospital (875 Washington Ave, Portland, OR 79468)
Job Title: Nurse's Aide
Job Description: Help the RNs take care of the patients. Fill out basic paperwork regarding patients, be able to take vital signs. No experience necessary—will train. Looking for someone who is friendly, patient, and doesn't mind working with sick people.

Company Name: Auto Land (75436 Harbor Blvd., Costa Mesa, CA 92627)
Company Description: Used car lot
Job Title: Salesperson
Job Description: Selling cars. Must be good with people and outgoing. No sales experience necessary.

Company Name: Choicemart (87645 Santa Maria, Houston, TX 77042)
Job Title: Customer Service
Job Description: Handling customer complaints, helping customer fill out proper paperwork to file complaint, entering the complaint information into the computer and setting up meetings to discuss the complaints with the proper department. Must have good oral and written communication skills. Must be good with people and have the ability to handle angry customers. Basic computer skills helpful.

Company Name: Villa Italia (756 Fifth Ave, New York, NY 06458)
Job Title: Food Server
Job Description: Serve food to customers. Must have restaurant experience, but serving experience not necessary. Will train.

C Choose one job that you would like to apply for from the descriptions in Exercise B. Tell your partner why you would be good for this job.

D Imagine that you are applying for the job that you chose in Exercise C. Write a cover letter to the company. (Answers will vary.)

_____

_____

_____

_____

_____

_____

_____

_____ ,

_____

_____

_____

_____

_____

_____

_____

_____

_____

Application 20-40 mins. ■■■

D Imagine that you are applying for the job you chose in Exercise C. Write a cover letter to the company.

Have students begin working on the application activity, Exercise D. Longer classes will have more time to peer-edit and perfect their letters in class. Shorter classes may have to do some work at home. If possible, have students type their resumes on a computer and print it out.

Refer students to *Stand Out 4 Grammar Challenge*, Unit 6, Challenge 4 for more practice with past perfect tense uses.

Activity Bank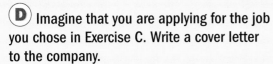

Lesson 4, Worksheet 1: Write a Cover Letter

Instructor's Notes

Objective: Prepare for a job interview
Vocabulary: *strength, weakness, conflict, benefit, eye contact, voice level, facial expressions, posture, willingness, self-evaluate, impression, mock, criteria*

AGENDA

Practice answering interview questions.
Think about important interview behavior.
Practice interviewing.
Complete a mock evaluation.

RESOURCES

Activity Bank: Unit 6, Lesson 5, Worksheet 1, and Extension
Reading and Writing Challenge: Unit 6

Grammar Challenge 4: Unit 6, Challenge 5; Extension Challenges 1-2

■ 1.5 hour classes   ■ 2.5 hour classes   ■ 3⁺ hour classes

Warm-up and Review   5-10 mins.

Ask some students to read their cover letters out loud.

Introduction   5 mins.

Tell students that they have now found the job they want, written their resume and cover letter, and sent them in. Ask students: *What's the next step?* State the objective: *Today we will practice interviewing for a job.*

Presentation 1   5-10 mins.

(A) Now that you have written your resume and your cover letter, it's time to get ready for the interview! The best way to prepare for an interview is to practice.

Have a brief discussion with students about interviewing for jobs. Ask how many of them have practiced at home before they have gone for an actual interview. Discuss the importance of practicing.

Practice 1   15-25 mins.

Look at the sample interview questions. How would you answer them? Discuss each question

with a group, then write your answers on a piece of paper.

Have each student write out his or her own answers.

Evaluation 1   10-15 mins.

Go over some of the questions and ask volunteers to tell the class how they would answer them. Discuss what makes a good answer and what makes a poor one.

Presentation 2   5-10 mins.

Have a volunteer ask you some of the interview questions. Give responses that you would give in a real interview.

Practice 2   10-15 mins.

(B) With a partner, practice asking and answering the interview questions. Since you are just practicing, it is OK to look at the answers you wrote in Exercise A.

Evaluation 2   10-15 mins.

Observe students as they practice the interview questions.

STANDARDS CORRELATIONS

CASAS: 4.1.5, 4.1.7 (See CASAS Competency List on pages 169–175.)
SCANS: **Information** Organize and maintain information, interpret and communicate information
Interpersonal Participate as a member of a team, teach others, exercise leadership, work with cultural diversity
Systems Monitor and correct performance
Basic Skills Reading, writing, listening, speaking

Thinking Skills Creative thinking, decision making
Personal Qualities Responsibility, sociability, self-management
EFF: **Communication** Read with understanding, convey ideas in writing, speak so others can understand, listen actively, observe critically
Decision Making Solve problems and make decisions, plan
Interpersonal Guide others, advocate and influence, cooperate with others
Lifelong Learning Take responsibility for learning, reflect and evaluate

Interviewing

GOAL ➤ **Prepare for a job interview**

 A Now that you have written your resume and your cover letter, it's time to get ready for the interview! The best way to prepare for an interview is to practice.

Look at the sample interview questions below. How would you answer them? Discuss each question with a group, then write your answers on a piece of paper.

(Answers will vary.)

1. Tell me about yourself.

2. Why are you applying for this job?

3. Why do you think you would be good at this job?

4. What is your greatest strength?

5. What is your greatest weakness?

6. Do you prefer to work alone or with other people?

7. Why did you leave your last job?

8. What did you do at your last job?

9. What did you like most about your last job?

10. Describe a situation where you had a conflict with another employee. How did you solve it?

11. What special skills do you have that would benefit our company?

12. What characteristics do you have that would make you a good employee?

13. Do you have any questions?

 B With a partner, practice asking and answering the interview questions. Since you are just practicing, it is OK to look at the answers you wrote in Exercise A.

Vocabulary   Grammar
Life Skills
Academic   Pronunciation

C In addition to your answers, job interviewers are also looking at other aspects of your interview. Read the list below. How would you rate yourself for each? (Answers will vary.)

Handshake	○ Fair	○ Medium	○ Excellent
Appearance	○ Fair	○ Medium	○ Excellent
Eye contact with interviewer	○ Fair	○ Medium	○ Excellent
Voice level (volume)	○ Fair	○ Medium	○ Excellent
Facial expressions	○ Fair	○ Medium	○ Excellent
Posture / body position	○ Fair	○ Medium	○ Excellent
Self-confidence / comfort level	○ Fair	○ Medium	○ Excellent
Willingness to volunteer information	○ Fair	○ Medium	○ Excellent
Appropriateness of responses to questions	○ Fair	○ Medium	○ Excellent
Effectiveness in describing strengths, skills, and abilities	○ Fair	○ Medium	○ Excellent

D Looking at the list above, which two aspects are your strongest? (Answers will vary.)

1. _____

2. _____

E Which two aspects do you need to work on the most? (Answers will vary.)

1. _____

2. _____

F Now it's time to practice. You will be interviewing for the job that you wrote your cover letter for. Work with a partner. Take turns being the interviewer and the interviewee.

Student A: Interviewer
Ask your partner at least ten of the questions on page 113. When the interview is over, fill out the Mock Interview Evaluation Form on page 115 in you partner's book.

Student B: Interviewee
Do your best to answer the questions without looking at your notes and try to do well on each of the aspects listed in Exercise C.

Presentation 3   15-20 mins. ■■■

(C) In addition to your answers, job interviewers are also looking at other aspects of your interview. Read the list below. How would you rate yourself for each?

Go through the list with students, explaining each item and how students should rate themselves. For example, demonstrate an excellent handshake, a medium handshake, and a fair handshake. Have students practice each item with you so they understand what it means to rate as excellent.

Practice 3   5-10 mins. ■

(Shorter classes can do these exercises for homework.)

(D) Looking at the list above, which two aspects are your strongest?

(E) Which two aspects do you need to work on the most?

Ask students to complete the blanks for themselves.

Evaluation 3   5-10 mins. ■

Ask some volunteers to say which aspects they are best at and which ones they need to work on the most.

Application   10-20 mins. ■■■

(F) Now it's time to practice. You will be interviewing for the job that you wrote your cover letter for. Work with a partner. Take turns being the interviewer and the interviewee.

Explain each role to students and what they are supposed to do. If they need more explanation, ask a volunteer to help demonstrate the activity with you in front of the class.

Application *(continued)*   10-20 mins. ■■■■

G Fill out the mock evaluation form about your partner.

Explain this form to students and show them how to fill it out. When students have finished, they should show their partners the mock evaluation forms, and answer any questions that their partner may have about the results.

Activity Bank

Lesson 5, Worksheet 1: Interviews

Lesson 5, Extension: Thank-You Letter

 Refer students to *Stand Out 4 Grammar Challenge*, Unit 6, Challenge 5 for practice using the past perfect tense with the simple past tense.

 Refer students to *Stand Out 4 Grammar Challenge*, Unit 6, Extension Challenges 1-2 for practice with non-restrictive adjective clauses and restrictive versus non-restrictive adjective clauses.

Instructor's Notes

GOAL ➤ **Prepare for a job interview**

G Fill out the mock evaluation form about your partner.
(Answers will vary.)

MOCK INTERVIEW EVALUATION FORM

Name of applicant: _____

Name of interviewer: _____

Date of interview: _____

Job applied for: _____

Rate the applicant on each of the following questions by writing *excellent*, *good*, or *fair*.

What kind of impression did this person make? _____
Did the person give answers that would make an employer want to hire him or her?

_____

Did the person have a friendly, enthusiastic, and positive attitude?

_____

Rate the applicant on the criteria below on a scale of 1 to 5.
(1 = poor, 5 = excellent)

CRITERIA   **Rating**

What suggestions can you give this person for how to make a better impression?

_____

	1	2	3	4	5
1. Handshake	___	___	___	___	___
2. Appearance	___	___	___	___	___
3. Eye contact with interviewer	___	___	___	___	___
4. Voice level (volume)	___	___	___	___	___
5. Facial expressions	___	___	___	___	___
6. Posture / body position	___	___	___	___	___
7. Self-confidence / comfort level	___	___	___	___	___
8. Willingness to volunteer information	___	___	___	___	___
9. Appropriateness of responses to questions	___	___	___	___	___
10. Effectiveness in describing strengths, skills, and abilities	___	___	___	___	___
11. Overall evaluation	___	___	___	___	___

Additional comments: _____

_____

_____

Review

A Write job responsibilities for the job titles. (Lesson 1)

Job Title	Job Responsibilities
administrative assistant	writes correspondence, schedules appointments
cashier	handles customer payment for goods
delivery person	drives truck, makes deliveries
dental assistant	assists dentist, cleans teeth
electrician	connects/fixes electricity in houses, offices
homemaker	cooks meals, takes care of children and house
receptionist	answers telephones, takes messages, greets people
salesperson	sells merchandise to customers

B List six characteristics you think an employer is looking for in an employee. (Lesson 1)
(Answers will vary. Possible answers below.)

1. well-organized
2. hardworking
3. a quick learner
4. efficient
5. dependable
6. works well under pressure

C Imagine you are looking for a job. Complete the table about your ideal job. (Lesson 2)
(Answers will vary.)

Information About Your Ideal Job	
Job title	
Job location	
Job skills	
Qualifications	
Hours	
Salary	
Benefits	

AT-A-GLANCE PREP

Objectives: All Unit 6 objectives
Grammar: All Unit 6 grammar
Academic Strategy: Reviewing
Vocabulary: All Unit 6 vocabulary

RESOURCES

Activity Bank: Unit 6, Lessons 1–5
Reading and Writing Challenge: Unit 6

Grammar Challenge: Unit 6, Challenges 1–5; Extension Challenges 1-2

■ 1.5 hour classes   ■ 2.5 hour classes   ■ 3⁺ hour classes

AGENDA

Unit objectives.
Review exercises.
My Dictionary.
Learner Log.

Warm-up and Review   5-10 mins. ■■■

In groups, have students come up with a list of things they should do to prepare for a job interview.

Introduction   5-10 mins. ■■■

Ask students to try to recall (in general) all the goals of this unit without looking at their books. Then remind them which goals they omitted, if any. (Unit goals: Identify skills and characteristics, conduct a job search, write a resume, write a cover letter, and prepare for a job interview.) Write all the objectives on the board from Unit 6. Show students the first page of the unit and mention the five objectives. State the objective: *Today we will be reviewing everything we have learned in this unit.*

Presentation 1   10-15 mins. ■■■

This presentation will cover the first three pages of the review. Quickly go to the first page of each lesson. Discuss the objective of each one. Ask simple questions to remind students of what they have learned.

Note: Since there is little presentation in the review, you can assign the review exercises that don't involve pair work or group work for homework and go over them in class the following day.

Practice 1   20-25 mins. ■■■

Note: There are two ways to do the review:
(1) Go through the exercises one at a time and, as students complete each one, go over the answers.
(2) Briefly go through the instructions of each exercise, allow students to complete all of the exercises at once, and then go over the answers. Stop and evaluate whenever it is appropriate for the class. (*See Evaluation 1 on pg. 118a.*)

Ⓐ Write job responsibilities for the job titles. (Lesson 1)

Ⓑ List six characteristics you think an employer is looking for in an employee. (Lesson 1)

Ⓒ Imagine you are looking for a job. Complete the table about your ideal job. (Lesson 2)

STANDARDS CORRELATIONS

CASAS: 7.2.1 (See CASAS Competency List on pages 169–175.)
SCANS: **Resources** Allocate time
Information Acquire and evaluate information
Interpersonal Participate as a member of a team, teach others, negotiate to arrive at a decision, work with cultural diversity
Systems Monitor and correct performance
Basic Skills Reading, writing, listening, speaking
Thinking Skills Creative thinking, decision making, problem solving, seeing things in the mind's eye

Personal Qualities Responsibility, sociability, self-management
EFF: **Communication** Convey ideas in writing, speak so others can understand, listen actively, observe critically
Decision Making Solve problems and make decisions
Interpersonal Guide others, cooperate with others
Lifelong Learning Take responsibility for learning, reflect and evaluate, learn through research

---

Practice 1 *(continued)*   25–30 mins.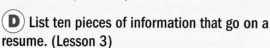

D List ten pieces of information that go on a resume. (Lesson 3)

E How would you answer these interview questions? Write your answers below. (Lesson 5)

Teaching Tip

Recycling/Review

The review process and the project that follows are part of the recycling/review process. Students at this level often need to be reintroduced to concepts to solidify what they have learned. Many concepts are learned and forgotten while learning other new concepts. This is because students learn but are not necessarily ready to acquire language concepts.

Therefore, it becomes very important to review and to show students how to review on their own. It is also important to recycle the new concepts in different contexts.

Instructor's Notes

D List ten pieces of information that go on a resume. (Lesson 3) (Answers may vary slightly.) Possible answers below.)

1. name
2. address/phone/email address
3. education (name of school and location, dates of education)
4. degree or certificate received
5. classes taken
6. work experience (name of employer, dates of employment, job title)
7. work responsibilities
8. language skills
9. computer skills
10. personal interests

E How would you answer these interview questions? Write your answers below. (Lesson 5)

1. What is your greatest strength? (Answers will vary.)

2. What is your greatest weakness?

3. What special skills do you have that would benefit our company?

4. What characteristics do you have that would make you a good employee?

5. What did you like most about your last job?

Review

F If you want to get a job, what are all the things you need to do from beginning to end? List them below. (Lessons 2–5) (Answers may vary slightly. Possible answers below.)

1. Write a resume.
2. Look for available positions.
3. Write a cover letter.
4. Apply for the job.
5. Prepare for the interview.
6. Interview.

G In this unit, you learned many things about getting a job. With a group, discuss the following. Complete the sentences to explain why each one is important. Share your answers with the class. (Lessons 1–5) (Answers will vary.)

1. Knowing what my skills are is important because _____

_____.

2. Finding information about the job I want is important because _____

_____.

3. Finding information about the company I am applying to is important because

_____

_____.

4. Writing a resume is important because _____

_____.

5. Writing a cover letter is important because _____

_____.

6. Practicing interviewing is important because _____

_____.

Practice 1 *(continued)*   25-30 mins.

(F) If you want to get a job, what are all the things you need to do from beginning to end? List them below. (Lessons 2–5)

(G) In this unit, you learned many things about getting a job. With a group, discuss the following. Complete the sentences to explain why each one is important. Share your answers with the class. (Lessons 1–5)

Evaluation 1   45-60 mins.

Go around the classroom and check on students' progress. Help individuals when needed. If you see consistent errors among several students, interrupt the class and give a mini-lesson or review to help students feel comfortable with the concept.

Presentation 2

5-10 mins.

My Dictionary

Ask students to brainstorm new vocabulary they learned in this unit. Have them do this without looking in their books.

Practice 2

15-20 mins.

(Shorter classes can do these exercises for homework.)

Take out your dictionary and add a section about yourself.

Make two lists—one for your skills and one for your characteristics. Write down anything you can do and anything that describes you. If you need to add definitions for any of the words, put them in the same section.

Whenever you are applying for a job or applying for school, you can pull out these lists as a reference.

Evaluation 2

5-10 mins.

Walk around the classroom and help students as needed.

Presentation 3

5-10 mins.

Learner Log

In this unit, you learned many things about getting hired. How comfortable do you feel doing each of the skills listed below? Rate your comfort level on a scale of 1 to 4.

Practice 3

5-10 mins.

Have students complete the Learner Log.

Evaluation 3

5-10 mins.

Walk around the classroom and help students as needed.

Application

5-10 mins.

Go over the reflection statements with students and have them complete the answers by themselves.

Assessment (optional)

Use the Stand Out 4 Assessment CD-ROM with *ExamView®* to create a post-test for Unit 6.

My Dictionary

Take out your dictionary and add a section about yourself.

Make two lists—one for your skills and one for your characteristics. Write down anything you can do and anything that describes you. If you need to add definitions for any of the words, put them in the same section.

Whenever you are applying for a job or applying for school, you can pull out these lists as a reference.
(Answers will vary.)

Learner Log

In this unit, you learned many things about getting hired. How comfortable do you feel doing each of the skills listed below? Rate your comfort level on a scale of 1 to 4.
(Answers will vary.)

1 = Need more practice   **2** = OK   **3** = Good   **4** = Great!

Life Skill	Comfort Level				Page
I can identify the characteristics of a good employee.	4	3	2	1	_____
I can identify job titles and skills.	4	3	2	1	_____
I can conduct a job search.	4	3	2	1	_____
I can write a resume.	4	3	2	1	_____
I can write a cover letter.	4	3	2	1	_____
I can prepare for a job interview.	4	3	2	1	_____
I can interview for a job.	4	3	2	1	_____

If you circled 1 or 2, write down the page number where you can review this skill.

Reflection

1. I learned _____.

2. I would like to find out more about _____.

3. I am still confused about _____.

Team Project

Create a job application portfolio.

Part 1: By yourself, you will create a job application portfolio, which will contain all the information you need to apply for a job and go to a practice interview.

1. List all of the information you want to include in your portfolio.

2. Create the different parts of your portfolio.

- All portfolios must include the following: a resume, a cover letter, and sample interview questions and answers.
- Other items that might be included in the portfolios: certificates, awards, transcripts, performance reviews, letters of recommendation.

Create a job advertisement and conduct interviews.

Part 2: With a team, you will write a brief job advertisement and interview other students for that job.

1. Form a team with four students. Choose positions for each member of your team.

POSITION	JOB DESCRIPTION	STUDENT NAME
Student 1: Company Owner	See that everyone speaks English and participates.	
Student 2: Department Supervisor	Write job advertisement and interview questions.	
Student 3: Company President	Ask interview questions.	
Student 4: Human Resources Director	Create evaluation form.	

2. Decide what company you work for and for what position you are hiring. Write a job advertisement for the position.

3. Prepare a list of interview questions that you will ask the applicants.

4. Decide what you are looking for in an employee and create an evaluation form.

5. Once your classmates have seen all of the job advertisements and decided on a job to apply for, interview and evaluate the applicants.

6. Choose the best person for the job.

Create a job application portfolio. Create a job advertisement and conduct interviews.

Each student will create his or her own job application portfolio. Each team will create a company and come up with an open position to hire for. The company will write questions, interview prospective employees, and hire the best candidate.

The team project is the final application for the unit. It gives students a chance to show that they have mastered all of the Unit 6 objectives.

Note: Shorter classes can extend this project over two class meetings.

15-25 mins.

Part 1: By yourself, you will create a job application portfolio, which will contain all the information you need to apply for a job and go to a practice interview.

Stage 1

List all of the information you want to include in your portfolio.

Stage 2

Create the different parts of your portfolio.

Explain what is needed in the portfolios by going over the lists with the class. If necessary, this can be set for homework before the team project begins.

Optional Computer Activity: Students may want to use a computer to write their resumes and cover letters.

Part 2: With a team, you will write a brief job advertisement and interview other students for that job.

Stage 1   5-10 mins.

Form a team with four students. Choose positions for each member of your team.

Have students decide who will lead each step as described on the student page. Provide well-defined directions on the board for how teams should proceed. Explain that all the students do every step as a team. Teams shouldn't go to the next stage until the previous one is complete.

Stage 2   15-25 mins.

Decide what company you work for and for what position you are hiring. Write a job advertisement for the position.

Have each team report to the class about its company and the position the company is hiring for. Ask a volunteer to put the ads together on one page to be distributed to the class.

Stage 3   10-15 mins.

Prepare a list of interview questions that you will ask the applicants.

Stage 4   15-20 mins.

Decide what you are looking for in an employee and create an evaluation form.

Stage 5   20-25 mins.

Once your classmates have seen all of the job advertisements and decided on a job to apply for, interview and evaluate the applicants.

This will take some careful planning to organize. Help teams prepare sign-up sheets with time slots for applicants to fill in. Tell each student he or she must interview with at least two companies.

Stage 6   15-20 mins.

Choose the best person for the job.

Have each team report to the class whom they have chosen to hire.

STANDARDS CORRELATIONS

CASAS: 4.8.1, 4.8.5, 4.8.6. (See CASAS Competency List on pages 169–175.)
SCANS: **Resources** Allocate time
Information Acquire and evaluate information, organize and maintain information, interpret and communicate information, use computers to process information
Systems Understand systems, improve and design systems
Technology (optional) Select technology, apply technology to exercise
Basic Skills Reading, writing, listening, speaking
Thinking Skills Creative thinking, decision making, problem solving, seeing things in the mind's eye, reasoning

Personal Qualities Responsibility, self-esteem, self-management, integrity/honesty
EFF: **Communication** Read with understanding, convey ideas in writing, speak so others can understand, listen actively, observe critically
Decision Making Solve problems and make decisions, plan
Interpersonal Guide others, resolve conflict and negotiate, advocate and influence, cooperate with others
Lifelong Learning Take responsibility for learning, reflect and evaluate, learn through research, use information and communication technologies (optional)

AT-A-GLANCE PREP

Objective: Identify appropriate and inappropriate
 workplace behavior
Grammar: Tag questions
Academic Strategy: Focused listening
Pronunciation: Rising and falling intonation
Vocabulary: *appropriate, inappropriate*

RESOURCES

Activity Bank: Unit 7, Lesson 1, Worksheets 1–3
Reading and Writing Challenge: Unit 7

Grammar Challenge 4: Unit 7, Challenge 1
Audio: CD 1, Track 24

■ 1.5 hour classes   ■ 2.5 hour classes   ■ 3⁺ hour classes

AGENDA

Discuss workplace behavior.
Classify behavior as appropriate
 or inappropriate.
Use tag questions correctly.

Preassessment *(optional)*   ■ ■ ■

Use the Stand Out 4 Assessment CD-ROM with
Exam*View*® to create a pretest for Unit 7.

Warm-up and Review   5 mins. ■ ■ ■

Have students look at the picture in their books
on page 121. Ask them what is wrong with this
picture, if anything.

Introduction   5–10 mins. ■ ■ ■

Write the words *appropriate* and *inappropriate*
on the board. See if students know what
these words mean. Ask them if the picture
shows appropriate or inappropriate workplace
behavior. State the objective: *Today we
will identify appropriate and inappropriate
workplace behavior.*

Presentation 1   5 mins. ■ ■ ■

Have students look at the situations listed in
Exercise A. Go over each one and make sure
students understand them.

Practice 1   10–15 mins. ■ ■ ■

 Imagine that you are at work. Think carefully
about each action below and decide if it is
appropriate (A) or inappropriate (I) workplace
behavior. Write *A* or *I* next to each statement.

Have students work individually to complete the
exercise. They should not share their decisions
with other students at this point.

 Discuss your answers with a group and think
of three more examples of both appropriate and
inappropriate workplace behavior. Share your
ideas with the class.

Have students discuss each situation in small
groups.

Evaluation 1   5 mins.

Have groups share their responses with the
class. Ask if any group had disagreements
among members about whether a situation
was appropriate or inappropriate.

STANDARDS CORRELATIONS

CASAS: 4.4.1 (See CASAS Competency List on pages 169–175.)
SCANS: **Information** Acquire and evaluate information, organize and
maintain information, interpret and communicate information
Interpersonal Participate as a member of a team, teach others, exercise
leadership, negotiate to arrive at a decision, work with cultural diversity
Systems Monitor and correct performance
Basic Skills Reading, writing, listening, speaking

Thinking Skills Creative thinking, decision making
Personal Qualities Responsibility, sociability, self-management
EFF: **Communication** Read with understanding, convey ideas in writing,
speak so others can understand, listen actively, observe critically
Decision Making Solve problems and make decisions
Interpersonal Advocate and influence, cooperate with others
Lifelong Learning Reflect and evaluate

UNIT **7**

On the Job

GOALS

➤ Identify appropriate and inappropriate workplace behavior

➤ Identify workplace actions

➤ Communicate problems to a supervisor

➤ Make ethical decisions

➤ Ask for a raise

LESSON 1

She's late, isn't she?

GOAL ➤ Identify appropriate and inappropriate workplace behavior

 Imagine that you are at work. Think carefully about each action below and decide if it is appropriate (A) or inappropriate (I) workplace behavior. Write *A* or *I* next to each statement.

<u>A</u> Ask a coworker for help.

<u>A</u> Ask for a raise.

<u>A</u> Ask your supervisor a question.

<u>A</u> Call in sick (when you are really sick).

<u>I</u> Send personal e-mails.

<u>I</u> Sit on your desk.

<u>A</u> Come back from break early.

<u>I</u> Smoke while you're working.

<u>I</u> Talk to a friend on the phone.

<u>I</u> Do Internet research for your child's school project.

<u>I</u> Take products home for your friends and family.

<u>A</u> Talk to your boss about a problem with a coworker.

<u>I</u> Arrive a few minutes late.

<u>A</u> Tell your boss you don't understand something he or she said.

 Discuss your answers with a group and think of three more examples of both appropriate and inappropriate workplace behavior. Share your ideas with the class.

 C Compare these two questions. Which is a tag question?

"Is she late for work?"

I have no idea, but I want to know.

"She's late for work again, isn't she?"

I'm not 100% sure, but I think this is true.

 D Read the questions and answers below about the tag question.

Tag question: She's late for work again, isn't she?

Q: Why is this called a tag question?
A: Because it's a question tagged onto the end of a sentence.

Q: When do we use tag questions?
A: When we are almost sure something is true, but we want to check and be 100% sure.

Q: When I'm asking a tag question, how do I know if the tag should be positive or negative?
A: If the sentence is positive, the tag is negative. If the sentence is negative, the tag is positive.

Q: What verb tense do I use in the tag?
A: Use the same verb tense in the tag that is used in the beginning of the statement.

E Study the chart with your teacher.

Tag Questions			
Positive statement	**Tag**	**Negative statement**	**Tag**
She works,	doesn't she?	She doesn't work,	does she?
She is working,	isn't she?	She isn't working,	is she?
She worked,	didn't she?	She didn't work,	did she?
She will work,	won't she?	She won't work,	will she?
She is going to work,	isn't she?	She isn't going to work,	is she?
She has worked,	hasn't she?	She hasn't worked,	has she?
She had worked,	hadn't she?	She hadn't worked,	had she?

Presentation 2   10–15 mins.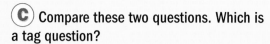

C Compare these two questions. Which is a tag question?

Have students look in their books at the two questions and the thought bubbles coming from each. Ask students how the two questions differ.

D Read the questions and answers below about the tag question.

First, have students read the questions and answers silently to themselves. Then go through the rules as a class, calling on two students to read each question-and-answer exchange.

E Study the chart with your teacher.

Using the examples in the chart, go back over the rules in Exercise D. To check students' comprehension, have students close their books. Read the first part of the tag question to students and see if they can come up with the appropriate tag.

Pronunciation

Intonation

In tag questions, a rising intonation often indicates that you are unsure of the answer. A falling intonation indicates that you are almost sure of the answer.

You work in the library, don't you? ↑*unsure of the answer*

You work in the library, don't you? ↓*almost sure of the answer*

Read the examples below to students. Read each example both ways so they can hear the difference. As you read each one, ask students if your voice went up or down at the end. Discuss the two possible meanings.

1. We called them, didn't we?
2. She is an engineer, isn't she?
3. You weren't in the office, were you?
4. He hasn't applied yet, has he?
5. He wasn't fired, was he?

Practice 2   5-10 mins. ■■

(Shorter classes can do Exercise F for homework.)

(F) Complete the questions with the correct tag.
Have students do this exercise by themselves.

Evaluation 2   5-15 mins. ■■

Go over the answers as a class.

Extra practice: Have students take the tag questions in Exercise F and reverse the positive and negative parts of each one. Reverse the parts of the first two sentences as examples, and then ask students to work in pairs to do the rest.

Presentation 3   10-20 mins. ■■■

Dictate the following tag questions to students, but don't give them the tag.

1. He sent the package yesterday, ____?
2. We'll get our paychecks tomorrow, ____?
3. They didn't eat the cake yet, ____?
4. Kayla hasn't ever missed class, ____?
5. You're just learning about tag questions, ____?

Have students complete the tags. Go over the answers as a class.

Prepare students for Exercise G by telling them they will hear the tag questions and have to circle the tag they hear.

Practice 3   5 mins. ■

(G) Listen to the tag questions. Fill in the circle next to the tag that you hear.

🎧 Listening Script   *CD 1, Track 24*

1. He arrived late yesterday, didn't he?
2. We'll leave early without telling the boss, won't we?
3. They didn't unload those boxes yet, did they?
4. Martina hasn't ever assembled computers, has she?
5. You're just learning how to write reports, aren't you?

✍ Refer students to *Stand Out 4 Grammar Challenge*, **Unit 7, Challenge 1 for more practice with tag questions.**

Evaluation 3   5 mins. ■

Go over the answers as a class. Play the recording again so students can hear the correct answers.

Application   10-20 mins. ■■■

(H) Write three tag questions about inappropriate workplace behavior.

(I) Write three tag questions about appropriate workplace behavior.

Activity Bank 💿

Lesson 1, Worksheet 1: Personal Grooming
Lesson 1, Worksheet 2: Tag Questions
Lesson 1, Worksheet 3: Appropriate Classroom Behavior

Instructor's Notes

_____
_____
_____
_____
_____
_____
_____
_____
_____
_____
_____
_____
_____
_____

F Complete the questions with the correct tag.

1. He isn't e-mailing a friend, _____is he_____?

2. Lisa and Jack have never missed a day of work, _____have they_____?

3. Maria works late every night, _____doesn't she_____?

4. Our coworkers will be fired next week, _____won't they_____?

5. My assistant is going to eat lunch during the meeting, _____isn't he_____?

6. She didn't finish her work, _____did she_____?

7. The supervisor said to wait until tomorrow to ask for a raise, _____didn't she_____?

8. He wore shorts to his interview, _____didn't he_____?

9. Roberto had stolen things before, _____hadn't he_____?

10. We'll have a business meeting next week, _____won't we_____?

CD 1
TR 24

G Listen to the tag questions. Fill in the circle next to the tag that you hear.

1. ○ did he?   ● didn't he?   ○ does he?   ○ doesn't he?
2. ○ won't she?   ○ will she?   ● won't we?   ○ don't we?
3. ● did they?   ○ did he?   ○ didn't they?   ○ didn't he?
4. ○ hasn't she?   ○ did she?   ○ didn't she?   ● has she?
5. ○ are you?   ● aren't you?   ○ isn't you?   ○ were you?

H Write three tag questions about inappropriate workplace behavior. (Answers will vary.)

EXAMPLE: <u>She told her boss he looked bad, didn't she?</u>

1. _____

2. _____

3. _____

I Write three tag questions about appropriate workplace behavior. (Answers will vary.)

EXAMPLE: <u>She wore a suit to the interview, didn't she?</u>

1. _____

2. _____

3. _____

The note was written by Jim.

GOAL ➤ **Identify workplace actions**

Where are these people?
What are they talking about?
What can you see on the desk?

CD 1
TR 25

A **Read and listen to the conversation.**

Raquel: Did you see the note I put on your screen?

Bruno: Was that note from you? I thought it was put there by Jim.

Raquel: Actually, the note was written by Jim, but I taped it to your screen. I wanted to make sure you got it before you left for lunch.

Bruno: I did get it. The orders were sent to me yesterday, and I'll have them ready for your signature before I leave today.

Raquel: Great! I'll sign them in the morning, and then you can send them to the finance department. Make sure they are sent by Package Express.

Bruno: I'll take care of it right away.

B **Answer the questions about the conversation.**

1. Who are the two people in the conversation? Who is the supervisor? A supervisor and an employee are having the conversation; Raquel is the supervisor.
2. What was the misunderstanding? The misunderstanding is about who left the note.
3. What was sent to Bruno? The orders were sent to Bruno.

C **Practice the conversation again, but this time, replace some of the words and phrases with the new words below.**

screen	➔	computer
note	➔	memo
lunch	➔	he day
the finance department	➔	human resources
right away	➔	as soon as possible

AT-A-GLANCE PREP

Objective: Identify workplace actions
Grammar: Passive voice
Vocabulary: *active, passive, misunderstanding*

RESOURCES

Activity Bank: Unit 7, Lesson 2, Worksheets 1–2
Reading and Writing Challenge: Unit 7

Grammar Challenge 4: Unit 7, Challenge 2
Audio: CD 1, Track 25

■ 1.5 hour classes ■ 2.5 hour classes ■ 3⁺ hour classes

AGENDA

Read and listen to a conversation.
Practice a conversation.
Identify sentences as active or passive.
Use the passive voice.

Warm-up and Review 10-15 mins. ■■■

Review the previous lesson by having students make two lists, one of appropriate and one of inappropriate workplace behavior. Then, have them practice tag questions by putting their ideas in the following sentences:

It's appropriate to _____, isn't it?
It's inappropriate to _____, isn't it?

Have students share their ideas with a partner or the entire class.

Introduction 5-10 mins. ■■■

Have students look at the picture in their books on page 124. As a class, discuss the boxed questions: *Where are these people? What are they talking about? What can you see on the desk?* State the objective: *Today we will identify workplace actions.*

Presentation 1 5-10 mins. ■■■

 A Read and listen to the conversation.

Play the recording as students follow along in their books.

Listening Script *CD 1, Track 25*

The listening script matches the conversation in Exercise A.

 B Answer the questions about the conversation.

Ask students the questions and go over the answers as a class.

Go over the instructions for Exercise C and show students how to substitute the words in the conversation.

Practice 1 10-15 mins. ■■■

 C Practice the conversation again, but this time, replace some of the words and phrases with the new words below.

Have students practice the conversation twice with one partner (switching roles), and then find other partners to repeat the process.

Evaluation 1 5 mins. ■■■

Ask two or three pairs of students to demonstrate the conversations for the class. Get students used to being in front of the class by asking them to come to the front of the room when they present.

STANDARDS CORRELATIONS

CASAS: 0.1.2, 0.1.6 (See CASAS Competency List on pages 169-175.)
SCANS: **Information** Acquire and evaluate information, interpret and communicate information
Interpersonal Participate as a member of a team, teach others, exercise leadership, work with cultural diversity
Systems Monitor and correct performance

Basic Skills Reading, writing, listening, speaking
Thinking Skills Decision making
Personal Qualities Responsibility, sociability, self-management
EFF: **Communication** Read with understanding, convey ideas in writing, speak so others can understand, listen actively, observe critically
Interpersonal Cooperate with others

Presentation 2   10-15 mins. ■■■

Write the following sentence on the board: *The note was put on the desk by his supervisor.* Underline *was put* and ask students if they know what verb tense this is.

(D) Study the chart. Compare the sentences in the passive voice with those in the active voice. What are the differences?

Help students understand the difference between an active sentence and a passive sentence.

Practice 2   5-15 mins. ■■

(Shorter classes can do these exercises for homework.)

(E) Decide if each sentence is active (A) or passive (P). Write *A* or *P* on each line.

(F) Rewrite each sentence in the active voice. (*Hint*: Use the simple past tense.)

Evaluation 2   10-20 mins. ■■

Go over the answers as a class. Ask volunteers to write the answers to Exercise F on the board.

Instructor's Notes

_____
_____
_____
_____
_____
_____
_____
_____
_____
_____
_____
_____
_____
_____
_____
_____
_____
_____
_____
_____
_____
_____
_____
_____
_____
_____
_____

D Study the chart. Compare the sentences in the passive voice with those in the active voice. What are the differences?

Passive Voice	Active Voice
The note was put there by Raquel.	Raquel put the note there.
The note was written by Jim.	Jim wrote the note.
The orders were sent yesterday. (We don't know who sent them.)	They sent the orders yesterday.

E Decide if each sentence is active (A) or passive (P). Write *A* or *P* on each line.

1. The copy machine was repaired last week. _P_
2. My manager wrote the report. _A_
3. The dishwashers were laid off by their supervisor. _P_
4. Was the package received? _P_
5. Eli designed the new brochure. _A_
6. The new office building was built last year. _P_
7. Our new employees were given an orientation. _P_
8. Kelli was given a raise last week. _P_
9. James and Brian started their own business. _A_
10. José quit. _A_

F Rewrite each sentence in the active voice. (*Hint:* Use the simple past tense.)

EXAMPLE: Three dishwashers were laid off by the supervisor.

<u>The supervisor laid off three dishwashers.</u>

1. Our new employees were given an orientation by the manager.

   <u>The manager gave our new employees an orientation.</u>

2. Kelli was given a raise last week by the owner of the company.

   <u>The owner of the company gave Kelli a raise last week.</u>

3. The package was received by the receptionist.

   <u>The receptionist received the package.</u>

LESSON 2

GOAL ➤ Identify workplace actions

G Study the chart below.

Passive Voice				
Example sentence	**Passive subject**	*be*	**Past participle**	(*by* + person or thing)
The note was written by Jim.	It	was	written	by Jim
The orders were sent yesterday. (We don't know who sent them.)	They	were	sent	

- Use the passive voice to emphasize the object of the action, or when the doer of the action is unknown or unimportant.
- To change an active sentence into a passive sentence, switch the subject and the object, and change the verb to the correct tense of *be* + the past participle. The word *by* is used before the doer of the action.

H Change the sentences from active voice to passive voice.

EXAMPLE: Our delivery person brought twelve bottles of water this morning.

Twelve bottles of water were brought by our delivery person this morning.

1. The receptionist bought all the supplies.

   All the supplies were bought by the receptionist.

2. The repairperson fixed the copy machine.

   The copy machine was fixed by the repairperson.

3. Someone stole his money and driver's license.

   His money and driver's license were stolen

4. A nurse took my blood pressure.

   My blood pressure was taken by a nurse

I Think of three things you did at work last week. Write three passive voice sentences.
(Answers will vary.)

   1. _____

   2. _____

   3. _____

Presentation 3   5-10 mins. ■ ■ ■

(G) Study the chart below.

Make sure students understand how to form the
passive voice, and when it is used. Go back to
the exercises on the previous page and look at
the passive voice statements to give them more
examples.

Practice 3   10-15 mins. ■

(Shorter classes can do Exercise H for
homework.)

(H) Change the sentences from active voice to passive voice.

Evaluation 3   10-15 mins. ■

Ask volunteers to write the answers on the
board. Correct them as a class.

(I) Think of three things you did at work last week. Write three passive voice sentences.

When students have finished, have them share
their sentences with a partner. If you think the
whole class would benefit from seeing more
examples, walk around the classroom and find
good examples from students' books and ask
those students to write their sentences
on the board.

Activity Bank

Lesson 2, Worksheet 1: Passive Voice
Lesson 2, Worksheet 2: Active or Passive?

Refer students to *Stand Out 4 Grammar
Challenge*, **Unit 7, Challenge 2 for more
practice with passive voice forms.**

Instructor's Notes

Objective: Communicate problems to a supervisor
Academic Strategy: Reading a flowchart
Vocabulary: *get someone's attention, politely, excuse me, pardon me, flowchart, solution, construction, shipment, lumber, door frames*

AGENDA
Read and listen to a conversation.
Get someone's attention.
Check for understanding.
Communicate problems.
Offer solutions.
Follow steps to solve problems.

RESOURCES

Activity Bank: Unit 7, Lesson 3, Worksheet 1
Reading and Writing Challenge: Unit 7

Grammar Challenge 4: Unit 7, Challenge 3
Audio: CD 1, Track 26

■ 1.5 hour classes   ■ 2.5 hour classes   ■ 3⁺ hour classes

Warm-up and Review   10-15 mins.

Have students take out the sentences they wrote in Exercise I from the previous lesson (page 126). Ask volunteers to write their sentences on the board. As a class, evaluate the sentences, making sure they are written in the passive voice. Then ask students to take out a sheet of paper and make the sentences active.

Introduction   5-10 mins.

Ask students to tell you about some problems they might face at work, possibly with a coworker or supervisor. Ask the class for suggestions on how to solve these problems. State the objective: *Today we will learn how to communicate problems to a supervisor.*

Presentation 1   10-15 mins.

(A) **Read and listen to the conversation.**

Have students close their books and play the recording for them. Ask them some basic

comprehension questions about what they heard. Next, have them open their books and follow along as you play the recording a second time.

🎧 **Listening Script**   *CD 1, Track 26*

The listening script matches the conversation in Exercise A.

Practice 1   5-10 mins.

(B) **Answer the questions about the conversation.**

Have students discuss the questions with the person sitting next to them.

Evaluation 1   5 mins.

Go over the questions and answers as a class.

STANDARDS CORRELATIONS

CASAS: 4.4.1, 4.8.1, 4.8.5, 7.3.2, 7.4.8 (See CASAS Competency List on pages 169–175.)
SCANS: **Resources** Allocate materials and facility resources, allocate human resources
Information Acquire and evaluate information, organize and maintain information, interpret and communicate information
Interpersonal Participate as a member of a team, teach others, serve clients and customers, exercise leadership, negotiate to arrive at a decision, work with cultural diversity
Systems Understand systems, improve and design systems
Basic Skills Reading, listening, speaking

Thinking Skills Creative thinking, decision making, problem solving, seeing things in the mind's eye
Personal Qualities Responsibility, sociability, self-management
EFF: **Communication** Read with understanding, speak so others can understand, listen actively, observe critically
Decision Making Solve problems and make decisions, plan
Interpersonal Resolve conflict and negotiate, advocate and influence, cooperate with others
Lifelong Learning Take responsibility for learning, reflect and evaluate, use information and communications technology (optional)

Taking action

GOAL ➤ Communicate problems to a supervisor

CD 1
TR 26

A Read and listen to the conversation.

Construction Worker: Excuse me, do you have a second?
Supervisor: Sure. What is it?
Construction Worker: Well, there's a small problem. The shipment of lumber didn't arrive, so we have to stop construction until it gets here. What would you like us to do?
Supervisor: There's nothing else you can do while you are waiting for it?
Construction Worker: No. We need that lumber to start working on the door frames.

Supervisor: OK. Well, why don't you guys take lunch early, and I'll call and see where the lumber is?
Construction Worker: Let me make sure I understand you correctly. You want all of us to go on lunch break right now while you call and find out where the lumber is?
Supervisor: That's right.
Construction Worker: When should we come back?
Supervisor: In about an hour.
Construction Worker: Thank you. See you in an hour.

B Answer the questions about the conversation.

1. What is the problem? A shipment of lumber didn't arrive, so work must stop.
2. What does the employee say to get the supervisor's attention? Excuse me.
3. Does the supervisor understand the problem? Yes.
4. What does he suggest they do to solve the problem? The workers will take a break while she calls to find out where the lumber is.

How to get someone's attention politely	How to check that you have understood
Excuse me, sir/ma'am/(name). Do you have a minute?	Let me make sure I understand you.
	What you are saying is . . .
Pardon me, sir/ma'am/(name). Can I talk to you for a second?	So what we/I should do is . . .

GOAL ➤ **Communicate problems to a supervisor**

C Read the flowchart. Do you agree with each step?

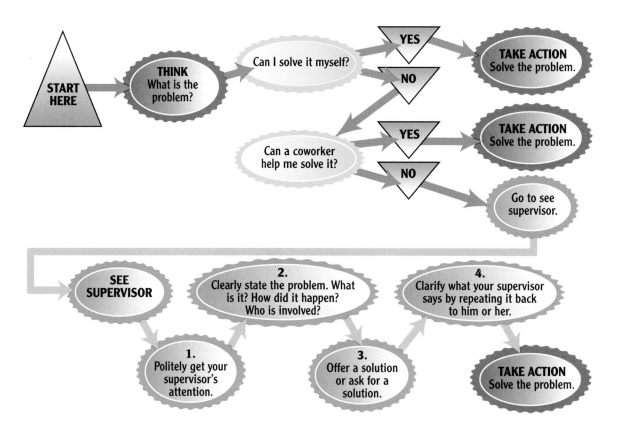

D Discuss these questions with a partner.

1. If you can solve the problem by yourself, what should you do? Take action and solve the problem.
2. If a coworker can help you solve the problem, what should you do? With your coworker's help, solve the problem.
3. When you go to see your supervisor, what is the first thing you should do? What is the last thing you should do? Politely get his/her attention. Clarify what he or she says by repeating it back.

How to offer a solution

Why don't we/I . . .
What if we/I . . .
Would it work if we/I . . .

E Look at the conversation on page 127. Did the construction worker follow the steps in the flowchart? Yes.

Presentation 2   10–15 mins. ■■■

C Read the flowchart. Do you agree with each step?

Go over the flowchart with students. Show them how the arrows guide them to the subsequent steps. Ask them questions about the flowchart as you are explaining it to make sure they understand.

Practice 2   10–15 mins. ■■

D Discuss these questions with a partner.

Evaluation 2   15–20 mins. ■■

Go over the questions as a class.

E Look at the conversation on page 127. Did the construction worker follow the steps in the flowchart?

Do this exercise together as a class.

Presentation 3   5-10 mins. ■■■

Look at the first situation in Exercise F with the class. Take students through the flowchart and have them come up with a decision about what Renee should do.

Practice 3   5-10 mins. ■

F With a group, read each situation below. Following the steps in the flowchart on page 128, discuss what you would do if you were in the situations.

Evaluation 3   5-10 mins. ■

Call on different groups to report what should be done in each situation.

Application   15-25 mins. ■■■

G Separate your class into two groups. Read your group's directions.

Divide the class into two groups and have each group get together and go through each of the three situations presented. Encourage students to look back at the useful language in the boxes on page 127 and 128 and to use these during the role-plays.

Group A: Supervisors
As a group, discuss how you would solve each of the employee's problems below. Be prepared to communicate this to the employee when he or she asks you.

Group B: Employees
As a group, discuss what you would say to your supervisor about each of the problems below. Remember the four steps from the flowchart.

H When you are ready, each supervisor from Group A should find an employee from Group B to talk to about the first problem. Make sure each employee talks to a different supervisor about each problem.

Have students get up and walk around the classroom to find someone to talk to. (If you want, each group could carry a different color card or wear a tag that says *supervisor* or *employee*.)

I Switch roles. The supervisors will become employees, and the employees will become supervisors.

Activity Bank

Lesson 3, Worksheet 1: Finding a Solution

 Refer students to *Stand Out 4 Grammar Challenge*, Unit 7, Challenge 3 for an overview of passive voice tenses.

Instructor's Notes

_____

_____

_____

_____

_____

_____

_____

_____

_____

_____

_____

_____

_____

_____

_____

_____

_____

_____

_____

_____

LESSON 3 **GOAL** ➤ **Communicate problems to a supervisor**

 F With a group, read each situation below. Following the steps in the flowchart on page 128, discuss what you would do if you were in the situations.

1. Renee is a cashier in a fast-food restaurant. A customer just came up to the counter and told her that she gave him the wrong change. He doesn't have his receipt, and she doesn't remember helping him. What should she do?
2. Mikhail came back from lunch and found a message marked *urgent* on his desk, but it wasn't addressed to him. He doesn't recognize the name of the addressee so he doesn't know what to do with it. What should he do?
3. James and Sara assemble telephones. For this particular group of phones, they have an uneven amount of parts and aren't able to finish 20 of the phones. What should they do?

G Separate your class into two groups. Read your group's directions.

Group A: **Supervisors**
As a group, discuss how you would solve each of the employees' problems below. Be prepared to communicate this to the employee when he or she asks you.

Group B: **Employees**
As a group, discuss what you would say to your supervisor about each of the problems below. Remember the four steps from the flowchart.

Problems
1. You just received your paycheck, and you notice that you didn't get paid for the overtime hours you worked.
2. There is an emergency phone call for you, but, if you leave your place, you will throw off the assembly line.
3. You are out installing cable TV at a customer's home, and the customer is unhappy with your service.

 H When you are ready, each supervisor from Group A should find an employee from Group B to talk to about the first problem. Make sure each employee talks to a different supervisor about each problem.

 I Switch roles. The supervisors will become employees, and the employees will become supervisors.

What should you do?

GOAL ➤ **Make ethical decisions**

> **ethics:** *n.* moral rules or principles of behavior for deciding what is right and wrong; *adj.* – **ethical**

A Each situation below describes an ethical question that you might face. What would you do? Check (✓) your answers and discuss them with a partner. (Answers will vary.)

1. You pay the cashier at the supermarket with a ten-dollar bill. He gives you change as if you had given him a twenty-dollar-bill. What would you do?

   ___ Tell her.   ___ Keep the extra money.

2. It's the night before the final exam at your school and you haven't had much time to study. A classmate has stolen the answers to the exam and offers to share them with you. What would you do?

   ___ Say no.   ___ Borrow the answers from him.

3. You go shopping and buy some books. When you get home, you realize that the clerk put an extra book in your bag that you didn't pay for. What would you do?

   ___ Go back   ___ Keep it.
   to the store
   and give
   the book back.

AT-A-GLANCE PREP

Objective: Make ethical decisions
Academic Strategies: Active reading, Writing a description of a situation
Vocabulary: *ethics, ethical, relevant*

AGENDA
Define ethics.
Respond to ethical dilemmas.
Read steps for making an ethical decision.
Make an ethical decision.
Write about an ethical dilemma.

RESOURCES

Activity Bank: Unit 7, Lesson 4, Worksheet 1
Reading and Writing Challenge: Unit 7

Grammar Challenge 4: Unit 7, Challenge 4

■ 1.5 hour classes ■ 2.5 hour classes ■ 3+ hour classes

Warm-up and Review   5–10 mins.

Talk about the application activity from the previous lesson with students. Ask students if it was easy or difficult and if they now think they feel better prepared to talk to a supervisor at work about a problem.

Introduction   5–10 mins.

Write *ethics* and *ethical* on the board. Tell students the following story: *Imagine that last week I gave you a test. When you got the test back, you saw that you missed 3 and got a B, according to what I had written at the top of your paper. When you went back and counted the wrong answers, you discovered that you had actually missed 5, which means you should have gotten a C. I made a mistake with your score. Would you tell me I made a mistake, or just keep your B?*

Discuss right and wrong decisions with students and define *ethics*. State the objective: *Today we will be looking at ethical dilemmas and learning steps to follow in order to make good decisions.*

Presentation 1   5 mins.

Tell students that in each situation in Exercise A, they are presented with a choice. Have them think carefully about each circumstance and make an honest decision.

Practice 1   10–15 mins.

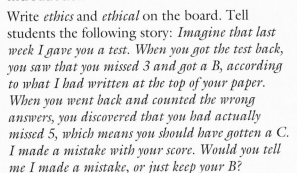 Each situation below describes an ethical question that you might face. What would you do? Check (✓) your answers and discuss them with a partner.

Have each student complete this exercise alone and then find a partner to share answers with. Remind students that there is no right or wrong answer and that they should try to answer truthfully.

Evaluation 1   10–15 mins.

Take a poll and see if the class agrees on the decisions.

STANDARDS CORRELATIONS

CASAS: 4.8.1, 4.8.5, 4.8.6, 7.2.2, 7.2.5, 7.2.7, 7.3.2, 7.3.4 (See CASAS Competency List on pages 169–175.)
SCANS: **Information** Acquire and evaluate information, organize and maintain information, interpret and communicate information
Interpersonal Participate as a member of a team, teach others, exercise leadership, negotiate to arrive at a decision, work with cultural diversity
Systems Understand systems
Basic Skills Reading, writing, listening, speaking
Thinking Skills Creative thinking, decision making, problem solving, seeing things in the mind's eye

Personal Qualities Responsibility, sociability, self-management
EFF: **Communication** Read with understanding, convey ideas in writing, speak so others can understand, listen actively, observe critically
Decision Making Solve problems and make decisions, plan
Interpersonal Guide others, resolve conflict and negotiate, advocate and influence, cooperate with others
Lifelong Learning Reflect and evaluate

Presentation 2   10-15 mins. ■■□

(B) In situations like the ones in Exercise A, you know what you should do, but do you always do it? Sometimes the decision is not easy, but there are steps you can take to help you make a good decision.

Go through each step with students. Then choose one situation in Exercise A and go through each of the steps again as it relates to the situation. See if the class agrees on a decision.

Practice 2   15-20 mins. ■■

(C) Using the steps above, discuss one of the situations in Exercise A with a group and decide what would be the best thing to do.

Evaluation 2   15-20 mins. ■■

Observe students as they resolve the dilemmas.

Presentation 3   5-10 mins. ■■■

(D) Read the situations below. Which one is the worst?

Call on volunteers to read the situations out loud. As a class, discuss which situation they think is the most ethically challenging.

Put students who don't normally work together into groups of four or five. Tell groups they will choose an ethical dilemma and go through the steps listed in Exercise B to reach a decision. Tell them all group members must agree on a single decision so they may have to negotiate and compromise.

Instructor's Notes

131a   Lesson Planner: Unit 7, Lesson 4

LESSON 4

GOAL ➤ **Make ethical decisions**

B In situations like the ones in Exercise A, you know what you should do, but do you always do it? Sometimes the decision is not easy, but there are steps you can take to help you make a good decision.

> **Steps for Making an Ethical Decision**
> 1. Identify the ethical issue or problem.
> 2. List the facts that are most relevant to your decision.
> 3. Identify the people who might be affected by your decision and how.
> 4. Explain what each person would want you to do about the issue.
> 5. List three different decisions you could make and what the outcome of each decision would be.
> 6. Decide what you will do.

C Using the steps above, discuss one of the situations in Exercise A with a group and decide what would be the best thing to do.

D Read the situations below. Which one is the worst? (Answers will vary.)

1. Ricardo, the night security guard, has access to all of the buildings at night. It is a slow night and he wants to check his personal e-mail using one of the available computers. The company has a strict policy about e-mail being used for business purposes only, but Ricardo is the only person in the building.

3. Kimberly, who works as a receptionist in the front office, has access to the copy machine to make copies for other employees. Her daughter, Alyse, needs some copies for a school project. She brought her own paper and needs 200 copies for her class. She needs to have the copies or she will fail the project. The copier does not require a security code and they don't keep track of who makes how many copies.

2. Emilia is a janitor who is in charge of cleaning the restrooms and refilling the supplies. She is the only one with a key to the supply closet. Her husband is very sick and she is having trouble making enough money to support her family. Often they can't afford food and they can't afford to buy toilet paper and soap.

4. Brandon works in Quality Control helping refurbish used computers. Once a year, his supervisor gives away computers to a local elementary school. He doesn't keep any record of this, and Brandon really needs a computer for his son who is just starting high school. His supervisor asks him to deliver twelve computers to a local school.

E Work with a partner and choose one of the situations from Exercise D. Follow the steps for making an ethical decision in Exercise B and answer the questions below.

(Answers will vary.)

1. What is the ethical problem?

_____

_____

2. What are the relevant facts?

_____

_____

3. Which people are involved and how would each person be affected?

_____

_____

_____

4. What would each person want you to do?

_____

_____

_____

5. What are three different possible decisions?

_____

_____

_____

6. What is your final decision?

_____

_____

F On a separate piece of paper, write a description of an actual situation where you had to make an ethical choice. What did you do? How did you feel afterwards?

Practice 3
10-20 mins.

E Work with a partner and choose one of the situations from Exercise D. Follow the steps for making an ethical decision in Exercise B and answer the questions below.

Have each pair read through the situations and choose one to work on. One partner should act as the secretary and write down the answers to the questions and the final decision.

Evaluation 3
5-10 mins.

Have each pair report its final decision to the class.

 Refer students to *Stand Out 4 Grammar Challenge*, Unit 7, Challenge 4 for practice with active to passive voice.

Application
10-20 mins. ▪▪▪

F On a separate piece of paper, write a description of an actual situation where you had to make an ethical choice. What did you do? How did you feel afterwards?

You may need to help students brainstorm if they are having trouble thinking of something to write about.

If students feel comfortable sharing their situations, ask for some volunteers to tell their experiences to the class.

Activity Bank

Lesson 4, Worksheet 1: Ethical Dilemma

Objective: Ask for a raise
Academic Strategies: Active reading
Vocabulary: *close the gap, cover your bases, contributions to the company, star performer, document, counterpart, Census Bureau data, rehearse, raise, deserve*

RESOURCES

Activity Bank: Unit 7, Lesson 5, Worksheets 1–3
Reading and Writing Challenge: Unit 7

Grammar Challenge 4: Unit 7, Challenge 5; Extension Challenges 1-2

■ 1.5 hour classes ■ 2.5 hour classes ■ 3⁺ hour classes

AGENDA
Talk about raises.
Read about how to ask for a raise.
Evaluate a memo asking for a raise.
Ask for a raise (in person or writing).

Warm-up and Review 5-10 mins. ■■■

Ask for volunteers to describe the ethical situations they wrote about in the previous lesson.

Introduction 5-10 mins. ■■■

State the objective: *Today we will learn about asking for a raise.*

(A) Discuss these questions with your group.

Put students in small groups and have them discuss the two questions.

Presentation 1 5-10 mins. ■■■

(B) Many people hesitate to ask for a raise. Can you think of some reasons why? List them.

Discuss the reasons as a class and have students write ideas in their books.

Have students look at the picture in their books. Ask: *What is happening in the picture?*

Practice 1 10-15 mins. ■■■

(C) Raj met with his boss yesterday to ask for a raise. Read about his experience.

Have students read this passage silently.

(D) Answer the questions.

Have students work with a partner to answer the questions.

Evaluation 1 5-10 mins. ■■■

Talk about the questions as a class.

STANDARDS CORRELATIONS

CASAS: 4.1.6, 4.4.1, 4.4.2, 7.2.1, 7.2.4 (See CASAS Competency List on pages 169–175.)
SCANS: Information Acquire and evaluate information, organize and maintain information, interpret and communicate information
Interpersonal Participate as a member of a team, teach others, exercise leadership, negotiate to arrive at a decision, work with cultural diversity
Systems Understand systems, monitor and correct performance, improve and design systems
Basic Skills Reading, writing, listening, speaking

Thinking Skills Creative thinking, decision making, problem solving, seeing things in the mind's eye
Personal Qualities Responsibility, sociability, self-management
EFF: Communication Read with understanding, convey ideas in writing, speak so others can understand, listen actively
Decision Making Solve problems and make decisions, plan
Interpersonal Resolve conflict and negotiate, cooperate with others
Lifelong Learning Reflect and evaluate, use information and communications technology (optional)

GOAL ➤ **Ask for a raise**

 Discuss these questions with your group. (Answers will vary.)

1. Have you ever received a raise at your job? If yes, what was it for?
2. Have you ever asked for a raise? If yes, did you get it? If no, did your manager or supervisor explain to you why you didn't get it?

B **Many people hesitate to ask for a raise. Can you think of some reasons why? List them.**

(Answers will vary. Possible answers below.)

They don't feel they deserve it; they are afraid the answer will be no; they are nervous

about talking with their supervisor.

C **Raj met with his boss yesterday to ask for a raise. Read about his experience.**

   Raj has been working for EJ Electronics as an assembler for two years. In the past year, he has come up with new ways to make the assembly line more efficient and helped increase productivity in his department. Raj thinks he deserves a raise. He has friends who work at other electronics companies, and he has been asking around to find out what different employees are paid. He believes that with his experience and his contributions to the company, his boss should give him a raise.

   First, Raj went to see Heidi in Human Resources and asked her what procedures he needed to follow to ask for a raise. She suggested that he make an appointment with his boss. So, last week, he asked his boss if the two of them could sit down and have a meeting. When his boss agreed, he began to gather his paperwork: job evaluations, memos from his supervisor about the new assembly-line configurations, his "Employee of the Month" award, and records of his attendance at work. He sat down and thought about all the questions his boss might ask him and he wrote out detailed answers. Then, he asked his cousin to help him practice by asking him those questions.

 Answer the questions. (Answers may vary. Possible answers below.)

1. Do you think Raj deserves a raise? Why or why not? Yes, because he has contributed positively to his company.
2. Who did he talk to first after he decided to ask for a raise? What did she tell him? First, he talked to Heidi in Human Resources. She told him to schedule a meeting with his boss.
3. What did he do to prepare for the meeting with his boss? He gathered paperwork and awards and practiced answering questions that he thought his boss would ask him.

E Read the following article about getting a raise. Underline the advice that could be useful for you.

How to Ask for a Raise

Men are still earning more than women—lots more. According to the most recent Census Bureau data, the pay gap between men and women is 27 percent. This means that a woman earns 73 cents for every dollar a man earns. In other words, a woman works four weeks to earn as much as her male counterpart earns in three weeks.

How can women close the gap? Knock on the boss's door and ask for a raise! Getting a raise is not as difficult as it might seem. Here are ten tips to assist women in negotiating their annual raise.

1. Be a star performer. Make yourself indispensable to the company. Document your successes by saving e-mails and letters, and then compile them into a portfolio. Make sure to take this portfolio with you when you go to your boss.

2. Do some research. Know what other men and women in your field are paid.

3. Focus on your contributions to the company. While the raise is certainly important to you, do not focus on how it will help your credit card debt.

4. Be informed. Know the company's policy on raises by asking your human resources director.

5. Timing is everything. Don't ask when the office is hectic; wait until the pace has slowed down and the moment is right.

6. Do your homework. Rehearse and prepare responses to counter any objections your boss might have. Know ahead of time what the difficult questions might be and have your answers ready.

7. Rehearse. If you can, role-play the scenario with a friend or colleague. This will help you to become more comfortable when you are actually face-to-face with your boss.

8. Be professional. Ask for a formal meeting with your boss.

9. Cover your bases. Make four points about your contributions prior to asking for the raise. Illustrate your ability:
• to find solutions,
• to go above and beyond your job responsibilities,
• to help others,
and, most importantly,
• to increase the company's profitability.

10. Don't take *no* for an answer. Negotiate more vacation time, stock options, 401K contribution, or flextime. Set goals and ask for another review in three months.

F Discuss these questions with a group. (Answers will vary.)

1. This article focuses on how women should ask for a raise. Do you think these same ideas apply to men? Why or why not?
2. Which aspect of asking for a raise do you think is the most difficult? Take a poll among your group members.

Presentation 2　　　5-10 mins. ■■■

Have students look at the title of the article, "How to Ask for a Raise." Have them speculate on what things they think the article might contain. Make a list of their ideas on the board.

Practice 2　　　15-20 mins. ■■

(Shorter classes can do Exercise E for homework.)

(E) Read the following article about getting a raise. Underline the advice that could be useful for you.

Encourage students to read for the main ideas rather than worrying about understanding every single word and phrase.

Have students reread the article and the story about Raj in Exercise C and underline any words or phrases they don't understand. Have a few students tell you which phrases or words they underlined and have them take you through the process of trying to discover the meanings through context.

(F) Discuss these questions with a group.

Evaluation 2　　　10-15 mins. ■■

Observe groups as they work.

Presentation 3 10-15 mins.

Write this question on the board: *Do you deserve a raise?* Make sure students understand *deserve*. Ask if any of them feel they deserve a raise at their job. If they say yes, ask them why. If none of the students answer yes, ask them to give you good reasons why anyone should get a raise.

G Read the memo that Rogelio wrote to his supervisor asking for a raise.

Have students read the memo silently to themselves. When they have finished, ask them basic comprehension questions about the memo, such as: *How long has Rogelio been working at the company? How many new employees did he train?*

Practice 3 10-15 mins. ■

(Shorter classes can do Exercise H for homework.)

H Read the letter again and check (✓) the items Rogelio included in his letter.

Have students do this exercise by themselves.

Evaluation 3 10-15 mins. ■

Go over the answers as a class.

I You can ask for a raise in person or by writing a letter or e-mail. What are the advantages and disadvantages of each method?

Have students discuss this question in small groups or discuss it together as a class.

Application 10-20 mins. ■■■

J Let's get ready to ask for a raise! First, answer these questions. (If you are a homemaker or a student, imagine that you get paid for what you do and are asking for more money.)

Go over each of the questions with students, giving them an example of a possible answer when necessary. Then have them work alone to answer the questions.

K Work with a partner to practice asking for a raise, or write a letter asking for a raise.

Ask students to raise their hands if they would prefer to practice writing a letter. Have those students move to the back of the class and begin working on their letters. Take the rest of the students and pair them up so they can practice asking for a raise in person.

Activity Bank

Lesson 5, Worksheet 1: Asking for a Raise
Lesson 5, Worksheet 2: Ask for a Raise—It's Your Turn
Lesson 5, Worksheet 3: Writing a Letter Asking for a Raise—Editing Checklist

Refer students to *Stand Out 4 Grammar Challenge*, Unit 7, Challenge 5 for practice with verbs with two objects.

Refer students to *Stand Out 4 Grammar Challenge*, Unit 7, Extension Challenges 1–2 for practice with two-word phrasal verbs, and practice with tag questions with indefinite compound pronouns and negative words.

Instructor's Notes

_____
_____
_____
_____
_____
_____
_____
_____
_____
_____
_____
_____
_____
_____
_____
_____
_____
_____

GOAL ➤ **Ask for a raise**

G Read the memo that Rogelio wrote to his supervisor asking for a raise.

Dear Mr. Michalski,

    I'm writing this letter to ask you to consider giving me raise. I have been working at Mitchel George Manufacturing for five years, and I really like my job here. I started out as a warehouse packer, and now I work in the shipping department.

    I feel like I deserve a raise because, in the past year, I have been given more responsibilities on my shift. I have trained ten new employees and become a team leader. I have increased efficiency in my department by implementing a new flow system that helps us pack and ship the boxes in less time. Therefore, I hope that you will consider giving me a raise.

    I would like to sit down and discuss this possibility with you as soon as it is convenient for you. Thank you for your time.

Sincerely,

Rogelio Rodriguez

H Read the letter again and check (✓) the items Rogelio included in his letter.

✓ *thank you* to his supervisor for reading the letter

✓ reason for the letter

✓ how long he has been working for the company

✓ what his job is

✓ how his job has changed since he has been there

✓ things he has done to help the company

I You can ask for a raise in person or by writing a letter or e-mail. What are the advantages and disadvantages of each method? (Answers will vary.)

J Let's get ready to ask for a raise! First, answer these questions. (If you are a homemaker or a student, imagine that you get paid for what you do and are asking for more money.)

(Answers will vary.)

1. Do you deserve a raise? Why or why not?
2. How long have you been working at your job?
3. When was the last time you got a raise?
4. Have you been working harder or working more hours?
5. Have you been given more responsibilities?
6. Have you gotten good reviews from your supervisors?

K Work with a partner to practice asking for a raise, or write a letter asking for a raise.

Review

(A) Add tags to the statements to make tag questions. (Lesson 1)

1. She is going to ask for a promotion, _____isn't she_____ ?

2. We will volunteer to help them finish, _____won't we_____ ?

3. Ken gets to work early every day, _____doesn't he_____ ?

4. Her sister can't pass her drug test, _____can she_____ ?

5. They won't get that project done, on time, _____will they_____ ?

6. The boss didn't talk to his employees, _____did he_____ ?

(B) List two examples of appropriate and inappropriate employee behavior. (Lesson 1)
(Answers will vary.)

Appropriate Employee Behavior:

1. ask a coworker for help

2. get to work on time

Inappropriate Employee Behavior:

1. smoke while you are working

2. talk to a friend on the phone

(C) Use the words given below to write sentences in the passive voice. You may have to add some words. (Lesson 2)

EXAMPLE: new office building / build / Lynn Street

   A new office building was built on Lynn Street.

1. childcare workers / give / a raise

   The childcare workers were given a raise.

2. machines / repair / mechanics

   The machines were repaired by the mechanics.

3. roses / cut / gardeners

   The roses were cut by the gardeners.

4. computer / buy / the finance department

   The computer was bought by the finance department.

5. reports / write / two weeks ago

   The reports were written two weeks ago.

6. package / sent / express mail

   The package was sent by express mail.

Objectives: All Unit 7 objectives
Grammar: All Unit 7 grammar
Academic Strategy: Reviewing
Vocabulary: All Unit 7 vocabulary

RESOURCES

Activity Bank: Unit 7, Lessons 1–5
Reading and Writing Challenge: Unit 7

■ 1.5 hour classes ■ 2.5 hour classes ■ 3⁺ hour classes

AGENDA

Unit objectives,
Review exercises,
My Dictionary,
Learner Log,

Grammar Challenge 4: Unit 7, Challenges 1–5;
Extension Challenges 1–2

Warm-up and Review   5-10 mins.

In groups, have students come up with a list of
things they should do before they ask for a raise.

Introduction   5-10 mins.

Ask students to try to recall (in general) all the
goals of this unit without looking at their books.
Then remind them which goals they omitted,
if any. (Unit Goals: Identify appropriate and
inappropriate workplace behavior, identify
workplace actions, communicate problems to a
supervisor, make ethical decisions, and ask for a
raise.) Write all the objectives on the board from
Unit 7. Show the students the first page of the
unit and mention the five objectives. State the
objective: *Today we will be reviewing everything
we have learned in this unit.*

Presentation 1   10-15 mins.

This presentation will cover the first three pages
of the review. Quickly go to the first page of
each lesson. Discuss the objective of each one.
Ask simple questions to remind students of what
they have learned.

Note: Since there is little presentation in the
review, you can assign the review exercises
that don't involve pair work or group work
for homework and go over them in class the
following day.

Practice 1   20-25 mins.

Note: There are two ways to do the review:
(1) Go through the exercises one at a time and, as
students complete each one, go over the answers.
(2) Briefly go through the instructions of each
exercise, allow students to complete all of the
exercises at once, and then go over the answers.
Stop and evaluate whenever it is appropriate for
the class. (*See Evaluation 1 on pg. 138a.*)

A Add tags to the statements to make tag
questions. (Lesson 1)

B List two examples of appropriate and
inappropriate employee behavior. (Lesson 1)

C Use the words given below to write sentences
in the passive voice. You may have to add some
words. (Lesson 2)

STANDARDS CORRELATIONS

CASAS: 7.2.1 (See CASAS Competency List on pages 169-175.)
SCANS: **Resources** Allocate time
Information Acquire and evaluate information
Interpersonal Participate as a member of a team, teach others,
negotiate to arrive at a decision, work with cultural diversity
Systems Monitor and correct performance
Basic Skills Reading, writing, listening, speaking
Thinking Skills Creative thinking, decision making, problem solving,
seeing things in the mind's eye

Personal Qualities Responsibility, sociability, self-management
EFF: **Communication** Convey ideas in writing, speak so others can
understand, listen actively
Decision Making Solve problems and make decisions
Interpersonal Guide others, cooperate with others
Lifelong Learning Take responsibility for learning, reflect and evaluate,
learn through research

Practice 1 *(continued)*   25–30 mins.

D What are two ways to politely get someone's attention? Write them below. (Lesson 3)

E Recall what you learned about communicating a problem to a supervisor. Circle the best answer. (Lesson 3)

Teaching Tip

Recycling/Review

The review process and the project that follows are part of the recycling/review process. Students at this level often need to be reintroduced to concepts to solidify what they have learned. Many concepts are learned and forgotten while learning other new concepts. This is because students learn but are not necessarily ready to acquire language concepts.

Therefore, it becomes very important to review and to show students how to review on their own. It is also important to recycle the new concepts in different contexts.

Instructor's Notes

D What are two ways to politely get someone's attention? Write them below. (Lesson 3)

(Answers may vary slightly.)

1. Excuse me, sir/ma'am/(name)

2. Pardon me, sir/ma'am/(name)

E Recall what you learned about communicating a problem to a supervisor. Circle the best answer. (Lesson 3)

1. What is the first step in communicating a problem to a supervisor?
   a. Take action.
   b. Think about what the problem is.
   c. Offer a solution.

2. What should you do if you can solve the problem yourself?
   a. Take action and solve the problem yourself.
   b. Ask a coworker for help.
   c. Offer a solution.

3. What should you do if you and your coworker can't solve the problem yourselves?
   a. Take action.
   b. Think about what the problem is.
   c. Go see your supervisor.

4. What is the first thing you should do when you talk to your supervisor?
   a. Ask for a solution.
   b. Think about what the problem is.
   c. Politely get his or her attention.

5. After your supervisor offers a solution, what should you do?
   a. Ask for a solution.
   b. Clarify what your supervisor has said by repeating it back to him or her.
   c. Take action and solve the problem.

Review

F What are the six steps to making an ethical decision? List them below. (Lesson 4)

1. Identify the ethical issue.
2. List the facts that are most relevant to your decision.
3. Identify the people who might be affected by your decision and how.
4. Explain what each person would want you to do.
5. List three different decisions you could make and what the outcomes would be.
6. Decide what you will do.

G Read the situation. Based on the steps you wrote above, what would you do? (Lesson 4)
(Answers will vary.)

> You work in a restaurant and you notice that your coworker is taking food off of the customers' plates before they are served—a French fry here, a carrot there. You know that your coworker is supporting a very large family and doesn't have enough money to feed everyone. What would you do?

_____

_____

_____

_____

H You read ten suggestions on how to ask for a raise. List them in your own words. (Lesson 5) (Answers may vary slightly.)

1. Make yourself valuable to the company.
2. Research what other people in your field are getting paid.
3. Focus on what you can do for your company.
4. Talk to HR to understand your company's policy on raise.
5. Chose the right moment to ask for a raise.
6. Be ready with prepared answers to difficult questions.
7. Role-play the conversation with a friend or coworker.
8. Ask for a formal meeting with your boss.
9. Illustrate what you have done for the company clearly before asking for the raise.
10. Negotiate if the answer is "No."

Practice 1 *(continued)*   25–30 mins. ■■■

F What are the six steps to making an ethical decision? List them below. (Lesson 4)

G Read the situation. Based on the steps you wrote above, what would you do? (Lesson 4)

H You read ten suggestions on how to ask for a raise. List them in your own words. (Lesson 5)

Evaluation 1   45–60 mins. ■■■

Go around the classroom and check on students' progress. Help individuals when needed. If you see consistent errors among several students, interrupt the class and give a mini-lesson or review to help students feel comfortable with the concept.

Presentation 2   5-10 mins.

My Dictionary

Ask students to brainstorm new vocabulary they learned in this unit. Have them do this without looking in their books. Write the word *synonym* on the board. Give students examples to help define it.

Synonyms are words that have the same or similar meanings.

Practice 2   15-20 mins.

(Shorter classes can do these exercises for homework.)

Can you think of synonyms for these words? Use a dictionary if you need help.

Now look in your dictionary and see if you can add synonyms to any of your entries.

Evaluation 2   5-10 mins. ■

Walk around the classroom and help students as needed. Ask volunteers to write vocabulary words and their synonyms on the board.

Presentation 3   5-10 mins. ■■■

Learner Log

In this unit, you learned many things about being on the job. How comfortable do you feel doing each of the skills listed below? Rate your comfort level on a scale of 1 to 4.

Practice 3   5-10 mins.

Have students complete the Learner Log.

Evaluation 3   5-10 mins.

Walk around the classroom and help students as needed.

Application   5-10 mins. ■■■

Go over the three reflection statements with students and have them complete the answers by themselves.

TB Assessment (optional)   ■■■

Use the Stand Out Assessment CD-ROM with Exam*View*® to create a post-test for Unit 7.

My Dictionary

Synonyms are words that have the same or similar meanings.

EXAMPLES: problem—*difficulty, hard time*
solution—*answer, explanation*

(Answers will vary. Possible answers below.)

Can you think of synonyms for these words? Use a dictionary if you need help.

fact   truth, information

decision   choice, resolution

rehearse   practice, prepare

illustrate   show, demonstrate, point out

contributions   help, assistance

Now look in your dictionary and see if you can add synonyms to any of your entries.

Learner Log

In this unit, you learned many things about being on the job. How comfortable do you feel doing each of the skills listed below? Rate your comfort level on a scale of 1 to 4. (Answers will vary.)

1 = Need more practice   **2** = OK   **3** = Good   **4** = Great!

Life Skill	Comfort Level				Page
I can identify appropriate and inappropriate workplace behavior.	1	2	3	4	____
I can identify workplace actions.	1	2	3	4	____
I can communicate problems to supervisors.	1	2	3	4	____
I can make ethical decisions.	1	2	3	4	____
I can ask for a raise.	1	2	3	4	____

If you circled 1 or 2, write down the page number where you can review this skill.

Reflection

1. I learned _____.

2. I would like to find out more about _____.

3. I am still confused about _____.

Team Project

Solve a company problem.

With a team, you will solve a company problem in an action committee and create a handout for the class.

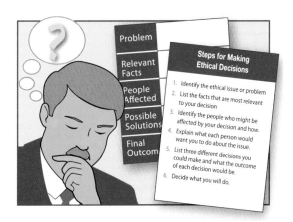

1. Form a human resources action committee with four or five students. Choose positions for each member of your team.

POSITION	JOB DESCRIPTION	STUDENT NAME
Student 1: **Human Resources Director**	See that everyone speaks English and participates.	
Student 2: **Secretary**	Take notes and write information for handout.	
Student 3: **Designer**	Prepare final handout.	
Students 4/5: **Spokespeople**	Report final decision to the class.	

2. With your group, carefully read the problem below.

3. Use the steps for making an ethical decision from page 131 as you consider each possible solution.

4. Make a final decision.

5. Create a handout explaining the process you went through to come up with your decision.

6. Report your final decision to the class.

> **Company:** RB Aerospace—Refurbishes and designs airplane interiors
> **Problem:** A group of employees discovers that the quality of some of the parts they are using is not up to standard. They are worried that this may cause safety problems when the aircraft is in use. They have mentioned it to the quality control supervisor, but the factory is on a tight schedule and if they don't deliver this contract on time, they may lose future contracts.

Solve a company problem.

Teams will form action committees to solve a company problem. They will create a handout explaining the process they went through to come up with their solutions.

The team project is the final application for the unit. It gives students a chance to show that they have mastered all of the Unit 7 objectives.

Note: Shorter classes can extend this project over two class meetings.

Stage 1   5 mins.

Form a human resources action committee with four or five students. Choose positions for each member of your team.

Have students decide who will lead each step as described on the student page. Provide well-defined directions on the board for how teams should proceed. Explain that all the students do every step as a team. Teams shouldn't go to the next stage until the previous one is complete.

Stage 2   15-20 mins.

With your group, carefully read the problem below.

Once groups have read the problem, go over it as a class to make sure everyone understands it.

Stage 3   10-15 mins.

Use the steps for making an ethical decision from page 131 as you consider each possible solution.

Stage 4   10-15 mins.

Make a final decision.

Stage 5   15-20 mins.

Create a handout explaining the process you went through to come up with your decision.

If possible, when students have finished creating their handouts, make copies for everyone in the class or at least one per group.

Optional Computer Activity: Students may want to use the computer to create their handouts.

Stage 6   15-20 mins.

Report your final decision to the class.

Help teams prepare for their presentations. Suggest that each member choose a different part of the handout to present.

STANDARDS CORRELATIONS

CASAS: 4.8.1, 4.8.5, 4.8.6. (See CASAS Competency List on pages 169–175.)

SCANS: Resources Allocate time

Information Acquire and evaluate information, organize and maintain information, interpret and communicate information, use computers to process information

Systems Understand systems, improve and design systems

Technology (optional) Select technology, apply technology to exercise

Basic Skills Reading, writing, listening, speaking

Thinking Skills Creative thinking, decision making, problem solving, seeing things in the mind's eye, reasoning

Personal Qualities Responsibility, self-esteem, self-management, integrity/honesty

EFF: **Communication** Read with understanding, convey ideas in writing, speak so others can understand, listen actively, observe critically

Decision Making Solve problems and make decisions, plan

Interpersonal Guide others, resolve conflict and negotiate, advocate and influence, cooperate with others

Lifelong Learning Take responsibility for learning, reflect and evaluate, learn through research, use information and communication technologies (optional)

AT-A-GLANCE PREP

Objective: Interpret civic responsibilities
Academic Strategy: Focused listening
Vocabulary: *civic responsibility, permit, jaywalking, public transportation, jury summons*

RESOURCES

Activity Bank: Unit 8, Lesson 1, Worksheet 1
Reading and Writing Challenge: Unit 8

Grammar Challenge 4: Unit 8, Challenge 1
Audio: CD 1, Track 27

 1.5 hour classes   2.5 hour classes   3+ hour classes

AGENDA
Understand and identify civic responsibilities.
Learn about getting a driver's license.

 Preassessment *(optional)*

Use the Stand Out Assessment CD-ROM with Exam*View*® to create a pretest for Unit 8.

Warm-up and Review   5-10 mins.

Ask students to recall what they learned in the last two units about jobs in the workplace. Have them make a list of the most important things they learned.

Introduction   5-10 mins.

Ask students to raise their hands if they can answer yes to the following questions: *How many of you drive a car? How many of you have a driver's license? How many of you vote? How many of you pay taxes?*

State the objective: *Today we will be interpreting civic responsibilities.*

Presentation 1   5 mins.

Write *driver's license, vote,* and *pay taxes* on the board. Ask students what these things have in common. Ask them if they can add any others to the list. Go over the instructions to Exercise A with students by focusing their attention on the pictures and the phrase box.

Practice 1   10-15 mins.

 A Why are these things important? Complete the sentences below.

Evaluation 1   5 mins.

Go over the answers as a class.

STANDARDS CORRELATIONS

CASAS: 5.6.3 (See CASAS Competency List on pages 169–175.)
SCANS: **Information** Acquire and evaluate information, organize and maintain information, interpret and communicate information
Interpersonal Participate as a member of a team, teach others, exercise leadership, negotiate to arrive at a decision, work with cultural diversity
Systems Understand systems, monitor and correct performance, improve and design systems
Basic Skills Reading, writing, listening, speaking

Thinking Skills Creative thinking, decision making, seeing things in the mind's eye
Personal Qualities Responsibility, sociability, self-management
EFF: **Communication** Read with understanding, convey ideas in writing, speak so others can understand, listen actively
Decision Making Plan
Interpersonal Cooperate with others

Civic Responsibility

GOALS

➤ Interpret civic responsibilities
➤ Apply for a driver's license and respond to a jury summons

➤ Communicate opinions about a community problem
➤ Interpret the electoral process
➤ Write and give a speech

LESSON 1

Solving problems

GOAL ➤ Interpret civic responsibilities

Vocabulary · Grammar
Life Skills
Academic · Pronunciation

A Why are these things important? Complete the sentences below.

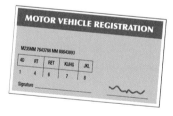

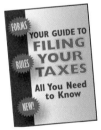

| jury summons | driver's license | ticket | car registration | taxes |

1. A _____ driver's license _____ permits you to drive a car.

2. _____ Taxes _____ help pay for government programs.

3. A _____ car registration _____ shows that you have paid to register your car with the state.

4. A _____ ticket _____ indicates that you have violated a traffic law.

5. A _____ jury summons _____ notifies you that the court needs you to appear for jury selection.

B A group of students from all over the country is attending a workshop about civic responsibility in the United States. Read their conversation and see if you can define *civic responsibility* with your teacher.

Bita: I never realized how difficult it would be to get adjusted to life in the United States. There are so many things to do.

Consuela: I know. Getting a driver's license and registering my car was very complicated.

Ranjit: In New York, we have good public transportation so I don't have to worry about a car. But I did get a jury summons the other day and I didn't know what I was supposed to do with it.

Ricardo: I got one of those last year and I couldn't understand it so I threw it away.

Minh: You threw it away? You can't do that. You have to respond.

Bita: What about tickets? The other day, I got a ticket for jaywalking. I want to fight it, but I don't know where to go.

Ranjit: I think you have to go to court, don't you?

Minh: The most confusing thing I've had to do is pay taxes. Can't they make those forms easier to understand?

Consuela: I agree. Last year, we paid someone to do our taxes.

C What five situations do the students mention?

1. getting a driver's license
2. registering a car
3. a jury summons
4. ticket
5. taxes

D Can you think of other situations you have had to deal with in the United States that are related to civic responsibility? Write them on the lines below. (Answers will vary.)

Presentation 2

5-10 mins. ■■■

B A group of students from all over the country is attending a workshop about civic responsibility in the United States. Read their conversation and see if you can define *civic responsibility* with your teacher.

Ask five volunteers to take one of the character's roles in the conversation and read the dialog to the class. Then, as a class, write a definition for *civic responsibility*.

Practice 2

10-15 mins. ■■

(Shorter classes can do Exercise C for homework.)

C What five situations do the students mention?

Have students get in small groups to find the five situations discussed in the conversation.

D Can you think of other situations you have had to deal with in the United States that are related to civic responsibility? Write them on the lines below.

Have students continue to work in their groups to complete this activity.

Evaluation 2

5-10 mins. ■■

Have each group report to the class. Make a list on the board of all the responsibilities mentioned.

Presentation 3   10-15 mins.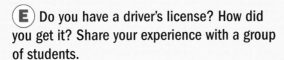

E Do you have a driver's license? How did you get it? Share your experience with a group of students.

Have students do this exercise in groups or discuss the questions as a class.

Prepare students for Exercise F by reading through the questions as a class.

F Bita calls Consuela to ask how to get a driver's license. Listen to the conversation.

After you've played the recording once, ask students if they think they understood enough to answer all of the questions. If not, play it again.

 Listening Script   CD 1, Track 27

Bita: *Is this Consuela?*
Consuela: *Yes. Who's this?*
Bita: *This is Bita from Bellingham, Washington.*
Consuela: *Hi! How are you doing?*
Bita: *I'm OK. A little busy with work and school, but I'm surviving. Hey, I was wondering if you could help me with something.*
Consuela: *Of course! What do you need?*
Bita: *Well, I think it's time for me to get a driver's license. Public transportation is taking up too much of my time and I need to be able to get around faster. I've been saving up to buy a car, but I still have to get my license. I remember the other day that you said you had gotten your license and registered your car, so I thought maybe you could give me some advice.*
Consuela: *Sure.*
Bita: *Well, I already have my driver's license from Iran. Do I still have to take the test?*
Consuela: *Yes, you'll have to take the written test and the driving test. Only people from other states in the United States can get the driving test waived.*
Bita: *OK, so how do I prepare for the written test?*
Consuela: *First, you need to go to the DMV and get a driver's handbook to study the rules of the road for the written test.*
Bita: *How many questions are on the test?*
Consuela: *In California, the written test has 36 questions. In Washington, it may be different.*
Bita: *How many questions do I have to get correct? And what if I don't pass it the first time?*
Consuela: *You can miss five questions, but you have three chances to pass the test. If you don't pass the first time, you can take it two more times.*
Bita: *OK. What about the driving test?*
Consuela: *First, you need to make an appointment. They won't let you test without one. Second, a licensed*

driver must accompany you to the DMV in the car that you'll use to take the test.
Bita: *And then they test me on my driving skills?*
Consuela: *Yep.*
Bita: *That should be easy. I've been practicing with my brother for over a year. So, how do I apply for the license?*
Consuela: *First, you have to get an application and fill it out. Then you have to take the application to the DMV.*
Bita: *OK, so what do I have to do next?*
Consuela: *Well, you have to take the written test, take a vision exam, show them proof of your social security number and your date of birth, give them your thumbprint, and have your picture taken.*
Bita: *How much does that cost?*
Consuela: *$12.*
Bita: *OK, I think I can do this.*
Consuela: *I know you can. Good luck! Call me and let me know how it goes.*
Bita: *I sure will. Thanks a lot, Consuela!*
Consuela: *Anytime.*

Practice 3   15-20 mins.

G With a partner, ask and answer the questions based on what you learned from the conversation.

Evaluation 3   10-15 mins. ■

Ask students to share the answers they discussed with their partners. If students want to hear the conversation again, play it for them.

Application   10-15 mins. ■■■

H In groups, ask and answer questions about situations related to the civic responsibilities that you listed on page 142.

Go over the example, then have students work in groups to talk about civic responsibilities.

Activity Bank

Lesson 1, Worksheet 1: Civic Responsibility

Refer students to *Stand Out 4 Grammar Challenge*, Unit 8, Challenge 1 for practice with *supposed to*, *required to*, and *allowed/ permitted to*.

 E Do you have a driver's license? How did you get it? Share your experience with a group of students.

 F Bita calls Consuela to ask how to get a driver's license. Listen to the conversation.

CD 1
TR 27

G With a partner, ask and answer the questions based on what you learned from the conversation.

1. If I already have my driver's license from another country, do I still have to take the test? Yes, you have to take both written and driving tests.

2. How do I prepare for the written test? Go to the DMV and get a Driver's Handbook to study the rules of the road.

3. How many questions are on the test? In California, there are 36.

4. How many questions do I have to get correct? You can miss five questions.

5. What if I don't pass it the first time? You may take the test two more times.

6. What do I need to know about the driving test? You need to make an appointment and a licensed driver must accompany you.

7. How do I apply for the license? Fill out an application at the DMV and turn it in.

8. Do I need to make an appointment to turn in my application? No, you don't.

9. What do I have to do when I turn in my application? You take the written test, take a vision test, give proof of your Social Security number and birthdate, give them your

10. How much does it cost?   thumbprint, and have your picture taken.
    It costs $12.

 H In groups, ask and answer questions about situations related to the civic responsibilities that you listed on page 142.

EXAMPLE: *Student A:* Have you ever gotten a ticket before?
            Student B: Yes, I got one for rolling through a stop sign.

A driver's license and jury duty

GOAL ➤ Apply for a driver's license and respond to a jury summons

 A Bita went to the DMV and got an application for a driver's license. Fill out the application.
(Answers will vary.)

DRIVER'S LICENSE APPLICATION

Name

Street/PO Box

City	State	Zip

Date of Birth	Sex ❑ Male ❑ Female	Height	Weight

License Number	Social Security No.	Restricted Code

	Eye Color ❑ Blue ❑ Brown ❑ Black ❑ Green ❑ Gray ❑ Violet ❑ Hazel	

Do you have any condition which might affect your ability to operate a motor vehicle, such as:

❑ Seizures or Unconsciousness	❑ Hearing or Vision Problem	❑ Have Your Driving Privileges Ever Been Suspended?
❑ Mental Disability	❑ Alcohol or Drug Problem	

***If any of the above are checked, a letter of explanation must accompany this application. Failure to do so may delay your license.

I certify that the above statements are true. Do you wish to be an organ donor? ❑ Yes ❑ No

Signed X	Date

Please check one of the following:
❑ Regular Driver's License (Class E)
❑ Out-of-State Transfer
 (Must surrender license from other state.)
❑ Applicant Under Age of 18
 *Must Provide School Enrollment Form
 *License Will Expire on 21st Birthday

DUPLICATE LICENSE FEE: $5.00
❑ Duplicate License
❑ Duplicate Class D License
❑ Address change: If you move, you must change your address on your driver's license within twenty days.
❑ Name Change: _____

FORMER NAME
*You must attach a copy of your marriage certificate, divorce decree, court order or birth certificate when changing your name.

DEPARTMENT USE ONLY
Your birth certificate must be shown to the examining officer as proof of your age.
The Applicant Named in This Application Passed the Examination Conducted.
At _____ Detachment This _____ Day of _____ 20 ___

Examiner _____ Unit Number _____

Restrictions _____

 B With a group, make a chart that explains how to get a driver's license step-by-step. Compare your chart with another group's chart.

Objective: Apply for a driver's license and respond
  to a jury summons
Academic Strategies: Active reading, using context clues
Vocabulary: *seizures, unconsciousness, mental disability,*
fair trial, jury, judge, jury selection, accused of a crime, case,
qualifications, disqualify

AGENDA

Fill out a driver's license application.
Explain in a chart how to get a
  driver's license.
Understand jury summons
  vocabulary.
Fill out a jury summons.

RESOURCES

Activity Bank: Unit 8, Lesson 2, Worksheets 1–2   **Grammar Challenge 4:** Unit 8, Challenge 2
Reading and Writing Challenge: Unit 8

■ 1.5 hour classes ■ 2.5 hour classes ■ 3⁺ hour classes

Warm-up and Review   5-10 mins.

Quiz students on the procedures they learned in
the previous lesson by asking them to take out
a sheet of paper and write down answers to the
following questions:

1. *If you already have your driver's license from*
   another country, do you still have to take the test?
2. *How do you prepare for the written test?*
3. *How many questions are on the test?*
4. *How many questions do you have to get correct?*
5. *What if you don't pass it the first time?*
6. *How do you apply for a license?*
7. *Do you need to make an appointment to turn*
   in your application?
8. *What do you have to do when you turn in your*
   application?
9. *How much does it cost?*

Introduction   5-10 mins.

Write *jury duty* on the board. See if students
can explain this term to you. Then ask if any
students have had experience with jury duty or
received a jury summons in the mail.

State the objective: *Today we will continue*
learning about applying for a driver's license by
filling out an application. Then we will learn what
to do when we receive a jury summons in the mail.

Focus students' attention on the application and
go over each section with them as they fill it out.

Presentation 1   10-15 mins.

(A) Bita went to the DMV and got an application
for a driver's license. Fill out the application.

Focus students' attention on the application and
go over each section with them as they fill it out.

Practice 1   10-15 mins.

(B) With a group, make a chart that explains
how to get a driver's license step-by-step.
Compare your chart with another group's chart.

Evaluation 1   5 mins. ■■■

Ask volunteer groups to write their charts
on the board.

STANDARDS CORRELATIONS

CASAS: 1.9.2 (See CASAS Competency List on pages 169–175.)
SCANS: **Information** Acquire and evaluate information, organize and
maintain information, interpret and communicate information
Interpersonal Participate as a member of a team, teach others, exercise
leadership, negotiate to arrive at a decision, work with cultural diversity
Systems Understand systems, monitor and correct performance
Basic Skills Reading, writing, listening, speaking
Thinking Skills Creative thinking, decision making, seeing things in the
mind's eye

Personal Qualities Responsibility, sociability, self-management
EFF: **Communication** Read with understanding, convey ideas in writing,
speak so others can understand, listen actively
Decision Making Solve problems and make decisions, plan
Interpersonal Cooperate with others
Lifelong Learning Take responsibility for learning, learn through research,
use information and communication technologies (optional)

Presentation 2   5-10 mins. ■■■

C Bita and Ranjit are chatting about jury duty in the United States. Read their conversation.

Choose two volunteers to read the conversation out loud. Ask students questions about the content of the conversation.

Practice 2   10-15 mins. ■■

D Discuss the following terms with your teacher. See if you can work out their meanings using the conversation above.

See if students can work out the meanings on their own before you begin a class discussion.

Have students read the conversation and underline any other unfamiliar words or phrases. Have them work out their meanings.

Evaluation 2   10-15 mins. ■■

Go over the meanings of unfamiliar words and phrases.

LESSON 2 **GOAL** ➤ Apply for a driver's license
and respond to a jury summons

C Bita and Ranjit are chatting about jury duty in the United States. Read their conversation.

Bita: Ranjit, I just got my new driver's license in the mail!
Ranjit: Congratulations, Bita! That's wonderful.
Bita: What are you looking at?
Ranjit: Oh, I just got a jury summons in the mail. Can you tell me what I'm supposed to do with it?
Bita: Sure. I've had at least three of them.
Ranjit: What are they about anyway?
Bita: Well, in the United States, anyone accused of a crime has the right to a fair trial, which means a judge and twelve people on a jury get to listen to the case and make a decision.
Ranjit: Oh, I get it. So, can anyone be on a jury?
Bita: No, you have to meet certain qualifications.
Ranjit: Like what?
Bita: First of all, you have to be a U.S. citizen and a resident of the county or city where the trial is taking place. Also, you have to be able to understand and speak enough English to participate in the jury selection and the trial.
Ranjit: Well, I think I can speak and understand enough English, but I'm not a citizen yet. Does that disqualify me?
Bita: I'm afraid so.
Ranjit: Darn. It sounds like fun to participate in a trial. So, what do I do with this form?
Bita: There should be a series of *yes/no* questions on it. Answer each of the questions truthfully. Then explain at the bottom why you are not qualified to participate. Some people who are citizens can be excused for other reasons, like financial hardship, medical conditions, or being older than 65. So, just fill out the form and then send it back in within ten days.
Ranjit: That's it?
Bita: That's it. Easy, huh?

D Discuss the following terms with your teacher. See if you can work out their meanings using the conversation above.

fair trial	judge	accused of a crime
jury	jury selection	qualifications

 LESSON 2 GOAL ➤ **Apply for a driver's license and respond to a jury summons**

E Read the jury summons with your teacher.

JURY SUMMONS

Please bring this upper portion with you when you report for jury duty.

JUROR	You are hereby notified that you have been selected for jury service in the State Trial Courts of _____ County. You are ordered to appear at the court for the following days: *May 3, 4, 5* Your Group Number: 75 Your Juror Number: 567

JUROR QUALIFICATION FORM
DETACH THIS HALF AND RETURN BY MAIL WITHIN 10 DAYS

Name _____

Address _____

City/State/Zip _____

Home Phone _____ Date of Birth _____

Employer _____

Occupation _____

Work Phone _____

Answer each of the following questions under penalty of perjury.

1. Are you a citizen of the United States? ☐ yes ☐ no
2. Are you currently a resident of _____ County? ☐ yes ☐ no
3. Are you 18 years of age or older? ☐ yes ☐ no
4. Do you read, write, speak, and understand the English language?
   (If another person filled out this form, please provide their name,
   address, and the reasons in the space provided below.) ☐ yes ☐ no
5. Have you ever been convicted or plead guilty to theft or any felony
   offense? ☐ yes ☐ no
6. Do you have a physical or mental disability that would interfere with
   or prevent you from serving as a juror? ☐ yes ☐ no
7. Are you 65 years of age or older? ☐ yes ☐ no

If you answered NO to questions 1, 2, 3, or 4, you are automatically excused from jury duty. Please write your reason below and send in the form.

Reason I cannot serve on jury duty: _____

_____

_____

 F **Fill out this jury summons with your personal information. What should you do with this form when you have filled it out?** (Answers will vary for filling out the form. Answer to question: bring the upper portion with you to jury duty, and mail the bottom portion back within 10 days.)

Note: If the information is too personal, just think about the answer and don't write it in your book.

Presentation 3   10-15 mins.   ■■■   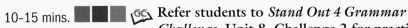 Refer students to *Stand Out 4 Grammar Challenge*, Unit 8, Challenge 2 for practice with causative verbs.

E Read the jury summons with your teacher.

Take students through the jury summons step-by-step.

Practice 3   15-20 mins.   ■

(Shorter classes can do Exercise F for homework.)

Have students practice asking and answering the seven *yes/no* questions on the juror qualification form with at least three other students. Demonstrate for them first by asking a volunteer the first two questions.

F Fill out this jury summons with your personal information. What should you do with this form when you have filled it out? *Note:* If the information is too personal, just think about the answer and don't write it in your book.

Evaluation 3   5-10 mins.   ■

Walk around the classroom and observe students filling out the summons. When students have finished, go over any common mistakes that you noticed when you were walking around.

Application   10-20 mins.   ■■■

Have students close their books. Write the following chart on the board.

	Requirements
To get a driver's license	
To be on jury duty	

Have students work in teams to complete the chart based on what they have learned in this lesson and the previous lesson.

Activity Bank

Lesson 2, Worksheet 1: Driving Safety
Lesson 2, Worksheet 2: Jury Summons Information

Instructor's Notes

_____
_____
_____
_____
_____
_____
_____
_____
_____
_____
_____
_____
_____
_____
_____
_____
_____
_____
_____
_____
_____
_____
_____
_____
_____
_____
_____
_____

Objective: Communicate opinions about a community problem

Academic Strategy: Writing a letter to a local official

Vocabulary: *graffiti, garbage, overcrowded freeway, gang, street corner, local official, facts, anecdotes*

AGENDA

Identify common community problems.
Identify solutions to community problems.
List problems in your community and possible solutions.
Write a business letter.

RESOURCES

Activity Bank: Unit 8, Lesson 3, Worksheet 1

Reading and Writing Challenge: Unit 8

Grammar Challenge 4: Unit 8, Challenge 3

■ 1.5 hour classes   ■ 2.5 hour classes   ■ 3ꞌ hour classes

Warm-up and Review   5-10 mins. ■■■

Review the jury summons process with students by calling on them to explain what to do if they receive a jury summons in the mail. If they don't give you enough information, ask for more. (Pretend you don't understand the process.)

Introduction   5-10 mins. ■■■

Ask students: *What are some problems in your community that you would like solved?* Write the problems that they mention on the board. State the objective: *Today you will be coming up with solutions for different community problems and writing a business letter to a local official.*

Presentation 1   10-15 mins. ■■■

 Look at the photos below and identify what these community problems might be.

Discuss the photo as a class and list the four problems on the board. Ask students if they have any of these problems in their communities.

Practice 1   10-15 mins. ■■■

 List the problems below. Discuss some possible solutions for each with a partner. Write one solution for each problem.

Evaluation 1   5 mins. ■■■

 Share your solutions with the class. Vote on the best solution for each problem.

STANDARDS CORRELATIONS

CASAS: 5.6.1 (See CASAS Competency List on pages 169–175.)

SCANS: Resources Allocate time, allocate money, allocate materials and facility resources, allocate human resources

Information Organize and maintain information, interpret and communicate information

Interpersonal Participate as a member of a team, teach others, exercise leadership, negotiate to arrive at a decision, work with cultural diversity

Systems Understand systems, monitor and correct performance, improve and design systems

Basic Skills Reading, writing, listening, speaking

Thinking Skills Creative thinking, decision making, problem solving, seeing things in the mind's eye

Personal Qualities Responsibility, sociability, self-management

EFF: Communication Convey ideas in writing, speak so others can understand, listen actively

Decision Making Solve problems and make decisions, plan

Interpersonal Resolve conflict and negotiate, advocate and influence, cooperate with others

Lifelong Learning Reflect and evaluate, learn through research, use information and communication technologies (optional)

Problems in your community

GOAL ➤ Apply for a driver's license and respond to a jury summons

Vocabulary Grammar
Life Skills
Academic Pronunciation

A Look at the photos below and identify what these community problems might be.

graffiti

trash/littering

traffic

overcrowded schools

B List the problems below. Discuss some possible solutions for each with a partner. Write one solution for each problem.

Problem	Solution
1. graffiti	repaint/remove
2. trash/littering	community clean-up programs
3. traffic	improve public transportation
4. overcrowded schools	build new schools/hire more teachers

C Share your solutions with the class. Vote on the best solution for each problem.

 Imagine you are meeting with a government official in your community. Practice
the conversation below.

Official: So, what do you think one of the biggest problems in our community is?
Resident: I think the biggest problem is <u>the number of homeless people who sleep
on the street</u>.
Official: Do you have any ideas about how to solve the problem?
Resident: Actually, our neighborhood came up with two ideas. One, <u>we would like
to spend our tax dollars to build a bigger homeless shelter</u>. And two, <u>we would like
to put a community group together to tell the homeless people about the shelter
and take them there if necessary</u>.
Official: Those are two great ideas. I'll bring them up at our next town hall meeting.

E What are some problems in your community? Work with a group to make a list. Then,
come up with two possible solutions for each problem. (Answers will vary.)

Problem	Solution
1.	1. 2.
2.	1. 2.
3.	1. 2.

 Work with a partner to practice the conversation in Exercise D again. This time,
substitute the information you wrote in Exercise E for the underlined information.

Presentation 2   5-10 mins.

 Imagine you are meeting with a government official in your community. Practice the conversation below.

Ask volunteers to read the conversation out loud, then have all of the students read the conversation out loud with a partner. Ask if students think these are good solutions.

Practice 2   10-15 mins. ■■

 What are some problems in your community? Work with a group to make a list. Then, come up with two possible solutions for each problem.

F Work with a partner to practice the conversation in Exercise D again. This time, substitute the information you wrote in Exercise E for the underlined information.

Prepare students to practice this conversation by showing them how to substitute their own ideas for the ones given in the conversation.

Evaluation 2   10-15 mins. ■■

Ask volunteers to perform the conversations for the class.

Presentation 3　　　　5-10 mins. ■■■

Go through each item in Exercise G and ask students why this information is important to include in a business letter to a local official. Make sure they understand what to write in each section.

Practice 3　　　　　15-20 mins. ■

(Shorter classes can do Exercise G for homework.)

G Prepare to write a business letter about a problem in your community. Choose one of the problems that you have discussed with your group or a different problem in your community. Before writing the letter, fill in the information below.

Evaluation 3　　　　　15-20 mins. ■

Walk around the classroom and help students as needed.

Application　　　　　10-20 mins. ■■■

H Now write a letter to a local official about the community problem and your solution. Format it like a business letter.

Activity Bank

Lesson 3, Worksheet 1: Writing a Letter to a Community Official—Editing Checklist

---

Refer students to *Stand Out 4 Grammar Challenge*, Unit 8, Challenge 3 for practice with passive modals in the past.

GOAL ➤ Communicate opinions
about a community problem

G Prepare to write a business letter about a problem in your community. Choose one of the problems that you have discussed with your group or a different problem in your community. Before writing the letter, fill in the information below. (Answers will vary.)

Date: _____

Your name and address: _____

_____

Official's name and address: (Research this information.) _____

_____

State the problem: _____

_____

_____

_____

Facts or anecdotes about the problem: _____

_____

_____

_____

Suggested solutions: _____

_____

_____

Closing: _____

_____

H Now, write a letter to a local official about the community problem and your solution. Format it like a business letter.

GOAL ➤ Interpret the electoral process

 A The students are chatting about local elections. Read their conversation. Do you agree with them? Why is it important to understand the electoral process?

Ranjit: Elections for a new mayor are coming up here in New York. Have any of you participated in an election before?

Bita: I haven't. I just became a U.S. citizen last year so I will finally get to vote in this election.

Ricardo: So, if we're not citizens, we don't need to pay attention to the elections, do we?

Bita: Oh, I disagree. Even when I wasn't a citizen, I participated in local town meetings and city council meetings.

Consuela: Why?

Bita: Because I live in this community just like everyone else and I want my voice to be heard.

Ranjit: I agree with you, Bita. I think it's important that we voice our opinions on local issues in our community. I've been listening to the candidates' speeches to see whom I would vote for. But I don't really understand how the election process works.

Bita: Let's look at the chart our teacher gave us.

B Read the flowchart and discuss it with your classmates and teacher.

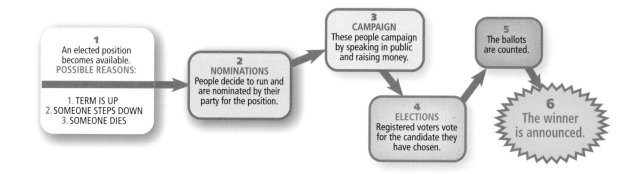

 C Work with a partner. One of you should explain the words in the box below. The other partner should then explain the electoral process using these words. Switch roles when you have finished.

> elected   position   to step down   term   ballots   to announce

AT-A-GLANCE PREP

Objective: Interpret the electoral process
Academic Strategies: Active reading, reading a
flowchart, writing a paragraph
Vocabulary: *elected position, step down, term, ballots,
announce*

RESOURCES

Reading and Writing Challenge: Unit 8
Grammar Challenge 4: Unit 8, Challenge 4

■ 1.5 hour classes   ■ 2.5 hour classes   ■ 3⁺ hour classes

AGENDA

*Understand and describe the
  electoral process.
Learn voter requirements.
Register to vote.
Write about the electoral process.*

Warm-up and Review   5-10 mins.

Ask students how they felt about writing a letter
to a local official. Take a poll and see how many
students would feel comfortable sending their
letter. Ask how many students would write
another letter in the future and actually send it.

Introduction   5-10 mins.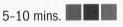

Ask students who the president is. Ask students
who the vice president is. Ask students how these
people got chosen to lead our country. State the
objective: *Today you will learn about the electoral
process and how to register to vote.*

Presentation 1   10-15 mins.

Have a brief discussion about local elections and
what happens in a community when elections
are coming up such as ad campaigns, voter
registration drives, and so on.

(A) The students are chatting about local
elections. Read their conversation. Do you agree
with them? Why is it important to understand
the electoral process?

Have students read the conversation silently.
Then call on two students to read the
conversation out loud. Answer any questions
students have about the conversation.

(B) Read the flowchart and discuss it with your
classmates and teacher.

Practice 1   10-15 mins.

(C) Work with a partner. One of you should
explain the words in the box below. The other
partner should then explain the electoral process
using these words. Switch roles when you have
finished.

Evaluation 1   5 mins.

Observe students as they work. Ask a few
volunteers to explain the electoral process.

STANDARDS CORRELATIONS

CASAS: 5.1.4 (See CASAS Competency List on pages 169-175.)
SCANS: Information Acquire and evaluate information, organize and
maintain information, interpret and communicate information
Interpersonal Participate as a member of a team, teach others, exercise
leadership, negotiate to arrive at a decision, work with cultural diversity
Systems Understand systems, monitor and correct performance
Basic Skills Reading, writing, listening, speaking
Thinking Skills Creative thinking, decision making, problem solving,
seeing things in the mind's eye

Personal Qualities Responsibility, sociability, self-management
EFF: Communication Read with understanding, convey ideas in writing,
speak so others can understand, listen actively, observe critically
Decision Making Plan
Interpersonal Guide others, cooperate with others
Lifelong Learning Learn through research, use information and
communication technologies (optional)

Presentation 2   1 min. ■■■

Explain the directions to Exercise D.

Practice 2   5-10 mins. ■■

(Shorter classes can do this exercise for homework.)

(D) Circle the best answer to each question about the electoral process.

If necessary, direct students back to the flowchart to find the answers.

Evaluation 2   5 mins. ■■

Go over the correct answers as a class.

Presentation 3   10-15 mins. ■■■

(E) Are you eligible to vote in an election? Read the list of requirements and check (✓) the ones that apply to you.

Go through each requirement with students and have them check the ones that apply to them.

 Circle the best answer to each question about the electoral process.

1. When does an elected position become available?
   a. when someone's term is up
   b. when someone steps down
   c. when someone dies
   (d.) all of the above

2. Who nominates people to run for office?
   a. their friends and family
   (b.) their political party
   c. their teachers
   d. the previous elected official

3. What does it mean to campaign?
   a. vote
   b. make posters
   (c.) speak in public and raise money
   d. count the ballots

4. When is the winner announced?
   a. before the elections
   b. after the nominations
   c. after someone dies
   (d.) when all the ballots have been counted

E Are you eligible to vote in an election? Read the list of requirements and check (✓) the ones that apply to you. (Answers will vary.)

Requirements	
U.S. citizen	❏ I am a U.S. citizen.
Resident of the state you live in	❏ I am a resident.
A person who is 18 years or older	❏ I am 18 years or older.
A person who is not in jail or on parole	❏ I am not in jail or on parole.

LESSON **4** **GOAL** > Interpret the electoral process

(F) If you checked all of the boxes in Exercise E, you are eligible to vote! What's the next step? You need to fill out a voter registration card. You can register to vote at these locations: a post office, a public library, the Department of Motor Vehicles (DMV), and other government offices.

(G) Fill out the voter registration card. (Answers will vary.)

Official Voter Registration Card

1. NAME _____

2. RESIDENCE _____

3. MAILING ADDRESS (if different from residence) _____

4. TELEPHONE NUMBER (_____) _____-_____

5. DATE OF BIRTH ____/____/_____

6. BIRTHPLACE _____

7. OCCUPATION _____

8. PRIOR REGISTRATION _____

9. POLITICAL PARTY (CHECK ONE)
❏ American Independent Party ❏ Democratic Party ❏ Libertarian Party
❏ Peace And Freedom Party ❏ Republican Party ❏ Decline To State
Other (Specify) _____

READ THIS STATEMENT BEFORE SIGNING:
I am a citizen of the United States and will be at least 18 years of age at the time of the next election. I am not imprisoned or on parole for the conviction of a felony. I certify under penalty of perjury under the laws of the state of california that the information on this affidavit is true and correct.

_____

Signature   Date

(H) Write a paragraph about the electoral process. Use some of these sequencing transitions in your paragraph.

After that,	In conclusion,	First of all,
At the next stage,	In summary,	Secondly,
Next,	Finally,	Thirdly,

Presentation 3 *(continued)* 10-15 mins. ▪▪▪

F If you checked all of the boxes in Exercise E, you are eligible to vote! What's the next step? You need to fill out a voter registration card. You can register to vote at these locations: a post office, a public library, the Department of Motor Vehicles (DMV), and other government offices.

Direct students' attention to the voter registration card and go through each item with them, making sure they understand how to fill it out.

Practice 3 10-15 mins. ▪

(Shorter classes can do Exercise G for homework.)

G Fill out the voter registration card.

Evaluation 3 10-15 mins. ▪

Walk around the classroom and help students as needed.

Application 10-20 mins. ▪▪▪

H Write a paragraph about the electoral process. Use some of these sequencing transitions in your paragraph.

📖 Refer students to *Stand Out 4 Grammar Challenge*, Unit 8, Challenge 4 for practice with gerunds and infinitives as subjects.

Lesson Planner: Unit 8, Lesson 4 **152a**

Objective: Write and give a speech
Grammar: Passive modals
Academic Strategies: Focused listening, active reading, writing a speech
Vocabulary: *running for office, tuition, gang violence, homeless, environmental awareness*

RESOURCES

Activity Bank: Unit 8, Lesson 5, Worksheets 1–2
Reading and Writing Challenge: Unit 8

Grammar Challenge 4: Unit 8, Challenge 5; Extension Challenges 1–2
Audio: CD 1, Track 28

■ 1.5 hour classes   ■ 2.5 hour classes   ■ 3⁺ hour classes

AGENDA

Analyze campaign speeches.
Who would you vote for?
Use passive modals.
Write a speech.
Give a speech.

Warm-up and Review   5-10 mins.

Without looking at their books, ask students to write down the six steps of the electoral process. Go over the answers as a class. How many students got them right?

Introduction   5-10 mins.

Ask students if they know who the mayor of their city is. Ask them if they have ever seen him or her on TV or in the newspaper. See what they know. State the objective: *Today we will listen to speeches from three different mayoral candidates, analyze the speeches, and write our own speeches to give to the class.*

Presentation 1   10-15 mins.

Prepare students for the listening exercise by telling them that they will be hearing speeches from three different mayoral candidates. Go over the list under Antonio Juliana.

Practice 1   10-15 mins.

(A) Listen to the speeches from three people running for mayor of your city. For the first speech, put a check mark (✓) next to everything the candidate promises to do for you. For the second two speeches, write down what they promise to do for you. You will hear each speech two times.

Note: Listening Script is on page 154a.

(B) Who would you vote for if you were interested in . . .

Have students complete this activity individually.

Activity Bank

Lesson 5, Worksheet 1: Sample Ballot

Evaluation 1   3 mins.

Discuss students' answers as a class.

STANDARDS CORRELATIONS

CASAS: 5.1.4, 5.1.6 (See CASAS Competency List on page 168.)
SCANS: **Resources** Allocate time, allocate money, allocate materials and facility resources, allocate human resources
Information Acquire and evaluate information, organize and maintain information, interpret and communicate information
Interpersonal Participate as a member of a team, teach others, exercise leadership, negotiate to arrive at a decision, work with cultural diversity
Systems Understand systems, monitor and correct performance
Basic Skills Reading, writing, listening, speaking

Thinking Skills Creative thinking, decision making, problem solving, seeing things in the mind's eye
Personal Qualities Responsibility, sociability, self-management
EFF: **Communication** Read with understanding, convey ideas in writing, speak so others can understand, listen actively, observe critically
Decision Making Solve problems and make decisions, plan
Interpersonal Advocate and influence, cooperate with others
Lifelong Learning Reflect and evaluate, learn through research, use information and communication technologies (optional)

What's your platform?

GOAL ➤ Write and give a speech

CD 1
TR 28

A Listen to the speeches from three people running for mayor of your city. For the first speech, put a check mark (✓) next to everything the candidate promises to do for you. For the second two speeches, write down what they promise to do for you. You will hear each speech two times.

Antonio Juliana promises to:

❑ clean up the streets

❑ lower tuition fees

❑ improve public transportation

☑ decrease gang violence

☑ get kids off the streets

☑ help the homeless people

❑ increase environmental awareness

Antonio Juliana

Gary Hurt promises to:

1. clean up the beaches

2. improve public transportation

3. create more parks and safe places for children to play

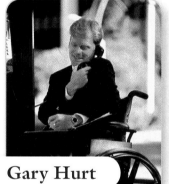

Gary Hurt

Kwan Tan promises to:

1. build more schools

2. lower tuition at community colleges

3. implement educational standards

4. start a parent-involvement program

Kwan Tan

B Who would you vote for if you were interested in . . .

the environment?   Gary Hurt

education?   Kwan Tan

safe streets?   Antonio Juliana

C Read Kwan Tan's speech.

Good evening and thank you for coming tonight! This community has given me so many opportunities and, in running for mayor, I hope to give something back to the city that welcomed me as an immigrant, educated me through my teen years, and supported me as I opened my first business.

First on my agenda is education. I will make sure your tax dollars are used to build more schools so our children won't have to sit in overcrowded classrooms. I'll lower the tuition at our community colleges so all of us will have a chance to continue and improve our education. I'll implement standards to ensure that schools are teaching our kids what they need to know. I'll start a parent-involvement program that encourages parents to participate actively in their kids' schools. Our children are the future of our community and we should invest time and money in their success.

Vote for me on Election Day and you'll have schools and a community to be proud of!

Kwan Tan for Mayor

Kwan Tan is:
★ A local business owner
★ A member of this community for over 25 years
★ A parent of two school-age children

A vote for Kwan will ensure for our community:
★ More primary and secondary schools
★ Improved standards of education
★ More parent involvement in schools
★ Lower community college tuition

★ **Vote for Kwan Tan** ★

D What changes would Kwan like to make? Do you think these are good ideas? Discuss your opinions with a partner. (build more schools, lower tuition at community colleges, implement educational standards, start a parent-involvement program)

E Study the chart with your teacher.

Passive Modals				
Example sentence	**Passive subject**	**Modal**	***be***	**Past participle**
More schools *should be* built.	schools	should	be	built
Taxes *need to be* increased.	taxes	need to	be	increased
Children *must be* protected.	children	must	be	protected
Parents *have to be* involved.	parents	have to	be	involved

Presentation 2　　　5-10 mins.

C Read Kwan Tan's speech.

Read Kwan's speech to your students. Ask them some basic comprehension questions about it.

Practice 2　　　10-15 mins.

(Shorter classes can do Exercise D for homework.)

D What changes would Kwan like to make? Do you think these are good ideas? Discuss your opinions with a partner.

Evaluation 2　　　10-15 mins.

Observe students discussing the changes and their opinions. Have students report back to the class.

Activity Bank

Lesson 5, Worksheet 2: Passive Modals

Presentation 3　　　5-10 mins.

E Study the chart with your teacher.

 Listening Script　　CD 1, Track 28

Antonio Juliana: *First of all, I want to thank you all for coming today. It is my pleasure to speak to you, and I hope that you will vote for me come Election Day. I'll be brief and to the point. My biggest concern is our streets. There is too much gang violence and I want to wipe it out. I think we can start by getting our children off the streets and taking care of the homeless people. It's time for us to regain our streets and feel safe again. Once this happens, we can focus on other problems like overcrowded schools and our public transportation system. I know you have a tough decision to make, but I hope that when you go to the polls next Tuesday, you'll put a check next to my name, Antonio Juliana.*

Gary Hurt: *I have been waiting for this day. A day when I could stand before you and tell you what I'm going to do if elected. These are not empty promises but things that WILL HAPPEN if you elect Gary Hurt as your mayor. The environment will be my number one priority. Our beaches will be clean again. Our public transportation system will be so good that you won't want to drive your cars anymore. I will use your tax dollars to create more parks and safe places for our children to play. Our city will be great once again if you vote for Gary Hurt!*

Kwan Tan: *Good evening and thank you for coming tonight! The community has given me so many opportunities and, in running for mayor, I hope to give something back to the city that welcomed me as an immigrant, educated me through my teen years, and supported me as I opened my first business.*

First on my agenda is education. I will make sure your tax dollars are used to build more schools so our children won't have to sit in overcrowded classrooms. I'll lower the tuition at our community colleges so all of us will have a chance to continue and improve our education. I'll implement standards to ensure that schools are teaching our kids what they need to know. I'll start a parent-involvement program that encourages parents to participate actively in their kids' schools. Our children are the future of our community and we should invest time and money in their success.

Vote for me on Election Day and you'll have schools and a community to be proud of!

Practice 3   15-20 mins. ■

(Shorter classes can do Exercise F for homework.)

(F) Write sentences to describe the issues Kwan Tan wants to change.

(G) Think of three problems that you would like to solve in your community. Write sentences about them using passive modals.

Evaluation 3   5-10 mins. ■

Ask volunteers to write their sentences on the board.

📖 Refer students to *Stand Out 4 Grammar Challenge*, Unit 8, Challenge 5 for more practice with passive modals, in the present.

📖 Refer students to Extension Challenge 1 for practice with passive modals in the past, and Extension Challenge 2 for practice with passive with *get*.

Application   10-20 mins. ■■■

(H) Kwan Tan's election speech has three parts. Look for each part in her speech.

(I) Imagine that you are running for mayor of your community. How would you introduce yourself? What problems would you like to solve? Write a speech that you would give if you were running for mayor. Practice it a few times alone and then give your speech to the class.

Give students an idea of how long their speech should be. (Two to four minutes is probably reasonable if you have a large class.) Depending on the amount of time you have, you may have to schedule the speeches over the next couple of class periods to give everyone a chance to give his or her speech.

F Write sentences to describe the issues Kwan Tan wants to change.

(Answers may vary slightly.)

EXAMPLE: Kwan Tan wants to build more schools.

She thinks that <u>more schools should be built</u>.

1. Kwan Tan wants to lower tuition fees at community colleges.

   She says that <u>tuition fees should be lowered at community colleges</u>.

2. Kwan Tan wants to implement standards in schools.

   She thinks that <u>standards need to be implemented in schools</u>.

3. Kwan Tan wants to encourage parents to participate in their kids' schools.

   She believes that <u>parents have to participate in their kids' schools</u>.

4. Kwan Tan wants to invest time and money in children.

   She emphasizes that <u>time and money must be invested in children</u>.

G Think of three problems that you would like to solve in your community. Write sentences about them using passive modals. (Answers will vary.)

1. _____

2. _____

3. _____

H Kwan Tan's election speech has three parts. Look for each part in her speech.

Introduction: She introduces herself and explains why she is running for office.

Body: She tells her audience what she plans to do if she is elected.

Conclusion: She reminds her audience to vote and tells them once again what changes she will make to the community.

I Imagine that you are running for mayor of your community. How would you introduce yourself? What problems would you like to solve? Write a speech that you would give if you were running for mayor. Practice it a few times alone and then give your speech to the class.

Review

 A Without looking back in the unit, try to recall what you learned about each of these topics. Write notes. (Lessons 1–5) (Answers will vary.)

Topic	I learned. . .
a jury summons	
a driver's license	
the electoral process	
voting	
giving a speech	

B Are the statements below true or false? (Lessons 1–5)

	True	False
1. You have to be 18 to apply for a driver's license.	○	●
2. You must respond to a jury summons.	●	○
3. You have to be a U.S. citizen to serve on a jury.	●	○
4. You don't have to speak English to serve on a jury trial.	○	●
5. People who want to run for office must be nominated.	●	○
6. Anyone who lives in the United States can vote.	○	●
7. You can register to vote at the DMV.	●	○
8. Only U.S. citizens can get involved in the community.	○	●

AT-A-GLANCE PREP

Objectives: All Unit 8 objectives
Grammar: All Unit 8 grammar
Academic Strategy: Reviewing
Vocabulary: All Unit 8 vocabulary

RESOURCES

Activity Bank: Unit 8, Lessons 1–5
Reading and Writing Challenge: Unit 8

Grammar Challenge 4: Unit 8, Challenges 1–5; Extension Challenges 1–2

■ 1.5 hour classes   ■ 2.5 hour classes   ■ 3+ hour classes

AGENDA

Unit objectives.
Review exercises.
My Dictionary.
Learner Log.

Warm-up and Review   10-15 mins.

Have students take out the speeches they wrote in the previous lesson and share them with a small group. Ask each group to vote on the best speech. Ask the writers of the best speeches to read their speeches aloud.

Introduction   5-10 mins. ■■■

Ask students to try to recall (in general) all the goals of this unit without looking at their books. Then remind them which goals they omitted, if any. (Unit Goals: Interpret civic responsibilities, apply for a driver's license and respond to a jury summons, communicate opinions about a community problem, interpret the electoral process, and write and give a speech.) Write all the objectives on the board from Unit 8. Show students the first page of the unit and mention the five objectives. State the objective: *Today we will be reviewing everything we have learned in this unit.*

Presentation 1   10-15 mins. ■■■

This presentation will cover the first three pages of the review. Quickly go to the first page of each lesson. Discuss the objective of each one.

Ask simple questions to remind students of what they have learned.

Note: Since there is little presentation in the review, you can assign the review exercises that don't involve pair work or group work for homework and go over them in class the following day.

Practice 1   20-25 mins.

Note: There are two ways to do the review: (1) Go through the exercises one at a time and, as students complete each one, go over the answers. (2) Briefly go through the instructions of each exercise, allow students to complete all of the exercises at once, and then go over the answers. Stop and evaluate whenever it is appropriate for the class. *(see Evaluation 1 on pg. 158a)*

(A) **Without looking back in the unit, try to recall what you learned about each of these topics. Write notes. (Lessons 1–5)**

(B) **Are the statements below true or false? (Lessons 1–5)**

STANDARDS CORRELATIONS

CASAS: 7.2.1 (See CASAS Competency List on pages 169-175.)
SCANS: **Resources** Allocate time
Information Acquire and evaluate information
Interpersonal Participate as a member of a team, teach others, negotiate to arrive at a decision, work with cultural diversity
Systems Monitor and correct performance
Basic Skills Reading, writing, listening, speaking
Thinking Skills Creative thinking, decision making, problem solving, seeing things in the mind's eye

Personal Qualities Responsibility, sociability, self-management
EFF: **Communication** Convey ideas in writing, speak so others can understand, listen actively
Decision Making Solve problems and make decisions
Interpersonal Guide others, cooperate with others
Lifelong Learning Take responsibility for learning, reflect and evaluate, learn through research

Practice 1 *(continued)*   25–30 mins. ■■■

C What are three problems in your community that you would like to solve? How would you solve them? Work with a small group to fill in the chart. (Lesson 3)

D There are six steps in the electoral process. Number them in the correct order. (Lesson 4)

E What are the four requirements to be eligible to vote? List them below. (Lesson 4)

F What are three places where you can register to vote? List them below. (Lesson 4)

Teaching Tip

Recycling/Review

The review process and the project that follows are part of the recycling/review process. Students at this level often need to be reintroduced to concepts to solidify what they have learned. Many concepts are learned and forgotten while learning other new concepts. This is because students learn but are not necessarily ready to acquire language concepts.

Therefore, it becomes very important to review and to show students how to review on their own. It is also important to recycle the new concepts in different contexts.

Instructor's Notes

C What are three problems in your community that you would like to solve? How would you solve them? Work with a small group to fill in the chart. (Lesson 3)
(Answers will vary.)

Problem	Solution
1.	
2.	
3.	

D There are six steps in the electoral process. Number them in the correct order. (Lesson 4)

__5__ Ballots are counted.

__4__ Elections are held.

__3__ Candidates campaign.

__2__ Candidates are nominated.

__6__ The winner is announced.

__1__ A position becomes available.

E What are the four requirements to be eligible to vote? List them below. (Lesson 4)

1. U.S. citizen

2. resident of the state you live in

3. 18 years or older

4. not in jail or on parole

F What are three places where you can register to vote? List them below. (Lesson 4)

1. post office

2. public library

3. DMV

Review

G Rewrite each sentence using a passive modal. (Lesson 5) (Answers may vary slightly.)

1. We must protect the environment.

   The environment must be protected.

2. They should reduce our taxes.

   Our taxes should be reduced.

3. They need to invest money in our education system.

   Money needs to be invested in our education system.

4. We have to reduce the speed limit.

   The speed limit has to be reduced.

5. They need to build more public transportation.

   More public transportation needs to be built.

6. We should protect our children from gang violence.

   Our children should be protected from gang violence.

H Imagine that you are running for mayor. What are your solutions for the following problems? (Lesson 5) (Answers will vary.)

1. Problem: gang violence

   Solution: _____

   _____

2. Problem: traffic

   Solution: _____

   _____

3. Problem: residents not using public transportation

   Solution: _____

   _____

4. Problem: homeless children

   Solution: _____

   _____

Practice 1 *(continued)*　　25–30 mins. ■■■□

G Rewrite each sentence using a passive modal. (Lesson 5)

H Imagine that you are running for mayor. What are your solutions for the following problems? (Lesson 5)

Evaluation 1　　40–55 mins. ■■■□

Go around the classroom and check on students' progress. Help individuals when needed. If you see consistent errors among several students, interrupt the class and give a mini-lesson or review to help students feel comfortable with the concept.

Presentation 2

5-10 mins.

My Dictionary

Ask students to brainstorm new vocabulary they learned in this unit. Have them do this without looking in their books.

Go back through each 'my dictionary' box in the book and remind students of all the vocabulary strategies they have learned. Then ask students to take a more in-depth look at the strategies on their own.

Practice 2

15-20 mins.

(Shorter classes can do these exercises for homework.)

In the past seven units, you learned many new ways to keep track of new vocabulary. Go back through your book and make a list of all the vocabulary strategies you learned.

Put a check mark (✓) next to the ones that are most useful to you.

Evaluation 2

5-10 mins.

Ask students to write the strategies on the board, and then ask volunteers to say which ones are the most useful to them and why.

Presentation 3

5-10 mins.

Learner Log

In this unit, you learned many things about civic responsibility. How comfortable do you feel doing each of the skills listed below? Rate your comfort level on a scale of 1 to 4.

Teaching Tip

Learner Logs

Learner Logs function to help students in many different ways.

1. They serve as part of the review process.
2. They help students to gain confidence and document what they have learned. Consequently, students see that they are making progress and want to move forward in learning.
3. They provide students with a tool that they can use over and over to check and recheck their understanding. In this way, students become independent learners.

Practice 3

5-10 mins.

Have students complete the Learner Log.

Evaluation 3

5-10 mins.

Walk around the classroom and help students as needed.

Application

5-10 mins.

Go over the reflection statements with students and have them complete the answers by themselves.

TB Assessment (optional)

Use the Stand Out Assessment CD-ROM with Exam*View*® to create a post-test for Unit 8.

My Dictionary

In the past seven units, you have learned many new ways to keep track of new vocabulary. Go back through your book and make a list of all the vocabulary strategies you learned.

Vocabulary Strategies I Have Learned

Vocabulary cards	Make a dictionary section about myself
Make your own dictionary	Use synonyms
Make related word lists	
Brainstorm new words	
Complete word family charts	

Check (✓) the strategies that are most useful to you.

Learner Log

In this unit, you learned many things about civic responsibility. How comfortable do you feel doing each of the skills listed below? Rate your comfort level on a scale of 1 to 4. (Answers will vary.)

1 = Need more practice   **2** = OK   **3** = Good   **4** = Great!

Life Skill	Comfort Level	Page
I can identify civic responsibilities.	1 2 3 4	_____
I can apply for a driver's license.	1 2 3 4	_____
I can respond to a jury summons.	1 2 3 4	_____
I can identify community problems and solutions.	1 2 3 4	_____
I can communicate opinions about community issues.	1 2 3 4	_____
I can write a letter to a local official.	1 2 3 4	_____
I can interpret and explain the electoral process.	1 2 3 4	_____
I can write and give a speech.	1 2 3 4	_____

If you circled 1 or 2, write down the page number where you can review this skill.

Reflections

1. I learned _____.

2. I would like to find out more about _____.

Team Project

Conduct an election.

With a team, you will prepare a candidate for an election. As a class, you will conduct an election.

1. Form a campaign committee with four or five students. Choose positions for each member of your team.

POSITION	JOB DESCRIPTION	STUDENT NAME
Student 1: **Campaign Director**	See that everyone speaks English and participates.	
Student 2: **Speech Writer**	Write candidate's speech.	
Student 3: **Candidate**	Give speech to class.	
Students 4/5: **Spokespeople**	Announce nomination. Introduce candidate. Create ballot.	

2. With your group, decide who will be running for school president. Announce the nomination to the class.

3. As a class, create a ballot with all the nominees' names on it. Make a ballot box for students to put their ballots in after they vote.

4. With your group, decide what issues are most important and write a campaign speech.

5. Candidates give speeches to the class.

6. Students all vote.

7. The teacher counts the ballots and announces the winner.

Conduct an election.

Each team will choose a candidate to run for school president. The team will prepare by writing a speech for their candidate. The candidates will give their speeches and the class will vote. The ballots will be counted and the winner announced.

The team project is the final application for the unit. It gives students a chance to show that they have mastered all of the Unit 8 objectives.

Note: Shorter classes can extend this project over two class meetings.

Stage 1 — 5 mins.

Form a campaign committee with four or five students. Choose positions for each member of your team.

Have students decide who will lead each step as described on the student page. Provide well-defined directions on the board for how teams should proceed. Explain that all the students do every step as a team. Teams shouldn't go to the next stage until the previous one is complete.

Stage 2 — 5-10 mins.

With your group, decide who will be running for school president. Announce the nomination to the class.

Ask for the campaign spokesperson to report to the class.

Optional Computer Activity: Students may want to use the computer to design their ads.

Stage 3 — 10-15 mins.

As a class, create a ballot with all the nominees' names on it. Make a ballot box for students to put their ballots in after they vote.

Have all the campaign spokespeople in the class get together to create a ballot with all the nominees' names on it. Tell them, they will need to have enough copies for the whole class to vote.

Stage 4 — 20-30 mins.

With your group, decide what issues are most important and write a campaign speech.

Stage 5 — 15-20 mins.

Candidates give speeches to the class.

Stage 6 — 5-10 mins.

Students all vote.

Stage 7 — 5-10 mins.

The teacher counts the ballots and announces the winner.

STANDARDS CORRELATIONS

CASAS: 4.8.1, 4.8.5, 4.8.6. (See CASAS Competency List on pages 169-175.)
SCANS: Resources Allocate time
Information Acquire and evaluate information, organize and maintain information, interpret and communicate information, use computers to process information
Systems Understand systems, improve and design systems
Technology (optional) Select technology, apply technology to exercise
Basic Skills Reading, writing, listening, speaking
Thinking Skills Creative thinking, decision making, problem solving, seeing things in the mind's eye, reasoning

Personal Qualities Responsibility, self-esteem, self-management, integrity/honesty
EFF: Communication Read with understanding, convey ideas in writing, speak so others can understand, listen actively, observe critically
Decision Making Solve problems and make decisions, plan
Interpersonal Guide others, resolve conflict and negotiate, advocate and influence, cooperate with others
Lifelong Learning Take responsibility for learning, reflect and evaluate, learn through research, use information and communication technologies (optional)

Stand Out 4 Vocabulary List

Pre-Unit
achievable P7
achieved P1
adjective P7
admission application P1
adverb P7
bar graph P6
conclusion sentence P8
creation P7
decide P7
educational P7
goal P1
interview P5
maiden name P1
meet P2
native speakers P4
noun P7
organization P7
paragraph P8
strategy P5
success P7
support sentence P8
topic sentence P8
verb P7
word family P7

Unit 1
accomplish 14
achievements 14
adjective clause 11
advice 8
allocate 14
architect 4
brainstorm 7
calm 10
carpool 7
cluster diagram 7
context 4
daily journal 10
daycare facility 8
deadlines 14
designed 4
determination 12
dreams 4
firm 4
focus 10
goals 4
habits 3
hopeful 10
in advance 13
influence 10
intern 5

jewelry 4
last-minute changes 13
medicine 4
obstacle 7
organized 13
overcome 7
partner 5
patience 12
perspective 10
positive influence 12
prioritize 14
qualifications 4
raise 4
realistic 14
reality 4
refugee 4
reliable 7
respond 8
retired 4
sacrificing 14
simultaneously 14
solution 7
suburban 4
surgeon 4
task 15
time management 13
toddler 8
to the last minute 13
troubled 10
used to 2
veranda 10

Unit 2
address 35
annual fee 27
APR 27
attractive 30
bargain 24
body 35
budget 22
budgeted amount 22
capacity 27
character 27
closing 35
collateral 27
complain 33
complaint 35
credit card 27
credit limit 27
creditworthiness 27
debit card 27
delivery time 24

digital camcorder 30
digital zoom 30
down payment 29
finance 21
grace period 27
greeting 35
image 30
introductory rate 27
late fee 27
LCD 30
loan 29
miniDV 30
miniDVD 30
monthly expenses 21
optical zoom 30
personal finances 21
persuade 30
price-matching 24
return address 35
salutation 35
shipping costs 24
shop around 24
signature 35
stabilization 30
still mode 30
trust 31
utilities 21
viewfinder 30
warranty 24

Unit 3
advantages 44
afford 53
amenities 41
asking price 41
attached garage 47
brand-new 41
central heating 50
closet space 50
closing 52
comparative 46
cozy 41
credit check 53
deposit 53
detached 41
disadvantages 44
enclosed 50
essential 50
expensive taste 45
financial commitment 53
floor plan 45
get approved for a loan 53

ideal 47
location 42
make an offer 51
market 41
master suite 41
mortgage 53
needs loving care 41
negotiate 41
nightlife 41
noisy 44
offer 41
on the way 47
outgrown 47
pay stubs 53
pile into 47
preferences 47
price range 48
priority 50
purchase price 53
putting away 47
realtor 47
seasonal views 41
secluded 41
single-family 41
superlative 46
survive 47
thought long and hard 47
within walking distance 47
working fireplace 41
works out of the home 47

Unit 4
airport 70
annunciation 66
Bingo 68
bulletin board 68
campground 70
clarification 72
community organizations 73
dress code 66
flyers 69
freeway 70
interstate 70
keep track of 74
local hangout 67
locate 61
map scale 70
marathon 68
notices 68
recycling 63
reservations 66
resources 61

Stand Out 4 Irregular Verb List

The following verbs are used in *Stand Out 4* and have irregular past tense forms.

Base Form	Simple Past	Past Participle
be	was, were	been
become	became	become
begin	began	begun
break	broke	broken
bring	brought	brought
build	built	built
buy	bought	bought
catch	caught	caught
come	came	come
do	did	done
drink	drank	drunk
drive	drove	driven
eat	ate	eaten
fall	fell	fallen
feel	felt	felt
fight	fought	fought
find	found	found
fly	flew	flown
get	got	gotten
give	gave	given
go	went	gone
grow	grew	grown
have	had	had
hear	heard	heard
hold	held	held
hurt	hurt	hurt
keep	kept	kept
know	knew	known
learn	learned	learned/learnt
lend	lent	lent

Base Form	Simple Past	Past Participle
lose	lost	lost
make	made	made
mean	meant	meant
meet	met	met
pay	paid	paid
put	put	put
read	read	read
ride	rode	ridden
run	ran	run
say	said	said
sell	sold	sold
send	sent	sent
set	set	set
show	showed	showed/shown
sit	sat	sat
sleep	slept	slept
speak	spoke	spoken
spend	spent	spent
spread	spread	spread
stand	stood	stood
steal	stole	stolen
take	took	taken
teach	taught	taught
tell	told	told
think	thought	thought
throw	threw	thrown
wake	woke	woken
wear	wore	worn
win	won	won
write	wrote	written

Used to

Example	Rule
Minh *used to* go to school during the day. Bita *used to* be an architect in Iran.	**Affirmative:** *used to* + base verb
Bita *did not use to* go to school at night. Minh *didn't use to* take care of his grandchildren.	**Negative:** *did + not (didn't) + use to* + base verb **Incorrect:** ~~I didn't used to go to school.~~
Did Minh *use to* work? *Did* Bita *use to* study English?	**Yes/No Question:** *did* + subject + *use to* + base verb **Incorrect:** ~~Did Bita used to live in Iran?~~
Where *did* Minh *use to* work? What *did* Bita *use to* study?	**Wh- Question:** *wh-* word + *did* + subject + *use to* + base verb
Used to + base verb expresses a past habit or state which is now different.	

Future Tense Using *Will*

Example	Rule
In the spring of 2009, *I will ask* my boss for a raise. In the summer, *I will look* for a job.	Future tense = *will* + base verb
In spoken English, people often use contractions: I will = *I'll*.	

Adjective Clauses

Main clause (Subject clause)	Relative pronoun	Adjective clause
This is the place	**where**	I grew up.
She is the person	**who (that)**	influenced me most.
A journal is something	**which (that)**	can help you focus on important things.
Main clause (Object clause)	**Relative pronoun**	**Adjective clause**
This is the woman	who (whom)	I met yesterday.
Here is the book	which	you gave me this morning.
Adjectival clauses describe a preceding noun. They can describe a subject noun or an object noun. If the noun is an object, you can leave out the relative pronoun.		

Contrary-to-Fact Conditionals

Condition (*if* + past tense verb)	Result (*would* + base verb)
If she *got* a raise,	she *would buy* a new house.
If they *didn't spend* so much money on rent,	they *would have* more money for entertainment.
If I *were* a millionaire,	I *would give* all my money to charity.
If John *weren't* so busy at work,	he *would spend* more time with his children.

- *Contrary-to-fact* (or *unreal*) *conditional statements* are sentences that are not true.
- The *if*-clause can come in the first or second part of the sentence. Notice how commas are used in the examples. (If you reverse the order of the condition and result clauses, omit the comma.)
- In written English, use *were* (instead of *was*) for *if*-clauses with first and third person singular forms of *be*.
- In spoken English, people often use contractions: I would = *I'd*; she would = *she'd*, etc.

Contrary-to-Fact Questions

Wh-Question	*Yes/No* Question
What + *would* + subject + base verb + *if* + subject + past tense	*Would* + subject + base verb + *if* + subject + past tense
What would you do *if* you won the lottery?	*Would* you give up your job *if* you won the lottery?

Passive Voice: Present Tense

Subject	*be*	Past Participle		Explanation
Ads	are	written	to sell products.	Since we know that ads are written by advertisers, the information "by advertisers" is not important.
The camera	is	advertised	on television.	Since we know that the store is advertising the camera, the information "by the store" is not important.
We use the passive voice to emphasize the object of the action or when the doer is not important.				

Questions Using Comparative and Superlative Adjectives

Question word	Subject	Verb	Adjective or Noun	Rule
Which	one place house	is	bigger? closer to work? the safest?	Use *be* when following the verb with an adjective.
		has	more rooms? the biggest floor plan?	Use *have* before a noun.

Long and Short Answers

Question	Short answer	Long answer	Rules
Which one is bigger, the condominium or the house?	The condominium.	The condominium is bigger. The condominium is bigger than the house.	• When talking about two things and mentioning both of them, use *than*. • When talking about two things, but only mentioning one of them, do not use *than*.
Which place has more rooms?	The house.	The house has more rooms. The house has more rooms than the condominium.	

Yes/No Questions and Answers

Do you want	air-conditioning? a backyard?	Yes, I do. No, I don't.
Do they need	a balcony? a garage?	Yes, they do. No, they don't.
Does the house have	heating? a pool?	Yes, it does. No, it doesn't.

Information Questions

Information	Example questions		
type of property	What type	of property	do you want? is it?
number of bathrooms number of bedrooms	How many	bedrooms bathrooms	do you want? does it have?
location	Where		is it?
price range	What		is your price range?
down payment (percentage)	How much		can you put down?

Embedded Questions

Introductory question	Embedded question	Rules
Can you show me	where *Orange Avenue is*?	In an embedded information question, the subject comes before the verb.
Do you know	if there is a library near here?	For *yes/no* questions, use *if* before the embedded question.
Can you tell me	when the library opens?	For questions with *do* or *does*, take out *do/does* and use the base form of the verb.
Why do we use embedded questions? They sound more polite than direct questions.		

Present Perfect Continuous

Example	Form
I *have been resting* for three hours.	*Affirmative sentence*: *has/have* + *been* + present participle
He *hasn't been sleeping* well recently.	*Negative sentence*: *has/have* + *not* + *been* + present participle
How *long have they lived/have they been living* here?	*Question*: *has/have* + subject + *been* + present participle

- To emphasize the duration of an activity or state that started in the past and continues in the present. Example: The president *has been sleeping* since 9 A.M.
- To show that an activity has been in progress recently. Example: You*'ve been going* to the doctor a lot lately.
- With some verbs (*work, live, teach*), there is no difference in meaning between the present perfect simple and the present perfect continuous. Example: They *have lived/have been living* here since 2000.

Note: Some verbs are not usually used in the continuous form. These include *be, believe, hate, have, know, like,* and *want*.

Present Perfect Simple

Example	Form
He *has seen* the doctor. I have moved four times in my life.	*Affirmative sentence*: *has/have* + past participle
They *haven't been* to the hospital to see her.	*Negative sentence*: *has/have* + *not* + past participle OR *has/have* + *never* + past participle
Have you *written* to your mother?	*Question*: *has/have* + subject + past participle

- When something happened (or didn't happen) at an unspecified time in the past. Example: She *has* never *broken* her arm.
- When something happened more than once in the past (and could possibly happen again in the future). Example: I *have moved* four times in my life.
- When something started at a specific time in the past and continues in the present. Example: They *have lived* here for ten years.

Direct Speech	Indirect Speech	Rule
"You have to exercise more."	The doctor *explained* (that) I had to exercise more.	• Change pronoun. • Change present tense to past tense.
"The most important thing is your health."	The doctor *said* (that) the most important thing was my health.	

Direct Speech	Indirect Speech
I want to lose weight.	I told *you* (that) I wanted to lose weight.
My test results are negative.	He notified *me* (that) my test results were negative.
It is important to check your heart rate.	My personal trainer said (that) it was important to check my heart rate.
I feel sick.	She complained (that) she felt sick.

- Some verbs are usually followed by an indirect object or pronoun. (*tell, assure, advise, convince, notify, promise, remind, teach, warn*)

- Some verbs are NOT followed by an indirect object or pronoun. (*say, agree, announce, answer, complain, explain, reply, state*)

Tag Questions

Positive statement	Tag	Negative statement	Tag
She works,	doesn't she?	She doesn't work,	does she?
She is working,	isn't she?	She isn't working,	is she?
She worked,	didn't she?	She didn't work,	did she?
She will work,	won't she?	She won't work,	will she?
She is going to work,	isn't she?	She isn't going to work,	is she?
She has worked,	hasn't she?	She hasn't worked,	has she?
She had worked,	hadn't she?	She hadn't worked,	had she?

Passive Voice

Example sentence	Passive subject	*be*	Past participle	(*by* + person or thing)
The note was written by Jim.	It	was	written	by Jim
The orders were sent yesterday. (We don't know who sent them.)	They	were	sent	

- Use the passive voice to emphasize the object of the action, or when the doer of the action is unknown or unimportant.

- To change an active sentence into a passive sentence, switch the subject and the object, and change the verb to the correct tense of *be* + the past participle. The word *by* is used before the doer of the action.

Passive Modals

Example sentence	Passive subject	Modal	*be*	Past participle
More schools *should be* built.	schools	should	be	built
Taxes *need to be* increased.	taxes	need to	be	increased
Children *must be* protected.	children	must	be	protected
Parents *have to be* involved.	parents	have to	be	involved

0. Basic Communication

0.1 Communicate in interpersonal interactions

0.1.1 Identify or use appropriate non-verbal behavior in a variety of situations (e.g., handshaking)

0.1.2 Identify or use appropriate language for informational purposes (e.g., to identify, describe, ask for information, state needs, command, agree or disagree, ask permission)

0.1.3 Identify or use appropriate language to influence or persuade (e.g., to caution, request, advise, persuade, negotiate)

0.1.4 Identify or use appropriate language in general social situations (e.g., to greet, introduce, thank, apologize, compliment, express pleasure or regret)

0.1.5 Identify or use appropriate classroom behavior

0.1.6 Clarify or request clarification

0.2 Communicate regarding personal information

0.2.1 Respond appropriately to common personal information questions

0.2.2 Complete a personal information form

0.2.3 Interpret or write a personal note, invitation, or letter

0.2.4 Converse about daily and leisure activities and personal interests

1. Consumer Economics

1.1 Use weights, measures, measurement scales, and money

1.1.1 Interpret recipes

1.1.2 Use the metric system (see also 1.1.4, 6.6.1, 6.6.2, 6.6.3, 6.6.4)

1.1.3 Interpret maps and graphs (see also 1.9.4, 2.2.1, 2.2.5)

1.1.4 Select, compute, or interpret appropriate standard measurement for length, width, perimeter, area, volume, height, or weight (see also 1.1.2, 6.6.1, 6.6.2, 6.6.3, 6.6.4, 6.6.5)

1.1.5 Interpret temperatures (see also 6.6.4)

1.1.6 Count, convert, and use coins and currency, and recognize symbols such as ($) and (.) (see also 6.1.1, 6.1.2, 6.1.3, 6.1.4, 6.1.5)

1.1.7 Identify product containers and interpret weight and volume

1.1.8 Compute averages (see also 6.7.5)

1.1.9 Interpret clothing and pattern sizes and use height and weight tables

1.2 Apply principles of comparison-shopping in the selection of goods and services

1.2.1 Interpret advertisements, labels, charts, and price tags in selecting goods and services

1.2.2 Compare price or quality to determine the best buys for goods and services

1.2.3 Compute discounts (see also 6.4.1)

1.2.4 Compute unit pricing

1.2.5 Interpret letters, articles, and information about consumer-related topics

1.3 Understand methods and procedures used to purchase goods and services

1.3.1 Compare different methods used to purchase goods and services

1.3.2 Interpret credit applications and recognize how to use and maintain credit

1.3.3 Identify or use various methods to purchase goods and services, and make returns and exchanges

1.3.4 Use catalogs, order forms, and related information to purchase goods and services

1.3.5 Use coupons to purchase goods and services

1.3.6 Use coin-operated machines

1.3.7 Interpret information or directions to locate merchandise (see also 2.5.4)

1.3.8 Identify common food items

1.3.9 Identify common articles of clothing

1.4 Understand methods and procedures to obtain housing and related services

1.4.1 Identify different kinds of housing, areas of the home, and common household items

1.4.2 Select appropriate housing by interpreting classified ads, signs, and other information

1.4.3 Interpret lease and rental agreements

1.4.4 Interpret information to obtain, maintain, or cancel housing utilities

1.4.5 Interpret information about tenant and landlord rights

1.4.6 Interpret information about housing loans and home-related insurance

1.4.7 Interpret information about home maintenance, and communicate housing problems to a landlord (see also 1.7.4)

1.4.8 Recognize home theft and fire prevention measures

1.5 Apply principles of budgeting in the management of money

1.5.1 Interpret information about personal and family budgets

1.5.2 Plan for major purchases (see also 1.5.1)

1.5.3 Interpret bills (see also 2.1.4)

1.6 Understand consumer protection measures

1.6.1 Interpret food packaging labels (see also 1.2.1, 3.5.1)

1.6.2 Identify consumer protection resources available when confronted with fraudulent practices

1.6.3 Identify procedures the consumer can follow if merchandise or service is unsatisfactory

1.6.4 Check sales receipts

1.7 Understand procedures for the care, maintenance, and use of personal possessions

1.7.1 Interpret product guarantees and warranties
1.7.2 Interpret clothing care labels
1.7.3 Interpret operating instructions, directions, or labels for consumer products (see also 3.4.1)
1.7.4 Interpret maintenance procedures for household appliances and personal possessions
1.7.5 Interpret information to obtain repairs

1.8 Use banking and financial services in the community

1.8.1 Demonstrate the use of savings and checking accounts, including using an ATM
1.8.2 Interpret the procedures and forms associated with banking services, including writing checks
1.8.3 Interpret interest or interest-earning savings plans
1.8.4 Interpret information about the types of loans available through lending institutions
1.8.5 Interpret information on financial agencies and financial planning

1.9 Understand methods and procedures for the purchase and maintenance of an automobile and interpret driving regulations

1.9.1 Interpret highway and traffic signs (see also 2.2.2)
1.9.2 Identify driving regulations and procedures to obtain a driver's license (see also 2.5.7)
1.9.3 Compute mileage and gasoline consumption
1.9.4 Interpret maps related to driving (see also 1.1.3, 2.2.1, 2.2.5)
1.9.5 Interpret information related to the selection and purchase of a car
1.9.6 Interpret information related to automobile maintenance
1.9.7 Recognize what to do in case of automobile emergencies
1.9.8 Interpret information about automobile insurance

2. Community Resources

2.1 Use the telephone and telephone book

2.1.1 Use the telephone directory and related publications to locate information
2.1.2 Identify emergency numbers and place emergency calls (see also 2.5.1)
2.1.3 Interpret information about time zones (see also 2.3.1)
2.1.4 Interpret telephone billings
2.1.5 Interpret telegram rates and procedures
2.1.6 Interpret information about using a pay telephone
2.1.7 Take and interpret telephone messages, leave messages on answering machines, and interpret recorded messages (see also 4.5.4)

2.1.8 Use the telephone to make and receive routine personal and business calls

2.2 Understand how to locate and use different types of transportation and interpret related travel information

2.2.1 Ask for, give, follow, or clarify directions (see also 1.1.3, 1.9.4, 2.2.5)
2.2.2 Recognize and use signs related to transportation (see also 1.9.1)
2.2.3 Identify or use different types of transportation in the community, and interpret traffic information
2.2.4 Interpret transportation schedules and fares
2.2.5 Use maps relating to travel needs (see also 1.1.3, 1.9.4, 2.2.1)

2.3 Understand concepts of time and weather

2.3.1 Interpret clock time (see also 2.1.3, 6.6.6)
2.3.2 Identify the months of the year and the days of the week
2.3.3 Interpret information about weather conditions

2.4 Use postal services

2.4.1 Address letters and envelopes
2.4.2 Interpret postal rates and types of mailing services
2.4.3 Interpret postal service forms and instructions on returned mail
2.4.4 Purchase stamps and other postal items and services
2.4.5 Interpret procedures for tracing a lost letter or parcel
2.4.6 Interpret a postal money order form

2.5 Use community agencies and services

2.5.1 Locate and utilize services of agencies that provide emergency help
2.5.2 Identify how and when to obtain social and governmental services (e.g., low-income housing, Social Security, Medicare), and how to interact with service providers
2.5.3 Locate medical and health facilities in the community (see also 3.1.3)
2.5.4 Read, interpret, and follow directions found on public signs and building directories (see also 1.3.7)
2.5.5 Locate and use educational services in the community, including interpreting and writing school-related communications
2.5.6 Use library services
2.5.7 Interpret permit and license requirements (see also 1.9.2)
2.5.8 (unassigned)
2.5.9 Identify child care services in the community (see also 3.5.7)

2.6 Use leisure time resources and facilities

2.6.1 Interpret information about recreational and entertainment facilities and activities

2.6.2 Locate information in TV, movie, and other recreational listings

2.6.3 Interpret information in order to plan for outings and vacations

2.6.4 Interpret and order from restaurant and fast food menus, and compute related costs

2.7 Understand aspects of society and culture

2.7.1 Interpret information about holidays

2.7.2 Interpret information about ethnic groups, cultural groups, and language groups

2.7.3 Interpret information about social issues (see also 2.7.2)

2.7.4 Interpret information about religion

2.7.5 Interpret literary materials such as poetry and literature

2.7.6 Interpret materials related to the arts, such as fine art, music, drama, and film

3. Health

3.1 Understand how to access and utilize the health care system

3.1.1 Describe symptoms of illness, including identifying parts of the body; interpret doctor's directions

3.1.2 Identify information necessary to make or keep medical and dental appointments

3.1.3 Identify and utilize appropriate health care services and facilities, including interacting with providers (see also 2.5.3)

3.2 Understand medical and dental forms and related information

3.2.1 Fill out medical health history forms

3.2.2 Interpret immunization requirements

3.2.3 Interpret information associated with medical, dental, or life insurance

3.2.4 Ask for clarification about medical bills

3.3 Understand how to select and use medications

3.3.1 Identify and use necessary medications (see also 3.3.2, 3.3.3)

3.3.2 Interpret medicine labels (see also 3.3.1, 3.4.1)

3.3.3 Identify the difference between prescription, over-the-counter, and generic medications (see also 3.3.1)

3.4 Understand basic health and safety procedures

3.4.1 Interpret product label directions and safety warnings (see also 1.7.3, 3.3.2)

3.4.2 Identify safety measures that can prevent accidents and injuries

3.4.3 Interpret procedures for simple first-aid

3.4.4 Interpret information about AIDS and other sexually transmitted diseases (see also 3.1.1)

3.4.5 Recognize problems related to drugs, tobacco, and alcohol and identify where treatment may be obtained

3.5 Understand basic principles of health maintenance

3.5.1 Interpret nutritional and related information listed on food labels (see also 1.6.1)

3.5.2 Select a balanced diet

3.5.3 Interpret food storage information

3.5.4 Identify practices that promote dental health

3.5.5 Identify practices that promote cleanliness and hygiene

3.5.6 Interpret information and identify agencies that assist with family planning (see also 2.5.3, 3.1.3)

3.5.7 Identify child-rearing practices and community resources that assist in developing parenting skills (see also 2.5.9)

3.5.8 Identify practices that promote mental well being

3.5.9 Identify practices that promote physical well being

4. Employment

4.1 Understand basic principles of getting a job

4.1.1 Interpret governmental forms related to seeking work, such as applications for Social Security (see also 2.5.2)

4.1.2 Follow procedures for applying for a job, including interpreting and completing job applications, résumés, and letters of application

4.1.3 Identify and use sources of information about job opportunities such as job descriptions, job ads, and announcements, and about the workforce and job market

4.1.4 Identify and use information about training opportunities (see also 2.5.5)

4.1.5 Identify procedures involved in interviewing for a job, such as arranging for an interview, acting and dressing appropriately, and selecting appropriate questions and responses

4.1.6 Interpret general work-related vocabulary (e.g., experience, swing shift)

4.1.7 Identify appropriate behavior and attitudes for getting a job

4.1.8 Identify common occupations and the skills and education required for them

4.1.9 Identify procedures for career planning, including self-assessment

4.2 Understand wages, benefits, and concepts of employee organizations

4.2.1 Interpret wages, wage deductions, benefits, and timekeeping forms

4.2.2 Interpret information about employee organizations

4.2.3 Interpret employment contract and union agreements

4.2.4 Interpret employee handbooks, personnel policies, and job manuals

4.3 Understand work-related safety standards and procedures

4.3.1 Interpret safety signs found in the workplace (see also 3.4.1)

4.3.2 Interpret work safety manuals and related information

4.3.3 Identify safe work procedures and common safety equipment, including wearing safe work attire

4.3.4 Report unsafe working conditions work-related accidents, injuries, damages

4.4 Understand concepts and materials related to job performance and training

4.4.1 Identify appropriate behavior, attire, attitudes, and social interaction, factors that affect job retention advancement

4.4.2 Identify appropriate skills and education for keeping a job and getting a

4.4.3 Interpret job-related signs, charts, diagrams, forms, and procedures, record information on forms, charts, checklists, etc. (see also 4.2.1, 4.3.4)

4.4.4 Interpret job responsibilities and performance reviews (see also 4.4.2)

4.4.5 Identify job training needs and goals

4.4.6 Interpret work specifications and standards

4.4.7 Demonstrate the ability to apply skills learned in one job situation another

4.4.8 Interpret job-related technical information, such as from service manuals and classes

4.5 Effectively utilize common workplace technology and systems

4.5.1 Identify common tools, equipment, machines, and materials required one's job

4.5.2 Demonstrate simple keyboarding

4.5.3 Demonstrate ability to use a filing or other ordered system (e.g., coded numbered)

4.5.4 Demonstrate use of common business machines (see also 2.1.7, 2.1.8)

4.5.5 Demonstrate basic computer skills use of common software programs, including reading or interpreting computer generated printouts

4.5.6 Demonstrate ability to select, set use tools and machines in order accomplish a task, while operating a technological system

4.5.7 Demonstrate ability to identify resolve problems with machines follow proper maintenance procedures

4.6 Communicate effectively in the workplace

4.6.1 Follow, clarify, give, or provide feedback to instructions; give and respond appropriately to criticism

4.6.2 Interpret and write work-related correspondence, including notes, memos, letters, and e-mail (see also 4.4.3)

4.6.3 Interpret written workplace announcements and notices (see also 4.4.1, 4.4.3)

4.6.4 Report progress on activities, status of assigned tasks, and problems and other situations affecting job completion (see also 4.3.4)

4.6.5 Select and analyze work-related information for a given purpose and communicate it to others orally or in writing

4.7 Effectively manage workplace resources

4.7.1 Interpret or prepare a work-related budget, including projecting costs, keeping detailed records, and tracking status of expenditures and revenue

4.7.2 Identify or demonstrate effective management of material resources, including acquisition, storage, and distribution

4.7.3 Identify or demonstrate effective management of human resources, including assessing skills, making appropriate work assignments, and monitoring performance

4.7.4 Identify, secure, evaluate, process, and/or store information needed to perform tasks or keep records

4.8 Demonstrate effectiveness in working with other people

4.8.1 Demonstrate ability to work cooperatively with others as a member of a team, contributing to team efforts, maximizing the strengths of team members, promoting effective group interaction, and taking personal responsibility for accomplishing goals

4.8.2 Identify ways to learn from others and to help others learn job-related concepts and skills

4.8.3 Demonstrate effective communication skills in working with customers and clients

4.8.4 Demonstrate initiative and resourcefulness in meeting the needs and solving the problems of customers

4.8.5 Demonstrate leadership skills, including effectively communicating ideas or positions, motivating and respecting others, and responsibly challenging existing policies

4.8.6 Demonstrate negotiation skills in resolving differences, including presenting facts and arguments, recognizing differing points of view, offering options, and making compromises

4.8.7 Identify and use effective approaches to working within a multicultural workforce, including respecting cultural diversity, avoiding stereotypes, and recognizing concerns of members of other ethnic and gender groups

4.9 **Understand how social, organizational, and technological systems work, and operate effectively within them**

4.9.1   Identify the formal organizational structure of one's work environment

4.9.2   Demonstrate how a system's structures relate to its goals

4.9.3   Identify sources of information and assistance, and access resources within a system

4.9.4   Assess the operation of a system or organization and make recommendations for improvement, including development of new systems

5.   Government and Law

5.1 **Understand voting and the political process**

5.1.1   Identify voter qualifications

5.1.2   Interpret a voter registration form

5.1.3   Interpret a ballot

5.1.4   Interpret information about electoral politics and candidates

5.1.5   Interpret information about special interest groups

5.1.6   Communicate one's opinions on a current issue

5.2 **Understand historical and geographical information**

5.2.1   Interpret information about U.S. history

5.2.2   Identify or interpret U.S. historical documents

5.2.3   Interpret information about world history

5.2.4   Interpret information about U.S. states, cities, geographical features, and points of interest

5.2.5   Interpret information about world geography

5.3 **Understand an individual's legal rights and responsibilities and procedures for obtaining legal advice**

5.3.1   Interpret common laws and ordinances, and legal forms and documents

5.3.2   Identify individual legal rights and procedures for obtaining legal advice (see also 5.3.1)

5.3.3   Interpret basic court procedures

5.3.4   Interpret laws affecting door-to-door sales (see also 1.6.2)

5.3.5   Interpret information about traffic tickets

5.3.6   Interpret information or identify requirements for establishing residency and/or obtaining citizenship

5.3.7   Identify common infractions and crimes, and legal consequences

5.3.8   Identify procedures for reporting a crime

5.4 **Understand information about taxes**

5.4.1   Interpret income tax forms

5.4.2   Compute or define sales tax

5.4.3   Interpret tax tables (see also 5.4.1, 5.4.2)

5.4.4   Interpret tax information from articles and publications

5.5 **Understand governmental activities**

5.5.1   Interpret information about international affairs

5.5.2   Interpret information about legislative activities

5.5.3   Interpret information about judicial activities

5.5.4   Interpret information about executive activities

5.5.5   Interpret information about military activities

5.5.6   Interpret information about law enforcement activities

5.5.7   Interpret information about local policymaking groups

5.5.8   Identify local, state and federal government leaders

5.6 **Understand civic responsibilities and activities**

5.6.1   Interpret information about neighborhood or community problems and their solutions

5.6.2   Interpret information about civic organizations and public service groups

5.6.3   Interpret civic responsibilities, such as voting, jury duty, taxes

5.7 **Understand environmental and science-related issues**

5.7.1   Interpret information about environmental issues

5.7.2   Interpret information related to physics, including energy

5.7.3   Interpret information about earth-related sciences

5.7.4   Interpret information about new technologies and scientific issues

5.8 **Understand concepts of economics**

5.8.1   Interpret economic information and statistics

5.8.2   Interpret information on economic issues and trends

5.8.3   Interpret information on world economic systems

6.   Computation

6.0 **Demonstrate pre-computation skills**

6.0.1   Identify and classify numeric symbols

6.0.2   Count and associate numbers with quantities, including recognizing correct number sequencing

6.0.3   Identify information needed to solve a given problem

6.0.4   Determine appropriate operation to apply to a given problem

6.0.5   Demonstrate use of a calculator

6.1 **Compute using whole numbers**

6.1.1   Add whole numbers

6.1.2   Subtract whole numbers

6.1.3 Multiply whole numbers
6.1.4 Divide whole numbers
6.1.5 Perform multiple operations using whole numbers

6.2 Compute using decimal fractions
6.2.1 Add decimal fractions
6.2.2 Subtract decimal fractions
6.2.3 Multiply decimal fractions
6.2.4 Divide decimal fractions
6.2.5 Perform multiple operations using decimal fractions
6.2.6 Convert decimal fractions to common fractions or percents

6.3 Compute using fractions
6.3.1 Add common or mixed fractions
6.3.2 Subtract common or mixed fractions
6.3.3 Multiply common or mixed fractions
6.3.4 Divide common or mixed fractions
6.3.5 Perform multiple operations using common or mixed fractions
6.3.6 Convert common or mixed fractions to decimal fractions or percents
6.3.7 Identify or calculate equivalent fractions

6.4 Compute with percents, rate, ratio, and proportion
6.4.1 Apply a percent to determine amount of discount (see also 1.2.3)
6.4.2 Apply a percent in a context not involving money
6.4.3 Calculate percents
6.4.4 Convert percents to common, mixed, or decimal fractions
6.4.5 Use rate to compute increase or decrease
6.4.6 Compute using ratio or proportion (see also 6.4.5)

6.5 Use expressions, equations, and formulas
6.5.1 Recognize and evaluate simple consumer formulas
6.5.2 Recognize and apply simple geometric formulas
6.5.3 Recognize and apply simple algebraic formulas
6.5.4 Recognize and evaluate logical statements

6.6 Demonstrate measurement skills (see also 1.1)
6.6.1 Convert units of U.S. standard measurement and metric system (see also 1.1.2, 1.1.4)
6.6.2 Recognize, use, and measure linear dimensions, geometric shapes, or angles (see also 1.1.2, 1.1.4)
6.6.3 Measure area and volume of geometric shapes (see also 1.1.2, 1.1.4)
6.6.4 Use or interpret measurement instruments, such as rulers, scales, gauges, and dials (see also 1.1.2, 1.1.4, 1.1.5, 4.3.3, 4.4.3)
6.6.5 Interpret diagrams, illustrations, and scale drawings (see also 1.1.4, 4.4.3)
6.6.6 Calculate with units of time

6.6.7 Solve measurement problems in stipulated situations
6.6.8 Interpret mechanical concepts or spatial relationships
6.6.9 Use or interpret switches and controls

6.7 Interpret data from graphs and compute averages
6.7.1 Interpret data given in a line graph (see also 1.1.3)
6.7.2 Interpret data given in a bar graph (see also 1.1.3)
6.7.3 Interpret data given in a picture graph
6.7.4 Interpret data given in a circle graph (see also 1.1.3)
6.7.5 Compute averages, medians, or modes (see also 1.1.8)

6.8 Use statistics and probability
6.8.1 Interpret statistical information used in news reports and articles
6.8.2 Interpret statements of probability

6.9 Use estimation and mental arithmetic
6.9.1 Use computation short cuts
6.9.2 Estimate answers

7. Learning to Learn

7.1 Identify or practice effective organizational and time management skills in accomplishing goals
7.1.1 Identify and prioritize personal, educational, and workplace goals (see also 4.4.5)
7.1.2 Demonstrate an organized approach to achieving goals, including identifying and prioritizing tasks and setting and following an effective schedule
7.1.3 Demonstrate personal responsibility and motivation in accomplishing goals
7.1.4 Establish, maintain, and utilize a physical system of organization, such as notebooks, files, calendars, folders, and checklists (see also 4.5.3)

7.2 Demonstrate ability to use thinking skills
7.2.1 Identify and paraphrase pertinent information
7.2.2 Analyze a situation, statement, or process, identifying component elements and causal and part/whole relationships
7.2.3 Make comparisons, differentiating among, sorting, and classifying items, information, or ideas
7.2.4 Identify or make inferences through inductive and deductive reasoning to hypothesize, predict, conclude, and synthesize; distinguish fact from opinion, and determine what is mandatory and what is discretionary

7.2.5 Evaluate a situation, statement, or process, assembling information and providing evidence, making judgements, examining assumptions, and identifying contradictions

7.2.6 Generate ideas using divergent (brainstorming) and convergent (focus) approaches, and also through creative imagination

7.2.7 Identify factors involved in making decisions, including considering goals, constraints, and consequences, and weighing alternatives

7.3 Demonstrate ability to use problem-solving skills

7.3.1 Identify a problem and its possible causes

7.3.2 Devise and implement a solution to an identified problem

7.3.3 Evaluate the outcome of an implemented solution and suggest modifications to the solution as needed

7.3.4 Utilize problem-solving strategies, such as breaking down the problem into component parts and generating alternative or creative solutions

7.4 Demonstrate study skills

7.4.1 Identify or utilize effective study strategies

7.4.2 Take notes or write a summary or an outline

7.4.3 Identify, utilize, or create devices or processes for remembering information

7.4.4 Identify or utilize appropriate informational resources, including the Internet (see also 4.9.3)

7.4.5 Use reference materials, such as dictionaries and encyclopedias

7.4.6 Use indexes and tables of contents

7.4.7 Identify or utilize test-taking skills

7.4.8 Interpret visual representations, such as symbols, blueprints, flowcharts, and schematics (see also 6.6.5)

7.4.9 Identify personal learning style

7.5 Understand aspects of and approaches to effective personal management

7.5.1 Identify personal values, qualities, interests, abilities, and aptitudes

7.5.2 Identify or use strategies to develop a positive attitude and self-image, and self-esteem

7.5.3 Identify or use strategies to cope with negative feedback

7.5.4 Identify sources of stress, and resources for stress reduction

7.5.5 Identify personal, family, and work responsibilities, and ways to accommodate them and deal with related problems

7.5.6 Identify or use strategies for communicating more successfully

7.5.7 Identify constructive ways of dealing with change, including showing flexibility and adaptability, and updating skills

8. Independent Living

8.1 Perform self-care skills

8.1.1 Recognize and/or demonstrate hygiene and grooming skills (see also 3.5.5)

8.1.2 Recognize and/or demonstrate dressing skills

8.1.3 Recognize and/or demonstrate dining skills and manners

8.1.4 Recognize and/or demonstrate selection and care of clothing and personal property

8.2 Perform home-care skills

8.2.1 Recognize and/or demonstrate meal and snack preparation tasks and activities (see also 1.1.1, 3.5.2)

8.2.2 Recognize and/or demonstrate dishwashing and meal clean-up activities (see also 3.5.5)

8.2.3 Recognize and/or demonstrate housekeeping and house cleaning tasks

8.2.4 Recognize and/or demonstrate laundry skills and related clothing-care skills (see also 1.7.2, 1.7.3)

8.2.5 Recognize and/or demonstrate yard and garden tasks and activities

8.2.6 Recognize and/or demonstrate general household repair and maintenance (see also 1.4.7, 1.7.4)

8.3 Use support services to assist in maintaining independence and achieving community integration

8.3.1 Identify and interact with persons in the home environment who can provide support in achieving goals (e.g., family, friends, caregivers)

8.3.2 Identify and interact with persons in the community who can provide support in achieving goals (e.g., neighbors, contacts from human service agencies and recreation facilities)

Photo Credits

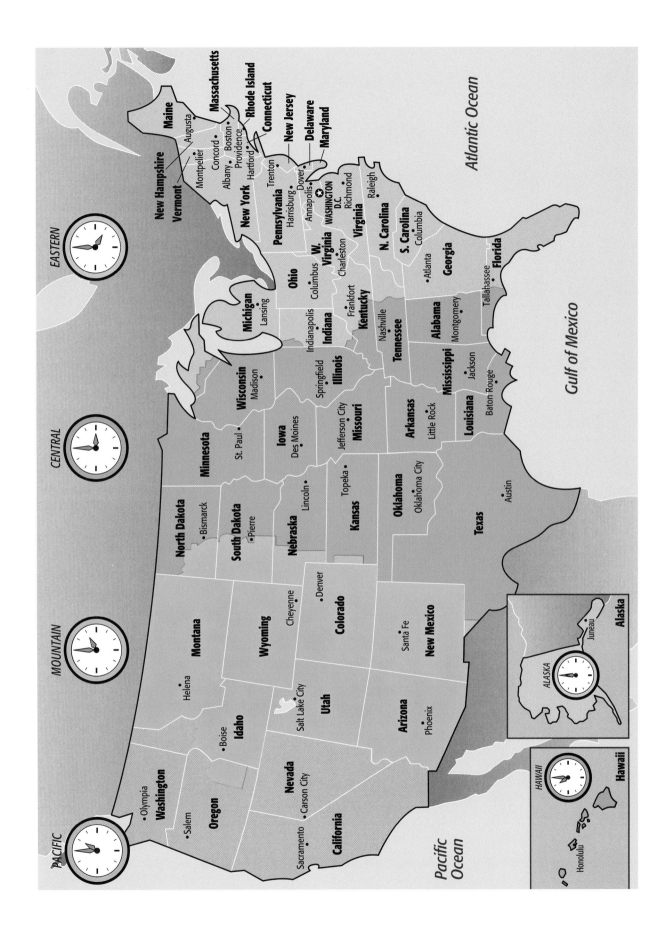

Activity Bank Contents (available on the enclosed CD-ROM)

Pre-Unit: Getting to Know You

Lesson	Worksheets*	Skill
1	1. Meet Your Classmates	Write three questions and interview four classmates.
	2. Admission Application	Fill out a college admission application.
2	1. Learning Strategies	Take a poll and create a bar graph.
3	1. Word Family Practice	Complete a word family chart. Write sentences using different parts of speech from the same word family. Write sentences from different word families.

Unit 1: Balancing Your Life

Lesson	Worksheets*	Skill
1	1. *Used to*	Complete exercises with *used to*.
2	1. Goal Practice	Put the steps it takes to reach a goal in order and fill out a goal chart.
	2. Goal Chart	Talk to someone about his or her goal. Write the steps it will take him or her to reach his or her goal and complete a goal chart.
	3. Personal Goal Chart	Fill out a personal goal chart for two goals.
3	1. Obstacles and Solutions	Work with a partner to give advice.
	2. Listening to Advice 🎧	Listen and write down the goals, obstacles, and advice you hear.
	3. A Letter of Advice	Read a letter asking for advice and respond to it.
4	1. Adjective Clauses	Complete exercises on adjective clauses.
	2. Parts of a Paragraph	Label the sentence types of a paragraph. Put sentences in the correct order to write a paragraph.
5	1. Time Management	Complete an outline on time management.

Unit 2: Consumer Smarts

Lesson	Worksheets*	Skill
1	1. Budget Practice	Calculate budget items and analyze one family's budget.
	2. My Budget	Create a personal budget.
2	1. Being a Smart Consumer	Paraphrase information from student book about being a smart consumer.
	2. Contrary-to-Fact Conditionals	Complete exercise and write a paragraph using contrary-to-fact conditionals.
3	1. Credit Card Application	Fill out a credit card application.
	2. Credit Card Team Project	With a team, create a credit card. Share the information with the class.
4	1. Analyze an Ad	Answer questions about an advertisement.
5	1. Complaints 🎧	Listen to customer complaints and write down what you hear.

Unit 3: Buying a House

Lesson	Worksheets*	Skill
1	1. Homes for Sale	Interpret ads.
2	1. Comparative and Superlative Adjectives	Complete a comparative and superlative adjective chart. Use adjectives to compare to homes for sale.
	2. Compare the Homes	Read statements about homes and put them in order from most expensive to cheapest and largest to smallest.
	3. Comparative and Superlative Questions	Complete exercises with comparative and superlative questions.
3	1. *Yes/No* Questions	Rewrite statements as *yes/no* questions. Answer *yes/no* questions.
	2. Information Questions	Rewrite statements as information questions.
4	1. Buying a House	Answer multiple-choice questions about buying a house.
5	1. Getting a Mortgage	Answer multiple-choice questions about the vocabulary and process of getting a mortgage. Put the steps of buying a house in order and write a paragraph.
Extension 1	Housing Bar Graph	Take a class poll of types of housing that students live in. Calculate percentages and make a bar graph.
Extension 2	A Business Letter	Write a business letter to a real estate agent.

Unit 4: Community

Lesson	Worksheets*	Skill
1	1. Embedded Questions	Write embedded questions. Practice asking and answering questions with a partner.
	2. Read for Information	Read a visitor's guide and come up with questions to ask based on missing information.
2	1. Practice Telephone Conversations	With a partner, practice telephone conversations, substituting information each time.
3	1. Making Suggestions	Get suggestions from your partner about places in your community. Then, rewrite your partner's suggestions.
4	1. Calling for Directions	Use shorthand to take directions.
5	1. Volunteer at the Animal Shelter	Read a newspaper article and answer multiple-choice questions about it. Use context clues to figure out the meanings of new expressions.
Extension	Class Telephone Directory	Make a directory of places in your community.

Unit 5: Health

Lesson	Worksheets*	Skill
1	1. Healthy vs. Unhealthy	Listen to people talk about their health and decide if they practice healthy or unhealthy habits.
	2. My Health Habits	Answer questions about personal health habits and make a bar graph.
2	1. Present Perfect and Present Perfect Continuous	Complete exercises with present perfect and present perfect continuous verbs.
3	1. Indirect Speech	Complete exercises using indirect speech.
4	1. Nutrition Label Practice	Read four nutrition labels and answer questions about the nutritional content of each food.
5	1. Healthy Life HMO	Read about an HMO. Complete exercises and work with vocabulary.
Extension	Write a Summary	Read an article about the common cold and learn how to write a summary.

Unit 6: Getting Hired

Lesson	Worksheets*	Skill
1	1. Characteristics	Choose appropriate characteristics for various jobs.
2	1. Job Search	Read job ads to look for information.
3	1. Write a Resume	Interview a partner and write a resume.
	2. Resume	Fill in a resume template.
4	1. Write a Cover Letter	Write a cover letter to send with a resume for a teacher's assistant position.
5	1. Interviews 🎧	Listen to four interviews and rate each applicant.
Extension	Thank-You Letter	Write a thank-you letter after an interview.

Unit 7: On the Job

Lesson	Worksheets*	Skill
1	1. Personal Grooming	Identify good personal grooming practices.
	2. Tag Questions	Complete statements with the correct question tags.
	3. Appropriate Classroom Behavior	Make a list of appropriate and inappropriate classroom behavior. Then, make a list of classroom rules.
2	1. Passive Voice	Complete sentences with verbs in the passive voice.
	2. Active or Passive?	Decide if statements are active or passive. Then, rewrite them in the opposite voice.
3	1. Finding a Solution 🎧	Listen to a conversation about a problem. Come up with a solution. Compare your solution to the given solution.
4	1. Ethical Dilemma	Come up with a solution for an ethical dilemma.
5	1. Asking for a Raise	Reread Raj's story on page 133 in the student book and rate him on the steps he took to ask for a raise.
	2. Ask for a Raise—It's Your Turn	Take notes on what you would do to ask for a raise.
	3. Writing a Letter Asking for a Raise—Editing Checklist	Write a letter asking for a raise. Use the checklist to make sure everything is included.

Unit 8: Civic Responsibility

Lesson	Worksheets*	Skill
1	1. Civic Responsibility	Create a matching activity for a partner. Answer questions about personal civic participation and then interview a partner about his or her civic participation.
2	1. Driving Safety	Read about driving safety. Complete a chart about what the reading says compared to the laws in students' state.
	2. Jury Summons Information	Answer questions about a jury summons.
3	1. Writing a Letter to a Community Official—Editing Checklist	Write a letter about a problem in your community. Use the checklist to make sure you included everything.
4	1. Register to Vote	Answer questions about registration eligibility.
5	1. Sample Ballot	Vote for one of the three candidates on page 153.
	2. Passive Modals	Rewrite candidates' statements using passive modals.

* Unit worksheets include low, mid-level, and high-level versions.